Critical Essays on
ELIAS CANETTI

CRITICAL ESSAYS
ON
WORLD LITERATURE

Robert Lecker, General Editor
McGill University, Montreal

Critical Essays on

ELIAS CANETTI

edited by

DAVID DARBY

G. K. Hall & Co.
New York

G. K. Hall & Co.
1633 Broadway
New York, NY 10019

Library of Congress Cataloging-in-Publication Data
Critical essays on Elias Canetti / edited by David Darby.
     p. cm. — (Critical essays on world literature)
    Includes bibliographical references and index.
    ISBN 0-7838-0455-5 (alk. paper)
    1. Canetti, Elias, 1905——Criticism and interpretation. I. Series.

PT2605.A58 Z645 2000
833'.912—dc21
                                           99-054643

For Jan

Contents

Publisher's Note

◆

Producing a volume that contains both newly commissioned and reprinted material presents the publisher with the challenge of balancing the desire to achieve stylistic consistency with the need to preserve the integrity of works first published elsewhere. In the Critical Essays series, essays commissioned especially for a particular volume are edited to be consistent with G. K. Hall's house style; reprinted essays appear in the style in which they were first published, with only typographical errors corrected. Consequently, shifts in style from one essay to another are the result of our efforts to be faithful to each text as it was originally published.

Introduction

♦

My whole life is nothing but a desperate attempt to overcome the division of labor and think about everything myself, so that it comes together in a single head and thus becomes one again. I do not want to know everything, I merely want to unify splintered things.

Elias Canetti, *The Human Province*

Almost 20 years have passed since the award of the Nobel Prize for Literature in 1981 suddenly and publicly promoted the works of Elias Canetti to the canon of World Literature. Although Canetti's earliest publication—the novel *Die Blendung* (*Auto-da-Fé*)—dated back to the mid-1930s, and his reputation as an author had grown gradually in both academic and popular circles since the 1960s, his name was in 1981, particularly in the English-speaking world, still anything but well known. He was, however, not without admirers in the academic and literary worlds, and these moved quickly, drawing on the available biographical data and the gradually developing body of critical work in German, to answer the seemingly simple question—"Who is Elias Canetti?"—that informed much of the initial response to the announcement of the Swedish Academy's decision.[1]

After almost two decades this situation has changed, and the questions that are now asked in academic circles have become both more varied and more sophisticated. In this interval Canetti has assumed his own place in the intellectual cosmos of the latter half of the twentieth century, the object of critical discussion, formal study, and not a little controversy. In the realm of scholarly literary criticism there has been a virtual explosion of interest in the form of essays, critical anthologies, volumes of conference proceedings, graduate dissertations, and monographs. And, as Canetti's reputation within the academy has grown, so too has his popular reputation, though still with far broader resonance in Europe than in North America. Not surprisingly, of course, the greater part of the scholarship to date is available only in German, the language in which Canetti himself wrote, and consequently, while virtually all his published works have been available in English translation during this period, relatively little of the growing corpus of critical material has been accessible to nonreaders of German. As far as the English-speaking world is concerned, there has been, especially in Great Britain where Canetti lived at the time and where in 1946 *Auto-da-Fé* was among the first German novels to be published in English translation after the Second World War, a persistent minority interest in Canetti's work from the immediate postwar period on.[2] However, while several books—on the one hand, studies of the novel, and, on the other, more general works surveying Canetti's life and works—were published in German in the 1970s, it was not until two decades later that the first general introductory monographs in English appeared.[3] The 1990s have also seen a series of more specialized book-length studies in English, though with a remarkably exclusive concentration on the novel *Auto-da-Fé*.[4]

Assembling the present critical anthology thus offers an exciting and timely opportunity to expand the scholarly discussion in English of the various parts of Canetti's formally diverse oeuvre. Most of the work collected here has never been published in English before. Of the interviews, essays, and reviews contained herein, 11 appear for the first time in English translation, having previously been published in German, and five new essays have been written by established Canetti scholars especially for this volume. Interspersed with these are a number of important essays that have previously been published in English but are brought together here in a more specialized context of studies on Canetti than that in which most of them first appeared. In selecting the component essays, reviews, and interviews, the net has been cast wide to include work that illuminates and opens discussion on all major parts of Canetti's oeuvre.[5]

In many ways Canetti's work resists generalization, and a degree of its fascination arises from the formal metamorphoses enacted in his writings over the years from the 1930s until the author's death in 1994. Over those decades Canetti repeatedly reinvents himself as a writer: beginning as a novelist and playwright, he subsequently emerges as scholar of the interrelation between crowds and power, then as travel writer, essayist, aphorist, and finally as autobiographer. Several essays in this volume discuss Canetti's concept of *Verwandlung* (metamorphosis, transformation) in varying ways. It is, however, more than just an anthropological category: it is also a practice essential to Canetti's own life as an author, and as such it underlies the organization of the present anthology, which in large part follows the chronological and generic configuration of his oeuvre. It is both because of and in spite of Canetti's generic metamorphoses, however, that too strict a principle of organization along such lines would do both the author and the scholarship devoted to his writings a significant injustice. Thus, while it makes sense in such an anthology to organize the critical studies of Canetti's earlier works into sections according to the genres in which Canetti writes, it becomes far less practicable or desirable to categorize the essays devoted more generally to the latter parts of the author's career as pertinent to only one work or group of works.

Despite its considerable formal diversity, Canetti's work is traditionally considered from a thematic perspective to be highly unified. One of the earliest postwar essays written in German about Canetti identifies four topics around which our author's interests circle: crowds, power, death, and metamorphosis.[6] In the ensuing decades these categories have provided the four compass points on which the critical, interpretative, and even biographical mapping of Canetti's career as an author has oriented itself, an orientation that determines the focus of several of the essays and interviews contained in this anthology. Of these categories, the latter two in particular require at the very least some brief, introductory explanation. First, Canetti's central concern with death focuses on the power its all-pervasive existence holds over human beings and human society. He explores how it distorts human relationships and is at the base of all evil in society; and he develops the terms of his much-cited *Todfeindschaft,* his enmity toward death, which has as its heroic—even Sisyphean—objective the liberation of humanity from that evil, the neutralization of the destructive power that the biological fact of death introduces into every dimension and function of human society. Second, under the heading of metamorphosis, Canetti refers to the potentially inexhaustible regenerative capacity that all animate beings possess to reinvent and transform themselves and their world in defiance of specialization, stagnation, petrifaction, and death. This of course includes human beings in their cultural practices, their intellectual and artistic activities, and their capacity to retell, revivify, and re-create the myths that determine their social and spiritual existence.

Within this thematic framework, general studies of Canetti's life and works have for the most part traced a coherent development in his writings. This runs from the dark early works of the 1930s, with their preoccupation with the ossification and destruction of the embattled individual subject; by way of the author's decades-long devotion to the study of crowds and power, of human societies and their myths; to the wisdom, love, and poise of the autobiographer celebrating the plurality of human life. He becomes the "keeper of metamorphoses," demonstrating in the practice of his own writing how all the human lives that have touched his own, that have contributed to his being, may be preserved in their full variety beyond the reach of death.[7]

Pivoting on Canetti's decision to abstain from "purely poetic work" (*CW,* v) in order to devote himself to the research and writing of *Masse und Macht* (1960; *Crowds and Power*), this schematic teleology relies on a distinction, which has had persistent and profound implications for the critical reception of this author, between two fundamentally different kinds of writing. It is suggested in the title of Dagmar Barnouw's 1987 essay on Canetti's life and works, "Elias Canetti—Poet and Intellectual," which follows this introduction. That his work as a whole has resisted categorization as either exclusively imaginative or exclusively reflective is in itself of course no unusual circumstance. After all, the oeuvre of many a writer, especially one whose career—like Canetti's—spans almost six decades, crosses that perceived divide, some works being attributable to the poet, others to the intellectual. Canetti's early friend and mentor Hermann Broch, whose reputation rests on his identity as a writer both of fiction and of a scientific work on the psychology of crowds, is an obvious and immediately relevant example of another such writer whose literary and intellectual roots, like Canetti's, lie in prewar Vienna. But the distinction between two Canettis—on the one hand, the driven author of the exuberantly inventive early novel and, on the other, the author of the long-researched and carefully deliberated anthropological-philosophical treatise—has proven to be neither as tenable nor as productive as some commentators have wished. The challenge for critics lies neither in the fact that Canetti's oeuvre bridges a perceived thematic or stylistic divide in the manner of Broch's work, nor even in the fact that he exploits or explores such a wide variety of generic forms in his works. It is, rather, that so many of his writings either call into question or actively undermine the implied or stated distinction between the work of the poet and that of the intellectual.

The consequences of this ambiguity permeate not only the publication history of the work but also the history of its scholarly and critical reception. With regard to *Auto-da-Fé,* for instance, which was first published in German in extremely unfavorable political circumstances in the mid-1930s, various early critical reviews and commentaries reveal their authors' inability to reconcile the irrepressible urgency of the narrative with the book's obviously heavy though largely unfathomable thematic substance.[8] Not until the third publication of the novel in German in 1963 did its commentators finally find the interpretative categories that would open their way into the novel. The timing was not mere chance: the German publication of *Crowds and Power* in 1960 had furnished a thematic framework that would sustain much of the critical work that has addressed the novel to date, leading *Auto-da-Fé* frequently to be read as the product of a fictional experimentation with ideas that were later worked out more fully and considerably less breathlessly in *Crowds and Power.* Representative of such commentary is Hans Magnus Enzensberger's review (translated for the present volume), which states *Auto-da-Fé* to be "a work of research undertaken with the means of the imagination."

The interpretations that have followed from this assumption play variations on a broadly historical theme. They see in the novel a representation of the implosion of received hierarchies of values; a depiction of the high-modernist experience of a fragmenting reality; an image of the decline of the Western subject, divorcing intellect from the real world in which people live; a prophetic vision of the susceptibility of Western civilization to the twin historical and human catastrophes of fascism and genocide, and so on. And, indeed, some of Canetti's own comments on the genesis of the novel have tended to support this kind of assumption.[9] There have, however, been sporadic warnings in the critical literature through the years against making a simple, too exclusive, and potentially reductive connection between these works at the expense of the study of the poetic, rhetorical, comic, and intertextual dimensions of *Auto-da-Fé,* and in the last decade a number of longer studies have chosen these other starting points for the investigation of this complex work of fiction.[10]

Similarly, assumptions about the oppressively cerebral nature of Canetti's three plays have burdened their respective performance, publication, and reception histories. Canetti's two early plays, *Hochzeit (The Wedding),* completed in 1932, and *Komödie der Eitelkeit (Comedy of Vanity),* completed in 1934, fell victim to the same historical circumstances that thwarted *Auto-da-Fé,* and they were neither performed nor successfully published in widely accessible form until the mid-1960s.[11] The catastrophic reception of their first performances in 1965 is recounted in the last part of the essay by Peter Laemmle, which has been translated into English for the present volume. The reasons that essay reveals for the public outcry are varied, having to do both with the texts and with the productions. The initial uproar subsided with time and these plays were occasionally performed in the following years, but their reputation as fundamentally untheatrical, as simply carrying too much of the intellectual baggage they share with *Crowds and Power,* persisted. It was not until the late 1970s and the 1980s that these plays were successfully staged under the direction of Hans Hollmann and received public recognition as stage-dramas.[12]

A similar criticism is discussed with regard to Canetti's third play—*Die Befristeten (The Numbered,* or *Life-Terms)*—in the essay on "Utopian Dissent," written by Dagmar Barnouw for this volume. Completed in 1952 during work on *Crowds and Power,* this play is often assumed to be simply too intellectual, too driven by the metaphysical concerns that preoccupied Canetti in the writing of his magnum opus, to be theatrically viable. In the conversation with Manfred Durzak, which appears (in English translation) in the section of this volume devoted to the dramas, Canetti himself contests this criticism as it pertains to all three plays. He does so in the context of a sketching of his theoretical and practical assumptions about his own dramas and about drama in general: a project, as Durzak notes, that Canetti had discussed elsewhere but never carried to publication. With regard to this, one is reminded of Canetti's oft-cited (by Laemmle, for instance) insistence on the essential dramaticality of his writings, when he states: "I believe that, at its core, everything I do is dramatic in nature."[13]

The text whose 1960 publication paved the way for the (re-)emergence of the novel and plays is, as indicated above, *Crowds and Power.* The product of more than 20 years of work, it provoked a mixed, sometimes bemused critical reaction. In its radically interdisciplinary approach to its twin subjects of crowds and their rulers, this study draws on a broad range of ethnographic documents—some well known and relatively modern, others more obscure, their field of reference extending into remote and near-forgotten history—and retells the stories found therein. In doing so it deliberately eschews both the professional idiom of the social sciences and the recognition of existing scientific theories of crowd psychology, and this refusal to participate in prior debates has led to persistent difficulties in this text's reception over the last four decades. Furthermore, as a work of cultural criticism, written in German and published in 1960, only 15 years after the defeat of Nazi Germany, it was subjected to early criticism regarding its silence with regard to modern experience, in particular the twentieth-century experience of dictatorship and mass movements: Communism and most especially National Socialism.

The early criticism of *Crowds and Power*, addressing with some force the perceived deficiency of Canetti's silence vis-à-vis modern history, provides the context of the intriguing and much-cited discussion of Canetti's text and its ideas between its author and Theodor W. Adorno. This conversation was broadcast on German radio in 1962 and is published for the first time in English translation in the present volume. In it Adorno, whose commitment is to the rational, scientific theorization of the experience of National Socialism, and Canetti, whose work recounts many stories of the myths and mores of ancient societies and whose approach defiantly resists the construction of closed theoretical systems, talk past each other in a way that is both frustrating and fascinating. The German print-publication of this conversation occurred in 1972 in a volume of collected interviews and essays that is usually read at least in part as Canetti's response to the early criticism of *Crowds and Power*. The range of reference of the essays in the volume *Die gespaltene Zukunft* (The divided future) extends from Confucius to Hitler, thus explicitly emphasizing the link between the distant and the recent past, a link that in Canetti's study remains almost completely implicit. This then is the background of Canetti's pointed advice to Adorno, with regard to *Crowds and Power*, that it would be quite wrong for "anyone to think that the significance of real crowds were not the decisive and the most important question of all."

Often characterized—be it with positive or negative intent—as being informed by a decidedly poetic form of anthropological practice, *Crowds and Power* has over the decades generally enjoyed a more positive reception among scholars whose work crosses the boundary—the division of labor—between literature and the social sciences. The work of Dagmar Barnouw in particular, whose initial writings on Canetti served to open up the field in the 1970s and whose influential contributions have continued to the present day, has argued consistently and persuasively for a integrated reading of Canetti's works and has contested the strict division of his oeuvre—be it with reference to form, topic, or methodology—between poetic and scientific writing, and she has placed *Crowds and Power* unambiguously at the thematic and stylistic core of that oeuvre. Barnouw thus defines this work as simultaneously "scientific . . . philosophical . . . [and] poetic."[14] It is, according to Barnouw, a text that challenges scientific specialization and argues for an approach that embraces all the kinds of knowledge of which an individual is capable, stressing the necessity of not being deterred from asking questions even in the face of their probable unanswerability. As Canetti himself writes with regard to his dedication to the "desperate attempt to overcome the division of labor": "It is almost certain that such an undertaking cannot succeed. But the very faint possibility that it might succeed makes any effort worthwhile."[15] In response, the scholarship that has found virtue in this difficult and controversial text has without exception recognized Canetti's synthesis of discourses as one of the principal achievements of *Crowds and Power.*

The essays on *Crowds and Power* included in the present volume all reflect this recognition. Iris Murdoch's 1962 review has the stamp of an author who enjoys a distinguished reputation as both an academic philosopher and a writer of fiction.[16] Similarly, Ritchie Robertson's 1991 essay is the work of a scholar whose interests in the modernist period go beyond any narrowly conceived definition of the study of literature. In his essay Robertson, embracing Barnouw's challenge, seeks to establish the context of Canetti's work within traditions of anthropological thought. And indeed, despite the difficulties this text has posed for its commentators, it would be wrong to assume that it has not over four decades found its place among the documents of the intellectual life of the late twentieth century. It is a work that one now finds increasingly often cited in diverse and unexpected places. The final essay in the section of this anthology concentrating on *Crowds and Power,* written for this volume by Hansjakob Werlen, explores some contemporary contexts in which Canetti's work has come to be quoted or invoked. If (to echo Canetti) this work really has "succeeded in grabbing this century by the throat" (*HP,* 185), the suggestion is that the century may now finally be beginning—albeit less dramatically—to come to grips with Canetti's thought.

The works that Canetti conceived and wrote during or after his work on *Crowds and Power* are remarkable for their generic diversity. As Canetti recounts in his conversation on *Auto-da-Fé* with Manfred Durzak (translated into English for this volume), his German publisher was eager to exploit the interest provoked in 1963 by *Auto-da-Fé,* and subsequent works were brought to press in relatively quick succession. Other than the drama *The Numbered,* his book publications with Hanser included several collections of notes and aphorisms, the first of which appeared in 1965, the most recent posthumously in 1996; the volume of travel sketches written after a 1954 trip to Morocco *Die Stimmen von Marrakesch* (1967; *The Voices of Marrakesh*); an extended essay on Franz Kafka's letters to Felice Bauer *Der andere Prozeß* (1969; *Kafka's Other Trial*); the volume of essays and interviews *Die gespaltene Zukunft* (1972), from which, as mentioned above, is drawn the conversation between Canetti and Adorno that is included in this anthology; the slim volume of character sketches *Der Ohrenzeuge* (1974; *Earwitness*); his collected essays *Das Gewissen der Worte* (1975, rev. 1976; *The Conscience of Words*); and his three volumes of autobiography *Die gerettete Zunge* (1977; *The Tongue Set Free*), *Die Fackel im Ohr* (1980; *The Torch in My Ear*), and *Das Augenspiel* (1985; *The Play of the Eyes*). It was the publicly acclaimed autobiography that led at last to the appearance of the septuagenarian author's still relatively unknown and exotic-sounding name in bestseller lists in the German-speaking world.

Reading through this catalog of rapid generic metamorphoses does not prepare one for the points of comparison that have been traced between these texts in the critical literature. From a formal point of view these generic distinctions conceal the predominance of shorter prose forms during most of this later period. Notes and aphorisms, essays, and character or travel sketches permit to varying degrees a kind of subjectivity of thought that other prose forms resist. They provide the space for the assaying of new ideas. In them the reader finds utopian or dystopian projections; invented or recorded stories of metamorphosis; models of how lives might be well or badly lived; depictions of forms of power and utopian sketches aimed at discovering ways in which its hold over people's lives might be escaped; investigations into the tyrannical power of death over individual human beings and the relationships between them; the sheer celebration of the infinite variety of human behavior; even whimsical fictions. Sometimes almost impenetrable in their meaning or implication, sometimes strikingly direct and amenable to quotation, they bind neither their author nor their readers to fixed interpretations. These are genres in which the boundaries between the imaginative and the reflective, the narrative and the argumentative, the poetic and the philosophical, blur and finally dissolve.

Commentaries on Canetti's work in these genres have focused on its resistance—indeed, opposition—to totalizing systems of scientific thought, final meanings, and universal theories or ideologies. These genres work around questions rather than seeking their definitive resolution, they celebrate the unanswerable and the mysterious, and they leave space for the silences and the other voices that surround their propositions and provocations. They aim to initiate their reader into the processes of Canetti's thinking, rather than to report on its products. To some extent the same is true also of the poetic anthropology practiced in the kaleidoscopic configuration of essayistic sections and subsections in *Crowds and Power*. Critics' praise for Canetti's work in short prose forms concentrates on the very same qualities of irreducibility, antisystemic thinking, and stylistic poignancy that have often been invoked by those commentators on *Crowds and Power* whose sympathies and interests lie with the poetic qualities of that text, qualities that seem so often to have frustrated or alienated social scientists and philosophers, not the least among them Adorno. It is of course important not to take the analogy too far: in their published form these more fragmentary texts lack the thematic concentration and organic structure of *Crowds and Power,* not to mention the tendency toward apodictic pronouncement that critics have noted in the 1960 text.[17] Often read as highly quotable companion pieces to *Crowds and Power,* many of the aphorisms and essays represent open-ended experiments around the same themes and topics discussed there, but the context of this work is more fluid, the invention of situations and narratives freer, the field of reference sometimes more familiar and contemporary, sometimes more fantastic.

Canetti's autobiography, recounting the first 33 years of his life up to the point of his leaving Vienna for London in 1938, heralds a return to work in a longer narrative genre. Read both as a sovereign act of personal remembrance and as a document of an intellectual world that has passed into history, there are two areas on which the dominant trends of the scholarship on these three volumes focus. The first is its relationship to the ideas of *Crowds and Power*: this autobiography provides a portrait of the author of both *Auto-da-Fé* and *Crowds and Power* as a young man, and of the forces at work in the intellectual, social, and personal environments in which he lived. It is this documentary function on which the reception of the autobiography initially focuses. The second, which gradually grows in significance alongside the critics' interest in the documentary, considers the organization of the autobiographical project in terms that once again stress the subjective, "literary" qualities of its narrative composition. Friederike Eigler's 1988 monograph, combining a focus on both of these areas, remains to date the most incisive and illuminative study of these texts.[18] Read from these two perspectives, the autobiography, like all of Canetti's writings, begins to oscillate indeterminately between the poles of the poetic and the documentary, the subjective and the objective. And though its overall effect is that of an extended narrative, formally it is perhaps not as radically different from his other late works as first appearances suggest, many of its short chapters being amenable to reading in isolation as self-contained, essayistic fragments.

Other commentators, including some whose essays are included in this collection, have begun to doubt the certainty of its documentary function. Pointing to the deliberation of its revelations and concealments, they explore the stylistic and structural artifice of the writing and question the factuality of characters and events that seem to fit the narrative a little too well to be true.[19] Taken further, this line of inquiry has led to the comparison of Canetti's text with the most famous German poetic autobiography of all, Goethe's *Dichtung und Wahrheit* (*Poetry and Truth*).[20] In a more surprising analogy, the autobiography is even read in part as a continuation of the young Canetti's project of a cycle of novels, of which he completed and published only *Auto-da-Fé*. Just as that book concentrated on the life and work of the extreme figure of the bookman Peter Kien, so the whole of Canetti's career— from the writing of the novel depicting a society's and a civilization's greedy, hate-ridden dance of self-destruction, through the years of silence and scholarship, to the emergence of the benevolent, loving founder of a new creed fundamentally opposed to the power of death—comes to be identifiable as the life, rich in metamorphoses and informed by a "passion for people," of another of his own projected fictional creations: the antithesis of the sterile bookman, the "Todfeind," the enemy of death.[21]

Not all critics pursue the implications of the artifice of the autobiography to the same positive end. Bernd Witte's and Gerhard Melzer's newly translated essays, found in the last major section of this anthology, represent a darker, more ambiguous interpretation that emerged as part of a controversial reevaluation of Canetti's career by a number of scholars beginning in the mid-1980s. In retracing the connection between, on the one hand, the textual strategies of selection and ordering at work in Canetti's later writings and, on the other, the strategies of power that the author unmasks in *Crowds and Power,* these critics argue that Canetti, the expert on power, himself becomes a power figure, ruling over his work and its interpretation with the final authority to determine who and what is included and remembered, and who and what is to be abandoned to the oblivion of exclusion. The difference between the Canetti that emerges from this reading and the redeeming, loving Canetti that emerges from that discussed just before can scarcely be overstated.

Who then is Elias Canetti? This simple question used to have a simpler answer than it does now. Biographical information, bibliographic data, and a narrow cluster of thematic foci used to provide an adequate framework within which to structure a functional answer, and Canetti's own writing on the early years of his life seemed to serve well enough to bolster this edifice. Barnouw's categories of the poet and the intellectual, which stand at the very beginning of the essays collected in this anthology, inevitably run intertwined though any integrated understanding of Canetti's life and achievement as a writer, simultaneously defining and complicating how he is to be read. General surveys of Canetti's work—dependent on the vision of a coherent progression from youth to maturity and from maturity to the wisdom and authority of age—rely without exception on the bildungsroman-like structure of the autobiography for their inspiration. This reliance, however, becomes problematic as soon as one acknowledges the extent of the poetic dimension of these texts. And it becomes especially problematic when that poetic artifice threatens to eclipse the documentary axis of the autobiography to the extent that such diametrically opposed interpretations can arise and be justified on the basis of one corpus of writing.

Is the Canetti of the autobiography the quasi-messianic savior, driven by a love for the variety of humanity? Or is he the absolute ruler over his text, wielding his expertise in power to vindictive ends? It is not my intention to attempt to answer these questions here. The reviews, essays, and interviews collected in the sections that follow contribute in a variety of ways both to the interpretation of individual texts and to an overall understanding of Canetti. In ending the anthology with Claudio Magris's essay, my intention is to leave the controversy unresolved. Rejecting the binary choice between the readings outlined above, Magris sees behind the autobiography a strategy of self-protective deception. His Canetti is the author who pretends to tell all, while in reality keeping everything essential about himself concealed and shrouded in ambiguity. This understanding of the author's life is in part reminiscent of what Canetti himself writes in the preface to *The Human Province* with regard to how the project of grasping a whole human life might be approached. As an alternative to grasping a life "in its full spiritual and intellectual context," he writes of his wish "that some men would record the leaps in their lives" (*HP,* vi). The idea of recording a life in this way makes a specific point with regard to how one might read the collection of the notes and aphorisms (spanning the years 1942 to 1972), at whose beginning it stands. The fragments of thought, imagination, and revelation contained therein present anything but a coherent and comprehensive "spiritual and intellectual context." But its significance goes beyond that, suggesting a reading of Canetti's life as one that itself consists of leaps, disjunctures, and sudden metamorphoses: the life of someone who inhabits a world that is graspable only in "splinters of astonishment" (*CW,* 3).[22] Such a reading defies the reduction of that life to any one simple identifying formula, with the consequence that Canetti will not be fixed so easily. There can be little doubt that he would have wanted it otherwise. With regard to his wish about how lives might be recorded, he concludes: "The loss of a superficial unity, inevitable in such an enterprise, cannot be regretted, for the true unity of a life is secret, and it is most effective when it unintentionally conceals itself" (*HP,* vi).

Notes

1. Ingo Seidler, "Who is Elias Canetti?" in *Cross Currents: A Yearbook of Central European Culture,* ed. Ladislav Matejka and Benjamin Stolz (Ann Arbor: University of Michigan Press, 1982), 107–23.

2. Elias Canetti, *Auto-da-Fé,* trans. C. V. Wedgwood (London: Cape, 1946); an American edition of Wedgwood's translation followed under the title *The Tower of Babel* (New York: Knopf, 1947).

3. Richard H. Lawson, *Understanding Elias Canetti,* Understanding Modern European and Latin American Literature (Columbia: University of South Carolina Press, 1991); Thomas H. Falk, *Elias Canetti,* Twayne's World Authors Series, no. 843 (New York: Twayne, 1993).

4. David Darby, *Structures of Disintegration: Narrative Strategies in Elias Canetti's "Die Blendung"* (Riverside, Calif.: Ariadne, 1992), hereafter cited in text as Darby 1992; Kristie A. Foell, *Blind Reflections: Gender in Elias Canetti's "Die Blendung"* (Riverside, Calif.: Ariadne, 1994); Robert Elbaz and Leah Hadomi, *Elias Canetti, or The Failing of the Novel* (New York: Lang, 1995); and Harriet Murphy, *Canetti and Nietzsche: Theories of Humor in "Die Blendung"* (Albany: State University of New York Press, 1997), hereafter cited in text as Murphy 1997.

5. In this context it is fitting to mention the only other collection of essays on Canetti published in English: *Essays in Honor of Elias Canetti,* trans. Michael Hulse (New York: Farrar, Straus and Giroux, 1987); hereafter cited in text as *Essays in Honor.* That volume, containing several important essays, is based on a collection issued by Canetti's German publisher in honor of the author's eightieth birthday: *Hüter der Verwandlung: Beiträge zum Werk von Elias Canetti* (Munich: Hanser, 1985). In selecting essays and reviews for the present anthology, I

have avoided duplicating work that appears in the 1987 volume (with the exception of some passages in the essay by Magris that are repeated there in another context). I have of course also drawn on important work done since the mid-1980s, work whose critical perspective is occasionally at odds with the overall celebratory tone of the earlier collection.

6. Hans Daiber, "Elias Canetti," *Neue Rundschau* 81 (1955): 605.

7. Elias Canetti, *The Conscience of Words,* trans. Joachim Neugroschel (London: Deutsch, 1986), 161; hereafter cited in text as *CW.*

8. The publication history of Canetti's novel is in itself extraordinary. Completed in early 1931—so midway between the economic crash of 1929 and the seizing of power by the National Socialist regime early in 1933—the novel was not published for almost another five years. By the time the book had been published in Vienna in 1935, its prospects in the German-speaking world—like those of its Jewish author—were already severely limited. This publication of the novel was thus short-lived, and it effectively disappeared from view with the annexation of Austria into the Third Reich in 1938, as did Canetti, who settled in London and devoted himself to researching his projected major study of crowds. The first postwar attempt to revive the novel's German fortunes was made in 1948. It was republished by the Weismann Verlag in Frankfurt am Main, this time in economic circumstances that could scarcely have been less auspicious, to which this publishing venture soon fell victim. It would be some years until the novel resurfaced in 1963, published in more favorable circumstances by the Carl Hanser Verlag, which has served ever since as Canetti's principal publisher. For a more detailed account of the reception of Canetti's novel, see Darby 1992, 1–12.

9. See for instance Canetti's essay "The First Book: *Auto-da-Fé*" (*CW,* 123–33).

10. See for instance Darby 1992, and Murphy 1997; a new essay, developing some of the ideas found in Murphy's 1997 book, is included in the present volume.

11. Prior to this a manuscript version of *The Wedding* had been published in Berlin in 1932 by S. Fischer; and *Comedy of Vanity* had been published in very adverse economic circumstances after the war (Munich: Weismann, 1950).

12. See Hollmann, "Working on Canetti's Plays" (*Essays in Honor,* 240–45).

13. Elias Canetti, "Gespräch mit Horst Bienek," in *Die gespaltene Zukunft: Aufsätze und Gespräche,* Reihe Hanser 111 (Munich: Hanser, 1972), 101 (my translation).

14. Dagmar Barnouw, "Masse, Macht und Tod im Werk Elias Canettis," *Jahrbuch der deutschen Schillergesellschaft* 19 (1975): 368 (my translation).

15. Elias Canetti, *The Human Province,* trans. Joachim Neugroschel (New York: Seabury, 1978), 34; hereafter cited in text as *HP.*

16. Murdoch's interest in Canetti has several dimensions, including (as critics surmise) her having modeled a character in the novel *The Flight from the Enchanter* on him.

17. See for instance Hansjakob Werlen's essay in the present collection.

18. Friederike Eigler, *Das autobiographische Werk von Elias Canetti: Verwandlung—Identität—Machtausübung,* Stauffenburg Colloquium 7 (Tübingen: Stauffenburg, 1988).

19. For example, Madeleine Salzmann, *Die Kommunikationsstruktur der Autobiographie: Mit kommunikationsorientierten Analysen der Autobiographien von Max Frisch, Helga M. Novak und Elias Canetti,* Zürcher germanistische Studien 11 (Bern: Lang, 1988); Waltraud Wiethölter, "Sprechen—Lesen—Schreiben: Zur Funktion von Sprache und Schrift in Canettis Autobiographie," *Deutsche Vierteljahrsschrift für Literaturwissenschaft und Geistesgeschichte* 64 (1990): 149–71; and David Darby, "A Literary Life: The Textuality of Elias Canetti's Autobiography," *Modern Austrian Literature* 25, no. 2 (1992): 37–49.

20. Robert Gould, "*Die gerettete Zunge* and *Dichtung und Wahrheit*: Hypertextuality in Autobiography and its Implications," *Seminar* 21 (1985): 79–107.

21. For example, Edgar Piel, *Elias Canetti,* Autorenbücher 38 (Munich: Beck, 1984), esp. 174–75.

22. The word "leap"—*Sprung*—echoes the term "Maskensprung," meaning a sudden switching of masks, with which Canetti defines a central concept in his theory of dramatic characterization. See for instance the conversation between Canetti and Durzak that appears later in this volume under the title "The Acoustic Mask."

LIFE AND WORKS

◆

Elias Canetti—Poet and Intellectual

Dagmar Barnouw

Canetti, Susan Sontag writes, "is both literally and by his own ambitions, a writer in exile."[1] Her recent enthusiastic review essay in the *New York Review of Books* is very welcome, because it provides a forceful introduction to an important European writer whose impact in this country has been very slight so far. Like many observations in her essay, however, her stylization of Canetti as a writer in exile is misleading. Canetti has been difficult to place, and partly for this reason recognition of his importance has come late; but he has not been subjected to the profound disruption of language and culture that exile has meant for so many writers. When he left Vienna in 1938 for London, where he has lived and written in German ever since, he went in a sense back to a language and a culture that had been important to him in his youth. He was born in Rustschuk, Bulgaria in 1905 into a large and lively sephardic family of merchants, who spoke Ladino, but from an early age he was very much aware of other languages spoken around him in his town of many nationalities. Preparing the child for the move to England in 1911 (to escape the tyrannical presence of his grandfather), his beloved and completely trusted father told the little boy: "In England everybody is honest ... if a man promises you something, he will do it, there is no need for him to shake hands on it."[2] The child, then, is promised a different usage of language, of the speech-act: language is no longer separated from action: rather, it serves to communicate and influence action.

England, even though he lived there for only two years, proved to be extraordinarily important for the child, because he started going to school and he learned to read. In England began the lifelong process of taking possession of the many worlds accessible in books, mediated by teachers. Canetti has been emphatically grateful to both, receiving what they had to give with a passionate urgent curiosity. Learning meant a concrete immersion, a feeling of physical involvement in the world between the covers of the book. The theme of transformation central to all his texts can be traced back to the child's somatic sense of changing: becoming smaller to fit himself between

Reprinted from *Major Figures of Contemporary Austrian Literature,* ed. Donald G. Daviau (New York: Lang, 1987), 117–38.

the bookcovers and into the pictures illustrating the stories and larger, more powerful, according to the expansive properties of the stories themselves.

England, as Canetti writes in the first volume of his autobiography *Die gerettete Zunge* (1977, *The Tongue Set Free*) is the country associated for him with books and with talking about them, sharing them, with the father's gentle reasoning. When he says that everything that he experienced later had already happened in Rustschuk, he is referring to the archetypical constellation of social relations, of passions and power, envy and desire, as the sensitive imaginative child observed them in the volatility and explosion of tempers in his family. Rustschuk was also particularly fascinating for its variety of sounds—one could hear eight different languages in one day, Canetti remembers—of tastes, smells, and images. The isolating reality of power, the immediacy of human diversity, the magically spontaneous interconnections of language were experienced by the child early and with surprising involvement. In England those frightening magical speech-acts receded; there language was not used mainly to manipulate and dominate, but to explore, to share, to gain access. Yet, like bad magic, a curse uttered by the grandfather punishing the disobedience of his son follows the small family to England: in October 1912, hardly settled in their new surroundings, his father dies suddenly of heart failure, caused, so his mother tells the children, by news about another crisis in the Balkans, signaling war that he dreaded and hated. The child had just been given a book about Napoleon with the admonition to read it "the right way," that is, critically; there had been no time to discuss it with his father: "Of all of Napoleon's victims, my father to me was the greatest, the most horrible,"[3] Canetti writes, remembering this traumatic event that proved to be of central importance for the direction of his work.

Having just gained a sense of language—English—as an opening, sharing activity, the boy was taken out of this nurturing environment by his mother, forced to learn German quickly during some months they spent in Lausanne, sufficiently well to survive in a school in Vienna where the mother had decided to live. The father's death had caused a deep-rooted hatred of destructive power in the child, affirmed by the mother's consistent and highly articulate denunciation of war, and the misuse of language was intimately connected with this complex of emotional and intellectual reactions. In Bulgaria the parents had spoken German as *their* language, reminding them of the happy time they had spent together in Vienna, constituting the realm of their privacy and intimacy, inaccessible to the demands of a complex intense family and a tyrannical patriarch, his grandfather, who had imposed a deeply resented business career on Canetti's father. When his mother now forces the boy to learn the language at any cost—and she comes across as a brilliant and remarkably cruel teacher—she also admits him to that intellectual and emotional intimacy and privacy so coveted by the child. It is not, as some critics have remarked, a magic concept of language with which the child operates; it is, rather, a surprisingly rational, social one: language, once more, is understood by the child as a supremely human activity in that it facilitates social intercourse, makes possible access to the other. The child is not interested in building his own worlds with language: from a very early age Canetti has been intent on understanding the world of the other and has seen himself, the needs of his own growing and developing self, in terms of the needs of the other.

In 1916 his mother moves her sons to Zürich. The boy is deeply impressed by a country that has managed to stave off the tidal waves of irrationality that he had seen overwhelming the crowds in the streets of Vienna at the outbreak of the war. Zürich was a paradise for the adolescent; he was left alone and given the peace and space to develop, to learn. From 1921 to 1924 he lived and went to school in Frankfurt because his mother thought the situation in Zürich too idyllic, too protected. He never forgot or forgave this violation, but he realized that what he saw and heard during this time of inflation, of mass unemployment and starvation, became, like his father's early inexplicable death, the major material force directing his work. From 1924 he lived mainly in Vienna, interrupted by visits to Berlin in 1928 and 1929. There he came into contact with artists like George Grosz and Isaak Babel and the influential leftist publishing house Malik for which he translated several of Upton Sinclair's novels. In 1929 he completed his studies with a dissertation in chemistry but decided to devote himself to writing henceforth.

In England where he arrived in January 1939, he continued to write in German, and the relative isolation—in terms of an audience—in which he worked did not differ from the situation in Vienna. He had a small circle of friends, admirers of his work,[4] and English was not really a foreign language to him. After the war he chose to stay in England, and he explained his decision to go on writing in German:

> The language of my mind will continue to be German, because I am Jewish. Whatever remains of that country, ravaged in every sense, I will protect in myself as a Jew. It is also *their* fate that is mine; but I bear a universal human inheritance. I want to give back to their language what I owe to it. I want my contribution to add to the reason for being grateful to them for something once again.[5]

Given the long period of time during which he did not publish anything, this certainty that he would find readers, that his "contribution" would be recognized, that his texts would indeed add to the reason for being "grateful" to the German language and German culture, is remarkable. Working on the social psychological analysis of power and crowds, he sees himself in a tradition of successful poetic communication. He had been sure of the importance of that activity as well as of his share in it from an early age: the fourteen-year-old dedicated a long badly written drama to his mother who "loved the poets" and considered reading the center of her life, signing it "in spe poeta clarus"; and with characteristic tenacity, passion, and patience he was to become just that. Poetic language for Canetti does not signify the writer's inevitable existence in exile, as it did for Walter Benjamin. It means, rather, a complex of intellectual, imaginative verbal energies distinguished from ordinary discourse, yet also connected with it, dependent on it and of very great importance to it. Canetti's trust in the concrete effectiveness of poetic language is as anachronistic (unzeitgemäß), as is his belief in the social responsibility of the poet,[6] especially as it is combined with his demand that poetic language be accessible, that it be willing to accommodate questions. Poetic language for him is emphatically not a privileged medium and yet central to all cultural and social activities. The reasons for this enlightened belief in the essential communicability of human affairs, mental and physical, in the importance of the rational dimension of social intercourse in any form, for this amazing abstinence from ideology in any shade or substance seems to be related to his early exposure to many different languages, cultures, and temperaments, a circumstance that saved him from ever feeling like an exile. In collaboration with his mother, for he almost always collaborated with her even when she seemed most forceful and tyrannical, even cruel, because she offered him reasons, he *chose* German as his language and never forgot the act of choosing nor the implications of this act: language, communication is a man-made achievement, not an a priori given, magically sustained phenomenon.

Canetti's precise and intense involvement with three languages—the Ladino spoken in his family, English and German—corresponds to the *locus* of his writing; between the conventional literary genres as well as between different fields in the social sciences. By the late thirties he had become known to a small important and influential circle of writers, critics, and poets in Vienna and in Berlin.[7] His first and only novel *Die Blendung*[8] (*Auto-da-Fé*) published in 1935 but completed in the fall of 1931, is an interesting counterpart to Heinrich Mann's *Der Untertan* [*Man of Straw*] (written in 1914 but not published until after the war had ended) in its "prophetic" extrapolation from existing aggressive verbal and nonverbal behavior. By looking at available evidence Mann anticipated the language of survival as it was used during the war; Canetti anticipated the language of total repression as it was to be used under Hitler's totalitarian regime. The main difference between these novels, which are strikingly similar in essential ways, for instance, in the handling of speech patterns in the fictional constructs of a social reality, lies in their reception: Mann's novel found many enthusiastic readers, whose response signaled a hoped-for cultural rebirth at the beginning of the Weimar Republic.[9] Canetti's novel, harsher, more extreme, and also more ambivalent in its indictment of his contemporaries, that is, Hitler's audience, than Mann's had been of the Emperor's subjects, came too late and too early to be effective. After the war *Die Blendung* returned to Germany via England and France where the response had been enthusiastic from small well-informed audiences.[10]

The novel and two early dramas written about the same time, *Hochzeit* (1932, The Wedding) and *Komödie der Eitelkeit* (1934, Comedy of Vanity)[11] record a confusing variety of what Canetti calls "acoustic masks," a character's speech habits that outline his individual functions and interactions in a group as distinctly as would a visual mask. Demands on the concentration of the reader/listener/spectator are high and exhausting. Canetti, who considers himself to be essentially a dramatist in all of his writings, developed the concept of the acoustic mask under the influence of Karl Kraus, the Viennese social and literary critic, writer of aphorisms, philosopher of language, poet, and journalist. For almost forty years (1899–1936) Kraus singlehandedly edited and from 1912 wrote *Die Fackel* (The Torch), the highly influential journal against what Kraus called "Journaille," a corrupted press that reflected and reinforced the general social verbal hypocrisy and physical cruelty. Above all he wanted his readers to doubt the official interpretation of their social reality, the conventions of language. Taking language "at its word," his judgments implicit in the "acoustic quotations," as Canetti calls them,[12] whether recorded in *Die Fackel* or flung out to the audiences crowding his immensely popular lectures, were irresistibly right: the world in which we live is seething with stupidity, greed, and cruelty and so is the corrupted language of daily life: "The fact that somebody is a murderer need not be proof against his [verbal] style. But his style may prove that he is a murderer," Kraus writes in his *Fackel* (October 1907). His anger made him expose the mechanics of a language of a social, indeed, criminal respectability; his compassion, literally fierce, mediated between despair and shame. In the unremittingly precise recording of its persecutor's "acoustic mask" the victim preserves his own painful individuality.

Canetti, who chose the title *Die Fackel im Ohr* (1980, *The Torch in My Ear*) for the second volume of his autobiography dealing with the ten years, 1921–1931, that he spent in Vienna, was particularly impressed by Kraus's adamant stance against war. He had started going to Kraus's lectures in 1924 and very quickly became an addict to these consummate performances of the "master of horror" using his weapon of "literalness" with deadly precision, putting contemporary language on a trial such as it could not possibly survive. Many years later when writing about his complex (but not ambivalent) relations to Kraus,[13] Canetti said that the horror of the atomic bomb was already contained in Kraus's satirical pandemonium of voices, of acoustic masks, with which he constructed a model of what very soon afterward presented itself to the incredulous gullible world as the Third Reich. From Kraus, Canetti learned the feeling of unrelieved social responsibility, bordering on obsession, and he learned to listen. From now on the voices of reality would pursue him; like Kraus he would never be set free again. The novel *Die Blendung* brings them to full expression, a virtuoso performance subjecting the reader to the relentless persecution by the monotonous, powerfully inarticulate acoustic masks of the housekeeper Therese and the janitor Pfaff, who destroy those around them with their material greed and raw urge for power. Indeed, the novel and the two early dramas are the most persuasive witnesses to the effectiveness of Kraus's methods of literalness (*Wörtlichkeit*). But more and more Canetti comes to see that the limitations of this most impressive of teachers lie precisely in his illuminating aggressive concentration on the sentence: the exposed subhuman imperfection of the quote, the inhuman perfection of the comment. Canetti explains the ultimately dangerous exclusiveness of Kraus's method by describing how his sentences form a "Chinese wall,"[14] a perfectly closed structure that has by its very perfection sapped the empire it was meant to defend: "For the ashlars he used for building were *judgments*, and all that had been alive in the area around there had entered into them."[15]

His mother, whose emotional and intellectual influence cannot be overestimated—the first volume of the autobiography, *Die gerettete Zunge: Geschichte einer Jugend* (*The Tongue Set Free: Remembrance of a European Childhood*), makes this abundantly clear—had directed him with judgments. He had admired their clarity and decisiveness and above all the fact that she always gave him a reason. So of course did Kraus. Given the profound influence and, for a time, response of absolute devotion, Canetti's recognition of the essential insufficiency of any judgment had far-reaching consequences.

Increasingly Kafka's influence asserted itself; along with Kraus he is the most important writer for Canetti. Canetti writes: "Many years after the influence had become effective with Kafka something new had come into this world, a more precise feeling for the fact that it is questionable, which is, however, not coupled with hatred but with reverence for life. The interaction between these two intellectual and emotional attitudes—reverence for something that has been recognized as questionable—is unique, and once one has come to know it, one is unwilling ever to do without it again."[16] That Canetti retained this feeling is documented by all the texts published since *Die Blendung: Masse und Macht* (1960, *Crowds and Power*), the study of sociopsychological, philosophical, anthropological phenomena concerning the relations between crowds and power in the magnetic field of death; the drama *Die Befristeten* (1964, The Deadlined);[17] aphoristic notes, collected in the volume *Die Provinz des Menschen* (1973, *The Human Province*), toward an open moral "system" set against the acceptance of death and as notations of intellectual poetic spontaneity meant to alleviate the sustained work discipline of *Masse und Macht*, decades in the making. There are also the gentle exposures of impotence, of children, of the poor, and of animals in the prose texts responding to travel experiences in Morocco *Die Stimmen von Marrakesch* (1968, *The Voices of Marrakesh*).

The book-length essay on Kafka's correspondence with Felice Bauer *Der andere Prozeß* (1968, *Kafka's Other Trial*) demonstrates through Kafka's superbly sensitive awareness of his own as of the other's life-center—the symbiosis of power and impotence—the fragmentary nature of human relationships too vulnerable to survive judgments and inflicted sentences. There are essays dealing with social and psychological aspects of all-powerful regimens and their attempts at total repression or destruction: on Albert Speer's memoirs, on an eyewitness to the apocalyptic explosion of the atomic bomb. A recent collection *Der Ohrenzeuge* (1974, *Earwitness: Fifty Characters*) goes back to acoustic masks from the world of *Die Blendung* with an added dimension of surreal ordinariness. Finally, there are the first three volumes of his autobiography,[18] which reveal the destructive (because limiting) properties of judgments, documenting Canetti's patient and passionate fascination for all the diverse forms of human life around him: everybody should be remembered, nobody should be excluded.

Canetti did not take too seriously the oft-noted "prophetic" quality of *Die Blendung*. "The prophets, lamenting, prophesy the known," he noted in 1945.[19] *Die Blendung*, referring to the burning of a scholar's magnificent library—the sinologist Peter Kien himself is the incendiary, having gone mad with intellectual and social isolation—is as much in anticipation of the burning of books ordered by Goebbels and carried out by enthusiastic university students in 1933 as it is reminiscent of the great burning of books in ancient China in the year 213 B.C. It was possible to predict such events by recording the voices of Viennese reality in the mode of Kraus, mastering horror and literalness. "My uncanny power was in chaos," Canetti notes in 1945. "I was as certain of that as I was of the world. Today even chaos has exploded. No structure was so senseless that it could not disintegrate into something even more senseless, and wherever I sniff, everything is heavy with the smell of extinguished fires."[20]

Chaos had been too safe in its brilliantly perfected presentation in the novel and the early dramas. The later work is set against chaos, its imagery simplified and purified, abandoning his earlier fascination for mimesis, the ultimately isolating mock surrender to the real. The differences between various voices have become more subtle, the nuances of the play with idioms and intonations more delicate. Yet these are voices recorded in many different places and periods of history, and in many different modes including the mythical. It is this greater restraint and subtlety that enabled Canetti to find meaning in speaking about contemporary totalitarian execution of power. Kraus had been permanently silenced by the "onset of hell" that he recognized very early in Hitler's regime. A poem published in the only issue of *Die Fackel* published in 1933 (October) "Man frage nicht" ("Don't Ask Me") ends with the well-known line: "Das Wort entschlief, als jene Welt erwachte" ("the word went to sleep when that world awoke"). One of the few antifascist writers who did not react violently to Kraus's remark, "Zu Hitler fällt mir nichts ein" ("I can't think of anything to say about Hitler") was Brecht, who understood that Kraus had been wise not to ask too much of satirical language. Brecht in his best works shared Kraus's method of capturing the weaknesses and the vices of men "in den Schlingen ihrer Redensarten" ("in the snares of their speech"); and he admired Kraus precisely for those acts of aggression that Canetti came to see as futile: "Als das Zeitalter Hand an sich legte, war er [Kraus] diese Hand" ("When the epoch laid its hand on itself, he was this hand").[21]

In an issue of *Die Fackel* in July 1934 Kraus had admitted: "The great theme of the onset of hell is too much for the passionate cowardice of him whose work had been done in vain: to talk of the devil."[22] Even the most severe, the most ingenious cross-examination of language had not disclosed what a totalitarian regime in a terrorized mass society was capable of. It is not within the satirist's imagination to find possible solutions or to foresee that the impossible would indeed happen. Kraus's achievement was to reveal the impossibility of "solutions," of social conventions that had been accepted as possible. Greatly indebted to him, Canetti went further. He stopped writing fiction, that is, imposing an interpretation before he had understood what had happened. In the preface to the first edition of *Aufzeichnungen 1942–1948* (Notes 1942–1948), which were not published until 1965, he states that in order to force himself not to turn away from "the naked world" for even one moment, he started to collect as much information as he possibly could about the different ways in which men had lived together and had explained their attempts at coexistence. His appetite for information was indeed ferocious, and he developed a very flexible concept of history—"I would give a great deal to get rid of my habit of seeing the world historically," he noted in 1950, two years after he had started writing *Masse und Macht*.[23] History like fiction was too much of a construct, an imposed interpretation suppressing other social possibilities. In his *Aufzeichnungen* he therefore recorded sketches of utopian social arrangements or conventions based on taking literally certain social problems that we have agreed to take for granted, above all the determination of human beings through rationed time and through the acceptance of death: cities in which men are born old and get younger, where they live as long as they are loved, where they have at least two ages simultaneously, for instance 19 and 57, where everybody disappears for periods of time so that nobody can be taken for granted alive or in death, where religion does not console but sustains an ever acute despair about the human condition, that is, consciousness of the passing of time and the imposition of destructive changes that are as inevitable as they are alien, as accidental as they are programmed.

The more Canetti experienced death as omnipresent during the war, the more he began to doubt its "natural law." Freud had developed his concept of a "Todestrieb," *thanatos,* under the impact of witnessing so much dying during the First World War, which he had opposed from the very beginning. Accordingly, Canetti feels he had to protest all the harder. "With one problem which is the most important to me, the problem of death, I have found only opponents among all thinkers. That may explain why my own opinion comes forward with the energy of belief and never declares itself without vehemence and eagerness," he states in the preface to *Die Provinz des Menschen.*[24] He is puzzled that he alone seems to question what appears to him so eminently questionable: "The incomprehensible accepted by everyone as if it contained a secret justification."[25] It cannot, it does not. To the analytic philosopher, relegating death to metaphysics, Canetti points out that death is the oldest fact, "older and more incisive than any language";[26] the human sciences, on the other hand, have abstracted the concrete social problem of death into a natural law as it poses such difficulties. And death is always seen as an absolute, by definition outside life, removed from considerations like fairness, function, proportion. But it is precisely these considerations that Canetti wants appreciated, and he startles the reader with his consistent common sense. What he says about the acceptance of death makes sense in that it refers to a shared experience. Yet, strangely, the making sense itself seems the most startling, the calm assertion of the obvious the most provoking. Life is too short to accommodate all there is to know about potential, constructive change, about motion and surprise that is essentially human: "Who will give me the news when I no longer am, who will tell me?" Canetti asks.[27] He refuses to be excluded from the human future, and it is not so much the futility of such refusal that makes it so poignant, but its justification. If there is so much to know, so many worlds to enter, why should anyone be excluded?: "Death would not be so unjust if it were not *fated in advance*. Each of us, even the most evil, can claim the excuse that whatever he does never comes close to the badness of this predetermined sentence. We must be evil (*böse*) because we know that we shall die. We would be even more evil (*böser*) if we knew from the beginning when," Canetti writes in 1952, the year he completed the drama *Die Befristeten* (1964, The Deadlined).[28] Those scheduled for death in this play are for this very reason more evil, more distorted than the most grotesque characters from the early dramas or *Die Blendung*. Their surface normalcy, their calm, dulled voices are functionally deceptive: we have to identify with them so that we can then decide that we shall be different.

It is the shifting of differences and similarities, the merging, the diverging of the familiar and the alien that informs Canetti's texts after *Die Blendung*. For many years he did not "write," at least not in any form that would contain and solidify such fluidity. With amazing patience—friends and acquaintances in London remarked on its quixotic substance[29]—he collected information that eventually went into *Masse und Macht*, remaining true to his concept of human time: if he did not actually *have* the time to let the riches of information and insight accumulate, he ought to take it. All he permitted himself to write then were the *Aufzeichnungen*, spontaneous notations of his perception of social reality, his subjunctive mode of existence sustained in the remarkably self-reliant, as it were, natural assertion of each sentence: "His image of happiness: to read and write quietly a whole life long, without ever showing anybody one word of it, without ever publishing one word of it. Everything he has noted for himself is to be left in pencil, not to be worked on, as if it were not there for anything particular; like the natural course of a life that does not serve any limiting purpose but is fully itself and traces itself the way one walks and breathes: spontaneously."[30]

This perspective helps to explain the curiously open quality of Canetti's language, which is accessible to the reader and accommodating to thoughts, images, phenomena, and other voices. The speaker admits to being wary of the incisiveness of critical thought, the separation, the shock almost: "One sees thoughts stretching their hands out of the water, one thinks they are crying for help. What an illusion! Down below they live in perfect agreement and intimacy. Try it and pull out a single thought!"[31] It is rather the connections, the bringing together of the disparate, that Canetti concentrates on in his postwar texts. At the same time he insists on clarity and rational access: thoughts living together in undisturbed intimacy are also clearly defined individual articulations; interacting thoughts must not become "matted." The concentration on small units in perception and expression practiced in the *Aufzeichnungen* proves very useful to the writing of *Masse und Macht*. The complexity of the self, reflected in experience, is preserved in these small units of articulation that are not so powerful as to force it into any manipulable pattern. It can then be preserved as something growing, not completed: "The important part of each thought is what it leaves unsaid, how much it loves what has not been said, and how close it comes to it without touching it."[32]

The tentative movements of thoughts, the open but carefully organized verbal complexes in which the abstract and the concrete merge, the exploration of images shared, accessible in idiomatic speech, defy the construction of a system but not a consistent search for order, a clearly articulated emphasis on values. "Rarely has anyone been so at home in the mind, with so little ambivalence," Sontag writes,[33] trying to illuminate Canetti's peculiar achievement. In the contemporary intellectual context of cultural despair it is important to stress Canetti's passionate fascination with the potential of the human mind. But in order to understand the mixed nature of his texts and their surface directness, the writer's roaming curiosity *and* undogmatic insistence on selecting that which is useful to know, it is also important to point out that this fascination is nurtured by the achievement of others before him. It is precisely because others were so at home in the mind, trusting the potential of intellect and imagination, that Canetti, writing as our contemporary, can do without ambivalence.

Canetti's concept of the crowd, its power and its mystery, is based on intense personal experience, as are all his social concepts. He witnessed his first great demonstration on the occasion of Rathenau's assassination in 1922. In his autobiography dealing with the twenties, he mentions the very strong physical attraction exercised by the crowd on the individual (his) body, like gravitation, but also different in the sense that the bodies pulled into the crowd are not lifeless and therefore unchanged but undergo a complete change of consciousness. It was this change Canetti found as decisive as mysterious a phenomenon: "It was a mystery which has never released me, pursuing me for the best part of my life, and though I finally did find some clues, much has remained mysterious," he writes from the distance of almost sixty years.[34] The decision to write a book about the phenomenon of crowd behavior crystallized in 1925 in reaction to reading Freud's "Massenpsychologie und Ich-Analyse" ["Group Psychology and the Analysis of the Ego"], a text by which he was repelled at first reading and still is today, fifty-five years later, because its author was not so much interested in understanding the dynamics of the crowd as in keeping it at a distance. What Freud's analysis lacked was recognition of a phenomenon which to Canetti seemed no less elemental than libido or hunger. To stress the fundamental aspect of the crowd, its dynamics and energies, the young Canetti used the term "Massentrieb" (drive of the masses), which he regarded as important as the sexual drive.[35]

In July 1927 the Vienna Palace of Justice was burned, an experience that proved to be highly important to the witness Canetti. The violent motions of flames and bodies merge: the fire assumes the properties of the crowd, the crowd spreads like fire. Distinct against the leaping flames and the convulsive body of the crowd Canetti sees a man flinging up his arms, lamenting the burning of all the files: " 'But they've shot down people,' I said angrily, 'and you're talking about files!' He looked at me as if I wasn't there and repeated plaintively: 'The files are burning! All the files!' "[36] This memory went into the book-burning scene in *Die Blendung:* The incendiary, Peter Kien, a highly respected sinologist, is driven to this act of self-destruction by his petty-bourgeois persecutors, because in his scholarly isolation he accepts the destruction of others; his books are closer to him than human beings. His brother Georges, a very successful psychiatrist, had come to save him from his tormentors and had succeeded in restoring Peter's library damaged by their greed. He also chased away the predatory housekeeper Therese and the janitor Pfaff. Finally he suggested to his brother, whose illness he does not really understand although he seems to be able to control it, the idea and the image of magnificent self-consuming destruction: the fire and the crowd. Peter had been complaining about his isolation, which takes the form of a very grave but not exclusively neurotic misogyny. Georges, seeing only individual rather than social illness, approaches the problem by trying to persuade Peter that love is an obstacle to efficient work. Consider the termites, he says: most of them have been freed from sexual drives because such drives would cause too many disturbances in a very crowded society. But then he projects what might happen if the individual termites, blind cells in an organism beyond their grasp, rebelled against such limitation. In describing the rebellion, spreading like fire, destroying the whole colony, he gets carried away, creating images of passionate energy for such self-destruction that prove much more persuasive than his admonition to his brother to be reasonable and accept certain necessary limitations. The termites are victims of a grandiose delusion comparable to Peter's setting fire to his own library. Georges professes to an ever stronger belief in science, the rationality of the termite colony in its normal state, but the incendiary power of his rhapsodic description of the erupting crowd—like fire—moves Peter to act.

Georges, the psychiatrist, lives among the mad, is loved by them, needs their love. Rather than healing them, he tries to understand them, that is, to lose himself in their madness, which he diagnoses as the crowd within them that does not find satiation.[37] On the basis of Georges's comments the Austrian Marxist, Ernst Fischer, who knew Canetti in Vienna, criticized his concept of the individual's victory over and against death by immersion and dissolution of the self in the mass, the crowd, a totality. However, Canetti is not Georges, and he is not Peter. He shares characteristics with both brothers, but he is distinctly critical of them. He is fascinated by crowds and increasingly searches for documentation in cultural and political history—for instance, in the geneses of religious movements where crowds have often played a highly important part. He does not, however, suggest the collective of the crowd as a refuge or remedy for the threatened individual in a mass society. He is interested in analysis, not in evaluation or justification.

Peter's self-immolation—he burns to death with his books—is the result of his and his brother's failure to act with social responsibility. Peter becomes guilty by completely withdrawing from the world of demented housekeepers and janitors desperately fighting for their share; Georges does so by manipulating the mentally ill. Both worlds are horrible *and* comical—Canetti mentioned Gogol's influence on *Die Blendung*[38]—and they document the immensely difficult coexistence of individuals in a mass society, caught in their differences, their inequality. The destructiveness of the petty bourgeois has its roots in his imperturbable isolation. His asocial acts show an aggressive potential which can be fully brought out in certain mass movements where, through crowd manipulation, his obsessive "me, me" can be whipped into collective orgasmic attacks on reasonable, civilized social conventions. Georges is unaware of this danger because he cannot imagine that he would ever be in a situation beyond his control. Peter becomes aware of it too late. It is only when his sensibility has been sharpened by illness that he understands how dangerous Pfaff really is. The acoustic masks of the housekeeper and of the janitor document above all their grotesque inarticulateness. Their specific distortions, their mental mutilations are taken seriously, but there is no attempt to explain them. They are closed off to each other, to the intellectuals Peter and Georges, and to the intellectual reader. They appear as typical examples of petty-bourgeois authoritarian repression, greed, and aggression, whose acts are predetermined. Yet the imaginative variations of their monomaniac, monotonous masks, which are recorded with such precision, give them exotic distinctness: they are as alien as they are familiar.

Isolation so extreme that the result is chaos: the early plays, *Hochzeit* (1932, The Wedding) and *Komödie der Eitelkeit* (1964, Comedy of Vanity), demonstrate chaos so effectively that they have had great difficulties with their audiences, still causing theatrical scandals in the 1960s. Canetti said that the dramatic element is central to all his texts: the recording of voices, making them heard.[39] He clearly sees a relation between the acoustic mask, the physiognomy of a speaker made up of his particular five hundred words, and the visual masks used in the early cult theater, as well as to the animal masks so important to "primitive" cultures. The concept dramatic means for Canetti the interplay of fixation and transformation. In *Hochzeit* the fixation is greed, people owning objects as well as one another; in *Komödie der Eitelkeit* it is the self carried to the extreme because of a curious kind of social prohibition: there are no mirrors allowed in this particular dystopian society. However, the mirror does mirror the self not only in relation to itself, but also in relation to the other. Deprived of the possibility of looking at oneself, to prepare oneself for being looked at by the other, to anticipate and to a degree to control such an instant of interaction, proves to be disastrous in that it solidifies isolation to the point of madness. The different acoustic masks in "concert" display variations and transformations of greed and self-mania, a cacophonous chorus, almost overwhelming in its chaotic diversity.

What did the eruptions of murderous aggression manipulated by demagogues haranguing a crowd with nationalistic racist rhetoric have in common with crowd behavior during socially justifiable demonstrations or strikes? It was not, as Canetti saw it, the relation between the crowd and a leader; there were other much more important mechanisms. In London Canetti set out to understand more about them. He learned about crowd behavior in seventeenth-century England from the historian Veronica Wedgwood (who was sufficiently fascinated by *Die Blendung* to take upon herself the immense labor of an excellent translation). He received stimulation and information from the social anthropologists Mary Douglas and Franz Baermann-Steiner; he was fascinated by Arthur Waley's erudition. "I will have to say, though, that especially during the English period it was experiences with books which became as important, sometimes more important than those with people," Canetti stated much later.[40] Above all, he mentions the importance of myths, "countless collections of myths." A critic interviewing him in his London study describes the room as "not filled with, but consisting of books." And there was not one question touched on in a long far-ranging conversation that Canetti did not have an answer for—and the reference to a book.[41]

The list of texts, of scholarly studies, sources, reports, and documents that Canetti read and used for *Masse und Macht* is very long and very varied. The book is striking in its openness to a large number of different voices based on an intellectual attitude of not taking anything for granted, of mistrusting categories: "One ought not be duped by other people's beliefs; and to the conclusions reached by extensive reading one ought to grant time and air to breathe," Canetti notes while working on *Masse und Macht*. He also remarked: "To be so alone as to overlook no one anymore, no one, nothing."[42] He wants to learn to understand myths as if he believed in them. It is of central importance to give the phenomenon one's undivided attention, to concentrate on the individual voice.

The result of such concentration is not, as one might expect, chaos but a specific kind of order based on a highly personal selective perspective, which could be called poetic. The fusion of anthropological, sociopsychological documents, observations, and insights with the poetic sense for the concreteness and literalness of the image, for the significant substance of the phenomenon puts *Masse und Macht* between literary genres and between different distinct social sciences. It also removes it from the influence and protection of ideological models. The long list of texts that were important to the making of Canetti's analysis does not include Marx or Freud. In an interview in 1972, when asked about his position toward Marx and Freud and about a possible collection of his own and Lévi-Strauss's approach to myths,[43] Canetti explains how he had tried to avoid a conceptual system. After having stuffed himself (*vollgestopft*) with the experience of phenomena, he had used a terminology that had developed during the course of the study, retaining as much as possible the concrete energy and vividness of the phenomenon. Canetti agrees fully with Lévi-Strauss's insistence on the cultural achievements of so-called primitive societies, but in his concentration on individual myths he differs sharply from Lévi-Strauss's comparatist categorization of myths, which he rejects as a compulsively collecting and speculating rather than as a meaningfully ordering activity. His own respect for the achievement of a particularly interesting myth made him develop a unique way of retelling it, thereby clarifying the conflict central to its conceptual grid and its imagery and justifying its exemplariness.

The concept of objectivity informing *Masse und Macht* does not deny the importance of the person who looks and listens—the author, the reader, the myth-makers, chroniclers, and observers of historical events. The first sentences in *Masse und Macht* deal with the primordial social fact of fear of physical contact.

There is no analysis of psychological mechanisms, rather the reader is told of, is shown concrete repellent energies creating spaces around bodies. The main characteristic of the crowd—for the observer Canetti—is the reversal of such fear, directing energies toward the dense unification of bodies. It is only in the dense mass of bodies, in the crowd, that physical fear of the other body is benumbed and the limits of the physical self seem lifted or at least expanded. The heavier the mass of bodies, the denser the shared body of the crowd, then the less substantial the weight, the less the burden of individuality. The perspective is that of a mobile narrator, as Canetti was, for example, in mixing with the crowd on that day in July 1927 when the Palace of Justice was burned. He formed part of the crowd, is fascinated, *and* he observes. He is partly immersed but retains some distance, recording the puzzling formations and motions of the crowd, its drive to grow and to attract more bodies and at the same time the futility of this drive visible in violent discharges, eruptions, and dispersions. He sees and explains the familiar phenomenon of crowd vandalism as a radical attack on all boundaries: "Windows and doors belong to the houses. They are the most vulnerable part of their exterior, and once they are smashed the house has lost its individuality: anyone may enter it and nothing and no one is protected anymore. In these houses live the supposed enemies of the crowd, those people who try to avoid it. What separated them has now been destroyed and nothing stands between them and the crowd. They can come out and join it, or they can be fetched."[44] The crowd's rush against limits, translated into physical borders, helps to approach the initially incomprehensible aggression enveloping the individual who is temporarily immersed in the crowd, his violent dash against a house that is of no (personal) importance to him, and his single-minded pursuit of people he has never seen or known before.

The first chapter offers particularly precise observations of concrete crowd behavior. The properties of the crowd, its rhythms of motion, its blockades, are related to the rhythm of one's own footsteps, the menace of the other's footfalls, also to the steady rhythmic motions of large herds of animals in flight, to ecstatic tribal war dances. There are also the invisible crowds described in accounts of visions occurring in myths and legends: in the vision of a Siberian shaman space is filled with the anxiety of naked human beings, clinging together in clusters, spirits swirling among them like snowflakes. Persian stories tell about crowds of demons moving against one another; the thirteenth-century historian Cäsarius von Heisterbach reports on the huge crowds of devils pressing hard on a sinful priest on his deathbed.

Canetti is interested in demonstrating that and showing how the myths dealing with crowds make meaningful statements about sociopsychological behavior. Systems of signs change historically, as do the relations between signifiers and the signified. As he includes the phylogenetic aspect in his concept of history, he is aware that the signified—the experience connecting crowds and power in the field of force determined by death—has changed very little, whereas the signifiers have changed dramatically as there exists a very complex, richly articulated social historical consciousness. Meaningful social activity has been documented through many centuries in the most various forms, and it is this variety and complexity, accessible, as Canetti believes, to the unprejudiced reader, that is the essentially human achievement: the ability to sustain and demonstrate transformation. Canetti disagrees with Lévi-Strauss's forceful archaeological exploration of myths and the reconstitution of their meaning: his is an ingenuity of the visible rather than the hidden, of observation rather than speculation. Where Lévi-Strauss deals with a confrontation of sense and nonsense, Canetti traces the changes, the developments of meaning, the metamorphosis of social conflict.

The social world as much as the physical world presents a challenge; it can be understood, and such understanding can be shared so that it can be questioned. Canetti's method is informed by that openness to the reader's questions and that desire to be as clear, as accessible as possible, that calm conviction that communication is possible and that language is a highly satisfying method, not so much in terms of scientific rigor and caution, but in terms of the curiosity directed toward the other, the fascination for the wonders of the (social) world. These wonders are not created by the self, though it does of course participate in them; but they are there to grasp, and it is the act of grasping that bestows significance and substance on the self. There is a curious mixture of assertiveness and modesty in Canetti's method of dealing with the past and of presenting documents of social behavior: assertiveness, because there is no question that they are worth our consideration, and modesty, because the worth is theirs and not the interpreter's.

The most important human metamorphoses refer to animals. In understanding man's ability to undergo transformation as centrally human, Canetti both establishes and erases a clear demarcation between animal and man: rather, he is fascinated by complexly organized transitions.[45] Consider his argument for the connection between metamorphosis and consciousness in the context of an analysis of a special sub-form of the crowd, the "Increase Pack" (*Vermehrungsmeute*).

> Man's weakness lay in the smallness of his numbers. It is true that the animals dangerous to man often lived singly or in small groups as he did. Like them he was a beast of prey, though one which never wanted to be solitary. He may have lived in bands about the size of wolf-packs, but wolves were content with this and he was not. In the enormously long period of time during which he lived in small groups, he, as it were, incorporated into himself, *by transformations,* all the animals he knew. It was through the development of transformation that he really became man; it was his specific gift and pleasure. In his early transformations into other animals he acted and danced many of the species which appeared in large numbers. The more perfect the representation of such creatures was, the intenser his awareness of their numbers. He felt what it was to be many and, each time, was made conscious of his own isolation in small groups.[46]

Potential faculties are always developed in interaction with the other, in this case the animal, by metamorphosis. This basic social fact is as important in the earlier stages of human development as in the later much more complicated stages of mass societies and their difficulties in communicating, as Canetti deals with them in *Komödie der Eitelkeit.* Contemporary mass societies, classless, hierarchically structured, rapidly changing but in many areas of social organizations profoundly afraid of change, grant little space to the individual's and the group's need and potential for transformation because this threatens the precariously balanced multitude of rigid arrangements which makes up our highly complex social systems. In the chapter "Verwandlung" (Transformation), Canetti traces particularly distinct forms of transformation:

metamorphosis—often connected with hysteria and mania—to escape the multiplication and consumption of self in the double figure of the totem, the experience of mass and transformation in delirium tremens, imitation and simulation, figure and mask, and finally the prohibitions on metamorphosis and the institution of slavery.

This chapter presents the argument that the advantage as well as the threat of metamorphosis were much more clearly present in the social consciousness of earlier periods—an example would be the reaction to mental illness. As is shown in the myths of Proteus, or of Peleus and Thetis, a sudden arrest of the process of transformation was understood as imprisonment, as becoming a prey. The totem is of special interest because it makes possible the selection of a specific metamorphosis, connected with the activated influence on the totem animal, the self, which can then be ordered to multiply.[47] Figure and mask accentuate processes of metamorphosis, but also its limits; for Canetti the figure shows the process *and* the result of metamorphosis, the mask only the final stage. In drama the mask can become a figure and then mediate between the audience and danger. If it remains unchallenged in its formal perfection—the fascination of the mask has its roots precisely here— then its limitations, rigidity, and determination set against temporal flux, the medium of experience, will have a negative influence. Canetti's emphasis on the social importance of transformation is supported by his plea for social pluralism. His curiosity is directed neither to the finite nor to the infinite but to the ever-changing scene of social conventions and conflicts; the only measure he recognizes records relatively and proportionally.

Canetti's method of retracing complex social phenomena to their earlier simpler more obvious forms is even more striking and provocative in the case of the command: it is the command to flee emitted by the stronger animal threatening to kill the weaker one. In the second volume of his autobiography he remembers his mother giving orders to a maid and making a point of rewarding her with food for those tasks that were especially difficult for the highly pregnant woman. His mother was proud of the fact that she did more than she "had to" according to her contract with the maid and complained that she could do the work better herself. It had been generous of her to hire the maid at all in her condition. The maid of course was very well aware of this and showed her gratitude by trying especially hard to comply with all the orders of the mistress. This perfectly ordinary incident becomes in Canetti's clarifying presentation an archetypical constellation of repression. He does not explicitly judge his mother, although her method of dealing with people had been shown to be a source of disagreements between them. He demonstrates his own uneasiness in the vividly remembered, tense and awkward verbal and physical behavior of unequals toward each other. An order, whether giving or receiving it, leaves a sting in the mind and the body, a profound irritation to the social balance of the self.

This sting isolates the individual and destroys his autonomy; it can be resolved only in the experience of merging with the crowd where the command strikes everybody simultaneously. The phenomenon of the demagogic orator, exciting his listeners and thereby creating a crowd, has to be seen in this context. Hitler had understood this connection. The extraordinarily aggressive, regressively cruel slogans that nobody took seriously in *Mein Kampf* became effective as threatening commands as soon as they were shouted at large audiences, which could then become one huge body receiving them.

Like death the giving and receiving of commands is a social problem of central importance, and the peculiar effect of Canetti's method in *Masse und Macht,* in his essays, in *Die Befristeten,* in his aphorisms, and in his autobiographical texts lies in the stunning concreteness sustained by his perspective, the urgent vivid obviousness of deeply flawed social conventions. Because impotence is so unbearable, so destructive to the individual, Canetti insists on paying attention to it. If he had his way, it would not be explained away so easily, nor would the really intolerable pain of annihilation by death. A strong pedagogical impulse has motivated his writing since the war, but what he has taught himself about social conflicts is well worth sharing and he knows how to share effectively: he does not lecture, he demonstrates.

Among the many sketches about social alternatives collected in the *Aufzeichnungen* there are projections of *Umkehrungen* (reversals), of the giving/receiving direction of commands: humble human beings before the thrones of animals; the poor are given the rich as a present; the gods on their knees, asking to be forgiven for having survived too many humans; the owner of a restaurant in the power of the hungry children of Marrakesh, whom he had always brushed off like flies. In *Masse und Macht* he quotes from an ancient Indian treatise on sacrifices: "For whatever food a man eats in this world, by that food he is eaten in the next world."[48] The original situation is reversed: the victim finds, kills, and eats his devourer. The sting cannot be removed.

Like Kafka, Canetti postpones the abstracting, simplifying, metaphorical ordering of a highly complex, diverse social reality. He confronts it literally, that is, somatically. It is bodies that he sees, hears, and feels; it is through his body that he does so. The "unrealistic" aspects of his statements on death, the singlemindedness of his search for evidence documenting the disastrous consequences of human inequality, his insistent denial that there are no "givens" in the realm of social intercourse have led some readers to overstress the "utopian" quality of his texts, his passion for the life of the mind. Canetti is not interested in projecting the impossible, in speculating about absolutes. It is not the best life he is after, nor a life without death. It is a better life for more people and to him this means a longer life, better chances, more time to develop the human potential through transformation. It is ultimately to accept more fully the responsibility for this potential.

Notes

1. Susan Sontag, "Mind As Passion," *The New York Review of Books,* Vol. XXVII, No. 14 (25 September 1980), 47–52. Sontag's essay is a collective review of the Canetti texts made available in English to date by Seabury Press. Sontag does not seem to be aware of the large number of articles and books on Canetti published in Germany and Austria during the past decade. For detailed bibliographical information see Dagmar Barnouw, *Elias Canetti* (Stuttgart: Metzler, 1979) (Sammlung Metzler, Band 180), pp. 115–136. My references unless stated otherwise are to the German texts; the translations are my own.

2. Elias Canetti, *Die gerettete Zunge. Geschichte einer Jugend* (München: Hanser, 1977), p. 50.

3. Ibid., p. 61.

4. See below, p. 18.

5. Elias Canetti, *Die Provinz des Menschen. Aufzeichnungen 1942–1972* (München: Hanser, 1973), p. 73.

6. See Canetti's essay, "Der Beruf des Dichters," in *Das Gewissen der Worte* (München: Hanser, 1976), pp. 257–267.

7. See Elias Canetti, *Die Fackel im Ohr. Lebensgeschichte 1921–1931* (München: Hanser, 1980), p. 197 ff.

8. *Die Blendung* has been translated into many languages: into English: *Auto-da-Fé,* translated by C. V. Wedgwood (London: Jonathan Cape, 1946) and, *The Tower of Babel,* translated by C. V. Wedgwood (New York: A. Knopf, 1947); into French: *La Tour de Babel,* translated by Paule Arhex (Paris: B. Arthaud, 1949).

9. Interview with Dagmar Barnouw in August 1978.

10. See Idris Parry, "Elias Canetti's Novel 'Die Blendung,' " in *Essays in German Literature* 1, ed. F. Norman (University of London: Institute of Germanic Studies, 1965), pp. 145 ff.

11. The early dramas have not yet been translated into English. [This situation has been remedied with the publication of the following volumes: *"Comedy of Vanity" and "Life-Terms,"* trans. Gitta Honegger (New York: PAJ Publications, 1983); *The Wedding,* trans. Gitta Honegger (New York: PAJ Publications, 1986). *Ed.*]

12. Elias Canetti, "Karl Kraus, Schule des Widerstands," in *Das Gewissen der Worte* (München: Hanser, 1976), p. 41.

13. Ibid., p. 44.

14. *Die chinesische Mauer* is the title of volume III of selected texts from *Die Fackel* (Wien: August Langen, 1910).

15. Elias Canetti, "Karl Kraus, Schule des Widerstands," p. 47.

16. Elias Canetti, *Die Provinz des Menschen,* p. 306.

17. [There exist two English translations of *Die Befristeten:* as *Life-Terms,* in *"Comedy of Vanity" and "Life-Terms,"* trans. Gitta Honegger (New York: PAJ Publications, 1983); and as *The Numbered,* trans. Carol Stewart (London: Marion Boyars, 1984). *Ed.*]

18. The third volume of Canetti's autobiography, *Das Augenspiel* (München: Hanser, 1985), has not yet been translated into English. [This situation has been remedied: *The Play of the Eyes,* trans. Ralph Manheim (New York: Farrar, Straus and Giroux, 1986). *Ed.*]

19. Elias Canetti, *Die Provinz des Menschen,* p. 80.

20. Ibid., p. 79.

21. Quoted in Werner Kraft, *Karl Kraus. Beiträge zum Verständnis seines Werkes* (Salzburg: Müller Verlag, 1956), p. 13.

22. Karl Kraus, *Die Fackel XXXVI* (July 1934), No. 890–905, p. 33.

23. Elias Canetti, *Die Provinz des Menschen,* p. 159.

24. Ibid., p. 8.

25. Ibid., p. 291.

26. Ibid., p. 346.

27. Ibid., p. 305.

28. Ibid., p. 166.

29. See Iris Murdoch, "Mass, Might and Myth," *The Spectator,* 7 September 1962, pp. 337 f. Robert Neumann, *Ein leichtes Leben. Bericht über mich selbst und Zeitgenossen* (München: Desch, 1963). [Murdoch's review is reproduced elsewhere in the present volume. *Ed.*]

30. Elias Canetti, *Provinz,* pp. 217 f.

31. Ibid., p. 10.

32. Ibid., p. 43.

33. Susan Sontag, "Mind as Passion," p. 52.

34. Elias Canetti, *Die Fackel im Ohr,* p. 94.

35. Ibid., p. 168 f.

36. Ibid., p. 275; see also pp. 276–282.

37. Elias Canetti, *Die Blendung* [München: Hanser, 1963], p. 454.

38. See Manfred Durzak, *Gespräche über den Roman. Formbestimmungen und Analysen* (Frankfurt: Suhrkamp, 1976), p. 95. [The conversation in question is reproduced in English translation elsewhere in the present volume. *Ed.*]

39. Elias Canetti, *Die gerettete Zunge,* p. 101.

40. Letter to Dagmar Barnouw, 10 June 1978.

41. Joachim Schickel, "Aspekte der Masse, Elemente der Macht. Versuch über Elias Canetti," *Text und Kritik,* Heft 28 (Elias Canetti) (October 1970), 13.

42. Elias Canetti, *Die Provinz des Menschen. Aufzeichnungen 1942–1972,* p. 60. Also ibid., p. 39.

43. Elias Canetti, *Die gespaltene Zukunft* (München: Hanser, 1972), pp. 104–131.

44. Elias Canetti, "Destructiveness," in *Crowds and Power* (New York: The Viking Press, 1963), p. 20.

45. See Ernst Fischer, "Bemerkungen zu Elias Canetti *Masse und Macht,*" in *Literatur und Kritik,* 1/H. 7 (1966), 12–20.

46. Elias Canetti, "The Increase Pack," in *Crowds and Power,* p. 108.

47. By contrast Lévi-Strauss sees totemism as a pure function of the differentiation of man from animal.

48. Elias Canetti, "The Reversal," in *Crowds and Power,* p. 324.

AUTO-DA-FÉ

◆

Auto-da-Fé

HERMANN HESSE

When starkly realistic means are applied to the presentation of fantastic things, the effect is usually a potent one. So it is that this remarkable novel by a very gifted young writer is not only full of tension but also gives the impression of skill and mastery, although the question remains completely open as to whether it deserves to be called a true work of literature or rather just a brilliantly written page-turner, an energetic demonstration of virtuosity.

In the space of well over 500 large pages the novel tells of the undoing of the life of an eccentric scholar and pathological bibliophile after he allows a woman to enter the unworldly, solitary, and loveless life he leads. He marries his housekeeper, and from that moment on he is lost and done for: his isolated but by no means meaningless or empty life is piece by piece upset, disrupted, and wrecked, until he is destroyed. The novel recounts each complex station of this process with great skill, but its writing has a certain breathless and harried quality. And here one senses a contradiction: what lends strength and zest to a shorter story has a tormenting effect over the course of such a long book, and that results in an interesting, but discomforting, tension between the tempo of the book and its length. But perhaps this is not the only tension that compromises and unbalances the effect of the story. Perhaps it is also the discrepancy between the actual content of the novel, which is pathological in nature, and the breadth and expansiveness of its narrative treatment.

Technically the narrative is masterful. There is an organic progression through the three parts of the novel ("A Head without a World," "Headless World," and "The World in the Head"), the texture of detail is consistently dense, and the psychology is logically coherent, if somewhat overwrought. There is many a novelist whom I rate much higher as a writer, who could learn much from this new author—insofar as the writing of literature can be learned. One has to admire this new novelist if only for the reason that he never loses his breath; but it is precisely in this flawlessly smooth performance that there is something not quite right: the book has a rhythm that is often reminiscent not so much of the sound of breathing as of the sound of an engine running.

Translated by David Darby for this volume from Hermann Hesse, review of *Die Blendung*, by Elias Canetti, *Neue Zürcher Zeitung* (Literarische Beilage), 12 January 1936, 3. Reproduced here by permission of the *Neue Zürcher Zeitung*.

Auto-da-Fé

Hans Magnus Enzensberger

It seems superfluous to warn naive readers about this book. Naive readers sense trouble from a distance and rely on their instincts. *Die Blendung* (*Auto-da-Fé*) is now in print for the sixth time: the novel appeared in Austria in 1936, in England in 1946, in America in 1947, in Germany in 1948, and in France in 1949. On each occasion the critics have accorded it respectful praise. Naive readers have rigorously avoided it, and for a simple reason: *Auto-da-Fé* is an unbearable book, a literary monstrosity.

The story it tells suggests nothing of that. It is simple, almost vacuous. Dr. Peter Kien—a victim of his own delusions, an independent scholar by profession, and "the greatest sinologist of his age"—lives in his enormous library as if in a clam-shell, alienated from the whole world, silent and alone, a godless Trappist. His housekeeper, a woman called Therese, breaks open the shell and annihilates the scholar in the course of a vicious, merciless, no-holds-barred struggle.

So, on one side the world of pure intellect and on the other the narrow confines of petty-bourgeois existence? This well-worn theme of German narrative literature, with a history stretching back to romanticism, suggests an interpretation of Canetti's parable, but one that does not quite fit. Two overused concepts—"idealism" and "materialism"—going around and around, chasing each other's tails. If that were all there were to this book, we would be dealing with a philosophical conjuring act that could scarcely command our interest.

It is not its insubstantial premise that makes Canetti's "Description of a Struggle" unique but rather its escalating intensity.[1] The antagonists, and in this novel there are only antagonists, fight each other literally to the point of madness. It is neither the scholar nor the housekeeper who is on trial, but rather all sense of normality. All figures in the story, from the sewage-worker to the police officer, from the building superintendent to the psychiatrist (since the book would not be complete without a psychiatrist), are simultaneously insane and normal. No kind of inhumanity is unknown to them.

Translated by David Darby for this volume from Hans Magnus Enzensberger, review of *Die Blendung*, by Elias Canetti, *Der Spiegel*, 7 August 1963, 48–49. Reproduced here by kind permission of Hans Magnus Enzensberger and of the Spiegel-Verlag Rudolf Augstein.

A few years before Hitler's assumption of power, the surrealists published a letter to all the psychiatrists of the world. They challenged the doctors to open the gates of their institutions and to release all their patients. The distinction between mental illness and "normality," so they wrote, was an arbitrary one. Furthermore, they continued, every delusion was a creative utterance whose suppression was misguided.

Such insights are not new to the psychiatrist of Canetti's novel: "Among the mentally diseased he grew into one of the most comprehensive intellects of his time.... [H]e merely simplified them in order to make them healthy.... They were the only true personalities."[2]

But it is not until Canetti that the full implications of the surrealists' discovery are explored. His madmen have the face of everyman, and the battles they wage in their dives and tenement buildings throw shadows of gigantic historical proportions. Canetti shows the omnipresence of paranoiac structures; his novel is a tangle of delusory systems whose development evinces the most acute sharpness of perception. His depiction of them is unique in literature.

Any description from the outside would be hopeless from the start. The author surrenders himself to the thoughts and words of his characters and mimics their logic, which is simultaneously both mad and internally coherent, with an extreme of precision. To achieve this effect, Canetti employs a style situated between free indirect discourse and interior monologue:

A respectable woman like her. Sometimes things do come out, and then you go to gaol. A respectable woman doesn't go to gaol. Things would be much better, if you didn't have to go to gaol at once. The least little thing gets about and round come the police and you go to gaol in a minute. They don't care whether a woman can bear it. They poke their noses into every mortal thing. What business is it of theirs how a wife gets on with her husband? A wife has to put up with everything. A wife isn't human. And her man's no use for anything. Is it a man? It's no man at all. Nobody'll miss such a man. The best thing would be if her friend took an axe and hit him on the head in his sleep. But he locks his door every night because he's afraid. Her friend must think out how to do it himself. He says, nothing will come out. She won't do such a thing. A respectable woman like her. [AdF, 100–101]

So run the thoughts of Therese. The tone, reminiscent of the lemures and somewhere between Nestroy and Herr Karl, is unmistakably Viennese, and it does not require the countless Austrianisms in the book to locate its intellectual home on the banks of the beautiful black Danube.[3]

In any case, the semiaudible murmuring of the characters and their insane soliloquies are the only outstanding formal feature of Canetti's novel. Its syntax is simple to the point of banality. The complicated twists and meanderings of the psychoses are achieved by means of the domino-like stacking of primitive sentences.

As long as the author cites his characters, one can look at it in terms of technique and even see it in positive terms. But where his own voice emerges, virtue becomes his downfall. The language has a thin taste, a taste of paper. Clouds of dust rise from the brittle pages: "He was tall, strong, fiery, and sure of himself; in his features there was something of that gentleness which women need before they can feel at home with a man. Those who saw him compared him with Michelangelo's Adam. He understood very well how intelligence and elegance could be combined. His brilliant gifts had been brought to fruitful effectiveness by the policy of his beloved" [*AdF,* 396].

It is not quite clear why people have tried to make out of the author of such sentences a second Kafka, a second Joyce. Such vociferous comparisons do Canetti an injustice, serving only to pillory the poverty of his language.

Despite all its intensity, *Auto-da-Fé* gives the impression of being long-winded and horribly monotonous. It is not the storyteller but rather the story itself that is to blame for the fanatical tedium, the murderously compulsive repetition of this book. It is precisely its unrelenting logic that makes it sterile: the more deeply the novel commits itself in that direction, the less chance it has of succeeding.

Nevertheless, Canetti's failure remains thought-provoking. Aesthetic criteria are incapable of approaching this book, since *Auto-da-Fé* is a work of research undertaken with the means of the imagination. A few years ago Canetti—the anthropologist—provided the theoretical key to this work in the form of his scholarly study *Masse und Macht* (Hamburg 1960 [*Crowds and Power*]). That examination concerns itself with tribal chiefs, *Führers,* and other madmen who are blinded by the same delusion as the housekeeper Therese and her master: the delusion of power. And those who are seduced by that delusion do not read books.

Notes

1. [This reference is to Franz Kafka's story "Beschreibung eines Kampfes." *Ed.*]
2. [Elias Canetti, *Auto-da-Fé,* trans. C. V. Wedgwood (New York: Farrar, Straus and Giroux, 1984), 398; hereafter cited in text as *AdF. Ed.*]
3. [Johann Nepomuk Nestroy (1801–1862) was a comic actor and satirical dramatist of the Viennese popular theater. Herr Karl is a satirical character created by the writers Helmut Qualtinger and Carl Merz in the early 1960s, whose darkly comic monologues in Viennese dialect were performed on stage by Qualtinger (also a renowned actor) and are published in Qualtinger and Merz, *Der Herr Karl und weiteres Heiteres* (1964). *Ed.*]

The World Can No Longer Be Depicted as in Earlier Novels

Elias Canetti, in Conversation with Manfred Durzak

1. Biographical Questions

Durzak: Dr. Canetti, as an author, you have generally—and, one might say, quite deliberately—kept your distance from the commercial aspect of literature and devoted yourself with untiring concentration to your work. And if one disregards the notes and aphorisms that you have published, that reflect not the story of your personal life but primarily that of your intellectual life, one could actually identify your continued silence about yourself and your personal circumstances as a fundamental characteristic of your writing. Further evidence of that is the fact that the personal diary which you keep, and which you wish to preserve from public scrutiny, is written in a shorthand code of your own invention, the key to which you have so far kept strictly to yourself. Given that background, it is surprising now to learn that you have been working on an autobiography. May one assume that this autobiography will present a documentary record of your artistic beginnings—and here I am thinking of you above all as the author of *Die Blendung* (*Auto-da-Fé*)—and at the same time a picture of the environment of intellectual turmoil in Vienna during the early part of the century?

CANETTI: That is something I am not yet willing to decide. But it is no doubt true that the desire to continue writing the autobiography will grow as the work progresses. I have only reached the thirteenth year of my life, and I am already noticing that there is more and more to write. I have the feeling that there is a mountain ahead of me, and that I would like to climb it from every side. I cannot yet say whether I will portray the rest of my life in as concentrated and consistent a form as I wish to portray the first 20 years. What I will no doubt do is distill out the most important encounters of my later life in Vienna and summarize them in individual chapters.

Translated by David Darby for this volume from "Die Welt ist nicht mehr so darzustellen wie in früheren Romanen: Gespräch mit Elias Canetti," in Manfred Durzak, *Gespräche über den Roman: Formbestimmungen und Analysen* (Frankfurt am Main: Suhrkamp, 1976), 86–102. Reproduced here by kind permission of the Carl Hanser Verlag.

DURZAK: You once said that for five years Karl Kraus was the most important presence in your intellectual world. Will, for example, your relationship to Karl Kraus be depicted?

CANETTI: I have already done that in part: the essay "Schule des Widerstands," which I wrote about Karl Kraus, addresses precisely that relationship.[1] I don't know whether I will expand that further, bringing in other personal details. In general my preference is to portray these encounters, clashes, or liaisons with really important people in a way that will bring out what is intellectually essential, leaving aside superfluous details.

DURZAK: I chose the example of Karl Kraus badly. What I mean is that that you have already depicted your relationship with Hermann Broch in some depth. And, beyond that, you have at several points commented on Robert Musil. So one already gets a certain picture of the age in which you lived as a young writer. But are there, in retrospect, other authors or philosophers whom you would consider very important from today's perspective, with a view to any affinities between their positions and your own, and who perhaps even had something of an influence on you?

CANETTI: My answer to that will probably disappoint you, since the most crucial influences of that time, even of my early years, were almost without exception people who had long been dead. Even after I moved to Vienna, I was subject to a remarkable mixture of influences from the most diverse foreign literatures, which had to do with my having grown up in various European cultures. Even in Vienna I read English and French writers, the German classics, and Chinese philosophers. They were by no means always people I had met in person. But there would probably be very much to say about people I knew personally. You mentioned Musil. If I were to summarize everything I have to say about Musil, it would fill a work at least as long as the Kafka essay with which you are familiar.

2. Counterinfluences

DURZAK: Of course my questions so far suggest a further question: namely, whether as a young author you were, so to speak, molded by contact with other writers, some of them perhaps already established, and so whether your autobiography will present material on that period to document that. In asking this question I am aware that you very much downplay the importance of influence. In your recent volume of notes and aphorisms, *Die Provinz des Menschen (The Human Province)*, there are two reflections on this question which state explicitly that influence is something of little substance. I will just quote the following sentences: "Usually, one has put new phrases into the world, but that is not the real effect; everything, no matter what, ultimately becomes a phrase, and something that has become conspicuously easy does not necessarily have to be bad."[2] Then you explain that actual influence cannot be controlled, that it occurs by means of a certain word's becoming a source of energy. At another point you advance the thesis, with great skepticism vis-à-vis the element of influence, that it is actually a mistake to ask about the influences on an author. Rather, one could characterize an author more precisely if one were to ask about counterinfluences. You write: "Instead of a literary history of influences, a literary history of counter-influences; it would be more informative. Counter-images, not always obvious, are often more important than model-images" [*HP*, 260]. My question now, applied to this autobiographical project, is: how would such a literary history of counter-influences look, taking Elias Canetti as its subject?

CANETTI: The difficulty I have in answering your question is that I would have much more to say than I can mention now. I possessed a general hostility to what I found to be a highly repugnant intellectual atmosphere characteristic of Vienna at the time when I lived there as a young person. This aversion was of course reinforced by Karl Kraus, who opposed it sharply and who was really contemptuous of everything that was fashionable and successful in Vienna. I believe that, quite apart from the question of influence, it was in my own nature to measure myself against the great authors: Gogol, Stendhal, Dostoyevsky, Aristophanes. So the sentimental, essayistic Viennese literature of the time could only be repulsive to me. My decision to write *Auto-da-Fé* was a deliberate attempt to dissociate myself from that. There are authors of that time who even today are considered "literary," of whom I have an extremely low opinion. One is Stefan Zweig. He was the worst. Werfel was more gifted than Zweig. He was perhaps the most sentimental of the authors who are considered Austrian. I knew him well, I was often a guest in his house. There was something almost operatic in his immense sentimentality: a tendency to translate everything that reached his ears into an aria. At parties at his house it would often happen—he had a good tenor voice, he liked to sing—that he would suddenly break out in song, he would drop down on one knee before a beautiful lady and sing her a wonderful aria. I think much of that found its way into his novels. His love of the opera was not without its consequences. He is for me the epitome of the operatic author, which is another reason why I find him bad. He was certainly a counterimage, albeit one I did not take too seriously.

3. Brecht as a Moral Counterimage

DURZAK: Were there other counterimages beyond the immediate literary surroundings of Vienna? I am thinking of Berlin, where you spent several months in 1928 and 1929.

CANETTI: My first visit to Berlin was in the summer of 1928, and I spent three or four months there. It happened by chance, because I was working for a very well-known publisher in order to support myself a student. He immediately introduced me to all the literary people who were there at that time, and not only literary people. All at once I met so many of them that I was almost overwhelmed by the experience. That is when I met Brecht as well. He found it tiresome that I had come with a certain overwrought idea of literature and with some quite strict moral precepts that derived in part from Karl Kraus and that I was always speaking about how unsullied a writer must be, how completely free of any material influence. These orations got on his nerves of course, and so he used to provoke and ridicule me with especially cutting and cynical comments.

DURZAK: Can you cite an example?

CANETTI: One example was his always telling me that, yes, he was already writing for money, that, for a contest, he had just written a poem praising a car, and that he had been presented with a car for his efforts. With my strict ideas about what a poet had to be, I was as horrified as if he had told me: "I have just killed a person, and I couldn't care less!" He enjoyed doing things like that. Or when he used to speak about people's working habits. He found it very amusing that I was, at that time, still absolutely convinced that a writer, a poet, had to close himself off completely in order to work in a concentrated way. So he used to say to me: "I can only work when people phone me; I keep the telephone right by my desk." He would always come up with things like that. It was cruel, and it simply amused him to ridicule this green, rather overwrought young person. That had a very good influence on me.

DURZAK: Would that be an example of a counterinfluence?

CANETTI: As strange as it sounds, that was perhaps the strongest counterinfluence that I ever experienced. For before I went to Berlin I had already read about him in Vienna. People spoke about him a lot, there was a lot of interest in him. Back then I read poems by him that made an enormous impression on me. Even today his poetry means more to me than his plays. This same poet was now telling me about how he conducted himself, how he lived, and doing so with a deliberate cynicism. He exaggerated of course and presented things in a much worse light than he really believed they warranted. That was—if I may say so—already a counterimage. I resolved then, upon my return to Vienna, to live more than ever as Karl Kraus demanded: one was to be rigorously pure, one was not to write for money, and above all not to publish anything, or at least to publish only what one had worked on for years and could put one's name to in good conscience. To that extent this encounter worked not as an intellectual counterimage, but, if you like, as a moral counterimage.

4. THE INFLUENCE OF BERLIN ON *AUTO-DA-FÉ*

DURZAK: Dr. Canetti, in discussing your two sojourns in Berlin during the time immediately prior to the conception of *Auto-da-Fé,* you have touched on a biographical episode whose crucial importance for the genesis of *Auto-da-Fé* has, as far as I can see, been neglected. As an author, how would you evaluate in your own mind the importance of these stays in Berlin?

CANETTI: The acuity and variety of the talents who were in Berlin at that time and who displayed themselves quite publicly impressed me enormously, so much so that I was completely confused by it all. It completely overwhelmed me. *Auto-da-Fé* was also in part a product of this remarkable conflict between my Viennese beliefs and my Berlin experiences. That is something that in general has not been considered in any of the studies that have been written on *Auto-da-Fé,* for the reason that it was not public knowledge. But there were, I believe, many interesting things, even psychologically very relevant things, to be found there. George Grosz was one of the people in Berlin who was very important to me. He took care of me and took an especially warm and generous interest in me. I was very young, quite unknown, a student. I could not have been of any importance to him. In spite of that he welcomed me with open arms. The other was a Russian author who was visiting—Isaac Babel—whom I consider the most important Russian writer since the Revolution. I got to know him there. He was a man whom I took most deeply into my heart and who took care of me in a most incredible way, although I really could not have been of any importance to him at the time.

DURZAK: What form did the contrast between Vienna and Berlin take for you, and, above all, what consequences did it have for the conception of your novel, which began to take shape soon afterwards?

CANETTI: I knew no writers in Vienna, I lived alone, and, since they were all scorned by Karl Kraus, I hadn't wanted to know any. Now suddenly I found myself in Berlin, among the new, the interesting, and also the famous. I moved only among these people, who all knew each other. They led fast and intense lives. They went to the same bars, spoke about one another without inhibition, loved and hated one another for all the world to see, their idiosyncrasies revealed themselves as soon as they spoke, it was as if they would pummel one with the force of their personalities. I was in a state of the most volatile excitement, and at the same time I was shocked. I took note of so much that it was bound to confuse me. I was seeing many things that I had always loathed. Everything was possible, everything was happening. I had never before had the feeling of being so close to the world at all its points at the same time, and this world, which I was unable to come to terms with in three months, seemed to me a world of madmen. This world fascinated me so very much that I was unhappy when the time came to return to Vienna in

October. I had neither resolved nor mastered any part of the huge tangle that lay within me. My second stay (in the summer of 1929), which again lasted about three months, was somewhat less feverish. I took the time to write a lot of things down. This time, when I returned to Vienna in the autumn, the amorphous tangle began to unravel. But what preoccupied me most of all after my return from Berlin, what would no longer leave me alone, were the extreme and obsessed people I had met there. One day the thought came to me that the world could no longer be depicted as in earlier novels, so to speak from the perspective of one writer. The world had disintegrated and, only if one had the courage to show it in its disintegration would it still be possible to give a true idea of it. But that did not mean that one should set to work on a chaotic book in which nothing could be understood any longer. On the contrary: one had, with the most rigorous logic, to invent extreme individuals like those of which the world indeed consisted and to juxtapose these utterly eccentric individuals with one another in their respective forms of isolation.

DURZAK: So in some sense the conception of *Auto-da-Fé* represents the crystallization of this experience.
CANETTI: I conceived the plan of a Human Comedy of Madmen and projected eight novels, each centered on a figure on the edge of insanity. Each figure was different from each of the others, the differences reaching right into their language, right into their most secret thoughts. Each experience was such that no other would have been able to experience it. Nothing could be interchangeable, nothing could intermingle. I told myself that I was building eight spotlights that were lighting up the world from the outside. For a whole year I worked on these eight figures in no particular order, just according to whichever one attracted me most at any given moment. There was a religious fanatic among them, a technological dreamer who only lived in the planes of space, a collector, a figure obsessed by truth, a spendthrift, an enemy of death, and finally also a pure bookman.

5. The Burning of the Palace of Justice in Vienna

DURZAK: But the Berlin experiences are not the only ones to have had an impact on the conception of *Auto-da-Fé*. The spectrum of your experiences in Vienna may well have had a still more important impact on the shaping of the novel. I am aware that there is here a very complex interweaving of stimuli. You have already drawn attention to individual factors. For instance, the burning of the Palace of Justice in Vienna in the summer of 1927 had a certain importance for *Auto-da-Fé*.
CANETTI: Shots had been fired in the Burgenland, and workers had been killed. The court had acquitted the murderers. This acquittal was reported—

no, trumpeted aloud—in the pro-government press as a "just verdict." More than the acquittal itself, it was this contempt for any feeling of justice that triggered an enormous unrest in the working people of Vienna. From all the districts of Vienna, columns of workers converged, their ranks closed, on the Palace of Justice, which just by virtue of its name embodied injustice for them. The Palace of Justice was on fire. The police received the order to shoot. There were 90 dead. That was 46 years ago, and I can still feel the excitement of that day in my bones. I became a part of the crowd, I was completely absorbed into it, I did not feel the slightest resistance to what it was doing.

DURZAK: It is not difficult to find here the obvious superficial connections to your novel: the fire with which Kien finally destroys himself and his library, the crowd experience that, seen from the perspective of Kien's brother Georg in the novel, indeed has positive features and that above all Broch characterized as very important for you in his speech introducing one of your early readings in Vienna.[3]

6. The Characters of *Auto-da-Fé*

DURZAK: Can one not recognize the unmediated presence of everyday Viennese reality in the very conception of the novel's characters? I have in mind here Kien's housekeeper Therese.

CANETTI: The original model for her was as real as the bookman was unreal. In April 1927 I had rented a room in the Hagenberggasse on a hill above Hacking outside Vienna. I went to have a look at the room; the housewife opened the door and took me upstairs where there was nothing but this room. She herself lived on the ground floor with her family. I was very taken with the view: across a playground one could see the trees of the large garden of the Archbishop, and on the other side of the valley, on the top of the hillside opposite, one had before one's eyes Steinhof, the walled city of the insane. I discussed the details with the housewife by the open window. Her skirt reached all the way to the floor, she held her head at an angle, sometimes alternating which side it was on; the first speech she held is to be found verbatim in the third chapter of *Auto-da-Fé*: about "the young people these days" and "potatoes, which cost double already."

DURZAK: You mentioned that the central figure, the sinologist Peter Kien, is not modeled on a real figure. How did this figure come into being? The various changes of name he underwent suggest that this figure went through a considerable process of development.

CANETTI: The central figure of this book, known today as Kien, was called "B." in the first drafts, an abbreviation for "Büchermensch" (bookman).

Because I had him in my mind's eye as a bookman, to the extent that his connection with books was far more important than he was himself. His only characteristic was that he consisted of books; at that time there was nothing else to him. When I finally came to write his story in a coherent way, I gave him the name "Brand." This name already held the clue to his fiery end. In October 1931, a year later, the novel was finished.

DURZAK: Then you changed the name of the central figure again.
CANETTI: In the course of the work Brand had changed his name to Kant. But I had reservations because he shared this name with the philosopher. So the title that the manuscript bore was a provisional one: "Kant fängt Feuer" (Kant catches fire).

DURZAK: Doesn't the final name, Kien, go back to some advice you received from Hermann Broch?
CANETTI: Quite uncharacteristically for him, Broch absolutely insisted that I give up the name Kant. I had always intended to do so, but now it happened at last. I named him Kien, and something of his flammability went into his name.[4] Along with Kant, the title "Kant fängt Feuer" also disappeared, and I decided on a new and definitive title: *Auto-da-Fé*.

7. INFLUENTIAL AUTHORS

DURZAK: It would be misleading to assume that the literary works of Broch, who was at that time just beginning to make a name for himself as a writer, could have had any influence on the conception of your novel. But while writing *Auto-da-Fé* you did encounter one of the most important stories of another writer who made a very strong impression on you. I am referring to Kafka.
CANETTI: I had finished writing the eighth chapter of *Auto-da-Fé*, today entitled "Death," when Kafka's *Die Verwandlung* (*The Metamorphosis*) fell into my hands. Nothing more fortuitous could have happened to me at that point in time. In it I found, perfected, the very antithesis of the noncommittal literature that I so detested: it possessed the rigor that I craved for my own writing. In it something had been achieved that I wanted to find on my own.

DURZAK: Are there yet other authors who were in some sense important to you during your work on *Auto-da-Fé*?
CANETTI: Gogol had a great influence on *Auto-da-Fé*, Stendhal too. Gogol's *Dead Souls* and *Le Rouge et le noir* (*The Red and the Black*) were actually the books I most enjoyed reading at the time I was writing *Auto-da-Fé*.

DURZAK: Those are—to say the least—quite diverse kinds of influences. In the case of Stendhal it was probably of all things the density, the concentration of the language, that attracted you. How could one define the corresponding importance of Gogol?

CANETTI: In Gogol's case it was the freedom of his imagination. The fact that he allowed himself to invent whatever he wanted. I still love him today. He is even now one of my favorite writers. Among the Russians I actually like him best, although Dostoyevsky, whose work I knew very well and still read again and again, is probably the greater of the two. Personally, however, Gogol appeals to me more.

8. Acoustic Masks

DURZAK: One very important linguistic influence on *Auto-da-Fé* and on your first two plays is of course probably the linguistic environment of Vienna with the countless nuances of its dialect. You once tried to explain that with reference to a specific theory of linguistic mimesis. I am referring to the theory of the acoustic mask, which throws light on the essentially scenic, and thus dramatic, conception of many of the episodes in *Auto-da-Fé*. In an interview with the Viennese newspaper *Sonntag* in 1937 you began to explain this theory.[5] How do things stand now regarding its genesis? What are its roots?[6]

CANETTI: The main influence was of course that of Karl Kraus. There is no doubt about that. The specifics are those I discussed in my essay on Karl Kraus. Of greatest importance were his public readings of Nestroy, which really opened one's ears to the sounds of Vienna.

DURZAK: That has to do, then, with the dialect quality of Nestroy's language?

CANETTI: Yes, and above all with the fact that that dialect was a constant element of one's environment in Vienna. Of course the readings of *Die letzten Tage der Menschheit* (*The Last Days of Mankind*) also impressed me very much, but Nestroy impressed me still more, because without these readings I would perhaps not have been so keen to go into those little pubs where I would sit for hours on end and sometimes even all night—they closed at four in the morning—and listen to how people spoke. That training continued for years, and it was very important to me. . . .

DURZAK: But there is something else in Nestroy: the element of improvisation. The truth of the matter is that his texts were not intended primarily as literary texts but rather as stage-scripts, and as an actor he changed them continuously, improvised, brought in new things.

CANETTI: I think this element, of which I was aware, contributed to the growth of my interest in these things. I did not intend to take acoustic masks and use them in the way that I had heard them. I wanted to have a reservoir of them, to have heard as many as possible. There were some that were more important to me, and some that led me directly to literary characters....

DURZAK: So there were several elements that had an influence on this theory of the acoustic mask: Nestroy via the readings by Karl Kraus, Karl Kraus himself, and beyond that biographical material, specific people.
CANETTI: There is yet another element that had an extremely strong influence on me: the Japanese Kabuki theater.

DURZAK: Yet it is true that, in an acoustic mask, a mimetic quality is retained, intact, regardless of all abstraction and concentration. The mimetic element is present, meaning the quite concrete mirroring, or representation, of something real.
CANETTI: Some basic elements of the mimetic remain, and perhaps that is also one of the main reasons why the acoustic masks became so important to me. There seemed to me to be an element of reality in them that has by no means yet been exhausted, that has not been used up, that is usable and has enormous dramatic potential; an attempt to reopen access to reality where it has not been exhausted. That is probably what especially attracted me to them.

DURZAK: What happens if one tries to apply the principle of the acoustic mask to the interpretation of *Auto-da-Fé*?
CANETTI: It is certainly possible to do that. But there is more to it in *Auto-da-Fé* because we are also concerned with trains of thought involving the use of a specific vocabulary. The connections between thought and speech are of course manifold. Indeed, there is scarcely anything separating the two, it is a fluid transition. And the acoustic masks become literally part of the person. After all, it is already the case that the figures consist of their acoustic masks.

9. THE NEW LANGUAGE

DURZAK: Looking at *Auto-da-Fé*, one could say that the acoustic mask serves the purpose of satirizing speech. It is always employed to critical effect. But what is the situation with regard to another level of language, which is presented in the idea of a new language, indeed a language mysticism, in the episode of the gorilla-metamorphosis? Is this a central theme?
CANETTI: You mean the story in the last part of *Auto-da-Fé*?[7] I don't know whether I was conscious of how crucial this story is.

DURZAK: I remember your once telling me that very interesting story about the film, the ape-film, which you and Broch saw together.
CANETTI: The Ingagi-film with the children?

DURZAK: And you said that you would still recognize the cinema where you had seen the film.
CANETTI: In Penzing, near the railway station. I told you that? I have scarcely ever mentioned it to anyone.

DURZAK: The film seems interesting to me, with respect to the gorilla episode in the novel. Anyway, this ape motif plays a large role in a still-unpublished story of Broch's. The new language that is spoken at this point in the novel also has a certain function vis-à-vis the aesthetics of novel writing. It suggests a critique of the fine language of the conventional novel. One could mention Thomas Mann here as an exemplary target for this attack on the conventional novel.
CANETTI: Perhaps I even had him in mind, although I had just read *Der Zauberberg* (*The Magic Mountain*), which had made a great impression on me for thematic reasons. I know no other book that depicts this slow advance of death in such a way. It is a book that I would still endorse. Nevertheless, I had strong objections to his kind of novel.

DURZAK: It seems to me that you are talking about two stylistic principles: on the one hand, an elaborate circumlocution, putting everything in fine words, behind which reality disappears; and on the other, a precision of wording, a condensation of reality in language, and an intensification of this process—and here I am thinking also of the Joycean concept of epiphany— which one could potentially characterize as a kind of language-mysticism.
CANETTI: That is a remarkable connection to make.

DURZAK: One of which you were not aware? Didn't it play quite a large role while you were writing the novel?
CANETTI: Not with regard to form. What did play a role was that the conception of the brother, the psychiatrist, seemed insufficient to me, in that he is the greatest expert in metamorphosis, while Kien rejects metamorphosis, being completely incapable of it. That seemed insufficient to me. I needed something more. And so I made use of two things that were important for the composition of his intellect. The first thing I gave him was my preoccupation with crowds. That was still at a very early stage, in which the concepts were by no means sufficiently differentiated, but I was very fascinated by the subject. I lent him the things that attracted me to the crowd in a positive way, although I knew very well that what I was working on, a real investigation of crowds, would also have to include negative aspects. But I gave him this sensation of merging with a larger entity and of the strong pull that

crowd events exert on the individual human being. The second thing was that, in contrast to Peter Kien, I conceived him as a successful man, a man who enjoyed success with women and who was in this respect "smoother." Later, when he became an important psychiatrist, it became impossible to imagine him just as this smooth success story. I needed him to undergo a conversion, a turning away from the smoothness of his profession as a gynecologist, in which everything came to him so easily, to something that was intellectually more exciting, more interesting. Then I suddenly had the idea that he would have to meet a creature that had its own unique language. That could lead to this conversion. So I brought him into contact with this banker's wife who belonged, so to speak, to his earlier life, and I confronted him with this primitive, gorilla-like being. Anyway, when I started to think about the language of the gorilla, I realized that it was very important to me, and I later wrote down a lot about it for myself. But it began quite spontaneously from a need to form this character. I can't put it any differently. But one could think it through quite differently and put it into an important intellectual context, a context that later indeed came to exist.

10. ON THE RECEPTION OF *AUTO-DA-FÉ*

DURZAK: Dr. Canetti, you have worked for decades in relative seclusion from what might be called the literary world, and *Auto-da-Fé* too has taken a long time to find its audience. Your—if one may put it that way—isolation as a writer and the delayed reception of your literary work have certainly also to do with the particular circumstances of the times, with the circumstances of your life—for instance, the fact that you have lived for a long time, and still do live, in England—and even with particular circumstances regarding publishers. But now your works have attracted considerable attention. What is the reason for that? How do you see that yourself? Does it have to do with a reorientation in Germany, or with a reorientation on your part? Do you see any logic behind it? Is it even possible to postulate such a logic?
CANETTI: I have of course thought about that and often tried to find reasons for it. Certainly it has to do in part with circumstantial matters: that the works were not available, that *Auto-da-Fé* therefore came to be republished. Without doubt that plays a role. Another factor is that I acquiesced a little and published some of the smaller things that are more understandable. I think that the reception of my work would have had to wait still longer, had it not been for these little yellow books of the Reihe Hanser.[8] There would definitely have been people who would have read my things. Some would have tackled *Masse und Macht* (*Crowds and Power*). But the other works are easier. I would say, the personal tone of the notes and aphorisms has given some people the impression that these books are not really the product of such an

objective, inflexible mind but of a person capable of every possible emotion and feeling. That was not my intention in writing the notes and aphorisms, but I believe they may have contributed to this impression. Of course there are also other reasons. I believe, for example, that *Auto-da-Fé* was kept away from the German literary public for a period of time—by people who wished to create a new German literature. Many of them knew *Auto-da-Fé*. I am learning of that now, they are telling me of it now. Back then, for all of 15 years, nobody spoke of it. It was, I think, often unconscious. It belonged to the process of those people's own struggle with the past. And I think that, for many, the impression of *Auto-da-Fé* as an isolated work was stronger than they wished to admit. That may sound presumptuous, but it is only meant as an explanation. Once I spoke with Jakov Lind, who told me that he had at one time been unable to write. Then Erich Fried gave him *Auto-da-Fé*. Suddenly he thought: this is another way of writing. Then he wrote his volume of novellas, *Seele aus Holz* (Soul of wood), in which he was clearly under the influence of *Auto-da-Fé*. But he was an emigrant, he told me the exact story without any attempt to obfuscate. I have learned that there are people who do not like to speak of their origins, who want to hide them, and other people who often speak of them. I am one of the latter, since I always like to speak of the people who have influenced me. I do not mean to suggest that one kind of person is better than the other.

11. A Writer in Exile?

DURZAK: Dr. Canetti, you have described—perhaps I exaggerate—your exclusion from the literary life of the postwar era, and talked of the marginalization of your novel as part of that. Would it be justified to see in that the effects of a more general situation that afflicted you among many others, namely the situation of exile? With regard to your work after 1938, could one even characterize you as an writer in exile?

CANETTI: I have never actually seen myself as a writer in exile. That may have to do with the fact that, by birth, I do not come from one of the German-speaking countries, that I spoke three languages before I spoke German. Rather, I was a writer in exile inside German literature—the term is inaccurate here, but anyway there is something appropriate in its inversion. Anyway, the truth is that I always spoke English and French, just as I spoke German, and that I had always been interested in the literature of these countries. When I came to England it was not difficult for me to use the English language. I did not, like so many other emigrants, have first to trouble myself with the language; for me it was, rather, a language that came quite naturally. But I developed a very remarkable connection to the German words that I used much less while living in London. What evolved, then, was in fact a much more intensive engagement with the German language, a still greater passion for the language, because I was not always living and breathing it. If one can characterize that as the effect of exile, then one could put me in that group. But I do not believe that it is right to do so. Because it seems to me to be a crucial characteristic of modern literature as a whole that authors live in countries quite different from those in which they have grown up. Think of Joyce, to name one major example, who wrote about Dublin all his life but who wrote in Trieste, or Zurich, or Paris. Think of Beckett, who lives in Paris and even writes in French. This situation is becoming more and more common. More and more authors need that distance from their real substance. Are they writers in exile? That would be a question one would have to examine carefully.

Notes

1. [Elias Canetti, "Karl Kraus: The School of Resistance," in *The Conscience of Words* (London: Deutsch, 1979), 29–39. *Ed.*]
2. [Elias Canetti, *The Human Province*, trans. Joachim Neugroschel (New York: Seabury, 1978), 245; hereafter cited in text as *HP. Ed.*]
3. [Hermann Broch, "Einleitung zu einer Lesung von Elias Canetti in der Volkschochschule Leopoldstadt am 23. Januar 1933," in *Canetti lesen: Erfahrungen mit seinen Büchern,* ed. Herbert G. Göpfert (Munich: Hanser, 1975), 119–21. *Ed.*]
4. [The German word "Kien" translates as "resinous wood." *Ed.*]
5. [A lengthy extract of Canetti's 1937 interview is cited elsewhere in an essay by Peter Laemmle and in another conversation between Canetti and Durzak, both of which appear in English translation later in this volume. *Ed.*]
6. [The following exchanges are abbreviated for publication here. In the German-language version they duplicate, with some minor differences in wording, a section of another discussion between Canetti and Durzak, a full translation of which appears later in this volume. *Ed.*]
7. [The episode in question is found in the chapter "A Madhouse." *Ed.*]
8. [The Reihe Hanser (Hanser series) was a new paperback series featuring relatively short books and using eye-catching yellow and black covers. *Die Stimmen von Marrakesch* (1968; *The Voices of Marrakesh*) was the first book published in the series; later on came the first book-publication of *Der andere Prozeß* (1969; *Kafka's Other Trial*), *Alle vergeudete Verehrung* (1970; All the squandered veneration), *Die gespaltene Zukunft* (1972; The divided future), and a two-volume edition of *Masse und Macht* (1973; *Crowds and Power*). *Ed.*]

Auto da fé: Reading Misreading in Elias Canetti's *Die Blendung*

Patrick O'Neill

To read is also, always and necessarily, to misread. Few novels demonstrate the consequences of this interpretive maxim so graphically as Elias Canetti's remarkable novel *Die Blendung* (1935)—translated into English as *Auto da fé*—whose central character is the professional (and obsessional) reader Peter Kien, forty years old, "man of learning and specialist in sinology" (12), perhaps even the greatest living scholar of ancient Chinese philosophy.[1] "Countless texts owed their restoration to him" (20). Revered and envied by his peers as the unchallengeable authority in his field, the reclusive Kien "preferred to express himself in the written rather than the spoken word. He knew more than a dozen oriental languages ... No branch of human literature was unfamiliar to him" (20).

Kien's readerly skills fail him entirely, however, when it comes to the world beyond the walls of his private library. Completely misreading almost everyone with whom he comes in contact, he is successively deceived and defrauded by a shrewish wife, a conniving dwarf, and a brutish ex-policeman. Only the intervention of his psychiatrist brother—a professional reader of misreadings—seems capable of saving the day. Safely restored to his precious library, Kien promptly barricades it against intruders—and burns it to the ground. "When the flames reach him at last, he laughs out loud, louder than he has ever laughed in all his life" (522).

I

Kien regards the world beyond the library as at best a regrettably necessary evil, to be kept in its place by a rigidly unchanging routine that assigns only a minimum of time to such daily irritations as sleeping and eating. Even his

Reprinted by permission of University of Toronto Press Incorporated, from *Acts of Narrative: Textual Strategies in Modern German Fiction,* by Patrick O'Neill (Toronto: University of Toronto Press, 1996), 76–96. © University of Toronto Press Incorporated 1996.

scrupulously timed daily walk is preceded by a lengthy selection of the books he will carry with him in his briefcase in order to mitigate even such a momentary absence from his only proper milieu. *Die Blendung,* entirely predictably, is the story of the inevitable destruction of this all too fragilely protected intellectual idyll at the hands of that everyday world it affects to ignore, a theme that might, of course, lend itself just as easily to a tragic as to a comic treatment. Canetti unambiguously chooses the latter option, and *Die Blendung,* from beginning to end, displays its credentials as a remarkable comic performance. A latter-day Don Quixote, Kien is presented by Canetti's narrator as far less a character than a caricature.[2] The world that destroys him, however, is also peopled almost entirely by caricatures, and of these the most notable examples are certainly provided by the redoubtable trio of Therese Krumbholz, Siegfried Fischerle, and Benedikt Pfaff.

Therese Krumbholz has been in Kien's employ as a housekeeper for eight years without his ever having paid the slightest attention to her. In a momentary fit of weakness Kien one day very grudgingly lends her one of his least treasured books to read, only to discover her strategically adopted regard for learning to be so high that she reverently reads every page at least a dozen times before continuing, "otherwise you can't get the best out of it" (51). Suddenly recognizing the perfect potential guardian of his library should such an emergency as a fire ever occur, Kien, seizing the moment, immediately proposes marriage. Therese, however, whose most striking personality trait is a highly starched and perennially worn bright blue skirt, turns out in fact to be a formidable adversary, largely because of her indomitable stupidity. With a vocabulary of only about fifty words, as Kien once scathingly estimates, she is rarely silent once she becomes the lady of the house. "When she had reached the end, she began at the beginning" (122). Disappointed by Kien's total rejection of the physical joys of matrimony, Therese soon gives way to delicious fantasies mostly involving Kien's immediate death and her inheriting vast sums of money. Having badgered a demoralized and exhausted Kien into making out a will in her favour, she is highly indignant that the sum involved falls so far short of her expectations and promptly improves the situation considerably by adding several zeros to the unsatisfactory figure (147). When this solution proves to be less permanent than she had hoped, she resorts to starving Kien for several days, beats him black and blue for good measure, and eventually ejects him bodily from house and home.

Kien escapes Therese's clutches only to fall immediately into those of Siegfried Fischerle, a misshapen, hunchbacked Jewish dwarf who lives by his wits and the avails of prostitution. Fischerle is characterized by a rapaciousness at least the equal of Therese's and by an overwhelming passion for chess. In Fischerle's view, all that stands between him and the world championship is the lack of adequate funds, and Kien is exactly the kind of involuntary patron he has long been looking for. He swiftly worms his way into Kien's confidence, ruthlessly exploits his accelerating dementia, plays on his multiple fears and weaknesses, and helps himself with great liberality to his money whenever possible. Fischerle's long-cherished dream is to escape to America, trounce the reigning chess champion, have his hump removed, and live in a mansion with a millionaire's daughter. Thanks to Kien's involuntary largesse, he eventually sees himself in a position to begin this odyssey, buys himself a suit of appropriate quality and pattern—"black and white checks" (393)—for a man of his anticipated standing, spends an afternoon learning American (399), and indulges in a first-class ticket to Paris. At the last moment, Fischerle—or Doctor Fischer, as his newly forged passport now more appropriately has it—decides to return to his room for a forgotten address book containing the names of all possible competitors for the world title that is now rightly his. There he unfortunately encounters one of his wife's customers, a "blind" beggar whom he has grievously insulted just a few days before and who promptly throttles the would-be world champion and savagely hacks off his hump with a blunt bread-knife—considerately shoving the corpse under the bed before resuming his interrupted love-making with the wife of the deceased.

The third member of the trio through whom Kien traumatically experiences the outside world is the caretaker Benedikt Pfaff. Kien originally sees Pfaff (like Fischerle) as an ally, for Pfaff has no time for the jumped-up Therese, whom he classifies with elegant simplicity, as he does all the other undesirables he encounters in the course of his duties, as a "shithead" (95). Pfaff's favoured method of reasoning with such "suspects" (95) of this kind as are incautious enough to attempt to venture past his porter's lodge is to fling himself on them from his lair and beat them senseless. A now-retired policeman, Pfaff is wholly devoted to Kien, since before his eviction the latter has paid him a handsome monthly tip to ensure his undisturbed privacy. In happier days, Pfaff, "the kind father" (413), had conscientiously terrorized, beaten, and sexually exploited both his wife and his daughter, partly for their own good, partly to remind them of the respect due to himself as husband, father, and breadwinner. His wife "died under his hands. But she would certainly have pegged out of her own accord in the next few days anyway. A murderer he was not" (414). When his daughter dies too some years later, he walls up the bedroom in which they were all three once so happy together and sadly devotes his fists to the re-education of uninvited visitors. Pfaff's success as guardian of the gate is largely due to his patented method of observation: all day long and much of the night he squats at a knee-high peephole in the wall of the entrance hall and watches the trousers and skirts that pass by. An instant evaluation of any previously unseen garment guarantees either safe passage or instant demolition for its wearer. When Kien, dazed from his experiences in the outside world, instinctively returns to his former address, he is first greeted with joy by Pfaff on account of the expected continuation of the monthly tip, then press-ganged into service at the peephole, and finally held to ransom in Pfaff's boarded-up lair for the price of his meals.

Like Kien himself, Therese, Fischerle, and Pfaff are far less characters in any realistic sense, capable of change and development, than they are caricatures, identified by just two or three static characteristics. Therese is characterized mentally by her stupidity, cupidity, and entirely groundless vanity, physically by her stiff blue skirt, in which she seems less to walk than to glide ominously as if on castors, her unusually large ears, and her pronounced body odour. Fischerle is characterized mentally by his cunning, his venality, and his contempt for anyone he can outsmart—which means most people, "for they're all fools" (374); physically by his dwarfish stature, his hump, and a gigantic nose. Pfaff is characterized mentally by his stupidity, his obsequiousness in the face of authority, and his belief in force as the answer to all problems; physically by his gigantic fists, his red hair, and his great roaring voice. All three are united not only by their consuming greed for money but also by their total disregard of the rights of other people: Therese happily leaves her husband for dead, Fischerle ruthlessly exploits his wife and routinely cheats anyone who can't stop him, Pfaff beats his wife to death and sexually abuses his daughter for years. Therese and Pfaff, for all that, both see themselves as pillars of society: Therese is proud to be a "respectable person" (33), as opposed to the "riffraff" (30) that are everywhere rampant; Pfaff, as one-time policeman and servant of the state, swears by law and order and the sanctity of family values. Fischerle, for his part, lives only for the day when, rich and famous, he will be in a position to occupy his rightful place in the scheme of things.

Therese, Fischerle, and Pfaff are the three most closely described inhabitants of the unnamed Vienna represented in Canetti's novel.[3] There are numerous others who make briefer but still memorable appearances: the smooth Herr Grob (whose name means "rough"); tiny Herr Groß ("great") and his domineering mother; Fischerle's wife, known as "die Pensionistin" or "the Capitalist" because of her steady income from a particular long-term customer; his friend "die Fischerin" ("the Fishwife," as C. V. Wedgwood felicitously translates it), so called because, a misshapen, hunchbacked dwarf herself, she is hopelessly in love with Fischerle; his murderer, Johann Schwer, alias "der Knopfhans" / "Johnny Button," obsessed by the fact that his professional blindness prevents an appropriately violent reaction (except eventually in Fischerle's case) when he plainly sees buttons rather than coins being thrown into his beggar's hat; and the police Kommandant, perpetually devastated by the size of his hopelessly underdeveloped nose.

It is among this collection of Dickensian grotesques populating the world beyond the library—"Here be monsters"—that Kien, the scholar and thinker, is obliged to move, at his peril, once he is ejected from his own book-lined world. To take Kien at face value as the representative of intellect in a hostile world, however, is to oversimplify drastically the complexity of the discursive situation presented in *Die Blendung*. Kien has completely rejected the outside world, the world of the "mob" (18), devoted as he is to his service in the cause of truth. Knowledge and truth were for him identical terms. You drew closer to truth by shutting yourself off from people. Daily life was a superficial clatter of lies ... He had always known this, experience was superfluous. (18)

Before Therese finally outflanks him, he adamantly rejects the thought of ever taking a wife: "Each is a specialist first and foremost as a woman, and would make demands which an honest man of learning would not even dream of fulfilling" (15). As far as Kien is concerned, he is a scholar first, last, and always, and his entirely indiscriminate contempt for other people in general is founded on their unprincipled failure to emulate him in likewise adopting a rigidly unswerving course towards the truth and then adhering to it at all costs: "*His* ambition was to persist stubbornly in the same manner of existence. Not for a mere month, not for a year, but for the whole of his life, he would be unchangingly true to himself" (18).

Kien's preferred method of dealing with this rejected world is to ignore it. "Every passer-by was a liar. For that reason he never looked at them" (18). He achieves similar success with this method when he learns to ignore Therese's newly acquired furniture (an inconvenience he had previously avoided) by training himself to walk around the apartment with his eyes firmly closed except when he is sure he is standing in front of a bookcase (78). "The furniture exists as little for him as the army of atoms within and around him. *Esse percipi,* to be is to be perceived. What I do not perceive does not exist" (79). Therese herself, unfortunately, is not quite so easy to rationalize out of existence. As an alternative strategy, Kien heroically attempts to mobilize his library in its own defence, addressing his army of books in martial terms before turning their twenty-five thousand backs to the wall—since that is exactly where the world of learning now finds itself in the face of an advancing tide of "slime from the bog of illiteracy" (102). A victim of his own eloquence, he succeeds only in falling from the library ladder and spending six bedridden weeks a helpless victim of Therese's unending tirades (120). Once she turns to actual blows, Kien has to resort to yet more rigorous methods of defence and turns himself to stone: "His eyes were fixed on the distance. He sought to close them. From their refusal to do so he recognized that he was the granite image of an Egyptian priest. He had turned into a statue" (179). Only Therese's incurable ignorance, which extends also to matters Egyptian, causes this excellent plan to fail also.

Kien is likewise no match at all for the wily Fischerle. Kien cannot, of course, afford to be without his research library, so when Therese expels him from it he goes to enormous pains to reassemble the entire library by visiting bookshops—and carrying the volumes thus "acquired" in his head. In order to sleep, of course, he then has to unload the entire library every night, requiring ever-larger hotel rooms as the collection grows. Fischerle busily assists him in this endeavour, even suggesting various refinements to ensure as orderly a procedure as possible (217). He also informs Kien in confidence that the state pawn office, the ominously (and fictitiously) named Theresianum (231), houses a particular official whose sole duty and pleasure it is to devour on the spot all books pawned by their unsuspecting owners. Appalled by this barbarous plot—"How little do we see of the fearful misery which lies about us?" (241)—Kien immediately decides to devote his entire remaining fortune to saving the books, takes up sentry duty at the door of the establishment, and hands out ever larger sums of money to erring individuals wishing to pawn their books—and who are, of course, all in Fischerle's temporary employ.

Or rather, not quite all, for one day Therese and Pfaff, having in the meantime joined forces, also turn up with large parcels of Kien's own books to pawn. This apparition considerably disturbs Kien, for in the meantime he has been reliably informed, by one of Fischerle's henchmen, of Therese's unhappy death: " 'I'm sorry to say she's dead,' said the blind man with genuine regret, 'and sends you her kind regards' " (288). Faced with such solid evidence, Kien has concluded that he himself was undoubtedly responsible for her death, for after he so narrowly escaped her clutches by locking her into the apartment, he reasons, she must no doubt have died a slow and very likely excruciating death of starvation. Her sudden appearance at this point is therefore obviously a hallucination of some kind, he further concludes, presumably due to overwork—certainly not to remorse, for Kien accepts his guilt with great equanimity: "She deserved such a death. Even today I don't know for certain if she could read and write with any ease" (294). Some days later Kien strangles Pfaff's four singing canaries because their "blue" plumage reminds him of the fatal blue of Therese's skirt, which comes to symbolize all that is evil in the world for him. Throwing their corpses out the window, he also tosses out the little finger of his left hand, which he has just cut off to test the sharpness of his dinner knife. "Scarcely has he thus expelled everything from the room when the walls begin to dance. Their violent movement dissolves in blue spots. They are skirts, he whispers, and creeps under the bed. He is beginning to doubt his reason" (442–3).

The reader has no doubt entertained similar reservations for some time already. And at just this point in the proceedings a second Professor Kien is introduced, namely, Kien's brother Georg (or Georges), the brilliantly successful director of a large psychiatric hospital in Paris. In striking contrast to Kien's determined misanthropy, Georg's success rests above all on his ability to empathize completely with his disturbed patients, to enter completely into their individual fantasy worlds on their own terms, and to treat them with all the respect due as appropriate to a Napoleon or a Goethe or a Jupiter. "Thus he lived simultaneously in numberless different worlds" (446), a master of metamorphosis (455). Perhaps the most interesting of the many hermeneutic enigmas faced by Canetti's reader is why Georg, who has been so successful at entering into the fantasy worlds—the *Blendungen* or "delusions"—of his other patients, fails so spectacularly when it comes to his own brother.

II

Die Blendung was originally intended as one of a cycle of eight novels that would constitute a "Comédie Humaine an Irren" (Canetti 1975: 127), a "*Comédie humaine* of lunatics." In the entropically degenerate world it portrays, rapacity, stupidity, brutality, and cunning fight constantly for supremacy. Critics are virtually unanimous in their reading of Canetti's narrative on this level. This is a novel about the emergence of the monstrous out of the everyday (Moser 1983: 54), a diagnostic portrayal of the sickness of the times (Busch 1975: 31), a revelation of all that is inhuman in society (Piel 1984: 16), a pandemonium of latent aggression (Barnouw 1979: 21–2). The degree to which social order has disintegrated is perhaps best illustrated by the fact that both Therese, the incarnation of stupidity and greed, and Pfaff, the incarnation of brutality and violence, appeal entirely confidently to the concept of law and order. The direct consequences of this social anomie are portrayed in various vicious (and historically prophetic) mob scenes—as when "die Fischerin," for example, is savagely beaten up and left for dead because of her hump (371).

The title *Die Blendung* has various possible connotations: the action or result of literal blinding, figurative blinding (as by bright lights), or metaphorical blinding (as by the deceit of others or by self-delusion). The term can also denote a "blind" in the hunting sense, a shelter (or fiction) behind which to conceal one's true intentions—whether from others or from oneself. The novel plays with these various conceptions of blindness throughout.[4] One of Kien's greatest fears as a scholar, for example, is that of blindness, though the blindness he eventually falls victim to is metaphorical rather than physical; he deliberately "blinds" himself on several occasions, quite literally closing his eyes to a reality he does not wish to see; and he is involuntarily "blinded," has the wool pulled over his eyes, in almost all his encounters with other characters. With the possible exception of Georg, all the inhabitants of this narrative world are represented as cripplingly limited by their assorted obsessions, each of them living in an almost entirely isolated fictional world of his or her own creation. Their grotesquely curtailed characterization corresponds to the grotesque limitations they impose upon their own development by the single-minded rigidity of their assorted *idées fixes*—graphically emblematized by Pfaff's knee-high peephole.

The narrative abounds in instances of voluntary or involuntary self-delusion as a means of controlling a rejected reality, typified by Kien's apologia: "I know this truth is a lie" (342). The most significant implication of this ubiquitous *Blendung* is that any form of real communication is practically impossible: nobody in this monoglot world talks *to* anyone else, rather everyone talks *past* his or her interlocutor, talks in the end only to him- or herself. The world becomes a lunatic asylum, with each individual hermetically sealed inside his or her own fantasy, reading everything that happens completely unreflectingly in accordance with the dictates of this system. One of the most graphic illustrations is provided by the farcical police interrogation of Kien, who is fully prepared to defend his "murder" of Therese before any court, and is duly given that opportunity (though he is the only one who knows this) in the course of an interrogation (convened for quite different reasons) during which total confusion reigns, volubly enhanced by frequent interventions on the part of the murder victim.

Canetti's novel achieved recognition in the German-speaking countries only extremely belatedly, almost thirty years after its first appearance.[5] It has been variously noted that a central reason for this may be found in the wholly unflattering picture it paints of the role of the intellectual in society, in the egregious failure of its intellectual protagonist to come to any sort of terms with the barbarous world in which he lives.

Kien, in fact, quickly becomes tainted by the reality he so sedulously endeavours to ignore. He is immediately infected by Therese's greed for money, for example—not for any base reason, of course, but because he can buy more books with it. He quite happily accepts that he is, as he thinks, a murderer—though likewise in a good cause, of course. His delirious solution for the ills of the civilized world is a simple one: "A decree for the abolition of the female sex is in preparation" (430)—a view interestingly paralleling Fischerle's contention that "Women destroy men" (223) or Pfaff's that "Women ought to be beaten to death" (124). Pfaff's respect for law and order parodically reflects Kien's own fanatic devotion to order (19) in his daily routine. Forced by Pfaff to take his place at the peephole, Kien very soon becomes fascinated by the exercise and even considers the possibility of a brief monograph on his observations in the field (433). And in the end, of course, Kien becomes his own worst nightmare, a destroyer of books.

"Believe me, no mortal man is worth his weight in books!" (242–3), Kien, a crazed Don Quixote in a fantasy world of book-devouring "cannibals" (273), preaches in what he sees as his role as a more intellectually responsible Christ, saviour of books rather than of men (269). As long as he stays in his library, Kien's eccentric vision of the world is essentially unchallenged. With his expulsion from this paradise, his vision becomes entangled with numerous other and equally eccentric visions of the world. The three divisions of the narrative show Kien sliding increasingly rapidly from an ostensibly sovereign idealism ("Ein Kopf ohne Welt" / "A Head Without a World") through a hopelessly ineffective encounter with the real world ("Kopflose Welt" / "Headless World") into outright madness ("Welt im Kopf" / "The World in the Head").

Thematically, the reader's attention is thus drawn in turn to *Kopf, Welt,* and the reading of the latter by the former. Semiotically, a central strand— almost entirely ignored by Canetti criticism so far—is the parodic juxtaposition of three radically different portrayals of the intellectual in society. *Die Blendung* employs two main (and continually interlinked) strategies of narrative discourse: first, the systemic problematization of reading; second, as one aspect of this, the parodic evocation of the "intellectual" by a process of synecdochic, stereographic characterization. The character thus obliquely evoked is not so much that of Kien, who remains a caricature throughout; rather it is that of the intellectual per se, implied rather than portrayed by virtue of the interaction of Kien and those about him. The resultant and highly satirical portrayal of the intellectual in society emerges from a double procedure of contrast: Kien is contrasted on the one hand to Therese and Pfaff as representatives of the forces that militate against intellect, and on the other to Fischerle and Georg as representatives of intellect.

Therese and Pfaff are purely one-dimensional caricatures; Fischerle and Georg are both more complicated figures. Having fought and lost his epic battle with Therese in Part One of the narrative, Kien—whose apartment does not contain a mirror (18)—is doubly reflected discursively in what follows: first, more grotesquely, in the comico-pathetic figure of Fischerle in Part Two, and then, more essayistically, in the figure of his long-lost brother Georg in Part Three. The result is a composite picture of the intellectual as deliberate outsider, as trickster (with physical deformities to match the intellectual ones), and as would-be saviour of a world that energetically resists any such salvation.

Fischerle, in whom Kien immediately believes he detects a fellow spirit—"Chess is his library" (209)—functions as a distorted image of Kien, a grotesque (and criminally minded) Sancho Panza to Kien's equally grotesque Quixote. Like Kien, he is totally obsessed, specifically by his ambition to become world chess champion. Where Kien's intellectual interests are entirely disinterested, however, Fischerle's, indicatively, are purely a means to an end. His real ambition is to become as rich as possible as soon as possible, and any means he may have to employ are secondary to this end. He is easily able to outwit Kien, as we have seen, but his own delusion eventually takes him over completely, just as Kien's does him. Where Kien arrogantly ignores other people, Fischerle contemptuously exploits them. Kien's arrogance leads ultimately to his own death, since his total exclusion of other people from his world leads, so to speak, to a complete loss of immunity, a complete defence-lessness in the face of others. Likewise, it is his contempt for others that finally leads to Fischerle's death, as the result of a gratuitous taunt. It is indicative also that while very few readers are likely to feel any sympathy with either Therese or Pfaff, some readers may well feel that, for all his ruth-lessness and depravity, Fischerle is at least to some extent as much sinned against as sinning. Branded a natural victim in the dog-eat-dog world in which he lives by both his physical deformities and his Jewishness, Fischerle, as "cripple" (365), needs all the considerable intelligence at his disposal to survive. We may note a number of occasions when the discourse parodically connects Kien and Fischerle in the choice of words: Therese, for example, also calls Kien a "Krüppel" (134; in English, 171); Fischerle himself sees Kien as a fish and himself as a fisherman (199); "I'm not a dog, am I?" (198) are the first words we hear Fischerle utter, addressed to a Kien whom Therese also thinks of on occasion as a dog to be whipped; he even masquerades as Kien in his faked (but entirely accurate) telegram to Georg: "Am completely nuts" (377); and so on.[6]

Indicatively, perhaps, Georg never actually meets Fischerle, but becomes involved in his brother's affairs precisely as a result of that telegram, sent by Fischerle in Kien's name as a malicious joke just before his own unforeseen death. Since Georg is an outsider—and a psychoanalyst—his arrival on the scene seems to promise an imminent solution to the proliferating hermeneutic confusion (Dissinger 1971: 55). His failure provides the reader with the interpretive crux of the novel. For some readers, Georg fails quite simply because he never realizes that his brother, a "warywise Odysseus" (479), who refuses to reveal his madness, *needs* curing in the first place: Georg, that is to say, expects to find a world of lunatics only inside the walls of his asylum (Dissinger 1971: 98). Other readers are struck more forcefully by the fact that Georg, the master healer, prefers not to heal some of his favourite patients at all, judging their fantasized private worlds to be infinitely richer than the shared world of normality.

Georg's (putative) blindness to his brother's (metaphorical) blindness is ironically anticipated when he encounters a blind fellow passenger on the train from Paris to Vienna, remembers his brother's terror as a small boy with measles that he was going blind, and anticipates that Peter's present problems may well arise from a renewed fear of (actual rather than metaphorical) blindness as a result of too much reading. Dissinger notes that Georg, like Peter, also initially misreads both Therese and Pfaff (1971: 98). Georg, however, quickly corrects his reading in both cases and has little difficulty in saving his brother from this combined threat from without. The threat from within apparently escapes his diagnosis, however, and during the long and (grotesquely) learned debate with his brother he even inadvertently hastens Kien's self-destruction by citing as an example of a ludicrous and completely unlikely eventuality that Peter should voluntarily burn down his own library—an idea that in fact has long been present to Kien as a nightmare and now seizes the upper hand in his rapidly failing mind.

Kien, who had broken off all communication with his brother eight years previously (57), none the less thinks of him as his potential protector: he wishes Georg were there (57) as soon as he realizes his mistake in marrying Therese; a silent cry for help to Georg (520) is one of his last thoughts before the final flames reach him. Yet he also instinctively mistrusts Georg, the one person who might be capable of saving him. The brothers, unacknowledged patient and would-be doctor, are presented as being in many ways two sides of the same coin. Georg at one point observes that together they would constitute one real human being, "a spiritually complete man" (490). Rigidity and abstraction are Peter's milieu, flexibility and human sympathy are

Georg's: determined isolation as opposed to equally determined openness, abstraction versus empathy, misanthropy versus philanthropy, Peter's vain attempts at petrifaction versus Georg's constant metamorphosis in entering into the fantasies of his patients. Indicatively, where Peter wishes to be stone, Georg(es), whose name metamorphoses easily with his surroundings, is "a walking wax tablet" (464). But how sane is a psychoanalyst who at least selectively prefers insanity to sanity? While earlier critics understandably tended to see Georg as a wholly positive counterpart to Peter, Dagmar Barnouw, for example, argues that both of them behave with a completely irresponsible combination of political ignorance and arrogance (1979: 23). Georg, she argues, is an undisciplined dilettante delighted more by his own ingenuity as a healer than by any real interest in his patients, and consequently both irresponsible and potentially dangerous—as his behaviour with Peter shows.[7]

Kien, Fischerle, and Georg are all presented as master readers, master interpreters in their several specialized fields, whether oriental philology, chess, or the human psyche. Kien, the reclusive scholar, sees his field as a place of refuge from the real world; Fischerle, the crook, sees his field as a way to improve the real world in the most immediately practical way by making him rich and famous; Georg, the idealist, sees his field as a way to help people who need help, to make the world a better place for all. By the same token, however, all three are failed readers in one way or another.

Kien the celebrated scholar would certainly not have neglected to examine conflicting versions of a text before deciding on the correct reading—but he subscribes blindly, and eventually fatally, to a single and highly limited reading of the world he lives in. Fischerle, like Kien, becomes so completely enmeshed in his private vision of how the world works (or how it *should* work) that he forgets equally completely to apply even the elementary rules of his own area of specialized knowledge. As a chess player he would certainly not have carried out a single move with anything approaching the degree of reckless overconfidence that leads, off the board, to the immediate checkmate of his plans—in the form of his own savage murder. Georg, whose *métier* is the reconciliation of conflicting visions of reality, a brilliantly successful listener in his dealings with the mentally disturbed inmates of his asylum, likewise apparently fails to observe his own basic diagnostic rule as a psychiatrist in failing to enter into Kien's fantasy world—because he fails to recognize a patient when he sees one.

One of the major challenges presented to the reader of *Die Blendung* is to decide just how seriously this composite picture of the intellectual should be taken. One basic question to consider is to what degree Kien, Fischerle, and Georg really are the authorities in their respective fields they are presented—and accepted by most critics—as being. The role of narrative focalization in Canetti's text—the fact, that is to say, that so much of the text we read is presented by the "voice" of the narrator but seen through the "eyes" of particular characters—is crucial in this respect. The question of Fischerle's credentials as a chess player is a good example of the implications.

The reader may not be surprised that, true to his criminal instincts, Fischerle cheats even at chess. Indeed, Fischerle's credentials as a potential chess champion are openly undermined by the narrator when the dwarf is shown dazzling his drinking companions by demonstrating the mistakes allegedly made by reigning champions—but "He was by no means convinced of his own importance. He racked his brains furiously over the actual moves he concealed" (204). The reader tends to assign less importance to this information, however, than to the information that "during games his partners were far too much afraid of him to interrupt him with objections. For he took a terrible vengeance and would hold up the foolishness of their moves to general derision" (200). So strong and so persistent is Fischerle's conviction of his own skill, in other words, that the reader tends to ignore the possibility that the account of his victories, though presented by the narrator, may be envisioned solely through Fischerle's eyes—tends, in fact, to accept Fischerle's vision of how things should be rather than the narrator's statement of how they in fact are.

Doubts as to Kien's being a professor are likewise raised (and apparently rejected) at a very early stage, when the boy Franz Metzger observes in the dialogue with which the narrative commences that "My mother says you aren't a real Professor. But I think you are—you've got a library" (12).[8] The nine-year-old schoolboy's apparent correction of his mother's erroneous opinion is immediately reinforced by the fact that the narrator's initial reference to Kien is to "Professor Peter Kien" (12). Since the reader has no reason to assume at this point that the narrator is presenting anything other than verifiably authentic facts, this reference and many others like it will naturally be read as entirely valid. A systematic analysis of focalization in the text, however, has convincingly shown that the narrator's various references to the extent and quality of Kien's scholarship all occur in narrative contexts where Kien's focalization can be read as predominating (Darby 1992: 23).

That Kien owns a large library seems to be beyond dispute, if only because we see Therese and Pfaff attempting to pawn large numbers of his books. That Kien is a world-renowned scholar, however, may be no less a private fantasy than are Fischerle's dreams of glory—we note, for example, that Kien eschews all contact with professional colleagues, whom he ostensibly despises. That Georg is a psychiatrist also seems beyond dispute, if only because the telegram Fischerle sends to his clinic in Paris actually reaches Georg there. But what of the reports of his astonishing success? Is the reported fact that his eight hundred patients regard him as a "saviour" (454) to be taken as a statement of narrative fact on the part of a reliable narrator—or as evidence that Georg, like his crazed brother Peter, also sees himself as a new and improved version of Christ the Saviour?[9] Can readers trust their own reading? Can readers trust the narrative presentation on which they have no option but to base that reading? In the absurd world of *Die Blendung*—in which its readers too must dwell for the duration of their reading—the yardstick that divides reading from misreading, the normal from the abnormal, the sane from the insane remains systemically uncertain, systemically subject to *Blendung* in its application.

III

Kien, the absent-minded professor, falls successively into the hands of a shrew, a crook, a murderer, the police, and a psychiatrist, all of them likewise portrayed as comic figures—including even Georg, the famous psychiatrist who cannot tell sane from insane. In the case of Georg, however, the comedy is in quite a different key, the grotesque slapstick of the earlier episodes giving way to a more ironically tinged picture of a world entirely out of joint, a world in which disorder reigns supreme—and a world that is also, of course, the creation of the narrator. Canetti's narrator is a master of grotesque invention, one who lives, like Georg, in a multitude of worlds at once—and allows the reader to do so too, though naturally at the latter's own risk. It is entirely in line with the thematic thrust of *Die Blendung* that instead of character development we are given character confrontation, conflicting visions of the intellectual juxtaposed rather than harmonized; it is entirely in line with the semiotic thrust that Georg's therapeutic practice, as reported, functions as a *mise en abyme* of the narrator's presentational strategy. Georg's belief that he can probe the relationship of the individual and society from the behaviour of the patients he leaves happily insane—"In his own consciousness he would gradually draw the separate halves of the patient, as he embodied them, closer to each other, and thus gradually would rejoin them" (446)—is clearly paralleled by the narrator's practice, metamorphosing easily as he does, like Georg, between one exclusive fantasy world and another.

One can agree with Annemarie Auer when she sees *Die Blendung* as constructed essentially along entirely conventional lines, but hardly when she calls it a novel innocent of all experimentation (1983: 33). Canetti's narrator is one of the most devious in literature. The novel's elusiveness is in large part due to what one might describe as an ostentatiously backgrounded narrator. Indeed, the narrator is almost entirely "absent" from his own account, as Dissinger observes (1971: 23), leaving his characters to speak for themselves, whether in the form of interior monologue (on a relatively few occasions) or, much more frequently, that of narrated monologue (*erlebte Rede*). The central significance of the latter device in Canetti's novel is that it almost always employs the third person and past tense of (apparently) omniscient (and thus completely authoritative) narration but is focalized through a character rather than by the narrator—and thus effectively leads to systemic ambiguity as far as the reader is concerned. For the options of unambiguous identification of the focalization with *either* the narrator or the character are rare; what are stressed are precisely the grey and frequently entirely indeterminable areas in between. The crucial difficulty is in determining just when the particular focalization involved should be read as the narrator's presumably authoritative and reliable report and just when as the deluded fantasy of one of his characters. As we have seen, even a reference like "Professor Peter Kien" demands two entirely different readings, depending upon whether we see it as focalized by an authoritative narrator or by a deluded character. In a narrative which centres on the fundamental ambivalence of narrative focalization, indeed, every single sentence is in principle ambivalent. Constant ironic change of perspective is thus a central feature of this narrative, obliging the reader constantly both to identify with *and* immediately to question the readings of the characters (Dissinger 1971: 33). The novel ironically comments on its own technique in Kien's dismissive statement that "Novels are so many wedges which the novelist, an actor with his pen, inserts into the closed personality of the reader" (47).

It is hardly surprising that before the appearance in 1960 of Canetti's major anthropological study *Masse und Macht* (*Crowds and Power*), criticism of *Die Blendung,* whether at home or abroad, was characterized by and large by bewilderment—and quickly moved towards an exclusive reliance on the theoretical categories developed in Canetti's apparently "explanatory" later work concerning the relationship of the individual and the collective. Such readings, while of considerable value in non-literary terms, tend to underplay drastically the primarily literary status of the narrative. Avoiding this explanatory paradigm, David Darby persuasively analyses the text as primarily an open system of meaning, concentrating especially on the degree to which a continually shifting and radically ambiguous focalization systemically undermines the reliability of the narrative account and produces an informational disorder that overtly challenges the reader's powers of structuration throughout (1992: 24–38). The point in such instances—which are legion—is precisely their uncertainty, precisely their challenge to the reader.

"The narrator of *Die Blendung* provides no commentaries, offers no opinions, makes no attempt to provide the kind of insight into motivation and behaviour that calms and consoles," as Stevens aptly observes (1991: 114–15). Instead, without comment, he presents a monstrous world, peopled by monstrous characters—and leaves the reader to decide where to locate its edges. It is also, however, a comic world, based on disorientation and disproportion, bearing comparison with those of Céline, Beckett, or Heller. Several (at least) of the chapters are frankly comic set pieces, especially, for example, "The Thief" (316–32) or "Private Property" (333–64). Canetti's narrative is also a comedy on another level, however, in that there is a second "story" in progress of which the characters, by definition, can never know anything. Lacking almost entirely any character development, and with only a minimal plot, the narrative is held together on the level of discourse by a network of parodic linking devices. These are of two main kinds: first, a variety of discursive leitmotifs, such as the occurrence of the colours blue and red; and second, a variety of teasing discursive parallels between characters.

Dissinger, for example (1971: 135–38), meticulously traces the occurrence of the colours blue and red, associated initially with Therese's skirt and Pfaff's hair respectively—and by extension with the threat to the intellectual life constituted by Therese and Pfaff as representatives of the unthinking mob, an elemental force of destruction like (blue) water or (red) fire. Kien's implication in his own downfall is minimally hinted at by references to his "watery blue eyes" (195) and Georg's dream of him as a fighting cock, "der rote Hahn" (372), literally "the red rooster" (470), but in German also a traditional literary expression for a destructive fire. And so on. Other ostensibly symbolic series involve recurring numbers, mythological references, and repeated references to the relationship of individuals and collectives, parts and wholes. The point of all of this quasi-helpful information, however, is not that it leads the reader closer to some grand unitary meaning but rather that it teasingly offers the possibility of generating further meanings that may or may not be significant.

The narrator's parodic attitude is perhaps most evident in onomastic terms. Canetti, as we know, originally intended calling the novel, as a satire on the Cartesian *cogito,* "Kant fängt Feuer" / "Kant catches fire," then changed the protagonist's name first to Brand, then to Kien, in each case retaining the ominous connection with fire: Kien's very name contains his own destruction from the beginning (Canetti 1975: 124, 127, 135). The term *Kien,* derived from a root meaning "to hew, to split off," denotes a long, flat shingle of resinous wood split off from a larger log and originally used especially as a torch. Onomastically Kien (whose unusual height and striking emaciatedness are also frequently mentioned) is thus ironically marked from the beginning not only as both a potential fireraiser and a potential victim of fire, but also as one "split off." The phrase *auf dem Kien sein,* we may also note, means "to be alert," a quality scarcely attributable to Kien, who allows himself to be swindled by almost everybody with whom he comes in contact. To add insult to injury, Kien, stamped by his surname as wood, is even ironically linked to Therese, the embodiment of all that is inimical to his way of life— and whose surname is Krumbholz, literally "wood bender" (a term originally associated with the wheelwright's trade). The reader may even wish to see a trilingual pun on Kien's first name, Peter: parodically connecting the Greek *petros* "stone" (recalling Kien's unavailing efforts to become a statue) via English *rock* to German *Rock* "skirt," the most striking external manifestation of Therese's personality.

We find the same parodic play in the entirely inappropriate odour of onomastic sanctity doubly informing the reprobate "Benedikt Pfaff" (the two names literally meaning "blessed" and "cleric" respectively) as well as in the obsequiously smooth Herr "Grob" ("rough") or the tiny Herr "Groß" ("great"). We note the parodic inappropriateness of Fischerle's given name, Siegfried; note the fact that Georg (like Siegfried) is onomastically stamped as a dragon-slayer; notice that Georges from Paris loses his -es in Vienna, just as Fischerle, en route to Paris, loses his -le when he promotes himself to Doctor Fischer, an orthographic correlative of the hump he wishes to lose—and will soon lose to a kitchen knife, just as Kien cuts off his own finger. How seriously readers choose to take all this all too generously provided information is left entirely up to them.

The presence of such caricatures as carriers of the narrative action might likewise suggest that the central thematic thrust of the narrative should most appropriately be read as bluntly satirical. Such a reading is certainly possible—as when Dissinger observes that one of the novel's central themes is to show the folly of greed (1971: 63; 1982: 35)—but though this is demonstrably the case, recognizing it also constitutes only the very beginnings of an adequate reading. What is far more striking, at least for an approach that privileges the semiotics of narrative discourse, is the number of loose ends that teasingly escape any such tidily attempted hermeneutic closure and demand a more differentiated and a more open reading. Darby thus responds far more adequately to the semiotic demands of the text in his discussion of the various (quasi-)symbolic strategies that are employed by the narrator— the use of colours, the opposition of the individual and the social mass, the use of "significant" numbers, the play with proper names and mythological references—in concluding that their explanatory value is highly limited and their function essentially parodic, gesturing only vaguely towards possible systems of meaning but remaining fragmentary, hermeneutic red (or blue?) herrings for the benefit of readers hungry for closure (1992: 149–58).

IV

"Anyone can read" (134), as Therese sagely observes. Not just Kien, Fischerle, and Georg but also Therese (who rereads and rewrites her future by adding an appropriate number of extra zeros to her anticipated legacy), Pfaff (who rereads and rewrites the past by walling it up) and almost all the minor characters are *all* readers of texts deemed in need of emendatory rereading. *Die Blendung* overtly thematizes the problematics of reading and writing, overtly challenges its reader to demonstrate those powers of interpretive discrimination so signally lacking among its characters. Any text presents its readers to some degree with a similar challenge, of course; *Die Blendung* offers more than fair warning of the likelihood of hermeneutic failure through a discourse characterized by unreliability and indeterminacy.

The central enigma of the narrative, Georg's apparent failure as a reader, needs to be read in this context. The account of his career makes it clear that his psychiatric practice differs radically from an "official psychiatry" (443) whose aim is to replace a deviant reading of reality with a socially authorized one. Georg rejects this aim in favour of a radically different understanding of his role as psychiatrist, refusing to subject his patients' reading of reality, albeit deviant, to a unitary master-reading: "Understanding as we understand it is a misunderstanding" (455–6). In refusing to heal his favourite patients, in short, Georg shows himself to be the open reader Canetti's text demands.

At the same time, of course, Georg, revered by his (mad) patients as a "saviour," characterized by his (translingually unstable) name as both a dragon-slayer and a mover between worlds, completely unsuccessful in his attempt to cure his own brother, and possibly a brilliant success only in his own imagination, is heavily ironized by the narrator. Readers, for their part, are left in the end with several possible interpretations of Georg's reading, none of which, however, can be considered definitive. First, we may conclude that Georg, outwitted by his brother's lunatic cunning, simply does not realize that Kien is mad: in this case Georg is either completely incompetent or insane himself—or, like all the other characters in the novel, he lives in a world where the distinction has become unrecognizable. Second, we may conclude that Georg does realize that Kien is mad—and unsuccessfully attempts to treat him as he does his other patients, by all too successfully entering into his fantasy world, "including its intensely reductive, rational, hermeneutic reading" (Darby 1992: 138) of the external world. Third, we may conclude that Georg's failure is really a success, for, realizing that Kien is indeed mad, he none the less allows him not only to persevere in his rejection of the outside world but to take it to its logical conclusion: Kien's final *auto da fé,* after all, parodically conflates his total failure (as the destroyer of his own world) and his success in finally achieving complete (physical) unity with the world of his books in the flames that devour them both. Kien's final—and uninterpretable—laughter marks this conflation.

Darby aptly observes that while *Die Blendung* draws on the sensibility of literary modernism in its thematization of disintegration, it already displays facets of a postmodern consciousness in its parodic play with hermeneutic indeterminacy and the structuration of meaning (1992: 175–89). Reading and misreading, blindness and insight, are relative and mutually defining concepts, for all reading, however authorized or authoritative it may also be, by the nature of things necessarily also involves a concomitant degree of misreading, a degree of what Canetti's novel, ironically challenging its reader even in its title, memorializes as the perpetual possibility of *Blendung.*

Notes

1. Quotations in English, silently modified where necessary, are taken from *Auto da fé,* trans. C. V. Wedgwood (Harmondsworth, UK: Penguin, 1965). [The original version of this essay includes quotations in both English and German; the quotations in German that have

been retained here are from *Die Blendung* (Frankfurt am Main: Fischer Taschenbuch Verlag, 1965). *Ed.*]

2. That Canetti's reading of *Don Quijote* shapes the writing of *Die Blendung* has been noted by various critics, while Canetti himself enthusiastically acknowledges his admiration of Gogol (cf. Thomas 1991), and Barnouw compares the caricatural quality of his characters to the work of George Grosz (1979: 18).

3. The unnamed city bears numerous general resemblances to the real Vienna—and is significantly different in points of detail. Dissinger speaks of the setting as a caricatured Vienna, corresponding to its caricatured inhabitants (1971: 54).

4. Canetti's translators have opted for other resonances. C. V. Wedgwood's translation was called *Auto da fé* (London: Jonathan Cape, 1946) in England, *The Tower of Babel* (New York: Knopf, 1947) in the United States. Paule Arhex's French translation was also called *La tour de Babel* (Grenoble: Arthaud, 1949).

5. The contention that *Die Blendung* is a novel about reading is ironically reflected in the history of its reception: largely ignored when it first appeared in 1935 (Wien: Reichner), it was greeted with enthusiasm by foreign readers in both its English translation (1946) and its French translation (1949), was still largely ignored by German readers in its second edition of 1948 (München: Weismann), and advanced to the rank of modern classic only with its third German edition in 1963 (München: Hanser) and a subsequent pocketbook edition in 1965 (Frankfurt: Fischer).

6. Roberts (1975: 55–62) notes a number of other suggestive points of connection between Kien and Fischerle.

7. Barnouw (1979: 23–9). See also Roberts (1975: 118), Moser (1983: 56), and Thomas (1991: 126–7). Critics have differed radically on the question of Georg's sanity. For a summary of conflicting critical positions see Darby (1992: 142n41).

8. Franz Metzger, a budding scholar with an interest in things Chinese, is the only single character in the book who is not portrayed as suffering from a delusion of some sort, as Dissinger observes (1971: 96), though whether we should interpret this as some potential gleam of hope—a fourth face of the intellectual, perhaps?—or just as delusion postponed is left up to us.

9. Noting that Georg re-adopts the original German form of his name for his encounter with Peter, Darby (1992: 139) suggests that this may render suspect all of the passages dealing with him under the name "Georges"—and also notes the intriguing parallel that Canetti's autobiography *Die gerettete Zunge* (1977) refers several times to the author's younger brother "Georg," who had settled in Paris, while the volume is dedicated to "Georges" Canetti.

Literary Texts Cited

Canetti, Elias. *Auto da fé*. Trans C. V. Wedgwood. London: Jonathan Cape, 1946. Harmondsworth, UK: Penguin, 1965.
———. *Die Blendung*. 1935. Frankfurt am Main: Fischer Taschenbuch Verlag, 1965.

Critical Texts Cited

Identified in text by author and date of the edition cited.

Auer, Annemarie. 1983. "Ein Genie und sein Sonderling—Elias Canetti und *Die Blendung*." Durzak 1983: 31–53.

Barnouw, Dagmar. 1979. *Elias Canetti.* Sammlung Metzler 180. Stuttgart: Metzler.

Busch, Günther. 1975. "Der Roman des großen Erschreckens, *Die Blendung.*" Originally pub. 1963. Göpfert 1975: 31–34.

Canetti, Elias. 1975. "Das erste Buch: *Die Blendung.*" Originally pub. 1974. Göpfert 1975: 124–35.

Darby, David. 1992. *Structures of Disintegration: Narrative Strategies in Elias Canetti's* Die Blendung. Riverside, CA: Ariadne Press.

Dissinger, Dieter. 1971. *Vereinzelung und Massenwahn: Elias Canettis Roman* Die Blendung. Studien zur Germanistik, Anglistik und Komparatistik 11. Bonn: Bouvier Verlag Herbert Grundmann.

Durzak, Manfred, ed. 1983. *Zu Elias Canetti.* LGW-Interpretationen 63. Stuttgart: Klett.

Göpfert, Herbert G., ed. 1975. *Canetti lesen: Erfahrungen mit seinen Büchern.* München: Hanser.

Moser, Manfred. 1983. "Zu Canettis *Blendung.*" Durzak 1983: 54–71.

Piel, Edgar. 1984. *Elias Canetti.* Autorenbücher 38. München: Beck/Text + Kritik.

Roberts, David. 1975. *Kopf und Welt: Elias Canettis Roman* Die Blendung. München: Hanser.

Stevens, Adrian, and Fred Wagner, eds. 1991. *Elias Canetti: Londoner Symposium.* Stuttgarter Arbeiten zur Germanistik 245. Stuttgart: Verlag Hans-Dieter Heinz, Akademischer Verlag.

Thomas, Noel. 1991. " 'My Great Russian': Reflections on Reality and Unreality in Canetti's *Die Blendung* and Gogol's *The Overcoat.*" Stevens/Wagner 1991: 119–30.

The Uses of Parody: Gogol, Stendhal, and Kafka in Canetti's *Auto-da-Fé*

Harriet Murphy

Historically, it has always been relatively commonplace to interpret Canetti's *Die Blendung* (*Auto-da-Fé*) as a satire on the fragmented world associated with the decline of the Austro-Hungarian Empire. It is also often seen as the ultimate satire on the "Philosopher King" idea floated originally by Plato or the modern equivalent thereof, the godless intellectual. Most recently it has been seen as a metaphysical satire on the very impossibility of truth, Nietzsche style.[1] If such a reading might imply that the novel can now be co-opted for the postmodernist celebration of aesthetic nihilism, we need to be careful of the temptation to see it as "free" from the bonds of tradition and objective truth. Firstly, Canetti's reputation as a classical humanist precedes the contemporary preference for aesthetics "liberated" from ethics, and it rests on the view that he is deeply concerned with "values," with the kind of civilization and culture whose development is assumed to be an individual's responsibility and duty, for both his or her and society's own benefit. Canetti's version of classical humanism is thus at variance with the vision of postmodernism, not least because this tends to deploy tradition disingenuously, often in order to advance an agenda for the utopian society first dreamed of by the secular humanists of the Enlightenment, with their insistence on a world dominated by liberty, equality, and fraternity in relation to sex, class, and race. It is often argued that in such a society the individual merely runs the risk of merging anonymously with the collective. This essay joins with the classical humanist counteroffensive against the new ideology of collectivization at the heart of postmodernism, following the leads taken by Roger Kimball, Harold Bloom, and David Parker, whose critiques of contemporary theory in the humanities open up very interesting avenues for debate.[2]

We can begin by suggesting that Canetti's 1935 novel has something provocative to say to the terms of the present, largely divisive debate about the death of truth, because it believes in facetiousness as a weapon that can disable ideology. This essay looks at how a typical manifestation of the face-

This essay was written specifically for this volume and is published for the first time by permission of the author.

tious spirit informs Canetti's set-piece parodies of canonical scenes from canonical literary works by Gogol, Stendhal, and Kafka. Discussions of the use of parody in this novel have previously been limited because the reputation of the novel has been set in stone by the early view that it was a satire in the great tradition. Where the term parody has been invoked, critics have implied that it is merely yet another form of satire. According to readings by Kristie Foell and others, for instance, the novel contains parodies of Freud's theory of sexual desire, of the death instinct, of repression, and of the meaningfulness of dreams.[3] It also contains a parody of Otto Weininger's theory of the polarity of gender.[4] Plot and character in *Auto-da-Fé* render these ridiculous, disabling them through satire and exposing them as intellectually and culturally questionable. The satirical edge of the set-piece parodies of Freud and Weininger, then, is destructive. It is aimed at destroying the hold such theories have on the popular imagination, rejecting them as categories of truth. By contrast, the more traditional interpretation of the novel as a satire stresses that Canetti makes ample use of the literary category of the grotesque, only as a vehicle for a discussion of what it is that might constitute psychological and, by extension, cultural health and well-being in an ideal world. The satirical project here, then, is one that is constructive, or ameliorative in content. According to this interpretation, Peter Kien's life and suicide are seen as a psychopathological case study in Freudian repression, the key terms being madness, paranoia, or schizophrenia. The embodiment in human character of such drives is intended as a stern warning of the cost of the human commitment to pure intellectualism with its concomitant rejection of human community. Assumed to be true in this way, this repression is often placed in a historical context and seen in terms of socioeconomic or sociopolitical theories. Either Peter Kien is simply the victim of capitalist economics, which apparently reduces all human activity to commodity exchanges, as Dieter Dissinger has argued, or he is made historically significant and seen as symbolic of a moral and cultural decline inseparable from the rise of National Socialism, as David Roberts has argued.[5]

In this essay we can review contemporary theory's fascination with intertextuality, and with parody in particular, on the grounds that it has become commonplace to associate both with that elusive and fascinating quality, subversion. Linda Hutcheon's theory of parody, for instance, makes any number of claims for the largely sociopolitical power of parody, as it is practiced across the art forms of the twentieth century.[6] She assumes, along with many on the intellectual Left, that the credentials of those in positions of power in society should be liberal, in the classical sense of the word. There should be an overt commitment to those nonreligious or secular definitions of "equality," "freedom," and the "rights" of the individual originally promoted by the European Enlightenment. In practice this secular agenda is not as universalist as it appears, since emancipation is framed in terms of a struggle against hostile powers. It also promotes women, homosexuality, and non-Christian religions as types, rather than individuals, under the heading of "pluralism" and with the intention that the type should be given full legal and social backing to pursue "happiness." Hutcheon's endorsement of parody as a mode is, then, indicative of the role culture is expected to play in the intellectual Left's offensive with respect to the Establishment. Culture is expected to be capable of nonviolent, sociopolitical subversion of an Establishment viewed as a monolith and assumed to be uniformly hostile to its particular causes. Certain cultural forms and objects that practice parody offer hope to those who feel that the political Right has been unsympathetic to those apparent victims of aggression, like women, homosexuals, and non-Christians.

Canetti's intertextual negotiation of canonical texts in world literature has not received the attention it deserves, in spite of the fact that his personal preferences in world literature have been well publicized in his literary essays, his notebooks, and his autobiography.[7] I propose to investigate whether his literary response in *Auto-da-Fé,* in the form of parody, to literary writers like Gogol, Stendhal, and Kafka, as distinct from his intellectual response to theoreticians like Freud and Weininger, can contribute anything to the status of the traditional readings of the novel discussed above and to the general, sociopolitically motivated debate on parody now so popular within postmodernism. In this essay I look at Canetti's explicit use of Gogol, Stendhal, and Kafka in pivotal chapters of *Auto-da-Fé,* with the aim of showing the universalist basis of his humanism, one not vulnerable to exploitation for the purposes of promoting a specific ideological agenda such as Hutcheon's. Part 1 ("A Head without a World"), for instance, represents a complete and compelling parody of Kafka's *Die Verwandlung* (*The Metamorphosis*). It questions Kafka's version of truth and meaning because in Kafka's story these qualities are limited to a view of the human condition that affects only those who are suffering. In the justly celebrated chapter "Private Property," Canetti makes humorous and selective allusions to Gogol's *The Nose,* also parodying Gogol's attitude to truth and meaning in the process. Gogol remains committed, for instance, to a view of the human condition that is proto-totalitarian, given the drift of the narrative, which suggests that all human experiences *should* be both personally fulfilling and socially functional. References in the same chapter to *Le Rouge et le noir* (*The Red and the Black*) color Peter Kien's attempt to mount his own defense before a nonexistent jury at the police station, since they invoke, humorously, Julien Sorel's self-defense before a formal jury during a legal trial at the end of Stendhal's novel. Once again, these references constitute a parody of Stendhal's attitude to truth and meaning, on the grounds that Stendhal, by no means a democrat, remains deeply wedded to the idea of the superiority of a certain type, the elitist, sensitive soul. This is the type represented by Julien Sorel, who is filled with contempt and resentment for those individuals who show no signs of sensitivity, like Monsieur de Rênal. These strategies do not just suggest that Canetti assumes a familiarity in his readers with the most famous scenes of some of the most famous works in world literature, although they obviously do express a simple determination to affirm the place of the classics in high culture. They point to a more ambitious desire, one that helps to illuminate aspects of the claim to radicalism made by those who promote multiculturalism, moral relativism, and aesthetic nihilism under the heading of postmodernism and who see in this contemporary movement the most intellectually, artistically, and morally respectable corpus of thinking of the present time, if not of all time.

Canetti's novel is radical by any standard because its parodies are high-spirited and highly civilized, bearing no traces of defeatism or nihilism. They selectively target the pretension to truth and meaning only where these are shorthand for nondemocratic views of the world or for dogmatism, both of which are often symptomatic of a thinking that presents a partial point of view as if it were a comprehensive vision of the world. The danger of confusing the one with the other is clearly only latent in the obviously partial visions of Canetti's preferred authors, and it remains relatively innocent. Yet the high spirits of these parodies do not condemn all writers who opt for a partial vision, nor do they seek to sponsor reactions that are emotional and sensational and likely to incite confrontation or hostility, thus disrupting and frustrating the social contract. The infectiously high-spirited parodies of Gogol, Stendhal, and Kafka represent simple and nonsensational cases of the issues raised when one mistakes a partial point of view for a comprehensive vision of the world. The sympathetic appeal of the high-spiritedness invites us to reflect rationally on the virtue of our taking seriously our responsibilities and duties as architects of the social contract. The parodies invite us to do this in the belief that our communities can remain civilized, sustained by consensus, rather than dominated by individuals intent on imposing their partial visions coercively on the group as a whole. Thus through the use of parody, not satire, *Auto-da-Fé* is able, by implication, to unmask the dangers of totalitarian ideology and of ideas abstracted from organic reality, history and tradition, to which they are usually hostile. It also exposes the dangers of the demagogue, the individual for whom ideology serves the pursuit of power rather than the welfare of the people, and of ideology that itself nowhere recognizes the value and importance of each unique individual. In its high-spiritedness *Auto-da-Fé* also argues effectively against those who believe that the individual is not capable of freedom that is both individually fulfilling and socially and morally responsible. The infectious quality of the high spirits communicates a belief in the power of the human will and the ability of individuals to intervene and interact in the social arena in ways that can solve human problems and promote the greatest amount of good for the greatest number of people.

Close analysis of the text indicates that the high spirits and exuberance that infuse Canetti's parodies carry this "argument" against the problems latent in strongly held points of view, in the high-minded, dogmatically inclined self-righteousness often inseparable from partial visions of reality, only because the high spirits and exuberance offer a highly effective antidote to such views and such feelings. The examples of the most typical form the high spirits and exuberance take in Canetti's parodies will demonstrate how morally and culturally ambitious Canetti's facetiousness is, in ways that have absolutely nothing in common with the claims made for parody in culture by Hutcheon. Firstly, my examples will reveal the abrupt and brittle quality of each of Canetti's sentences. These make demands on his reader's ability to concentrate carefully, to remain receptive to the world while in a state of high and productive tension, to listen. This high tension is comparable to vigilance, a quality Canetti assumes to be indispensable to the moral life, because it is sensitive to and thus able to do justice to the assumed vitality, richness, and complexity of material reality. Since facetiousness continually proclaims the value of interventions in speech, the novel also insists on the importance of talking. Secondly, since Canetti's sentences do not combine to produce relentless, semantic logic or rhetoric, as they are conventionally assumed to do in extended prose, but rather repeatedly destroy any attempts to produce momentum of this kind, they speak out against a danger inherent in semantic logic and rhetoric, the danger of a purely self-serving approach to "reality" intent on imposing itself by force from above. Canetti assumes that both semantic logic and rhetoric are vulnerable in ways that facetious conversation never can be, both to the charge of indifference to material reality and to that of a moral surrender whereby the kind of vigilance that makes us live in a state of perpetual sympathy with other human beings thought to be our friends is defeated. Canetti's facetious sentences thus defy the priority we give to semantic logic and rhetoric in society and culture in the full knowledge that they can destroy the universalist, democratic basis of humane communities, that spirit of listening and talking in sympathy, with faith in the importance of a common future. The reading proposed by this essay, then, agrees with conventional criticism that the novel offers us a moral tale, a provocative commentary on totalitarianism. The argument is different in substance, because, while conventional criticism claims this on the evidence of the character of Peter Kien and the direction and climax of the plot, this essay shows that the facetious spirit of the narrative as a whole, of which the literary parodies are just typical manifestations, constitutes an engaged fight against, and antidote to, totalitarianism, a fight that makes ambitious demands on the kind of offensive skills needed to defeat totalitarianism in nontextual life in its repeated appeal to our creative skills, our ability to listen and respond to challenges and threats in a productive spirit of sympathy.

In what way is it possible to see the whole of part 1 of *Auto-da-Fé* as a straightforward parody of *The Metamorphosis*? Canetti's novel recognizes all aspects of Kafka's plot, all characters, together with the main rhetorical points about human conduct raised by the story, only to stand them on their head. Canetti implies rather provocatively, and *pace* those that see *The Metamorphosis* as funny, that, while the ideas raised by *The Metamorphosis* are grave and serious, they are also defeatist about the individual and his or her place in the world. Canetti's facetiousness implies that this defeatism is both personally and socially divisive, since it does not promote the possibility of improving the quality of life in the present. Such defeatism is opposed to the possibility that life can rescue us from spiritual death. It is opposed to the qualities Nietzsche admired in Stendhal, namely the refined epicureanism that makes a connection between laughter and happiness, that relaxed openness which Stendhal called "la détente pour le rire." Canetti starts by taking over Kafka's idea of the isolation of an individual within an already socially isolated urban apartment, only to transform it into a scene of high comedy. Gregor Samsa retreats to his refuge after work. Peter Kien only ventures out of his apartment to go shopping for books. Furniture in the apartment in both works takes on a symbolic significance. Gregor Samsa hides behind his divan to shield himself from the aggression of his family. The divan in Canetti also provides a central focus. It comes to symbolize the sexually inactive nature of Peter and Therese Kien's weird marriage, and it is fought over by both. Just as Grete administers to the physical needs of Gregor, Therese administers to the physical needs of Peter Kien. The idea of expulsion from paradise or exile, so prominent in *The Metamorphosis* because of Herr Samsa's violent attacks, together with the idea of decline that results in death, is also taken over in *Auto-da-Fé*. Peter Kien is expelled from his apartment by his wife after a prolonged spell of violence in the chapter "Beaten" and returns only to damn his life as he commits suicide. Kafka's story, however, hinges on a dualism between body and soul, a form of which Canetti introduces into *Auto-da-Fé* at the beginning of his novel, only to exploit it for entirely different purposes. Gregor Samsa has the body of a vermin and the inner life of a soulful, sensitive man. The music scene alone makes a very strong rhetorical point about the superficiality of appearances, since it acknowledges the power, however ephemeral it may be, of the inner life. Peter Kien from the outset identifies himself as a victim of a version of this central dualism in Western culture, since he hates everything to do with the body, anything that is nonaesthetic or nonintellectual. The subtitles of the three parts of the novel—"A Head without a World," "Headless World," and "The World in the Head"—superficially endorse this whole tradition, since they insist on the separation of the mind from the world. Yet the facetiousness of Canetti's plot, his characters, and narration, as we shall soon see, dispenses altogether with this dualism, as it dispenses with every single one of the indestructible links vital to intellectually pretentious theories, any gesture towards the kind of semantic logic or speculative thinking on which Kafka's tale crucially depends.

Canetti's attack on the "big ideas" behind Kafka's story takes the form of an overt appeal to his reader's instincts for play, not speculative thinking, in terms of the style and content of his own writing. In terms of plot and character Canetti refutes Kafka's depressing theory that the economic necessity supposedly imposed on individuals by capitalism is capable of undermining the aesthetic or moral will. Canetti's representative capitalists have private money, it is true, but their utter dedication to the scholarly pursuit of culture is presented as an independent manifestation of human choice and commitment. Canetti does not surrender to theory, inasmuch as he does not claim that Peter Kien's special interests, which lie with sinology, and George Kien's special interests, which lie with medicine, with psychopathology in particular, are to be understood merely as an effect of "privilege." Canetti pays tribute to moral energy and vitality and gives credit where credit is due, taking issue in the process with those theoreticians of human experience whose version of capitalism is selective and undifferentiated enough to marginalize evidence of individual choices, individual success, or the reality of the uneven distribution of talent, ability, and willpower across humanity. If Kafka's tendency is to argue that there is inflexible logic everywhere that makes a mockery of the individual will, that is his choice, and one that should not necessarily stand for a general interpretation of the human condition as such. Canetti's impatience with Kafka is also apparent in his facetious reworking of the theory Kafka holds about work. Whereas Gregor Samsa, his mother, father, and sister are all physically exhausted as they work for a living, Canetti's Fischerle retains all his vigor and energy in spite of his work. Indeed, all Canetti's characters are endowed with considerable strength of personality, resilience, and decisiveness, with a variant of Stendhal's idea of the importance of wanting, of moral energy and determination to life (his dictum "apprendre à vouloir"). As such they represent a triumphant counterargument to Kafka's implied theory about the necessarily destructive impact of work, and the inevitable weakness of the human will in the face of outside pressure.

Canetti's facetiousness extends beyond a high-spirited reworking and subversion of Kafka's plot and characters. It spreads to the very language used in the dialogue in the novel, the spirit of which is often imitated by the narrator in the diegetic material in which the dialogue is embedded, in what Dorrit Cohn has admirably called the "stylistic contagion" of the narrative.[8] After reading Confucius, for instance, Peter Kien displays his determination to affirm life on his terms, as he proclaims, ludicrously:

> I will marry her! She is the heaven-sent instrument for preserving my library. If there is a fire I can trust in her. Had I constructed a human being according to my own designs, the results could not have been more apt for the purpose. She has all the elements necessary. She is a born foster-mother. Her heart is in the right place. There is room for no illiterate fools in her heart. She could have had a lover, a baker, a butcher, a tailor, some kind of barbarian, some kind of an ape. But she cannot bring herself to it. Her heart belongs to the books. What is simpler than to marry her?[9]

This example, both in its extraordinary originality as a theory of marriage and in its extraordinary exuberance as a set of existential propositions, is able, on the one hand, to convey Canetti's moral disapproval of the very serious forms of exploitation that mark the relationships in Kafka's story and, on the other, to provide an antidote to Kafka's seriousness by indulging his readers' sense of astonishment at the sheer unusualness of his invention. This sense of wonder is fully indulged by the narrator, who takes up the story, only to sustain the shocking strangeness of what has gone before, in a spirit of sympathy, as if he were listening carefully:

> Kien had no time to thank him for this last encouragement. He flung himself towards the kitchen, and seized violently upon the door. The handle came off in his hand. Therese was seated in front of the cushion and made as if she were reading. When she sensed that he was already behind her, she got up, so that he could see what she had been reading. The impression of his last conversation had not been lost on her. She had gone back to page 3. He hesitated a moment, did not know what to say, and looked down at his hands. Then he saw the broken door handle; in a rage he threw it to the ground. (*AdF*, 48)

Similarly, Canetti uses Kafka's material of covert and overt forms of verbal and physical violence in an apartment peopled by separate and warring factions. He does so not to make a mute point about the demise of decent family life and the failure of mutually satisfying human relationships but to create the kind of high comedy that simply could not exist without the pronounced moral willpower and strength of personality typical of Peter Kien, Therese, Fischerle, and Georges Kien, willpower and strength that are celebrated. In this sense, it positively approves of personality as a weapon of survival. Whereas Gregor Samsa is always the victim of the actions and words of his family, Peter Kien and Therese engage with each other verbally, as equals, each determined to promote strategies aimed at achieving his or her respective goals. Peter Kien informs Therese: "From now on I shall keep the door into your rooms locked. I forbid you to step over my threshold as long as I am here. If I want books from your rooms I shall fetch them myself. At one o'clock and at seven o'clock precisely I shall come to meals. I request you not to call me. I can tell the time myself. I shall take steps to prevent further interruption. My time is valuable. Kindly go!" (*AdF*, 66).

Once again, the narrator indulges the spirit of Kien's pronouncements as he continues: "He struck the tips of his fingers together. He had found the right words: clear, practical and superior. She would not with her clumsy vocabulary dare to answer him" (*AdF*, 66). Meanwhile, the narrator is equally indulgent, with respect to Therese, whose ability to resist victimization is astonishing: "I'm not going to eat in the kitchen like a servant. The mistress eats at table" (*AdF*, 60). It is for these reasons that Canetti refuses to lapse into the kind of melancholic self-pity that infuses the portrait of Gregor Samsa, because he accepts that relationships which have a basis in strength and equality are inevitably part of the drama of everyday life. The relationship between Peter Kien and Therese is presented as a battle of two equally powerful wills. The relationship between Gregor Samsa and the other members of his family does not allow for this kind of confrontation because it is not based on strength or equality, which is why the few confrontations that puncture the narrative are not about individual desires but about matters relating to the collective, the survival of the family unit. Gregor is merely economically crucial in terms of this wider project. He is socially irrelevant to family life and personally ineffectual in terms of determining positive human relationships. That this is the case is obvious from the small details that allude to Gregor Samsa's vicarious eroticism, his love of the portrait of the woman clad in fur, and the expression of desire for physical contact with Grete as she plays her violin. Because Gregor Samsa is never presented as wishing to challenge this status quo it is possible to talk about his evasion of conflict and his evasion of confrontation. He is complicit with a status quo that does nothing to acknowledge him as a human being in his own right. This is not the case in *Auto-da-Fé*. Examples of confrontation are rife, yet only because willpower and determination are acknowledged as sources of natural vitality in the world, to the extent that Canetti's work communicates the idea of life as a trial and a challenge to which we can rise, not one that defeats us as it punishes us for unspecified crimes by forces beyond our control. Finally, Canetti in no way appropriates the soulful version of Christianity so common in literature, on which Kafka relies so heavily. Concentrating on lack of fulfillment and on suffering rather than on the qualities that make life a celebration of goodness and the like, Kafka's central character becomes paralyzed, holding on to the "idea" of his superiority on the strength of the dualist conviction that the soul is superior to the body. Canetti's characters do not have to draw on this claim because they are strong and capable at the outset, endowed with the qualities that make it possible to determine life, not be determined by it. This is why we can call them pragmatists, who live for the moment, opportunists who take responsibility for the present, not defeatists living in the past. Examples of their pragmatism and opportunism are rife in conversational exchanges that are full of exuberant vitality. As a result Canetti's novel demonstrates how deeply resistant it is to speculative thought, those binary ideas of paradise and expulsion, Crucifixion and Resurrection, which we need to account for the world of *The Metamorphosis*. The novel believes in our ability to live fully in the present by relying on the dynamic liveliness of vibrant intelligence as a conversational tool, rather than the more personally hostile forms of speculative, suggestive, intellectual thought typical of the demagogue. The abrupt, brittle sentences used by Canetti's characters are vital in the war waged by the novel against speculative thought and in the struggle to affirm raw intelligence over and above intellectual thinking.

The chapter in which Therese plans to seduce Peter Kien into signing away his fortune, called "Judas and the Saviour," is a good example of Canetti's indifference to and boredom with those forms of dualist thinking to which intellectual thought is often prone. It is also proof of the continued interest in the kind of playfulness that keeps readers free from the burdens of pretentious, intellectual thinking. Canetti denies narratives based on a single premise—here the idea of Christianity as synonymous with suffering—by inverting their constituent parts, robbing them of all their conventional meaning, and turning them into a hilariously homely account, a pretext for the exuberance inseparable from facetiousness. Therese sympathizes with the Judas figure because she assumes he is annoyed with the redeemer for being so stingy with his money. She displays no understanding of the gravity of the biblical account of the Passion, death, and Resurrection of Jesus Christ, not because she is unintelligent but because Canetti is using her to make a case for the cultural value of facetiousness. This small detail alone demonstrates how Canetti's facetiousness works. It enjoys releasing us from reliance on established ways of interpreting the world, to remind us of the vitality of our own creative energies and the joy of being free from the burden of gravity. The scene is, *en passant,* blasphemous.

The case for seeing links between *Auto-da-Fé* and Gogol's *The Nose* is strong. A relatively weak link can be established on the basis of a small piece of evidence. In the chapter in *Auto-da-Fé* called "Private Property," Peter Kien is interviewed by the police for an unspecified crime. Readers are not invited to see him as a candidate for the position of criminal since from the outset he has been likened to Don Quixote, the man who lives in his imagination, innocently and charmingly. Fischerle, more likely to be thought guilty of a misdemeanor, is nowhere in evidence in the scene. The logical basis for the encounter between Peter Kien and the commandant, in terms of plot, is therefore missing. How are we then to interpret the commandant's exclusive concern with aesthetics, both with his own appearance in the mirror and with the awfulness of Peter Kien's frame once he undresses? He is perpetually feeling his nose, worried about the position of the cushion on his chair, which bears the words "Private Property." This is the point at which the scene makes an overt reference to Gogol's *The Nose* itself, since the central character Kovalyov laments the loss of his nose, referring to it as his private property. Now, Canetti's commandant is not concerned with ethics, with the deductive logic that makes it possible to establish what is a crime and what is a punishment. Further proof of his noninterest in justice, together with the narrative's preoccupation with the delights of pure diversion, comes as he affectionately thinks of his domestic concerns, his children's progress at school. His preoccupation with performance and effect is charming, such that we become complicit with the artistry of the narrative, its ability to create *ex nihilo,* to be fully gratuitous: " 'Clown!' yelled the Inspector. He trusted himself again to intervene, but he pronounced the word in English: the educated impression Kien had made on him was indestructible. He looked round him, to see if he was understood. The man with a memory transposed the word into the German pronunciation. He knew what it meant, but declared that the Inspector's was the correct form. From this moment he was under suspicion of secretly knowing English" (*AdF,* 309). These few lines give us a flavor of the interview scene at the police station and indicate how far removed it is from a serious attempt at an investigation into the machinations of crime, punishment, and justice. Kovalyov in Gogol's *The Nose* visits an inspector of police at a point when the reader has fully accepted that he has a genuine grievance. Kovalyov's interview is part of his quest to be reunited with his nose, to right what he and the reader accept is an injustice. The portrait of the inspector of police in Gogol's *The Nose* is a satirical set piece. He is neatly and memorably present as a ludicrous perversion of humanity and social usefulness: "The Inspector was a great patron of the arts and industry, but most of all he loved government banknotes. 'There's nothing finer than banknotes,' he used to say. 'They don't need feeding, take up very little room and slip nicely into the pocket. And they don't break if you drop them.' "[10] Not only does the inspector of police represent the noninterest of the police generally in the welfare of citizens, he is personally using his job to feather his own nest. Now these satirical overtones are nowhere present in the scene in which Peter Kien encounters the commandant. Again, Canetti virtually dismisses as irrelevant all the inflexible theories about the quality and function of the police in the body politic floated by Gogol in his portrait. The sheer absence of gravity in "Private Property" ensures that we never see the commandant's introversion as tantamount to a personal, social, political, or cultural problem. He is not a satirical set piece. Gogol's story, by contrast, identifies itself as a proto-Marxist text because it raises rhetorical questions about the socioeconomic and sociopolitical basis of power, of which the interview scene examined is a good, if problematic, example. Inasmuch as losing and finding your nose in life are utterly inexplicable and random events, it also succeeds as a piece of protomodernist writing. This package of desperate insights into the human condition is underlined by the fact that our representative rebel, the noseless Kovalyov, is parasitically dependent on institutionalized methods of problem-solving. He has neither the natural ability nor the willpower to initiate action. His instinctive reaction, when faced with a problem, is to assume that those in positions of authority and power should be expected to solve the problem. Although dissatisfied with the material status quo, with its so-called uneven distribution of wealth, power, and privilege, we soon realize that all characters in Gogol's fiction are equally guilty of one single assumption, namely that power lies in the hands of those further up the hierarchy.

Many of Gogol's pessimistic and unattractive first premises would be relentlessly awful were it not for the overt facetiousness characteristic of the narrator of the story, whose intrusive presence from beginning to end ensures that readers are distracted and insulated from the full intellectual force of the pessimism. The reader is continually under pressure to abandon notions of wholeness, integrity, and meaning commonly thought to be provided by character and plot, and no more so than at the end of *The Nose,* where elaborate diversionary tactics seem to triumph over meaninglessness. If Canetti's scene takes Gogol's raw material as a point of departure, it does so only to rob it of most of its rhetoric. However, the facetiousness both writers have in common is not of the same order. In Gogol the narrator's final facetious summing up of the story merely diverts the reader from the pessimistic first premises, providing purely temporary relief:

> And all this took place in the northern capital of our vast empire! Only now, after much reflection, can we see that there is a great deal that is very far-fetched in this story. Apart from the fact that it's *highly* unlikely for a nose to disappear in such a fantastic way and then reappear in various parts of the town dressed as a state councillor, it is hard to believe that Kovalyov was so ignorant as to think newspapers would accept advertisements about noses. I'm not saying I consider such an advertisement too expensive and a waste of money: that's nonsense, and what's more, I don't think I'm a mercenary person. But it's all very nasty, not quite the thing at all, and it makes me feel very awkward! (Gogol, 70)

Canetti's facetiousness is not confined to individual moments in the novel, as above; rather it is the motor of the novel in general. Nor is it as self-consciously slow and awkward as that of Gogol's narrator. It is not prone to despair, as Gogol's narrator's is, despite appearances to the contrary. By contrast it is, as my examples so far demonstrate, always offensive, powerful, and ambitious, because it recognizes how creativity and the spirit of hope can be compromised and suppressed by the inflexibility of rhetoric and logic. It proves by example that it is possible to be responsible to different energies, creative energies, like faith, confidence, and open-mindedness.

The tribute to *The Red and the Black* in "Private Property" concludes this essay's case for a new, ahistorical interpretation of *Auto-da-Fé* that acknowledges not the novel's negative psychopathology but rather its positive psychology, in particular the cultural virtues and strengths of facetiousness. Julien Sorel exemplifies many of the moral characteristics that Canetti attributes to his central characters: energy, ability, determination. Once again, Canetti plays with the framework of crime and punishment that becomes so important toward the end of *The Red and the Black,* when Julien Sorel is clearly guilty of the murder of Madame de Rênal. While on trial he interrupts court proceedings to take responsibility for establishing the truth, acknowledging in public his guilt, dealing carefully with all the theories that the court has circulated as to his motive. At all times he is perfectly mannered. He is clear that the murder was premeditated. As a scene it is typical of the heroic posturing of Julien Sorel, who has always been so preoccupied by his image. It is also a poetic moment, allowing Julien Sorel to die in dignity; it is a poetic prelude to his renewing his love for Madame de Rênal in prison; and it brings to an end the arguments the novel has made about changes in society in early modern France. Peter Kien's self-defense at the police station is deprived of any of these trappings of romanticism. It is also not situated in terms of any debate about society as an evolutionary force. *Auto-da-Fé* depends, in fact, on keeping at bay any of the conventional notions of healing, through love and death, on which *The Red and the Black* and romanticism rely so heavily, because these impose finality and place limitations on the kind of openness to the future conveyed by the facetious spirit.

Peter Kien begins his defense in such a rational way that it is difficult to see why so many commentators have classified it as a brilliantly realistic piece of psychopathology:

> You may well believe that I am the victim of an hallucination. I am not gener-ally subject to them. Scholarship demands a clear head, I would not read an X for U, or take any other letter for its fellow. But recently I have been through much; yesterday I had news of my wife's death. You are aware of the circum-stances. On her account I have the honour to find myself among you. Since then thoughts of my trial have ceaselessly occupied my mind. To-day [*sic*], when I went to the Theresianum, I encountered my murdered wife. She was accompanied by our caretaker, a very good friend of mine. He had followed her, as my representative, to her last resting place; I was myself unable to attend. (*AdF*, 302)

And so it goes on, charming and delightful and in its contents offering us very little in terms of logic, be it physical, emotional, or intellectual. Whilst mainstream criticism of *Auto-da-Fé* sees the above as evidence of his derange-ment, proof of Kien's inability to distinguish between the power of his own imagination and the reality of the world outside, the diegetic material in which the above monologue is embedded offers us evidence to the contrary. His defense ends with the plea: "Prove to me that she is dead" (*AdF*, 303). The narrator then takes over: "The spectators began to make words of his sounds. They became accustomed to his manner, and listened perplexed; one clutched at another in order to hear better. He spoke like an educated man, he was confessing a murder. As a body they could not believe in his murder, though each of them singly would have taken it to be true. Against whom did he want protection? In his shirt they let him alone; he was afraid. Even the Inspector felt powerless; he preferred to say nothing, his phrases would not have sounded literary enough" (*AdF*, 303). As a whole this understated, antidramatic, antisensational manner of the narrator encourages readers to participate and collaborate as an act of sympathy with the spirit of Peter Kien's own performance. It seems to promote core Nietzschean ideas, the view that the investment of the human will in reality is of paramount impor-tance, that the personal investment of individual artistry is crucial to the cre-ation of social reality. Literature is best suited to promoting this argument since it can focus on a very innocuous version of its application within the safe confines of a literary experiment. Here the pure fictionality and literal impos-sibility of Kien's defense is overt. Nothing Kien says can be corroborated intratextually or extratextually. Most critics apply a kind of logic here to which the spirit of the text is deeply resistant, because they deduce from the literal nontruth of his account that Peter Kien is mad. From this they deduce further that he is a man whom we should condemn. This reasoning reveals their own insensitivity to the playfulness of the facetious spirit, the general narrative strategy examined above, of allowing the narrator to imitate the voice of each character. The imitation destroys the distinction we like to make between the assumed normality and reliability of the empirical reality of the public world and the assumed vulnerability of the private world of each individual imagination to human eccentricity. The narrative, characterized by a consistent ambiguity of voice, refuses to distinguish between character and narrator, with the result that Peter Kien's performance to an audience at the police station, together with the narrator's own commentary on its reception, combine to create a masterpiece of sustained facetiousness. This contains a set of philosophical truths about the brilliance of the human imagination when it is freed from rhetoric and formal logic, and it relies on its own originality, its own ability to create connections *ex nihilo* that are utterly original and shocking enough in their originality to propel us out of our sleep of abstract reason, to face the future with a firm, rational grasp of the concrete nature of reality. The reader is thus schooled in the virtues of a highly ethical way of living fully in the world, continually kept alert and in a state of high tension by the sheer originality of the situation comedy at work, the propositions made by characters in speech, and the solidarity expressed by the narrator with the spirit of those propositions in the diegetic material. We learn that reality is an illusion that has to be sustained at all times by the work of an imagination utterly dedicated to communicating its defining principles to other human beings in the public sphere. The above scene is particularly successful in identifying the cultural importance of invention as an artistic skill in the quest to affirm life, to make it mean action, performance, initiative, because it repeatedly appeals to our instincts for play, repeatedly does violence to our tendency to rely on the well-trodden paths of speculative thought, and repeatedly rates the vibrance of natural intelligence over and above the lamentable dreariness of much intellectual thinking.

Finally, the examples of Canetti's facetiousness we have examined are all couched in extremely nonliterary language. This is part of the facetious project in itself. Facetiousness is sociable by nature, associated by most with the spoken as opposed to the written word, which is why it tends to dispense with overtly literary formulations. Typically it prefers conversation, where it works by inviting everyone to venture to make displays not of mediocrity but of brilliance and wit. Facetious conversation thereby offers us a particularly immediate and effective way of expressing our love of and our ability to enjoy being with one another, of affirming a social contract that is alive because of the consensus that sustains it. It relishes solidarity and the importance of caring for the general well-being of others because it acknowledges our desire for, and ability to relate with, one another in the immediate present, and in ways that bring about mutual happiness. Facetiousness makes clear its preference for frequent displays of virtuoso wit in dialogue and its indifference toward the formality of semantic logic and rhetoric in monologue. Its greatest challenge is to defy the power of those established ideas that take themselves seriously and assume that reality can be accounted for comprehensively and conclusively. Such ideas are viewed as a natural enemy of the cause of civilization. So Canetti's facetiousness is morally responsible, because in it the power of established ideas over the imagination is fully recognized only so that those ideas can be turned on their head. This is why facetious people and facetious writing always trivialize the pretensions of gravity and seriousness where these manifest themselves in a monotonous repetition of predictable ideas assumed to represent definitive estimates of reality. The estimates of reality on which Canetti focuses, whether about marriage, or the responsibility for conducting an official investigation, or the question of whether or not someone is dead or alive, are all self-consciously trivial. And they are trivial enough to succeed in making the serious, humane, and civilized points about reality that I discussed at the outset under the heading of Canetti's democratically based humanism, his vision of a community of sympathetic individuals held together by a desire and an ability to help create a world in which people collaborate with one another freely, in order to protect and promote the welfare of the greatest number.

The virtue of facetiousness, therefore, is that it aims, for highly serious reasons, to trivialize those pretensions to comprehensiveness, high moral seriousness, and dogmatism inseparable from "big ideas," together with the semantic logic and rhetoric used to present them. It would be wrong to assume that this suggests Canetti is an aesthetic anarchist. The facetious spirit is too forward-looking and positive about the future, too sociable in its interest in life, in talking and listening, too rational in its openness to the world, and too consciously resistant to the enemies of life. The novel knows that all predictable ideas tend to be inflammatory, because they invariably promote a promised land in some distant future. The appeal to the future is a rhetorical move that itself presupposes a vision of the past, usually identified as uniformly wrong. Facetiousness recognizes that this kind of thinking promotes intellectual reductiveness and hostility because the version of history to which it is linked has its roots in a kind of specifically dialectical thinking that is inclined to trivialize and oversimplify. The pervasive influence of Hegel and Marx on theory and ideology is thus recognized, inasmuch as the simplicity of dialectical reasoning is recognized to be both seductive and beguiling yet also responsible for misleading people. It encourages individuals to think that the cause(s) of humanity require(s) abstract ideas that speak of the past and the present only in terms of how these must be changed by drastic action, by reform or revolution, in an unspecified future and that simultaneously postpone commitment to life in the present and trivialize the importance of responsibility for life in the present.

Facetious people tend to object to an attitude to humanity that is based on hostile confrontation of this kind, not because they are anarchists, nor because they are socially irresponsible, still less because they are wedded to a conservative position that makes them insensitive to others. Rather they reject the appeal to hostile confrontation because they have a vested interest in life, in experience and experiences, not ideas. Facetious people know that the best human experiences require cooperation, not confrontation; they require personal commitment and intervention, and they require positive human qualities like discrimination, sympathy, and love of all forms of the concrete. Thus facetiousness is a practice that is inseparable from the original storytelling we have examined. The ability to tell stories in an original manner presupposes the ability to make the best of the myriad forms the concrete takes in life, when life is dedicated to experience, not speculative thought. Stories, originally told, presuppose an investment of the imagination that is sympathetic, which is why such stories are more often than not characterized by and known for their wit and style rather than judged to be factually right or wrong. Facetiousness is opposed to the kind of abstraction that denies the value of individual subjectivity because it always prefers our instincts for play to our ability to indulge in speculative thinking. Facetiousness proves by example how valuable faith in subjects and subjectivity is in personal and social terms, in the confidence and knowledge that an alliance between the two can produce originality and creativity, or positive consequences in both personal and social terms. It prefers these qualities to the repetitive sameness that characterizes stories which are not told originally, like those to be found in ideology and theory, because it associates sameness with the demise of the possibility of happiness, both personal and social. Facetiousness has no time for those whose creativity is limited to the ability to provide mere neutral paraphrases of the work of other writers deemed to be masters, on whose "insights" they are parasitically dependent, because it has faith in our ability to be fully original creators and independent, if not free, thinkers. Facetiousness is thus not only opposed to the private and solipsistic pleasures to which reading is normally thought to give rise. It recognizes that "big ideas" rarely help to perpetuate both the art of civilized exchanges between equals and the quest for improving the quality of life in the here and now, typical of sociable communities that are convinced of the importance of speaking and listening in equal measure. We can conclude, then, by agreeing that Canetti's face-tiousness is a force in the war to reevaluate all values, a version of Nietzsche's "Umwertung aller Werte." But facetious writing still adheres to the possibil-ity of a fully objective truth, in the disciplined appeal it makes to our instincts for intellectual play on the assumption that intellectual play performs a civi-lizing function in listening and talking, in human communities. In this Canetti is opposed to Nietzsche, whose writings give such confident support to fully subjective truths and to anarchistic individuals who despise commu-nities. Canetti's facetious writing can thus offer a provocative commentary on the kinds of fixed ideas that are vital to all forms of explicit and implicit total-itarianism, such as those that underlie the celebration of parody as a mode, now prominent to such an extent in both postmodernist theory and practice across the art forms that they have come to constitute established orthodoxy in many quarters of the Academy.

Notes

1. This essay amounts to a critical commentary on the thoroughly libertarian reading of Canetti's novel promoted recently by my *Canetti and Nietzsche: Theories of Humor in "Die Blendung"* (Albany: State University of New York Press, 1997).

2. Harold Bloom, *The Closing of the American Mind: How Higher Education Has Failed Democracy* (Harmondsworth: Penguin, 1988); Roger Kimball, *Tenured Radicals: How Politics Has Corrupted Our Higher Education* (New York: Harper and Row, 1990); and David Parker, *Ethics, Theory and the Novel* (Cambridge: Cambridge University Press, 1994).

3. Kristie A. Foell, *Blind Reflections: Gender in Elias Canetti's "Die Blendung"* (Riverside, Calif.: Ariadne, 1994).

4. Otto Weininger (1880–1903), author of *Geschlecht und Charakter* (1903; *Sex and Character*).

5. Dieter Dissinger, *Vereinzelung und Massenwahn: Elias Canettis Roman "Die Blendung"* (Bonn: Bouvier, 1971); and David Roberts, *Kopf und Welt: Elias Canettis Roman "Die Blendung"* (Munich: Hanser, 1975).

6. Linda Hutcheon, *A Theory of Parody: The Teachings of Twentieth-Century Art Forms* (New York: Methuen, 1985).

7. Canetti repeatedly remarks on the formative influence of Gogol, Stendhal, and Kafka and on the importance of the works covered by this essay.

8. Dorrit Cohn, *Transparent Minds: Narrative Modes for Presenting Consciousness in Fiction* (Princeton: Princeton University Press, 1978).

9. Elias Canetti, *Auto-da-Fé,* trans. C. V. Wedgwood (New York: Farrar, Straus and Giroux, 1984), 47–48; hereafter cited in text as *AdF*.

10. Nikolai Gogol, *Diary of a Madman and Other Stories,* trans. Ronald Wilks (Harmondsworth: Penguin, 1972), 57; hereafter cited in text.

DRAMAS

◆

The Acoustic Mask:
Toward a Theory of Drama

ELIAS CANETTI, IN CONVERSATION WITH MANFRED DURZAK

DURZAK: Dr. Canetti, the literature on your work refers again and again to the concept of the acoustic mask, as a key to the distinctive linguistic structure not just of your plays but also of your narrative magnum opus *Die Blendung* (*Auto-da-Fé*). In an essay on Karl Kraus—who is perhaps one of the most important literary influences on you—you speak of Kraus's technique of "acoustic quotation." That essay reads: "Karl Kraus had a gift for condemning people out of their own mouths, as it were. However the origin of this mastery—and I don't know if the context has already been seen clearly—lay in something that I should like to call the 'acoustic quotation.' Kraus was haunted by voices . . . but with one distinction: The voices pursuing him *did exist,* in the Viennese reality."[1] One is certainly not mistaken in identifying the technique of acoustic quotation found in Kraus as one of the origins of your theory of the acoustic mask. As far as I know, the only place where you have dealt with your theory of the acoustic mask at any length is in an early essay that appeared in the Vienna newspaper *Sonntag* on 19 April 1937.

CANETTI: It was not an essay, but rather an interview on the occasion of a reading of *Hochzeit* (*The Wedding*) that I was to give in Vienna in April 1937, I believe.[2]

DURZAK: I know you have been working on a book on your theory of drama for a long time but have not published anything from it. That early text, of which to date only extracts have been available—in the introduction to the selection of your work published by Erich Fried in 1962 under the title *Welt im Kopf* (World in the head)—and that had for all intents and purposes disappeared in its original form, seems to me so important that I would like briefly to call it to mind. It reads:

Translated by David Darby for this volume from Elias Canetti and Manfred Durzak, "Akustische Maske und Maskensprung: Materialien zu einer Theorie des Dramas. Ein Gespräch," *Neue deutsche Hefte* 22 (1975): 497–516. Reproduced here by kind permission of the Carl Hanser Verlag.

Drama lives in language in a quite unique way. If the words were not so easily misunderstood, one could almost say: it lives in languages. For I consider the most important element of dramatic composition to be the "acoustic mask." It's not easy to sum up this idea clearly in a few sentences. I have to touch on thoughts that have occupied me for years and that I intend to publish in a lengthy work on the nature of drama.

Go into a pub, one in your neighborhood for instance, sit down at any table, and make the acquaintance of a complete stranger. Initially you will have no choice but to say a few accommodating sentences to get him started. But as soon as he is really talking—and he'll be happy to talk, that's why he goes to this pub—you must rigorously hold your tongue and listen to him carefully for several minutes. Make no attempt to understand him, don't try to get to the bottom of what he means, don't try to empathize with him. Pay attention quite simply to the external form of his words. This advice will only take you so far. It serves only to let you experience once and for all and as quickly as possible what I just now referred to as the acoustic mask.

You will discover that your new acquaintance has a quite idiosyncratic way of speaking. It isn't enough to say: he speaks German, or he speaks in dialect; so does everyone, or almost everyone, in this pub. No, his way of speaking is unique and unmistakable. It has its own pitch and tempo, it has its own rhythm. One sentence differs little from another. Certain words and phrases recur again and again. His whole language consists of only 500 words. He manages quite expertly with them; those are *his* 500 words. Someone else, whose vocabulary is equally impoverished, speaks in another 500. If you've listened well, you will be able to recognize him the next time by his language, without seeing him. The shape he has taken in his speech demarcates him on all sides and differentiates him from all other people as clearly as does his physiognomy, for instance, which is just as unique. The linguistic shape of a human being, the things that remain constant in his speech, this language that came into being with him, that is his alone, and that will pass away only with him— this is what I call his acoustic mask. Now this doesn't mean that the dramatist has to be a strolling phonograph, recording the diction of as many people as possible and then assembling dramas as needed from the available collection of acoustic masks. In fact that would be just another of the many ways of mechanically plagiarizing life, none of which have the slightest thing to do with art. But the dramatist must be able to *hear;* he must have a good deal of linguistic life within him; what is heard must both completely blend together and completely separate out again into its component parts, so that each form that emerges in due course is clear and effective precisely in its acoustic mask.[3]

Dr. Canetti, how would you describe in detail the genesis of your theory. What are its roots?[4]

CANETTI: The main influence was of course that of Karl Kraus. There is no doubt about that. The specifics are those I discussed in my essay on Karl Kraus. Of particular importance were his public readings of Nestroy, which really opened one's ear to the sounds of Vienna.

DURZAK: That has to do, then, with the dialect quality of Nestroy's language?

CANETTI: Yes, and above all with the fact that that dialect was a constant element of one's environment in Vienna. Of course the readings of *Die letzten Tage der Menschheit* (*The Last Days of Mankind*) also impressed me very much, but Nestroy impressed me still more, because without these readings I would perhaps not have been so keen to go into those little pubs where I would sit for hours on end and sometimes even all night—they closed at four in the morning—and listen to how people spoke. That training continued for years, and it was very important to me.

DURZAK: But isn't it the case with Nestroy that the dialect is used artificially? There are various forms of linguistic characterization that employ dialect. There is, for example, the quite exaggerated, elevated literary language that is used by Nestroy to critical and satirical effect.

CANETTI: But that elevated language is also something that one hears in Vienna. Of course with Nestroy it is intensified and put to use in an outrageously witty and clever way. But it is not uncommon to hear it in Vienna. There are people who try to speak like that.

DURZAK: But there is something else in Nestroy: the element of improvisation. The truth of the matter is that his texts were not intended primarily as literary texts, but rather as stage-scripts, and as an actor he changed them continuously, improvised, brought in new things.

CANETTI: I think this element, of which I was aware, contributed to the growth of my interest in these things. I did not intend to take acoustic masks and use them in the form that I had heard them. I wanted to have a reservoir of them, to have heard as many as possible. There were some that were more important to me, and some that led me directly to literary characters. You are familiar with Emilie Fant in the *Komödie der Eitelkeit* (*Comedy of Vanity*). That was the acoustic mask of Alma Mahler, of whom, I believe, I have spoken to you. She was a vulgar, common person. Of course, in terms of social standing she became somebody quite different, but to me she really seemed like the madam of a bordello. And then she did finally take on something of that role. Oh and those feigned tones in which she spoke of her child, Manon, the paralyzed daughter of Gropius, the way in which she paired her off, arranged her engagement in her condition, spoke of the child again and again, put her on display. There were masks that I could not otherwise shake off, that pursued me, that really tortured me.

I could not free myself of certain masks in any way other than by later forming them into characters, of course quite transposed as in the case of Emilie Fant. There is yet another case of direct imitation in *Comedy of Vanity.* You remember the character François Fant, that enormously arrogant and spoilt person. That was a very bad Viennese writer by the name of Paul Frischauer. He spoke like that. A mask that I couldn't rid myself of and that is reproduced more or less verbatim. All the other masks in the *Comedy* are, I believe, freely invented.

DURZAK: So there were several elements that had an influence on this theory of the acoustic mask: Nestroy via the readings by Karl Kraus, Karl Kraus himself, and, beyond that, biographical material, specific people.

CANETTI: There is yet another element that had an extremely strong influence on me: the Japanese Kabuki theater. Have I ever told you that story? There was a Japanese Kabuki theater that gave a week of guest performances at the Vienna Volksoper. They performed the same thing every evening. Of course I did not understand a word of Japanese, but those sharply defined characters, and above all their intonation, made an enormous impression on me. I don't know whether one can really speak here of an acoustic mask, but the sound made it seem like one to me. I went again and again, every evening. What I enjoyed was closing my eyes and still knowing exactly which character was speaking. Perhaps the masks were somewhat more stylized than in my plays. There were further acoustic elements that of course were very interesting, that did not necessarily have to do with what I would call a mask but that also made a strong impression on me. In one play there was the figure of a farmer—he was very bowlegged—who appeared with a large leather purse on his belt. He was attacked by robbers. They took his money, and he was slain. Then his daughter arrived, looking for him. She made noises like a bird: "Oh tatata, oh tatata!" These calls to her father, laden with fear for her father, were very moving. It was not like the functional expression of a European in such a situation. It sounded like something much more fixed, almost formulaic, despite what had happened. Later on something different happened. A young man appeared in the play, the farmer's son. He knew nothing yet of his father's death and had trodden on a thorn, driving it into his foot. The son sat down and pulled out the thorn. This caused him great pain, and his voice was as plaintive as if the physical pain had been real. And then someone came and gave him some news. I didn't know of what. And suddenly the plaintive tones and the crying changed. From the change I knew that he had learned of his father's death, that he was no longer bemoaning anything physical but rather the death of his father. This was confirmed when I took the trouble to find out. That was enormously moving.

That is not an acoustic mask in the strict sense, but it did nevertheless somehow amplify the element of the acoustic, which was so important for me, and it made me even more aware of it. It proved to me, for instance, that one can express, purely in sound, everything that goes on inside a human being, that one did not have to see this peasant boy to know that he was first in pain and then in mourning for the loss of someone close to him.

DURZAK: Now that we are talking of linguistic phenomena, I am reminded of the distinction made between semantics and semiotics. Semantics has to do with the received meanings that one identifies with certain words: certain fields of association, of meaning, that switch in when a word is uttered. But semiotics means something quite different: a sign-function that is no longer necessarily connected to a word's received meaning. Referring to your example, could one not say that certain acoustic signs likewise assume a semiotic quality and so have nothing more to do with specific interjections that are uttered when one is in pain or suffering in some other way? This however raises the important question: how is it that you, in the situation you have described, had the impression that what was being expressed had to do with quite specific human phenomena? What is the element that creates the connection to understanding.

CANETTI: The switching of masks [*Maskensprung*]. That plays a large role in the concept of the acoustic mask. But that is an imprecise answer to your question. Perhaps we will return to that later.

DURZAK: Yet it is true that, in an acoustic mask, a mimetic quality is retained intact, regardless of all abstraction and concentration. The mimetic element is present, meaning the quite concrete mirroring, or representation, of something real.

CANETTI: Some basic elements of the mimetic remain, and perhaps that is also one of the main reasons why acoustic masks became so important to me. There seemed to me to be an element of reality in them that has by no means yet been exhausted, that has not been used up, that is usable, and that has enormous dramatic potential; an attempt to restore access to reality where it has not been exhausted. That is probably what especially attracted me to them.

DURZAK: What are the parallels between this technique and Brecht's alienation techniques, which also trace connections back to Chinese and Japanese theater? I believe he too mentions the Kabuki theater. Can one compare your approach to Brecht's?

CANETTI: I would say that the Oriental theater has influenced both Brecht's and my work. But, as I see it, we are concerned with two different things. Brecht, you see, is concerned with the gulf between the spectator and what is presented on stage. I don't believe in that at all. My understanding of drama is in this respect the opposite of Brecht's. I do not want this gulf. I want shock, I want horror, an openly acknowledged participation, such as there was in ancient drama. What Brecht's theory champions may be useful for the things he wishes to achieve, but I am not even sure whether his plays are good when he applies his theory. I believe the strongest places in his plays are those where he is a dramatist in the old sense, as in *Mutter Courage (Mother*

Courage) when the girl drums on the roof.[5] That is immensely powerful, this deaf-mute girl. What does that have to do with alienation?

DURZAK: Alienation in the sense that there no longer exists a possibility of communication. A specific sign, the drumming, takes its place. That is, the sign is something that does not belong directly to this person; rather, it represents a means of expressing a mode of human behavior.

CANETTI: But its effect is different. In practice exactly the opposite happens. One is so affected that one becomes more strongly involved in this drumming than one would if Brecht had described the situation in definite and clear terms. As it is, the effect is stronger. And that is where I disagree with Brecht's theory.

DURZAK: That throws light on the fact that there is a difference between you and Brecht, and that Brecht's intention differs from his execution, above all here in the example of the mute girl Kattrin, as the alienation effect is obscured when the quality of human spontaneity comes to the fore in this sign of the drumming.

CANETTI: It makes the scene tremendously effective. As much as Brecht may have deliberately aimed for what you have just described, he achieves precisely the opposite effect.

DURZAK: So one could say then that you basically try to achieve a comparable effect in realistic theater by means of new techniques of linguistic concentration. You hold fast to the mimetic function of the theater, not with regard to the representation of reality but rather with regard to language. But you dispense with any extensive apparatus of representation and character formation, even linguistic character formation. There is only concentration, abbreviation, concision. At bottom there is also a gestural quality, which, while its intention and effect are quite different, is nevertheless reminiscent of Brecht.

CANETTI: Here I want also to say something about another, much more fundamental, formative factor that I have not yet mentioned at all. Everything I was able to read about the drama of primitive peoples—the presentation of totem animals, say, or the play of dead figures—has fascinated me. Those things, as I have argued in *Masse und Macht* (*Crowds and Power*), are products of metamorphosis. These figures are part kangaroo, part human being, but also both at the same time. I have sought to make my acoustic masks correspond to the visual aspect of the masks of such figures, which is not very easy.... Strolling around a city, as I used to walk around Vienna, without any destination, quite aimlessly, I actually had the impression of hearing numerous animal voices. But they were the voices of species that were not yet known and whose creation is actually the task of the dramatist. That seems to me to be the most creative essence of drama, and it goes back very far to an early time, very strongly colored by myths. The discovery of a new figure composed of acoustic masks, a distinct being. What one first hears from a real creature is something mimetic-naturalistic, but the figure that has now come into being is something new, if only because something has been omitted, because not everything that goes to make up a fully rounded human being is included in the picture. Thus one arrives at new figures, and one peoples a whole city as if it were a jungle. Here is another connection with Brecht, who also depicted the city as a jungle. But I mean it literally, absolutely literally. For Brecht it is a metaphor.

The most powerful experience that I ever had—more powerful than Kraus, more powerful than his readings, more powerful than the Kabuki theater—was a gramophone record of animals by Julian Huxley. There is a book by him called *Animal Language,* which appeared just before the outbreak of the First World War. I came across it quite by chance. So I listened to it, some time after I had written my first play. That was the strongest confirmation I received that I was on the right track.

One gramophone record contains the voices of individual animals. The other consists of two parts. One part is called "African Animals by Day," the other "African Animals by Night." The record called "African Animals by Night" depicts—purely acoustically—a lion going out hunting, then its encounter with its quarry, a zebra, which it kills. So one hears the nagging of the zebra, and then all the other animals as they appear on the scene: birds, animals, and then, around the carcass of the zebra, the predators. Then come the voices of a tiger, a serval, a jackal, various hyenas, of which one—it has a voice like laughter—laughs. Then the record ends with this truly insane laughter, the voice of this hyena.

This has the form of a drama not only in terms of what happens—for it is a hunt, the killing of an animal—but also in terms of its voices. I had the feeling that this was the greatest document of what I actually wanted that I had ever come upon. The many voices that exist in the African jungle are for me precisely the model for what I want to do in drama. That needs of course to be rephrased and is much more complex. I don't know whether I have made that clear enough.

DURZAK: One could of course argue that what is missing, despite all the acoustic forcefulness on the level of animal language, is an element of reflection.

CANETTI: A very important objection, and, as you have noted yourself, there is not much reflection present in the two plays whose writing derived directly from this theory, so in which there was no reason to suppress the acoustic mask. In *The Wedding* and *Comedy of Vanity* the reflection is actually to be found in the inventiveness and in the composition of the scenes. And that is extraordinarily important to me. I do not want a lot of reflection. It is much more important to me that there be an idea—what I call the *Grundeinfall,* or basic premise. I would never begin a drama without a completely new *Grundeinfall,* one I am certain has never been used before. So I want every play I write to be completely new. I want to start from a premise that, to the best of my knowledge, did not exist beforehand, that had never yet been used. What should happen is the following: I want to play variations on this premise. The *Grundeinfall* is the intellectual component. The variations—which really take the form of storytelling—should be quite simple, almost as simple as the animal recording, if that were thinkable. You remember how simple the scenes are. And the effect should be this—and here there comes into play an element that one could perhaps associate with Brecht (I never did so, though later I thought about him a great deal): what alienates is the nature of this premise, to coin the word "alienation." It is not a word I use at all. This is something we find in Aristophanes, and the origin of the kind of comedy that is always based on a new premise is to be found there.

DURZAK: The amazing thing is that Dürrenmatt refers to Aristophanes in the same way and, like you, insists on the poetic importance of a basic premise.
CANETTI: Yes, there is a parallel there. He does it differently, but the points where I like him are those where he does exactly the same thing: say, in *Der Besuch der alten Dame (The Visit).* I like it, it is a good play. In it he does something similar, even if it is a different kind of premise. But sometimes he comes even closer to my ideas.

DURZAK: In *Der Meteor (The Meteor),* for instance, where the premise addresses the impossibility of dying?
CANETTI: Yes, that comes closer to my kind of premise. I really sensed an affinity here. But what is different is that, unlike Dürrenmatt, I am concerned with the richness of variations, how these variations come into being, so to speak, out of the play's form, how a crystal comes into being. The play must be very tightly structured, it must contain nothing superfluous. It must have a form as solid as if it were a physical object. The audience should be struck first of all by the premise, which should be a remarkable one: that one knows when one is to die, as in *Die Befristeten (The Numbered),* or the idea that all mirrors are to be destroyed, as in *Comedy of Vanity.*[6] That should give the listener a jolt, and he should then find himself in a society that is not quite his own, that is somewhat altered, but not so very much. What I would like to achieve—I don't know whether I succeed in this, but it would actually be my real goal (you will see why I emphasize that, because it is something where I also think somewhat differently from Brecht, although I would perhaps have the same goal in the end)—I would like the spectator himself to work with this premise, to complete the variations on the theme just as if he had been able to think them up for himself. For I am of the opinion that a really good premise can be thought through by anyone, more or

less well. Everyone could reflect: yes, how would it be if there were no mirrors? What would happen? What happens should provoke the feeling: yes, that's actually what I thought. So first he gets jolted into the somewhat strange world, and then he makes himself at home in it by working out everything that happens. That is actually my real goal. It is more complex than anything in Brecht. I may be expressing this somewhat unapologetically and bluntly—of course Brecht is an important writer—but we are talking about how I see him: I find his conception too primitive. It is much too primitive to assume that one can teach people something by forcing them to think, by holding them at a distance and making them rely on their own reasoning; I think that just irritates them: they resist the very things that they would have liked to think, the conclusions that they would have liked to draw, just because they are under duress. What happens is quite different from the idea that people participate creatively in the working out of the variations. Have I said that clearly?

DURZAK: Yes, as far as the intention is concerned. But the question is: does it work? How do things stand with regard to the performance of your plays and the reaction of the audience. I have heard you read *The Wedding*. It was actually for me the most fascinating thing I have ever witnessed on a stage. It was more theatrical, it was scenically more impressive than a performance by actors.

CANETTI: Yes, that is my misfortune. I have no experience in the theater. I thought these things out for myself. I thought them out in such a way that I can read these plays myself. The danger is, of course, that it then becomes something autonomous. The difficulty lies in transferring that to the stage. There must be people who can do it. Then one would see whether it has this effect. I am convinced that people are thinking things through while I am reading. Perhaps you would confirm that. That one, so to speak, runs a little way ahead, that some things then seem obvious, that one then wishes to pursue them further.

DURZAK: The concept of the premise, the *Grundeinfall*, represents a structural element essential to all three plays. While in *The Wedding* and in *Comedy of Vanity* the principle of the acoustic mask appears in tandem with the concept of the *Grundeinfall*, it scarcely has any significance in the last play, *The Numbered*.

CANETTI: Yes, the idea in *The Numbered* is that the figures exist only in relation to their numbers. The life-number they possess is precisely the thing that distinguishes them. That goes beyond the acoustic mask.

DURZAK: The question arises here: where is the element that guarantees the mimetic quality of language? If it is no longer language, as it is in the acoustic mask, what is it?

CANETTI: That element is not present. This is a different play. The intention of the play, what I wanted to do in the play, was to work out all the variations on the relationship of human beings to death, without discussing them philosophically. So I had to effect an extreme reduction. I would actually say that *The Numbered,* of all the dramatic texts I know, represents drama at its most abstract.

DURZAK: Is that not a double-edged knife? Of course one can aim at a very strong reduction, one can play out these variations and thereby avoid abstract terminology, but the variations offer an excess of reflection in quite compact form. Basically it remains a very philosophical, reflective play: that is, it becomes philosophical at the very moment of its reception, the moment the audience tries to break open what is presented in quite compact and concentrated form, devoid both of abstraction and of any great philosophical conceptual framework.

CANETTI: That is absolutely correct. If one examined the play, one would also come upon something that up to now nobody has understood: why the final scene has to be as it is. It is an attempt to counteract that. This scene is supposed to transport people back to the place of anyone who is just experiencing death. This experience of death is, so to speak, torn open after all the possible variations have been played out. And the original situation is then a unitary one, before it divides, before the interpretations separate. At the end The Friend, who is speaking about his sister as if she were still there and he could feel her, could have gone mad with grief. But he could also be religious and believe that she still existed somewhere. The variations have not yet all been developed. It is the basic seed of this experience before it divides up into possible consolations, into insuperable grief. That should still be present in this last scene. The last scene is thus actually the first. There have been friends who said: it is not true that the play contains every relationship to death. But we have talked it through, and I have been able to convince each one of them that it really is so. Whereby there are, of course, some very emotional scenes, more emotional than in the other plays: the mother at the grave of her child, unable to imagine that her child is no longer alive; the young Ten, who is allowed to do whatever he wants because he is dying; the pair of lovers. They are actually very concentrated dramas in themselves. When one has been though all these scenes, when one has experienced the powerlessness, the disintegration of this society that believes it has abolished the fear of death; when one has experienced the opposite, the reversal—I do not wish to talk about reversal now, it is an especially important theme—then at the end one returns to this original situation. So one is actually supposed to be left again with this original situation. My intention was that the thinking can begin again at this point.

DURZAK: Nevertheless there remains a difficulty if one approaches *The Numbered* from the outside. The fact is that certain linguistic-mimetic and satiric-theatrical qualities in your first two plays facilitate the audience's work. But your last play seems to have much stronger connections with the theoretical work with which you were preoccupied: that is, with the basic ideas of *Crowds and Power.* Can one say that your dramatic work falls into two halves: on the one hand the first two plays and on the other the third? Bracketing out your intention in the third play, could one in fact not argue that you have written something along the lines of a philosophical parable, a discussion piece, a drama to be read, where the ideas are in fact more important than the form.

CANETTI: Here I can only speak of its actual performances. While there have so far been only few productions of *The Wedding*—such as that in Cologne—which have really worked well theatrically, I witnessed the first performance, in English, of *The Numbered,* which was extraordinarily effective on stage. It really happened—this was in Oxford—that it was talked about for months, in the seminars at the university. It really captured people's attention and got them talking. It was quite astonishing. Then the production in the small theater, downstairs, in the Josephstadt—not a bad production, but not as good as the English one—also had quite a strong effect. I would say that most people reacted to it. Then of course there was a completely unsuccessful production in Berlin, which I did not see—in the workshop of the Schiller-Theater—and on which I had no influence. People told me that everything was done wrongly.

DURZAK: So, based on the Oxford production, in what way and in what aspects is the play theatrically effective?

CANETTI: This play shares certain advantages with conventional dramas. There are only a few central characters. In my other plays there is little depth to any of the characters. Here, the characters of Fifty, The Friend, and The Keeper of Lockets are very important. The plot is for the most part played out between these three figures. There is something else I would like to mention: a radio play was made out of the play for Cologne. It was performed a few years ago, shortened of course, with music by Bernd Alois Zimmermann. It was extraordinarily accurate; I was sent a copy of it. I have seldom received so many letters, from listeners. Now of course you could say: that was a radio play.

DURZAK: That points somewhat in my direction, since there is a certain kind of radio play that often displays the qualities of a drama of reflective ideas. I am thinking of Siegfried Lenz's "Die Zeit der Schuldlosen" (The age of the innocent), basically also a philosophical drama of ideas, intensified in the form of a parable and as such very successful as a radio play.

CANETTI: I am personally convinced that *The Numbered,* if it is staged correctly (that is to say, in a manner consistent with my intentions), is the most effective in performance of the three plays. That was not my intention. It did not turn out that way because I wanted it to. I have done numerous readings of it, even though it contains no acoustic masks.

DURZAK: What is striking here is actually the following: your starting point is always language, that is as true of *Die Blendung* (*Auto-da-Fé*) as it is of *The Wedding* and *Comedy of Vanity*. Now in *The Numbered* you employ a specific idiom that is deliberately simple. The language is certainly concentrated but no longer identifiable with a specific cast of characters. The idiom is thus an abstract one.
CANETTI: Not really. I wanted—I don't know whether I have written this to you—an idiom that does not identify itself as such in any way. It is supposed to be neither an elevated nor an exaggerated or consciously brash everyday language, something colorless, something that does not distract one from the inventiveness of the scenes. They were important to me as scenes, each of which was supposed to work out a relationship to death. It was a renunciation of language—of course not absolutely—if you want to put it that way, because I was dispensing with everything that language had ever been to me. I did not use acoustic masks in my notes and aphorisms either, but they are nevertheless carefully shaped.

DURZAK: That is an interesting formulation, basically a paradox: a renunciation of language. On the other hand, you concede that your distancing from dialect, in which both *The Wedding* and *Comedy of Vanity* are rooted, is originally connected with your long absence from the linguistic area in which *Auto-da-Fé* and your first two plays were written. Could one not now connect this idea of renouncing language with your situation in exile? And, even if contrary to your intention, has not a kind of connection come about, which has had an effect on the language that you used in *The Numbered*? When was *The Numbered* written?
CANETTI: The play was finished in 1953.

DURZAK: So you had been abroad for quite a long time before that. It is interesting that there are parallel phenomena with respect to other authors who have lived abroad for many years. One finds something basically similar in Broch's *Der Tod des Vergil* (*The Death of Virgil*): that gave birth to a completely new artistic idiom, not in the sense of a reduction and concentration such as one finds in your writing but actually in the sense of a proliferation of language.
CANETTI: That is not quite true of me. I would like to say it were. It is very tempting, but it is not quite correct. For, you see, the deliberate work I conducted over decades was what I formulated in *Crowds and Power* and what is in the notes and aphorisms. Shortly afterwards I wrote *Die Stimmen von Marrakesch* (*The Voices of Marrakesh*). There you also find a very simple language, but different from that in *The Numbered*. That still has its own colors, despite

the reduction. That, if you like, is the real effect of exile on my writing: the very concentrated and pointed language of *Crowds and Power*. My model for that was very much Lichtenberg, whom I have read constantly in exile. Just as I once enjoyed listening to Kraus in Vienna, I have always read Lichtenberg in exile. But the case of *The Numbered* is different. One sees it even within the negation. The truth is simply that the play was written under the effect of a specific death, a death that stretched over a year and a half. I did not write the play in one go—my other plays were written quite quickly—but rather over the course of the fatal illness of a friend of whom I have told you. He was in hospital in Paris for a long time, where I visited him and witnessed the progress of his illness. I believe, because it touched me so closely, I wanted to avoid any language that was too deliberate. It was a kind of asceticism. Both the impression under which the play was written—that was drawn out over a long period—and the artistic intention were going in one direction. I wouldn't say that I consider the language of *The Numbered* to be characteristic of the other things I have written since my emigration. In other books there definitely is an influence in your sense: when one examines the language of *Crowds and Power*, of my notes and aphorisms, and of other things that I have not published, there is quite clearly a turning away from the color of the language spoken in Vienna.

DURZAK: Earlier you mentioned that the concept of inversion, of reversal, is very important for your plays. Do you mean that in the Aristotelian sense?
CANETTI: No, I mean something different.

DURZAK: I was thinking of the Aristotelian concept of peripeteia.
CANETTI: It is not very far removed from that, but my meaning is actually more precise. In the structure of the dramas you will see that very often one scene corresponds to another, using the same characters but with the opposite outcome; so, for instance, the teacher couple in *The Wedding* who are so worried about the child, and who then later, in the catastrophe scene, drop the child, causing it to die. Or there is the absolutely loveless scene between the business couple Max and Gretchen, who conduct negotiations about the house, whereby the man's love is reckoned in as part of the payment. Later, when the house falls down, and the possible speculation threatens to assume enormous proportions, it suddenly turns into a genuine love scene: the two of them understand each other so well that they submit to a kind of rapture. That is the reversal corresponding to the earlier scene. Or the old landlady who cannot speak at the beginning, who can only master these few sounds, and then can suddenly speak at the end. Reversals completely encircle the play. This technique of reversal seems to me enormously important and essentially dramatic. Later, in my examination of the command and other processes in *Crowds and Power*, I realized that this could probably be explained in part by reference to my theory of punishment. It is too complicated to

explain in detail now. There are verifiable psychological reasons why reversal in drama is something of special importance. There are many instances of it in *The Numbered*. It is full of reversals. The scenes, say, with the two young men at the beginning, than the reversal later, and so on.

DURZAK: Isn't that something quite different from the Aristotelian peripeteia that always occurs shortly before the catastrophe begins?

CANETTI: I have studied Greek dramas very carefully, and I have concluded that there are reversals in my sense even in Greek drama, indeed more often than one thinks, and that the Greek tragedies that impress me most are those that contain the most reversals. Nevertheless I sometimes have the feeling that some of the theoretical things in Aristoteles are—I would say—wrongly expressed, that he means something correct but expresses it in a different way. I believe he reaches conclusions that contain some truth about the Greek dramas he has in mind but his conclusions are not concrete enough. A distant connection could even be made here with peripeteia.

DURZAK: The theoretical connection in Aristoteles is the plot. He develops four models of how the plot can reach a specific, in each case different, end, having to do respectively with recognition, with anagnorisis, and with complete change, reversal, peripeteia. So it can happen a) that the catastrophe is recognized in advance and changed, b) that it is known in advance and nevertheless not prevented, c) that it is not recognized and despite that still prevented, or d) that it is not recognized and not prevented. This is very convincing within Aristotle's theoretical framework. Of course it is abstracted since his intention is to produce a specific poetological model. But could one not say that what you have characterized as reversal with regard to your own plays could perhaps be understood as the concept of character development? This is traditionally applied to the dramatic hero, at least in nineteenth-century theater, less so in the theater of the eighteenth century where one is still working to a great extent with a fixed arsenal of types. I mean type in the sense that the protagonist undergoes no development of any kind but goes through the whole play unchanged; even when reality defeats him, he does not change. No reversal takes place, while development implies that he is a different person at the end from at the beginning.

CANETTI: Your mentioning that is very important, for I am against development in drama. For me drama functions beyond time, and everything that introduces temporal sequence into drama is undramatic. The changes that characters undergo are sudden. That is what I call mask-switching (*Maskensprung*). Here I am thinking, for instance, of things that are already found in primitive drama. There it can happen that a figure appears—there are immensely interesting things—with a mask, some dangerous spirit; suddenly the mask is removed, and the face that appears behind it is another mask. So there are multiple masks, and I call that *Maskensprung*. I believe that is very important in drama.

DURZAK: But doesn't that utterly destroy the mimetic effect? You remove the element of time, and you thereby destroy something like the principle of individuation in drama. If you have these switches, if behind each mask there emerges another mask and not the face that one considers characteristic of a specific person, doesn't drama completely lose itself in the domain of the symbolic?

CANETTI: No, it would lose itself if what I call *Maskensprung* were something used too widely, incessantly, and for many purposes. Whether one can make use of a mask-switch at all, and when, depends on the premise and on how the scenes are thought out. It is only one technique. It is a technique to be used in places where one would talk in a conventional bad drama of a crucial character development. I would make use of a mask-switch to show that the identity of a person has changed.

DURZAK: I understand: development works with psychological material; everything is justified and causal. You reject that completely.

CANETTI: I reject that. Of course it sometimes happens nonetheless, but I reject it on aesthetic grounds.

DURZAK: So what you present in a mask-switch is the completely new face of a person, without any derivation or development linking the two.

CANETTI: There is a connection. It cannot be explained psychologically but only in terms of the relationship between the two masks. Of course that depends on what else is happening in the scene. One can only show that concretely, and that has to be done with some precision. You see, we are mentioning quite a few points here, about which there is very much to say.

DURZAK: Yes, that is a new point of view, this concept of mask-switching.

CANETTI: It is new. I do not know whether you remember the short chapter in *Crowds and Power* about masks. Irrespective of drama, that is theoretically a new way of looking at masks. I have already outlined many things here.

DURZAK: Dr. Canetti, I know how important your plays are to you, that you have said more than once that you most enjoy writing plays, and that, at its center everything you write is of a dramatic nature. The external circumstances of your life, in particular your situation in exile, have meant that it has taken decades for your plays to start to find their place in theater repertoires. That phase has now begun. Has there nevertheless been any kind of response on the part of other German dramatists, in particular those of a younger generation?

CANETTI: Martin Walser recently came to see me in London. I didn't know him at all. He was very open and said suddenly, to my greatest astonishment, that he had read the five scenes of *The Wedding* that had once been printed in the journal of the Weismann Press, very early on, and indeed that he had done so with great excitement and that that had been important for his form of drama.[7]

Notes

1. [Elias Canetti, "Karl Kraus: The School of Resistance," in *The Conscience of Words,* trans. Joachim Neugroschel (London: Deutsch, 1986), 31–32. *Ed.*]

2. ["Leergegessene Bonbonnièren—Das Reich der Schatten—Die akustische Maske: Elias Canetti und das heutige Theater," *Der Sonntag,* 18 April 1937. *Ed.*]

3. [I am indebted to Paul M. Malone for his collaboration on the translation of this extended quotation. A slightly different German version of this passage is cited by Peter Laemmle, whose 1975 essay, translated by Malone, appears elsewhere in the present volume. The most significant difference is that Laemmle's version states: "It's easy to sum up this idea clearly in a few sentences." *Trans.*]

4. [The next several exchanges duplicate, in unabbreviated form here, almost identical passages that appear in abbreviated form in the conversation between Canetti and Durzak to be found earlier in this volume. *Ed.*]

5. [The reference is to the eleventh scene of Brecht's play. *Ed.*]

6. [There are two published English translations of *Die Befristeten.* The title used here is that of Carol Stewart's translation, *The Numbered* (London: Marion Boyars, 1984); Gitta Honegger's translation, entitled *Life-Terms,* appears in a volume together with *Comedy of Vanity* (New York: PAJ Publications, 1983). *Ed.*]

7. [These scenes appeared in the journal *Die Fähre* (1947). The Weismann Verlag (Munich) published editions of *Auto-da-Fé* (1948) and *Comedy of Vanity* (1950) in very adverse economic circumstances and with little commercial success. *Ed.*]

The Power and Powerlessness
of the Earwitness:
The Dramatic in Canetti's Early Plays

PETER LAEMMLE

Lend me your ear for my unuttered speech!

Grillparzer, *Des Meeres und der Liebe Wellen*
(The Waves of Sea and Love)

"I believe that, at its core, everything I do is dramatic in nature."[1] This statement of Canetti's might seem surprising in light of his complete oeuvre, including *Die Blendung* (*Auto-da-Fé*) and *Masse und Macht* (*Crowds and Power*), which in fact seems rather to tend toward the epic and the philosophical. Canetti's often-attested preference for the dramatic genre must seem unusual, indeed almost a misjudgment of his own talent, considering that the reservations about his dramas—that is, about their performability—are as grave as ever. They have hitherto been only moderate successes for Canetti, and the spectacular failures of the 1965 premieres of *Hochzeit* (*The Wedding*) and *Komödie der Eitelkeit* (*Comedy of Vanity*) at the Braunschweig Staatstheater have evidently only confirmed the prejudices. They are the prejudices of theater practitioners. They fear that Canetti's plays are too cerebral; they speak of a basic untheatricality; they doubt whether the basic premise of each play holds water. This outlook, which might well be symptomatic for German theater circles, has been formulated with considerable clarity by Günther Rühle. Referring to the two Braunschweig productions—with all due respect for the author—Rühle writes of *The Wedding*: "Canetti's plays have the weakness of any play whose construction is given only cursory thought: symptoms and correspondences to a premise are sought and incorporated. The theme is not developed organically"; and of *Comedy of Vanity*: "Canetti's material: if one read it as an aphorism, one would say: Make it a comedy. Seeing it as a comedy, one says: That would make an admirable aphorism."[2]

Translated by Paul M. Malone for this volume from Peter Laemmle, "Macht und Ohnmacht des Ohrenzeugen: Zur Kategorie des Dramatischen in Canettis frühen Stücken," in *Canetti lesen: Erfahrungen mit seinen Büchern,* ed. Herbert G. Göpfert (Munich: Hanser, 1975), 47–61. Reproduced here by kind permission of the Carl Hanser Verlag.

Such misunderstandings arise because Canetti's plays simply cannot be adequately described and produced against the background of a traditional theory of drama, unless they are reduced to familiar individual elements: to the Brechtian *Lehrstück,* to echoes of the *Volksstück* à la Horváth, to the relentlessness and blackness of the theater of the absurd. Such attempts remain mere attributions, speculations. They are also historically inaccurate. Canetti had still read nothing of Horváth when he wrote his dramas.[3] His models were—though in an indirect, mediating manner—Aristophanes, Nestroy, and, with all the signs of a sublimated love-hate relationship, Karl Kraus.

It is striking that Canetti's scenic imagination comes much more obviously to light outside his dramas. In *Auto-da-Fé* there are scenes that from their construction and their (petty-bourgeois) milieu could have come from one of Labiche's comedies: Therese's appearances in the furniture store or the interrogation of the protagonists at the police station (the key scene of the whole book). The combination of acoustic and visual elements in these events gives the reader the impression of dramatic composition.

In Canetti's notes and aphorisms, which contain not only reflections but also quite concrete observations and minute scenes of everyday life, there is one passage in particular that remains in my memory. It sounds like the stage directions for a play, set in an imaginary space, which in its motionlessness assumes nightmarish, surreal traits.

> A pub in which all have gone mute. The patrons sit mutely, alone or in groups, and down their drinks. The waitress mutely hands you a menu, you point to a spot, she nods, brings you what you want, and puts it mutely on the table. Everyone looks wordlessly at everyone else.... Someone stands up. What is he going to do? Everyone is scared. A child, like a painting, opens its mouth wide, but no shriek sounds out. The parents say nothing and close his mouth. The light goes out, one hears a smashing. The light goes on again.... A cat leaps on the table and dominates the place.[4]

It is therefore no coincidence—and certainly not due to lack of ability—that in his dramas Canetti suppresses plot in favor of the linguistic element, speech and counterspeech (although there is in the plays, strictly speaking, no dialogue, but only monologue; spoken signals from separate, mutually alien worlds). The privileging of speech above all other forms of human communication and interaction derives from Canetti's theory of language: a theory that results in a revealing literalness. Named the "acoustic mask," this theory stands at the center of his conception of the dramatic (a conception that, until it is made available in context, as occasionally promised, can only be pieced together from individual remarks in his work). For Canetti, the diction of each individual is the essence of the physiognomy of his intellect, psyche, and character. In speech one finds the quintessence of all human behavior.

It should not be overlooked that Canetti approaches a possible definition of the dramatic from the psychological side. He is interested above all in what goes on *between* people, in all possible forms of encountering and missing each other, which for him means understanding and misunderstanding each other. *Auto-da-Fé* is about how people deal with each other, about acts of aggression and projection, about fear, envy, cunning, exploitation—and it is about power in all its guises. Even though Canetti's observations never avail themselves of psychological terms, they can nonetheless easily be traced back to them. Admittedly, much of their particular quality would then be lost: the frightening concreteness of this psychopathology of everyday life. The anti-Freudian, sworn enemy of psychoanalysis, is himself perhaps one of the greatest psychologists since Freud; his gift for the radical observation of people (radical in its precision) could be the real unifying insight of his work, which only at first glance appears so heterogeneous. Canetti's passionate interest in all processes of the human field leads so far in *Crowds and Power* (where he analyzes the social, objective aspect of human behavior) that he attributes anthropomorphous traits to crowd symbols from the realm of nature (sea, river, rain, wind). The sea, rivers, rain, and wind have characteristics, emotions, behaviors like people. The anthropomorphous view thereby even determines the beauty of the poetic image, as for instance in the expression, "The sea never sleeps."[5]

It is crucial for the understanding of Canetti's dramatic works that his idea of the dramatic is structured less aesthetically than psychologically: "Drama is, of all human possibilities of summing-up, the least untruthful" (*HP*, 13). With regard to Canetti, one could modify the classic Aristotelian definition, which describes the drama as that artistic genre in which "men in their actions are imitated," as follows: the dramatic is the field in which men in their actions are no longer invented but rather observed; that is, where the realm of the mimetic is omitted in favor of an authenticity that manifests itself in speaking. In this sense Canetti's early plays *The Wedding* and *Comedy of Vanity* are precursors of a newer theater (Marie-Luise Fleisser and Franz Xaver Kroetz come to mind) that makes the acting characters' manner of speaking into its real dramaturgical agent.[6] In terms of psychology there are surely also points of contact with Brecht, as for instance when Brecht says that "the new theatre creates (and derives its life from) the joy of conveying human relationships"; by contrast, in their treatment of the gestural, scenic element, the two authors differ considerably.[7]

The statement of Canetti's cited at the beginning proves justified, then, if one understands that he broadens the idea of the dramatic to mean the actions of people, their interactions, their collisions as individuals or en masse. Seen in this light, Canetti's dramas are a piece of concrete psychoanalysis; that is, they make visible the reactions to drives that are unconscious, displaced, or sublimated under external moral pressure. The indignation that his plays have occasionally provoked in their audience only demonstrates how close he comes in them to the truth about the human condition.

THE ACOUSTIC MASK: LITERALNESS AND HORROR

Psychoanalysis cannot be taught because it is innate in everyone, because it is a characteristic of the human being, as, for instance, sight and hearing are.
Georg Groddeck, *Schriften zur Literatur und Kunst*
(Writings on literature and art)

In his notes and aphorisms, Canetti reproaches analysts for not really listening to their patients at all but only hearing what they already knew anyway (*HP,* 217). The psychologist Canetti knows the old rule of thumb that states that every man betrays himself, if one only lets him speak long enough. As a person, Canetti has the rare characteristic of concentrated listening, with which he forces his interlocutor to just such concentration in speech. Many of Canetti's experiences with people are acoustic in nature; in an autobiographical prose work, "Unsichtbarer Kristall" (Invisible crystal), he reports how, in his Viennese apartment, the ecstatic outcry of the crowds in the adjacent soccer stadium fascinated him. "The cry of the crowd in the distance ... became so important to me that I strove not to miss a single game. While others, as was natural, went to the stadium knowing which side they were on and what they were screaming for, I heard this cry without meaning and without bias, so to speak, in my room.... I believe that in the six years I lived in this room, my decision to explore the crowd ... [was] nourished in a mysterious way by the cries of the crowd."[8] Canetti's somewhat uncanny contemporary, for whom listening is a profession and who only occasionally, to rest from his "work," "claps blinders on his ears and refrains from storing up the hearable things," is the eponym of Canetti's collection of characters: this prose piece, "Der Ohrenzeuge" ("The Earwitness"), is surely a self-portrait of the author, encoded with charming irony.[9]

The Earwitness Canetti is a pupil of Karl Kraus. In his essay "Karl Kraus: Schule des Widerstands" ("Karl Kraus: The School of Resistance"), the following aspect (which can be paraphrased, though quite inadequately, in Luther's phrase "Heed the speech of the common folk") appears most important to Canetti: "Kraus was haunted by voices ... the voices pursuing him *did exist* in the Viennese reality. He could hear them everywhere, on streets, squares, in restaurants. Most writers knew how *not* to listen.... But since *his* ear was constantly open (it never closed, it was always in action, it was always listening) he also had to read ... newspapers as though he were *hearing* them. When he quoted them, he seemed to be letting voices speak: acoustic quotations."[10]

Through Karl Kraus the young Canetti (whose sensitivity to the shadings of language, to the appeal of individual words, was especially strongly marked by his own complicated polyglot linguistic situation) learned to pay attention to his linguistic environment.[11] As Canetti himself says, Karl Kraus "opened [my] ear" (*CW*, 34). The fact that the Earwitness Canetti, in his expeditions through the Vienna of the early thirties, not only perceived the dictions of different social milieus (they are authentically recalled—in the dialect as well—in the early plays and again in *Auto-da-Fé*) but also made individual bizarre acoustic finds is demonstrated by the sentence "And then he pulled me to th' altar 'n' kissed me and he was so nice."[12] This stands almost at the end of *The Wedding*, when the house has already collapsed (this sentence is a utopian countersentence to the outbreak of chaos). Canetti picked up this sentence in passing from the conversation of two old women. "I couldn't get rid of this sentence, it pursued me in my sleep, and I mean that literally.... From this sentence came, about half a year later, *The Wedding*. I took it up unchanged in the play as a kind of good luck charm.... I could go so far as to say that the play was created in honor of this sentence. I still love it today. To me it is as if I had heard it yesterday. I wanted it to have the power to protect us against later destruction."[13]

Canetti has made the "acoustic quotation"—like Karl Kraus in *Die letzten Tage der Menschheit* (*The Last Days of Mankind*)—into the essential satirical feature of his plays. Satire is for him, too, first of all satire of language. The intentions and motivations underlying the satire are, admittedly, decidedly different in the two authors (and here is also to be found the cause of Canetti's later rejection of Kraus). In his own theory of language, however (although the magical tendency of his consciousness of language could stem from the religiously conditioned faith in the word of his Sephardic childhood home), Canetti may be greatly influenced by Karl Kraus. Karl Kraus's idea that language is "the great betrayer" of human character, that in language the "depravity of the soul" finds expression, is the linguistic-critical satirical starting point of Canetti's early plays.[14] The characters of *The Wedding* and *Comedy of Vanity* define themselves and their social origin through the language they speak (be it reduced or be it rhetorically exaggerated). The wrong tones predominate. They are the linguistic equivalent of the wrongheaded life and consciousness of these distraught petty bourgeois whose distress is expressed in their relationship with language. The idea that thought and language are one, naturally, has a specific Viennese tradition. It extends from Nestroy's plays, which Canetti came to know through Kraus (in Nestroy's *Zu ebener Erde und erster Stock* [On the ground floor and upstairs] there are not only two playing levels onstage but also two levels of speech, "upstairs" and "downstairs"), up to the Viennese linguistic positivists (Wittgenstein writes in the *Tractatus logico-philosophicus*: "The limits of my language mean the limits of my world"[15]). A sign of the essentially dramatic character of *Auto-da-Fé* is that in this novel the typification of the figures is performed in their own language (after Kien holds his monologue in the police station, enriched with book-learning and rhetorical figures, all present recognize from his language that he "wasn't a servant"). "The tone, reminiscent of the lemures and somewhere between Nestroy and Herr Karl," attributed by Hans Magnus Enzensberger to this book, also characterizes the language of Canetti's plays, and not only when he avails himself of obvious Austrianisms.[16]

The reconnaissances of the Earwitness, the experiences of the linguistic theorist, yield an idea of the dramatic that Canetti formulated in 1937, some years after writing his plays, in the Viennese newspaper *Der Sonntag*. This interview, under the heading "Acoustic Mask," is probably the most important testimony of the dramatist Canetti on his own behalf.

Drama lives in language in a quite unique way. If the words were not so easily misunderstood, one could almost say: it lives in languages. For I consider the most important element of dramatic composition to be the acoustic mask. It's easy to sum up this idea clearly in a few sentences. Go into a pub, sit down at any table, and make the acquaintance of a complete stranger. Initially you will have no choice but to say a few accommodating sentences to get him started. But as soon as he is really talking—and he'll be happy to talk, that's why he goes to this pub—you must rigorously hold your tongue and listen to him carefully for several minutes. Make no attempt to understand him, don't try to get to the bottom of what he means, don't try to empathize with him. Pay attention quite simply to the external form of his words. This advice will only take you so far. It serves only to let you experience once and for all and as quickly as possible what I just now referred to as the acoustic mask.

You will discover that your new acquaintance has a quite idiosyncratic way of speaking. It isn't enough to say: he speaks German, or he speaks in dialect; so does everyone, or almost everyone, in this pub. No, his way of speaking is unique and unmistakable. It has its own pitch and tempo, it has its own rhythm. One sentence differs little from another. Certain words and phrases recur again and again. His whole language consists of only 500 words. He manages quite expertly with them; those are *his* 500 words. Someone else, whose vocabulary is equally impoverished, speaks in another 500. If you've listened well, you will be able to recognize him the next time by his language, without seeing him. The shape he has taken in his speech demarcates him on all sides and differentiates him from all other people as clearly as does his physiognomy, for instance, which is just as unique. The linguistic shape of a human being, the things that remain constant in his speech, this language that came into being with him, that is his alone, and that will pass away only with him—this is what I call his acoustic mask.

Now this doesn't mean that the dramatist has to be a strolling phonograph, recording the diction of as many people as possible and then assembling dramas as needed from the available collection of acoustic masks. In fact that would be just another of the many ways of mechanically plagiarizing life, none of which have the slightest thing to do with art. But the dramatist must be able to *hear;* he must have a good deal of linguistic life within him; what is heard must both completely blend together and completely separate out again into its component parts, so that each form that emerges in due course is clear and effective precisely in its acoustic mask.[17]

The rather static character of the "acoustic mask" is transformed by the sudden "change of masks" (*CP,* 375). By this Canetti means the linguistic development of the characters, the leap within a character from one mask to another (Holz). In *The Wedding,* for example, this is always the case when a character changes his manner of speaking according to which one of the other characters he is speaking to.

Canetti later anchored the principle of the "acoustic mask" in *Crowds and Power* anthropologically as well (in the chapter "The Figure and the Mask"). It is important above all that here he brings into play the idea of "the opposite of transformation," which in his usage means nothing other than unmasking.[18]

In his early plays, the satirist Canetti rigorously pursues the unmasking of human behavior and characteristics. He dissects the real motives of the action behind the facade of bourgeois propriety. In *The Wedding* all humane considerations end in the face of a raging avarice directed with equal lack of inhibition at money and at sexual objects, an avarice that reduces everything to a mere commodity. The grotesque contortions and humiliating situations to which people are prepared to submit themselves, when they are forbidden to satisfy their narcissism and look for ways to do this secretly, are demonstrated in *Comedy of Vanity,* whose language leaves nothing to be desired in its directness and explicitness (this is where Canetti's reading of Aristophanes has left its most obvious traces).

It is this literalness, at which humor freezes and veers round into blank horror, that probably induced the audience of the Braunschweig productions (both plays were taken off again relatively quickly) to their vehement campaign of protest. Evidently the spectators discovered in the stylized "acoustic mask" of both plays, distorted into recognizability, their own language. This confrontation mobilized the resistance and the hostility of the audience, which announced the degree of its dismay precisely by means of disruptive maneuvers (led, by the way, by students from the dueling societies).

During the premiere, near the middle of the play ... furious protests from the audience broke out. The scene in question in *The Wedding* portrayed a three-man-conversation that identified woman as a manipulable object of cupidity; there was hardly a sentence in it that was not related to this basic theme and to its appropriate structure. The noise grew to a considerable volume and resulted in a nervous tension among the actors that did not serve the flow of the plot. It came to a heated discussion among the theatergoers, whereby the sentence was heard: "This sullies the honor of German womanhood!"—a remark that put the latent grotesquerie of the text far in the shade. This, like all the other signs of emotion from the stalls and from the circle, was evidently the result of an identification diametrically opposed to the character of the play.[19]

The fact that the satire hits its mark only proves the power of the Ear-witness. It is no accident that Canetti has called him, in ironic exaggeration, the "executioner himself" (*E,* 44).

THE CHEERFUL MISANTHROPE

It is not to be believed how innocent people are when no one is eavesdropping.

Canetti, *Earwitness*

"Canetti's satirical temperament aims at shock and provocation, in order to shake up, to expose and thus to improve."[20] The moral impetus that is here superficially and naively attributed to the plays has in fact hung as a favorite label on Canetti's work for quite some time. Adorno, too, who was one of the experts called to speak in the suit against the Braunschweig production of *The Wedding* (the suit was triggered by an anonymous complaint on the grounds of "creating a sexual nuisance"), wrote in his statement, among other things: "On the basis of an exact knowledge of the work of Elias Canetti ... I con-sider any intent on Canetti's part to be lascivious, to cause injury to modesty, or to deal in obscenity so thoroughly out of the question that the mere attempt to associate him with such matters is ridiculous.... This play, written more than thirty years ago ... , if it is anything other than a pure work of art, is meant to moralize, and moreover its form unequivocally bears this out" (Bischoff, 78).

Whether one considers *The Wedding* to be a pandemonium of humanity in general (like Adorno) or an allegory of bourgeois society in its death throes (like Hans Heinz Holz), one will have to examine the psychological or politi-cal moralism that is at work in Canetti's plays for its origin and intent.[21] It is then obvious that a straightforward didactic element is lacking in his plays: Canetti does not want to improve and instruct his spectator. This is where he differs quite essentially from his model Karl Kraus. It would never occur to him to send onstage the moralist who, with raised index finger, editorializes an event whose moral intent is already evident—as Karl Kraus did with the character of the "Grumbler" in *The Last Days of Mankind.* Canetti's moralism has nothing to do with the defense of moral norms. It springs rather from a fear of what people can be capable of. But the fact that he has been hurt by people does not lead him to pass sentence on them. His form of satire thus loses the reproachful character that marked satire as a genre from Juvenal to Karl Kraus. To be sure, he too, like all satirists, rails against the current state of affairs, but he does not measure the bad present against a good past. The *laudatio temporis acti* that determines the moral counterexample of traditional satire is not to be found in Canetti. He is no disillusioned idealist, suffering almost masochistically from the (natural) contradiction between reality and ideal (Schiller, too, saw the satirist thus in his "Naive und sentimentalische Dichtung" ["Naive and Sentimental Poetry"]). That clearly conservative element that Walter Benjamin and Theodor W. Adorno discovered in Karl Kraus is completely foreign to Canetti.[22] His form of satire limits itself to revealing "the immediate contrast between essence and appearance."[23] The Earwitness, who participates himself in this contradiction, can do no more than show us human reality (therein may lie his powerlessness). Canetti measures the reality of humanity against some possible future development in which the present defective condition will be abolished. It is written in the notes and aphorisms: "Man will still become all and whole. The slaves will redeem the masters" (*HP*, 9). The moralism of the satirist Canetti only seems to have misanthropic traits. In truth, it derives its power from a utopian humanism.

Canetti never makes the characters of his plays into laughingstocks, not even when he shows them from their most repulsive side. At the most, he has "precisely exaggerated" them (*HP*, 262). It is not people that he wants to criticize but rather modes of human behavior. The break with Karl Kraus, to whom his plays owe so much, took place on this point. That homicidal tendency in satire (which Canetti in his recent lecture on Kraus so rightfully emphasized), that deadly contempt for humanity that nobody could withstand, that left nobody a chance, could not set an example for Canetti.[24] Before he wrote *The Wedding,* he had stumbled upon an author whose goodness, whose ability to feel pity (even while observing people pitilessly) was far more congenial to him: Georg Büchner. "The real moment that triggered *The Wedding* was my late encounter with *Woyzeck,* by Büchner. I was 26 when I read it in a single night, and that night I suddenly felt I achieved distance from Karl Kraus. . . . So the real occasion for writing *The Wedding* was a drama that already dates rather far back: namely Büchner's *Woyzeck*" (Holz).

ON THE PRODUCTION HISTORY OF BOTH DRAMAS

The Wedding received its premiere on 3 November 1965 in the Staatstheater Braunschweig; the director was Alexander Wagner. In the 1969–1970 season the play was staged three times: at the Städtische Bühnen in Cologne (under the direction of Karl Paryla), at the Vereinigte Bühnen in Graz (directed by Jan Biczycki), and at the Zurich Schauspielhaus (directed by Max P. Ammann). In the 1970–1971 season a production followed at the Vienna Volkstheater, directed by Bernd Fischerauer. In 1973–1974 the play was performed at the Städtische Bühnen in Bonn (director: Hansjörg Utzerath). Besides these, there was a production at the Dramaten Theater in Stockholm, which Donya Feuer directed. Ludwig Cremer adapted and produced *The Wedding* for television (ZDF, 10 May 1972).

Comedy of Vanity was produced twice. The premiere took place on 2 June 1965 in Braunschweig. The direction was by the Braunschweig artistic director, Helmuth Matiasek. Besides this, Hermann Kutscher directed the play in Graz (1972–1973 season); this production was also recorded and broadcast by the ORF.

The Braunschweig audience's protest at the premiere of *Comedy of Vanity* may also have been directed at the mise-en-scène, which rather violently politicized the play with film inserts from the Nazi period. (The use of film and photos of the scenes was in any case a fundamental error of the director, since the piece deals precisely with the prohibition of all mirrors and of any other possibilities whereby people can depict themselves.)

The disruptive actions against *The Wedding* were clearly motivated by the text of the play and especially, of course, by the promiscuous tendencies of the wedding guests. The very evening after the premiere of *The Wedding* the theater management, intimidated by the audience's reactions, came to an agreement with the author and director regarding several cuts. Indeed, the following performances were not disturbed again. Between the first and second performance, however, the theater received oral and written threats: for the second production a student demonstration using car horns was allegedly planned (cf. Bachmann, 114). An anonymous complaint "on the grounds of creating a sexual nuisance" was published on 4 November 1965 in the *Braunschweiger Zeitung.* The office of the district attorney determined that the originator of this advertisement wished to remain anonymous because, "given the cultural dictatorship under which we live," he feared "numerous journalistic slanders." Consequently, the theater management asked renowned personalities in domestic and foreign cultural circles for their opinions (among others, the following responded: Theodor W. Adorno, Peter Weiss, Günter Grass, Günter Eich, Reinhard Baumgart, Hermann Kesten, Fritz Bauer, and Martin Walser, as well as numerous prominent theater experts). Adorno's opinion ended with the words: "Even the so-called naive spectator, on whose behalf such complaints are no doubt lodged, can receive absolutely no other impression from the play than that a judgment has been meted out to a kind of Sodom and Gomorrah.... Anyone who takes umbrage at this play can only have come in order to take umbrage." Erwin Piscator called the inquiries against the piece a "blasphemy." On 29 November 1965 the state attorney's inquiry was discontinued (cf. Bischoff, 78 ff.).

Notes

1. Elias Canetti, "Gespräch mit Horst Bienek," in *Die gespaltene Zukunft: Aufsätze und Gespräche,* Reihe Hanser 111 (Munich: Hanser, 1972), 101.

2. Günther Rühle, "Skandal Nummer zwo" [review of *The Wedding*], *Frankfurter Allgemeine Zeitung,* 5 November 1965; Günther Rühle, "Ein Skandal in Braunschweig" [review of *Comedy of Vanity*], *Frankfurter Allgemeine Zeitung,* 9 February 1965.

3. Elias Canetti, "Die umstrittene Hochzeit," conversation with Hans Heinz Holz; hereafter cited in the text as Holz. This interview, which took place shortly after the Braunschweig premiere, contains important passages on Canetti's idea of the dramatic. The conversation is unpublished. Quotations are taken from a manuscript placed at my disposal through the kindness of the arts and culture editors of the *Basler National-Zeitung.*

4. Elias Canetti, *The Human Province,* trans. Joachim Neugroschel (New York: Seabury, 1978), 195–96; hereafter cited in text as *HP.*

5. Elias Canetti, *Crowds and Power,* trans. Carol Stewart (New York: Farrar, Straus and Giroux, 1984), 80; hereafter cited in text as *CP.*

6. The drama *Die Befristeten (The Numbered),* which was written only after the Second World War, could not be considered in connection with this essay. Thematically and in its dramatic conception it is very different from both the early plays.

7. 20 December 1944; in Bertolt Brecht, *Journals,* trans. Hugh Rorrison, ed. John Willett (London: Methuen, 1993), 338.

8. Elias Canetti, "Unsichtbarer Kristall," *Literatur und Kritik* 3 (1968): 65–66.

9. Elias Canetti, *Earwitness: Fifty Characters,* trans. Joachim Neugroschel (New York: Seabury, 1979), 44; hereafter cited in text as *E.*

10. Elias Canetti, *The Conscience of Words,* trans. Joachim Neugroschel (London: Deutsch, 1986), 32; hereafter cited in text as *CW.*

11. Cf. on this topic Manfred Durzak's essay "Versuch über Elias Canetti," *Akzente* 2 (1970): 169 ff.

12. [Cf. Elias Canetti, *The Wedding,* trans. Gitta Honegger (New York: PAJ Publications, 1986), 83. This sentence occurs on the very last page of the play, only four lines before the curtain falls. The line has been translated anew to suit the context of the article; Honegger's translation, perhaps wisely, makes no attempt to reproduce the spectrum of dialects in Canetti's German original and furthermore divides this sentence into two sentences. *Trans.*]

13. This quotation is from the program for the production of *The Wedding* at the Zurich Schauspielhaus (1969–1970 season).

14. Christian Wagenknecht, "Wortspiel bei Karl Kraus," *Palaestra* 242 (1965): 128–29 and ff.

15. Ludwig Wittgenstein, *Tractatus Logico-Philosophicus,* trans. C. K. Ogden (London: Routledge and Kegan Paul), 149.

16. Hans Magnus Enzensberger, review of *Die Blendung,* by Elias Canetti, *Der Spiegel,* 7 August 1963, 48–49. Enzensberger's review is notable for its remarkably malicious tone. [Enzensberger's review appears in annotated English translation elsewhere in the present volume. *Ed.*]

17. Cited from the program of the Zurich Schauspielhaus. [Cf. the version of this passage cited by Manfred Durzak in the conversation entitled "The Acoustic Mask," which precedes the present essay in this volume. Durzak's version states (perhaps more logically): "It's not easy to sum up this idea clearly in a few sentences." *Ed.*]

18. Cf. *CP,* 378. [Canetti's German coinage *Entwandlung,* cited by Laemmle, is translated by Stewart simply as "unmasking," which obscures the play on words with German *Verwandlung* ("transformation"); to make Laemmle's point more clearly in English, Canetti's gloss on the word, "the exact opposite of transformation," has been inserted in place of *Entwandlung* ("unmasking"). *Trans.*]

19. This report was written by the dramaturge of both Braunschweig productions, Claus-Henning Bachmann, under the title "Katastrophe, Massenwahn und Tabu," *Wort in der Zeit* 12 (1964): 44–50; hereafter cited in text.

20. Alfons-M. Bischoff, in his dissertation *Elias Canetti: Stationen zur Werk* (Bern: Lang, 1973), 80; hereafter cited in text. Bischoff's work is of obvious value for gathering together some hitherto unknown material (particularly about the plays). It is sometimes hasty in its conclusions, however, because whenever he has to pass a judgment of his own, he often reacts helplessly. Thus he writes that the language of the plays is of "enchanting brilliance" (!).

21.   Hans Heinz Holz, "Eine apokalyptisch Komödie," *Basler National-Zeitung*, 19 November 1969.

22.   Walter Benjamin, "Unmensch," from the essay "Karl Kraus," in *Illuminationen* (Frankfurt am Main: Suhrkamp, 1961), 394 ff.; likewise "Kriegerdenkmal," in *Einbahnstrasse* (Frankfurt am Main: Suhrkamp, 1965), 74–76; Theodor W. Adorno, "Juvenals Irrtum," in *Minima Moralia* (Frankfurt am Main: Suhrkamp, 1969), 280–83.

23.   Georg Lukács, "Zur Frage der Satire," in *Essays über Realismus* (Neuwied: Luchterhand, 1971), 90.

24.   Elias Canetti, "Der neue Karl Kraus" (lecture given at the Berliner Akademie der schönen Künste, 1974). [Since published in *CW,* 214–35. *Trans.*]

Utopian Dissent: Canetti's Dramatic Fictions

Dagmar Barnouw

1

In the twentieth century social imagination has been driven by dystopian rather than utopian energies, ostensibly because utopian possibility has receded before the "can do" of modern technology. Technocracy, however, has contributed not only to the increase of social and political problems but also to their solution. The real issue seems to be not so much the fact but the kind of creation, the various and ever-more rapid ways of change that, more than anything else, have lit up the age-old limitations of utopian models, their stasis and immutability. For the time being, utopian thought seems better served by the nonbinding reality of computer-created virtual worlds with their cheerfully mobile independence of time/space contingencies. It is no accident that almost all utopian communities since the eighteenth century have succumbed to the old utopian "corruptio pessima optimi"—a self-destruction intimately connected with these communities' sharp self-separation from the larger world.[1] Their spatial-temporal-ideological fortification and remoteness, their loquacious unanimity, their silenced contradictions ultimately turned them into dystopias.

Utopian fictions, nourished by the desire for paradisiacal origins, provided the model for this self-separation and limitation. Their radical exclusion of historical time—that is, the awareness of changing lifeworlds and lifetimes—had its source in the hope of regaining the innocence and wholeness of the beginning: the inviolability of community and the exemption from the destructive effects of time passing, finally the threat of death. Since More's *Utopia,* the elaborately constructed society on the artificial island "No-Place," Utopia has attracted the visitor/observer precisely with its radical artificiality. More's fiction was meant as a counterprojection to the economic chaos in early sixteenth-century England. As such it was conceived not as a social organism subject to temporal change but as the best possible social construct that would endure forever just as it had been planned at a certain point in time. This obvious contradiction at the core of the concept of Utopia has

This essay was written specifically for this volume and is published for the first time by permission of the author.

arguably been one of the main reasons for the fascination utopian fictions have held over the centuries. Rejecting the experiences of a shared temporal lifeworld, a shared past, the construct of utopian community is created as timeless and fully authorized—as good as, or even better than, paradise. Utopia becomes dystopia as soon as its radical constructedness becomes questionable—a process that requires a radical change in perception that eventually leads to dystopian self-destruction. It is not the visitor's different perspective that causes the breach that makes Utopia permeable to time and change. It is, rather, the insights of local dissidents trying to break out of the suprahistorical, inhumanly "perfect" construct: Zamyatin's mathematically constructed city of glass, Huxley's biochemically engineered stability defeating the fear of death, Orwell's Big-Brotherly rule by all-embracing psychological terror. The utopian dissenters' goal is the return to the contradictions, unresolvable conflicts, and contingencies of historical social experience changing in time. There are no travelers in dystopia who look at the hitherto unseen, listen to the unheard-of, and admiringly report on it. Rather, the inhabitants of utopia themselves begin to see the dystopian features of their community. Where the traveler to Utopia wishes to understand the logic of the construct offered for inspection and to reconstruct it as a whole in his narration, the dissenting inhabitant of Utopia dissects that logic and thereby removes it from representation. Dystopias are meant to be warning signals, appeals to the need for change. The more clearly they indicate that their artificiality is inherently self-destructing, the more effective they are.

Canetti's drama *Die Befristeten* (*The Numbered*), written while he was working on *Masse und Macht* (*Crowds and Power*), presents dystopia at its purest, because the construct, the new order, is revealed as a consummately planned and executed deception.[2] This is of course true for all ideological rule, all organized attempts to fit other persons into a system controlled by allegedly unchanging, unquestionable laws. The unmasking of ideologically based and constructed political rule as a lie is one of the preconditions for revealing the dystopian nature of a community. But in the dystopian society of *The Numbered*, where human temporal transformation is halted by the a priori determined duration of each individual's life, the dystopian symbiosis between ideological control and deception is at its most intimate and powerful: the deceptive state control over the subjects' life span is itself the source for the basic structures of social conduct. To Canetti, for whom the mass destruction of human life was the core experience of the twentieth century, the manipulation of lifetime in the society of *The Numbered* would indeed mean the ultimate bad place.

Like Canetti's dramas of the 1930s, *Hochzeit* (*The Wedding*) and *Komödie der Eitelkeit* (*Comedy of Vanity*), *The Numbered* is a *Lese-Drama*, a text to be read, a play for radio rather than for the stage, to be heard rather than seen. More clearly than the earlier texts, it is a also a teaching drama whose "message" suits to perfection the dystopian mode of decomposition, playing on the connection between utopian construction and dystopian self-destruction. This format does not necessarily make the text a more successful dramatic fiction, but it does make it a coherent and satisfying intellectual fiction.[3] Culled from the voices of the novel *Die Blendung* (*Auto-da-Fé*), blaring out accusations of social corruption, the two early dramas use their dystopian settings in intriguing but also problematic ways. This is partly due to the—at the time—overwhelming influence of Karl Kraus on Canetti. In his different roles as political journalist and dramatist, philosophical sociolinguist, and neo-idealist poet, and above all as a brilliantly gifted speaker who brought to life the voices of others in order to annihilate them, Kraus is powerfully present in all of Canetti's prewar texts.

Canetti celebrated this influence in later essays, emphasizing Kraus's "absolute," almost demoniacal social and political responsibility and his near fantastic ability to open his readers' and listeners' ears to the great plurality of Viennese voices.[4] But he also described here his attempts at freeing himself from the enslaving power of Kraus's "acoustic quotation" (*CW,* 32) by becoming a writer himself, the author of *Auto-da-Fé*. These attempts seem to me only partially successful in the novel, and they have much to do with its grandiosely flawed composition, which is repeated, if on a minor scale, in the two dramas. The great number of "acoustic masks" recorded by means of acoustic quotation in *Auto-da-Fé* do indeed represent a stunning symbiosis of the comical and the terrible: Kraus had forced Canetti to let himself be pursued, persecuted by the voices of Vienna, drawn to them as if into an explosive microcosm of the social and political ills of the war and the postwar period. The effectiveness of the novel and the early dramas depends on a sudden defamiliarization of these voices in the acoustic masks so that their "literalness" will reveal their "horror."[5] Canetti had experienced the—to him—unique speaker Kraus as a "master of horror" who forced his listeners to join together in a "uniform and unchangeable," an "absolute" stance against war (*CW,* 33). This fact in particular was, in the older Canetti's view, the core of the irresistible attraction that Kraus exerted on the young Canetti and the overwhelming majority of young Viennese intellectuals in the years between the two world wars.[6]

Instructively, the young writer's sensation of consisting of many figures was affirmed by both the plurality of voices that Kraus enabled his listeners to distinguish and the ordering power of his sentences as judgments, particularly in his antiwar teaching drama *Die letzten Tage der Menschheit* (*The Last Days of Mankind*). Kraus, his text as he read it, was for him justice (see *CW,* 137–38). He had learned from his master to select those voices from the contemporary Viennese Babel that most promptly and stunningly indicted themselves, since Kraus focused exclusively on acoustic masks in the moment of their capitulation. Quoting, he let the hunted allow themselves to be caught in the snares of their cant, and the fact of the catch itself confirmed the authority of his judgment. His enormous effect on audiences derived largely from his seemingly magical ability to pull even the most aggressive voices toward the snare that then closed on them as if with inexorable logic. In retrospect, Canetti finally understood and revolted against the superhuman effort and absolute superiority of the person who, in quoting others, became the author of the real, utterly contemptible meaning of their statements. The second volume of Canetti's autobiography, *Die Fackel im Ohr* (*The Torch in My Ear*), the title a play on the name of Kraus's influential journal *Die Fackel,* narrates the process of this revolt. Here the cruel brilliance of the master's performance of other voices is stunningly evoked in Canetti's description of the reaction of his enthralled listeners: their ecstatic aggressive laughter that mercilessly pursues all dissenters, the utopian unanimity in judging the wickedness of a corrupt world from which they were separated by light-years. It was a judgment that had itself become corrupt through the utopian exclusion and silencing of others.

This is an important insight into crucial limitations of Kraus's remarkable achievement. It is instructive that Canetti did not (wish to) apply it to his own work of the period before the Second World War, though his early texts could not deny Kraus's enduring influence. He consisted, as he said himself, of Kraus's sentences, both literally and figuratively, he had mimetically created himself in the master's image. Having listened to Kraus, he could no longer turn away from the voices reproduced by the master performer, and this hateful compulsion is reflected most clearly in the pandemonium of the voices of the novel. He may be rejecting the endless exposing of subhuman stupidity in the quotations and the inhuman perfection of the commentator who quotes them. He may understand the utopian exclusivity of the sentence that irrevocably distances the speaker from all that is stupid and wrong in contemporary social conduct. He may accuse Kraus of having built a "Great Wall of China" whose utopian perfection and impenetrability threatened to diminish and paralyze what it had been built to protect (*CW,* 35–36). The central theme of *The Torch in My Ear* is Canetti's seduction by Kraus's moral and intellectual absolutism and his gradual self-distancing from Kraus in finding his own way in *Auto-da-Fé* to the representation of the troubling reality of the 1930s. But if he wrote himself free in the novel, he did so only by showing how much and how well he had learned from Kraus. Moreover, Kraus's influence would linger on, albeit complexly transformed, in *The Numbered.*

2

When Canetti refers to the essentially dramatic nature of all his texts, he means his approach of letting others speak in their own voices.[7] He wrote *The Wedding* in the winter of 1931–1932 in response both to the social and political anxieties of these years and to Büchner's *Wozzeck.*[8] In Büchner's characters he found the same capacity for "self-denunciation" that determines the characters of *Auto-da-Fé* (*PE,* 15–18), and he was impressed by the unmediated vitality of Büchner's figures, be they victims or victimizers. The poet's justice, he argued, was not to condemn his characters; he can create their victims and show their impact on them. It seemed to him that Büchner had been successful in creating characters whose identity was not dimmed by their suffering and who yet exhibited the impact of that suffering. This is indeed a perceptive comment on a highly talented dramatist's strategies, but it has little to do with his own handling of the characters of *The Wedding* and *Comedy of Vanity.* Here, more clearly even than in *Auto-da-Fé,* he was the satirist who did not grant his figures, as did Büchner, the right to present themselves as they saw themselves, to express "the full value of the word 'I' " (*PE,* 16). The victims'—the author's—accusations stay in the foreground, always audible, and the figures remain stuck in their acoustic masks. Canetti stated in a 1937 interview with the *Wiener Sonntag* on the occasion of one of his readings from *The Wedding* that the "deeper laws of the drama" as they had become clear to him in the writing process required its structure to be derived from the spatial constellation of the characters as acoustic masks and to be as consistent and unique as the individual figures.[9] Many readers have justifiably doubted the theatrical effectiveness of the plays in view of the difficulties inherent in articulating structures of meaning through acoustic figures that are themselves— and by intention—so limited.[10] A good speaker reading the text—and by all accounts Canetti was an excellent one (Fried 15)—can help them and the structure of the play come to life by virtue of his transformative control.

Both prewar dramas are characterized by their allegorically clear contouring of antisocial speech and action and by the energy of a *Grundeinfall,* a completely new originary idea.[11] This new idea, as Canetti claimed rather grandiosely in that early interview, would "shed new light on the world as a whole," and the dramatic structure would have to derive from it, following the utopian principle of perfect construction in nowhere. The issue in *The Wedding* is the compulsion to possess objects and the concomitant exclusion of meaningful communication; in *Comedy of Vanity* it is the subject's narcissistic possession of the self that leads to destructive isolation and fragmentation. In both cases the *Grundeinfall* is overdrawn in its allegorical distinctness. In *The Wedding* the house is the most palpable presentation of the bourgeois status quo, the fetishized object at the center of everyone's wishes and desires. In *Comedy of Vanity* it is the forbidden mirror on which isolated, unauthentic characters fix their crazed desire for identity. In both cases the greed of the characters—to be in possession of objects, of themselves—is expressed by explosively inarticulate acoustic masks limited to accusations and threats. *The Wedding* reveals all social relations to be property relations: this is true no less of marital fidelity than of sexual promiscuity. The house condenses the omnipresent greed so that it becomes an icon of the craving for permanence and stability that then cannot but paralyze all human interaction. The figures' speaking, shouting past each other, comes to a climax when one of the wedding guests suggests a parlor game. As his name suggests, Horch (in Honegger's English translation, Hark) listens to and connects with other people, whereby his acoustic mask acquires more verbal range.[12] He asks everybody to come up with ideas how they would rescue the person dearest to them during an earthquake. But his appeal to the guests' humanity is at the same time an open admission—even a celebration—of lying as the core of all social communication. No reader, listener, or viewer can then be surprised when the characters' answers reveal the material and sexual greed that is fully realized when the earthquake actually happens. Their author has constructed an inhumanly perfect dystopia by having everyone's word and by leaving the dissenter nothing to say.

The dystopia of *Comedy of Vanity* is conceptually more complex and less predictable in its self-destruction. However, it shares with *The Wedding* (and *Auto-da-Fé*) the core problem of the author's excessive verbal control, which is central to the conceit of the acoustic mask. The drama's *Grundeinfall* is that the utopian taboo on all mirrors and photographs—which was intended to eradicate the antisocial vanity of the pre-utopian period—has instead intensified solipsism immeasurably. Thus more or less normal, if not particularly admirable, egocentricity has developed into pathological ego-addictiveness.[13] Very expensive brothels sell self-gratification instead of sexual intercourse by providing the forbidden experience of seeing oneself in a mirror. Casual eye contact with others has become masturbatory self-reflection. The utopian prohibition of self-images has undermined all mediation of social norms, since it has made affirmation of self-value impossible. Poor people who cannot afford the large admission fees charged by the brothels are begging for flattery in the streets. The maid Marie, presumably less corrupted by (pre-utopian) bourgeois self-presentation than other figures, laments that there are no more windowpanes to polish: they have all been replaced by frosted glass. She does not need a man in her bed, she tells the preacher; she needs a mirror in her room; she would only fight with the man anyway. In this mirrorless society people are constantly fighting because, unable to develop self-perception, they lack perceptiveness in relation to others.

The absence of mirrors has repressed the normally intersubjective and interactive ego-development that begins with the newborn's learning to make visual contact with other people. Marie's contempt for the man who does not expect from her some attention to her looks is to be seen as positive: her acoustic mask has traits of dissent. Remaking oneself (*sich zurechtmachen*) by rearranging one's hair, applying make-up in preparation for being seen by the other person requires a glance in the mirror. Self-esteem also means both appreciating the esteem of the other person and showing this appreciation in one's self-presentation. The preacher is not interested in these connections; he works with a religious recipe against the sin of using a mirror. Presenting

Marie with a mirror, he expects her to be horrified by the sinfulness of possessing it. But Marie is horrified by the consequences of what she sees in the mirror: the face that looks back at her is alien because it has developed independently of her and her relations to others, and it is therefore unacceptable. Ten years have passed without her looking at and arranging herself, without her tracing a gradual and then perceptible transformation. Marie rubs at the mirror in a rage and, finding it worse than useless now, gives it away to an old woman. She puts it to good use by charging high fees for healing the now common mirror deficiency syndrome, a sort of psychological paralysis caused by the withdrawal of self-images and the consequent lack of self-awareness and capacity for transformation.

These connections are both obvious and hidden, because none of the acoustic masks would have enough words—not to speak of language—to articulate them. Canetti again relies here too much on Kraus's symbiosis of literalness and horror, *Wörtlichkeit und Entsetzen,* which, in its complete authorial control of *Entsetzen,* disregards the potential of other speakers' *Wörtlichkeit.* The self-destruction of this society—the drama ends with a revolt of mirror-deprived individuals screaming "I" who smash all remaining mirrors and burn all images—is not brought about by dissenters able to speak intelligently about the dystopian corruption of what they had been told to see as the good (better) place. This self-destruction is too obviously the construct of its author, whose interest in its possible meanings is too limited.

The prohibition of mirrors, which is meant to weaken individual egocentricity, has not brought about the promised good (better) community but rather an extreme of social fragmentation and polarization. In their ever more rigid fixation on an increasingly hollow notion of selfhood, people have lost the ability to engage with each other as individuals and have been sucked into destructive mass-eruptions—the central theme that connects Canetti's prewar texts. Despite his unshakable belief in the theatrical effectiveness of the early dramas (see Barnouw 1996, 160–61), they have been performed very rarely. The reason given most frequently (and justifiably) is their *Kopflastigkeit,* their cerebral quality, the dominating role of conceptual patterns.[14] The novelty of the absolutely new *Grundeinfall* is too self-referential and the negativity of the grotesque characters too relentless: they could never have been— would never be—different, whatever their social environment. This is, of course, a systemic dystopian problem, but it is intensified here by the violent obviousness and rigidity of the acoustic masks that prohibit transformation. There is also a compactness of conceptual organization that can be taken apart and put together again at leisure by readers but that is not easily accessible to viewers limited by the short duration of a performance. The very weight of this compactness threatens to undermine the literalness of the *Grundeinfall*—the house and the mirror as allegories for social alienation and fragmentation—and thereby also its effectiveness as a warning signal.

3

The Numbered was not meant to work as a drama in the stricter sense. Apart perhaps from the greater immediacy of the dialogical structure, it might have worked just as well as an essay or story, were it not for Canetti's enduring preoccupation with the dramatic challenge of giving voice to others' voices. His experience of the war and of working with the materials that went into *Crowds and Power* had taught him to be appreciative of a greater variety of voices and to reproduce them accordingly. The social order of *The Numbered* is based on what is for temporal beings the most unfair, "unequal" aspect of their existence, the distribution of lifetime. At birth each is given a name that tells the number of the allotted years. Knowing the date of their death gives the Numbered a security that has eluded their pre-utopian ancestors. The new order is presented to them as the new freedom from the contingencies that plagued people in the past, since, freed from the randomness of death, they can really plan and arrange their lives as they see fit. The utopian improvement on the past turns out to be the basis of the power of the totalitarian regime under whose rule—the rule of death—intersubjective relations have been almost completely destroyed. In the prologue the reader or listener, who here takes the place of the utopian traveler, is informed that mankind's acquisition of the knowledge of "the moment" (of death) has been the greatest step forward in the history of the species. Before that people had been living in "barbarian" uncertainty, like animals more than humans. But, as the dissident Fifty comes to understand, it is the Numbered, the subjects of death, who, knowing their "moment," resemble animals that in their innocence of death are simply subject to the laws of nature. The pre-utopian barbarians, in contrast, had been able to elude the rule of death at least temporarily by not knowing beforehand when they had to die. Together with Fifty, the protagonist of the argument that dismantles the dystopian order, we discover that in this society every command is a death sentence and every death its execution. In rituals celebrating the utopian happiness of the Numbered as the status quo of the Unequal (*die Ungleichen*), the state ideology presents their liberation from the sting of death as mediating between the rule of natural laws and the dignity of the individual. Allotting to each Numbered a death that is both anonymous and personal, this ideology systematically hides the possibility both of death sentences and of their execution.

As the dystopias of *The Wedding* and *Comedy of Vanity* referred to the explosive social and political problems of the 1930s, so the dystopia of *The Numbered* reflects the troubling implications of limited lifetime for modern societies even, particularly, at their most stable and "normal." There is no great distance between the conduct of the Numbered vis-à-vis their limited lifetime and our own. Our private taboo where death is concerned is the public taboo of the Numbered. The very fact of this taboo obscures a fuller understanding of intersubjective relations.[15] Over many decades Canetti wrote down aphoristic projections—many of them potential dramatic *Grund-einfälle*—of societies that have not abolished death but have acknowledged it as a serious social problem. Not surprisingly, some of these create their own considerable difficulties: cities, in which people live as long as they are loved; where they disappear for longer or shorter periods; where one is born old and becomes younger; where everyone has at least two ages and can be for instance simultaneously 59 and 23 years old. In 1981 he asked: "A land where *some* of the dead return. Which, and why?"[16] Common to all these projections is the perceived need to keep open for everyone the potential of transformation and not to arrest this process prematurely by accepting too easily the death of others.[17]

Canetti's concern has not been an eternal life but rather a longer and better one, taking seriously, as few writers have done, the social and political implications of the experience of death, the arch-anxiety of time passing, the arch-desire for permanence. In his view a longer life should be a better one,[18] which means, to begin with, a consistent respect for each individual life. Everyone is owed the chance to live their life as long and meaningfully as possible. This has become a new and in some ways unexpected challenge to modern societies at the end of this century when astonishing developments in medical technology that increasingly do indeed prolong life have created ever greater ethical problems. Canetti's dystopian, dissenting perspective could be useful here because it illuminates so sharply certain important aspects of these questions. One of them is the new fact that the costliness of these new treatment protocols, which then are not available to everyone who needs them, has already created a new inequality with regard to available lifetime. Canetti could not have foreseen these developments, but they are intimately connected with his plea for an understanding of the quintessentially social dimension of the experience of death. His concrete concern in his dramatic essay was the most basic aspect of that dimension from which everything follows: the connection between the enduring inertia of social relations, the constant reassertion of a status quo, and our predictably limited life span that makes us all more easily disposable—at such and such a time we will reliably be gone. Being able to take for granted a certain duration for a generation's presence and then its absence has made it much easier to plan for the future—as in *The Numbered*. Instructively, such planning is increasingly seen to be "threatened" by the increase in life expectancy and the demographics of aging populations. At the same time we accept the determinant nature of aging as a constant decrease of the individual's vitality and "market value" and have made our arrangements accordingly. The degradation and gradual decline caused by the approach of death has been a social-psychological problem much discussed in Western societies at the end of this century, but it seems to be very difficult to deal with it concretely and intelligently, other than by making it easier to die.

Canetti has done a great deal to unmask the palpable physical cruelty at the core of many of the social abstractions of the problem of death, not least in his discussion of the survivor as victor with respect to the dead in *Crowds and Power.*[19] After the completion of *The Numbered,* he recorded reflections on the repulsive satiation of the victor, his gloating contentment at being alive where others were dead. And yet it was impossible not to be a victor over every person one had known well and survived. To go on living without being (in that sense) a victor seemed to him as impossibly difficult as "the moral squaring of the circle" (*HP,* 138). The state ideology of *The Numbered* offers a solution to this challenge that cannot but reveal itself to be dystopian but that can nevertheless be related to our situation in Western societies at the end of the twentieth century. If, at a certain age, we become less willing to let it be known exactly how old we are, if we keep secret our birthdays, our age, our probable number of remaining years, so too this information has been a lifelong secret kept by the state in the society of *The Numbered.* A priest who is also a state official, the Keeper of Lockets, fastens around the neck of every newborn a capsule protected by a strong taboo that contains the date of birth and, since the number of years each individual is permitted to live is announced in the name, thereby also the date of death. This official alone is permitted to open the capsule at death and confirm its correctly predicted date. Since, with the a priori determined lifetime, the approach of death can signify a socially weaker position, the public concealment of the birthday is quite welcome and becomes internalized, a private secret. Fifty, whose time will be up very shortly, tries to share his gradual insight into the real meaning of these rituals with other members of the Numbered. At issue is their understanding the illusory nature of their freedom from the fear of death and the absolute social injustice of their inequality with respect to their life span since it is based on a random distribution—and then rigid possession—of chronological time. Like Canetti for whom he speaks here, Fifty thinks monstrous the idea that we have been made a present of life (cf. *HP,* 244). His subversive restlessness and disbelief move him to unmask the "natural law" of death. The holy "moment" of death, with its utopian significance, is in dystopian reality nothing but an execution protected and covered by the instructions of the priest who is an official of the state.

Fifty, however, encounters great difficulties when he appeals to an extra-utopian reality principle. The illusory freedom of choice within the utopian limitations occupies the social imagination of the great majority of the Numbered and thus works as a reliable support for the ruling system. Carefully controlled "indiscretions" about the remaining amount of lifetime are spread like rumors about the stock market and further isolate the members of the Numbered. The few people who understand this situation have withdrawn into resignation and do not believe that Fifty will be able to achieve anything given the deeply rooted rule of death. The unequal limitations, the arbitrarily granted allotment of years, have created a hierarchy that operates as reliably as a machine and is enacted by the chorus of the Unequal that concludes the first part of the drama. To the Keeper of Lockets's ritual question whether they like being together they answer "no," because they will be separated and are waiting for "the moment" of separation. Deprived of the fear of death, this most human reaction, they have been deprived of the equality and the bonding with others in the face of its sting. Still alive, they are already as separated as if they were dead because death here is the great unequalizer. It is consistent with the logic of this new order that the dystopians only connect as equals when urging Fifty to desist from his heretical doubting of the rule of death by natural law.

Fifty is the quintessential dissenter in this quintessential dystopia. It is true, he is coresponsible for the enduring rule of death since he has accepted the status quo for a long time. But he can also see the situation more clearly than others because he has not kept track of the number of the years he has lived. Preoccupied with living, he really does not know when exactly he is supposed to die. Above all, his not wanting to die himself means also that he does not want others to keep on dying so cooperatively. Argument by argument, he reveals first his and then every death to be the result of a death sentence passed a priori and thereby the theocratic basis of the omnipotent rule of death. Without having to lie, he can admit as well as deny to the Keeper of Lockets the fiftieth return of his birthday. Most important, he can really negotiate his "moment" with the priest who represents the power of the state. Fifty's temporary respite comes from his proving that the taboo-protected moment of death is not determined by a law of nature enacted in religious terms but by the mundane needs of theocratic rule. Exposing the utopian political control by means of religious concepts like contrition, recantation, and grace, he can himself use them strategically. The truly revolutionary aspect of his dissent is its rigorous secularism.

As with all revolutionary acts, however, destabilizing energies create their own problems, and this fact becomes part of the play's dramatic logic. When Canetti compared Fifty to Brecht's Galileo, whose new physics destabilized not just the scientific but also the social and psychological self-perception of his contemporaries, he was not only drawing attention to the cultural importance of his own new insights (*HP,* 191). He was reflecting on the fact that the disintegration of familiar order, regardless how good or bad, brings with it uncertainties and thereby a greater vulnerability to new ideological systems—utopian constructs that always already carry the seed of their own dystopian decomposition. The young dramatist did not deal with this dynamic, notwithstanding his claims made in hindsight that, an act of dissent at the time, he had understood and revealed the dystopian aspects of Kraus's utopian pursuit of verbal purity. The utopian-dystopian dynamic has been as central to twentieth-century social politics as it has been destructive, and it was not addressed in the early dramas. With all their occasional verbal brilliance and their intriguing *Grundeinfälle* that seem to touch on important issues of their time, these texts now seem curiously innocent of that period's complexities and therefore dated.

Despite its limitations as dramatic fiction *The Numbered* has aged quite well; an intricate argument that seems as cogent and valid today as it was half a century ago is well served by the very "undramatic" pace and verbal sobriety of the text. Fifty has temporarily freed himself from "his" death forced on him by the power of the utopian state. At some point in time he will die; but first he has gained human time, lifetime—like all things human a relative gain and precisely for this reason not to be despised.[20] Most of the Numbered, however, are no longer capable of this insight. Their utopian socialization has left them so isolated that they cannot use this kind of liberation intelligently. Since their own potential for transformation has been so unjustly limited, they can longer see themselves in their interdependency with other persons' need for transformation. During his work on the text, Canetti reflected on the injustice of death as a death sentence inflicted a priori: "We have to be bad because we know we will die. We would be even worse if, from the very start, we knew when" (*HP,* 129). In the utopia of the Numbered, the fear of death has been muted by the religious presentation of the rule of death. Their wickedness shows itself in the inhuman indifference with which they simply accept as a law of nature what is, for conscious beings, the most unnatural thing: that there will be an end to consciousness. It turns out— logically in terms of the dramatic argument—that Fifty's most important opponent is not the Keeper of Lockets but his best, most sympathetic dialogue partner, Friend, and he—again logically—has the last word.

Friend has been open to Fifty's dissenting arguments because he has never stopped mourning his beloved sister Twelve. Under the rule of death mourning is subversive, not to be tolerated. When Fifty argues with a young woman who has just buried her child Seven that one should at least try to resist "the moment" in order to get the child more lifetime, she counters with the utopian prescriptions for motherly love that she had strictly followed. Beyond her "moment" the child is nothing but a shadow to the mother, no longer real. If the child went on living, it would no longer be her child but a ghostly witness to her crime against a society that imposes the death sentence in the case of heretical nonacceptance of death. The emotion of mourning alone signifies dissent and is punishable under the law, consequences that Friend has accepted courageously. But after Fifty's precarious victory—he broke the taboo and escaped—Friend implores him now to stop assailing the fact of death as law of nature. Fifty, however, naturally thinks and acts in cultural, that is, social terms. Instinctively, he includes others in the consequences of his revolt and logically this means here death as well as life. The precondition for not accepting death as a foregone conclusion is that everybody acknowledges the other person's right to their own life instead of death. But Friend is no longer capable of doing that. Immediately after Fifty's unmasking of "the moment" he sets off on a search for Twelve, who now might still be alive and grown into a young woman. Fifty tries in vain to keep him back, arguing that Friend ought to set her free, not continue owning her as he had tried to do when mourning her premature death. At the end of the drama Friend's decision to search for and find *his* sister is unshakable.

In Fifty's view, this in many ways understandable human desire to possess the other, reflected also in Friend's mourning more his loss of the sister than hers, was vulnerable to exploitation by the utopian rule of death. Abolishing the uncertainty regarding the time of death and thereby deadening its sting also meant numbing or, as in Friend's case, refocusing the pain of loss for the living. The utopian isolation, as Fifty has shown, negates this pain. Friend cannot understand all the implications of Fifty's dissenting view because it presents the social dimension of human life so literally. It was precisely Fifty's lack of desire to possess other people in life that enabled his insight into the social meanings of the experience of death: an indispensable insight because it makes this experience subject to human time and human measure. The underlying challenge of this and of all of Canetti's postwar texts—that we can truly share the world only if we overcome the desire to have power over others—is itself the most powerful and "unnatural" utopian desire and in that by no means harmless. Its absolutism echoes that of Kraus, if in more muted and soberly reflected form, and it has no doubt been central to Canetti's dissent, provocative and thoughtful, from the utopias of the status quo.

Notes

1. See Dagmar Barnouw, *Die versuchte Realität oder von der Möglichkeit, glücklichere Welten zu denken* (Meitingen: Corian, 1985), chaps. 1 ("Die Möglichkeit von Utopie: Wie betritt man eine andere Welt?") and 2 ("Die Realität von Utopie: Wie verhält man sich in einer anderen Welt?").

2. Translations of *Die Befristeten* have appeared under two different titles: the present essay refers to *The Numbered,* trans. Carol Stewart (London: Marion Boyars, 1984); an alternative version is found in *"Comedy of Vanity" and "Life-Terms,"* trans. Gitta Honegger (New York: PAJ Publications, 1983).

3. See Peter Iden, "Mich brennt der Tod," *Frankfurter Rundschau,* 24 August 1994; Hans Hollmann, "Erfinder der Akustischen Maske: Über Elias Canetti, den Dramatiker, Denker und Todesfeind," in *Wortmasken: Texte zu Leben und Werk von Elias Canetti,* ed. Carl Hanser Verlag (Munich: Hanser, 1995), 83–88; Wolfgang Hädecke, "Die moralische Quadratur des Zirkels: Das Todesproblem im Werk Elias Canettis," *Text und Kritik* 28, rev. ed. (1982): 27–32; and Reinhard Urbach, "Der präsumptive Todestag: Bemerkungen zu Elias Canettis *Die Befristeten,*" *Literatur und Kritik* 3 (1968): 404–8.

4. Elias Canetti, *The Conscience of Words,* trans. Joachim Neugroschel (London: Deutsch, 1979), 33–34; hereafter cited in text as *CW.*

5. Canetti identified *"literalness* and *horror"* as crucial components of the effect that Kraus achieved (*CW,* 31).

6. See Gerald Stieg, "Elias Canetti und Karl Kraus: Ein Versuch," *Modern Austrian Literature* 16, no. 3/4 (1983): 197–210.

7.   Elias Canetti, "Gespräch mit Horst Bienek," *Die gespaltene Zukunft: Aufsätze und Gespräche,* Reihe Hanser 111 (Munich: Hanser, 1972), 101.

8.   Elias Canetti, *The Play of the Eyes,* trans. Ralph Manheim (New York: Farrar, Straus and Giroux, 1986), 3–18; hereafter cited in text as *PE.*

9.   Quoted in Erich Fried, *Elias Canetti: Welt im Kopf* (Graz: Stiasny, 1962), 14; hereafter cited in text.

10.   See Dagmar Barnouw, *Elias Canetti: Zur Einführung* (Hamburg: Junius, 1996), 161; hereafter cited in text as Barnouw 1996.

11.   Regarding the former, see Dagmar Barnouw, " 'Noch ist das Lachen erlaubt': Dystopische Komik im Drama der Eitelkeit," *Sprache im technischen Zeitalter* 95 (1985): 200–206.

12.   Elias Canetti, *The Wedding,* trans. Gitta Honegger (New York: PAJ Publications, 1986).

13.   Regarding the play's *Grundeinfall,* the prohibition of mirrors, Canetti describes how, at the barber's one day, he was irritated by having to look into the mirror for the duration of the haircut but enthralled by the other customers' fascination with their own image (*PE,* 90).

14.   See Peter Laemmle, "Macht und Ohnmacht des Ohrenzeugen: Zur Kategorie des Dramatischen in Canettis frühen Stücken," *Canetti lesen: Erfahrungen mit seinen Büchern,* ed. Herbert G. Göpfert (Munich: Hanser, 1975), 48. [Laemmle's essay appears in English translation elsewhere in the present volume. *Ed.*]

15.   "The man who really knew what ties people together would be able to save them from death. The enigma of life is a social enigma. No one is on its track" (Elias Canetti, *The Human Province,* trans. Joachim Neugroschel [New York: Seabury, 1978], 194; hereafter cited in text as *HP*).

16.   Elias Canetti, *The Secret Heart of the Clock: Notes, Aphorisms, Fragments, 1973–1985,* trans. Joel Agee (New York: Farrar, Straus and Giroux, 1989), 96; hereafter cited in text as *SHC.*

17.   Canetti's stance against death has been vulnerable to many misunderstandings because of its radical originality, especially since it reflects, at the same time, a peculiarly perceptive, troubling common sense; see Barnouw 1996, 8–10, 201–17.

18.   "Is everyone too good to die? One can't say that. First everyone would have to live longer" (*HP,* 48).

19.   His reflections here are focused much more generally and do not refer to the guilt of the survivor common in situations of war and persecution.

20.   In 1985 the 80-year-old noted: "Here he stands, looking at Death. Death approaches him, he repels it. He will not do Death the honor of taking it into account. If he finally does break down in bewilderment—he didn't bow before Death. He called it by its name, he hated it, he cast it out. He has accomplished so little, it is more than nothing" (*SHC,* 150).

CROWDS AND POWER

◆

Crowds and Power

Elias Canetti and Theodor W. Adorno, in Conversation

ADORNO: I know that you are very critical of Freud and differ greatly from him on many points. But there is one methodological point on which you and he surely agree. That point is one that he emphasized most strongly when psychoanalysis was still in its formative stages and was still a cohesive project. Namely, that he had no intention of challenging or rejecting the conclusions of established scientists but only of adding something that those conclusions had overlooked. To be sure, he understood the reasons for this oversight as something essential, as something key to the way in which human beings coexist. I believe, if you wish, you might best be able to illustrate that point by referring to the central role that the question of death plays in your work, as indeed in many (in the broadest sense) anthropological works of our time; and so, in order to give our listeners too an idea, a model, of what has actually been overlooked with respect to the whole matter of death (if one may be forgiven for speaking so bombastically of this most elementary phenomenon), you might be able to identify those points—having to do with the experience of death—to which you attach so much importance. This would reveal the productiveness of your method and make clear not only that you write about things that have received little attention elsewhere but also that there is a danger precisely in the unquestioning way in which these matters have been presumed, a danger that you, in the spirit of enlightenment, seek to alleviate by bringing it to our attention.

CANETTI: It is perfectly correct that the consideration of death plays an important role in my investigation. If I might offer an example of what you have indicated, it would be the question of survival, to which, in my view, far too little attention has been paid. The moment of one person's surviving another is a *concrete* one, and I believe that the experience of such a moment has enormous consequences. I believe that this experience is masked by convention, by the things that one is *supposed* to feel when another person dies,

Translated by Bruce Krajewski and David Darby for this volume from Elias Canetti, "Gespräch mit Theodor W. Adorno," in *Die gespaltene Zukunft: Aufsätze und Gespräche*, Reihe Hanser 111 (Munich: Hanser, 1972), 66–92. The conversation was broadcast by radio in March 1962 and appears here by kind permission of the Carl Hanser Verlag.

but that, hidden beneath those things lie certain feelings of satisfaction, which can sometimes—for example, in the case of a fight—amount even to triumph, and that something quite dangerous can result if they happen often and accumulate. And this dangerous accumulation of the experience of others' deaths is, I believe, an absolutely essential seed of power. I am offering this example out of context, without elaboration. Since you have brought up Freud, let me be the first to admit that the way in which he approached things anew, without distraction or fear, made a deep impression on me in my formative period. It is certainly true that I no longer consider some of his findings convincing, and that I must oppose some of his specific theories. But for his way of approaching things I retain the deepest respect.

ADORNO: Here I feel the need to observe that you have touched on a very strong connection between the two of us. In the *Dialektik der Aufklärung* (*Dialectic of Enlightenment*) Horkheimer and I have analyzed the problem of self-preservation, of reason preserving itself. We realized that this principle of self-preservation, as it was classically and initially formulated by Spinoza, and which you call in your terminology the moment of survival (that is, the situation of survival in the succinct sense), is unstable. When this motive of self-preservation, so to speak, runs wild and severs the connections between the individual and the group, it transforms itself into a destructive power, into ruin, and simultaneously always into self-destruction too. You did not know our work on this subject, nor we yours. I do not believe that this correspondence is serendipitous. Rather, it may point to something more substantial, a crisis of self-preservation, of survival, run wild, which has become directly relevant to the present situation.[1]

CANETTI: I am very happy to learn that your deliberations have produced similar results to my own, and I believe that the fact that they have been reached independently contributes substantially to their persuasiveness.

ADORNO: I agree. On the other hand, I believe that there is a methodological problem, which for our purposes, namely of establishing the context of your thinking, must be taken into account. To a thinker such as myself, regardless of whether he calls himself a philosopher or a sociologist, your book is immediately conspicuous—and, if I may speak freely, a little outrageously so—for what I might call the subjectivity of its approach. By subjectivity I mean the subjectivity neither of the thought nor of the author but on the contrary: precisely the freewheeling quality of the subjectivity. I am fully sympathetic to the fact that this thinking does not bind itself by oath to scientific rules of play and does not respect the constraints of a division of labor. I mean by subjectivity rather the departure from the work of others in this area. Put more succinctly and more broadly, the departure from conceptual systems. Anyway, I am very aware that, not unlike Freud, you trace the fundamental concepts that you employ—crowds and power—back to real conditions, just as I would do, to real crowds and real powers, and so to real human experiences. Nevertheless, your reader will not quite lose the feeling that in your book's development the imagination, the idea of these concepts or facts (these categories blend together), is actually more important than the concepts or facts themselves. For instance, this is suggested by the concept of the invisible crowd, which plays a large role in your work. And now I would like to direct a really simple question to you, which might give our listeners a clearer idea of what is at stake. The question regards how you evaluate the real meaning of crowds and also of power, or of those holding power, in relation to the merely ideational constructs, in relation to pictures: in psychoanalytic terms, the imagoes of crowds and power that have occupied your work.

CANETTI: Let me digress somewhat in answering that. *(ADORNO: I believe that would be very helpful.)* You mention my concept of the invisible crowd. Well, I would perhaps say here that invisible crowds are not discussed until the fourteenth short chapter of the book, that they are thus preceded by 13 other chapters in which I deal intensively with real crowds. The book's approach is, I believe, as real as it can be. I begin with what I term the fear of being touched. I believe that the individual feels endangered by others and thus has a fear of being touched by the unknown and that he attempts by any means available to protect himself from that, by creating space around himself, by taking care not to come too close to others.[2] Every human being has had the experience of trying to avoid bumping into others, of disliking it when others bump into him. Whatever preventative measures he adopts, the human being never fully loses the fear of being touched. And in view of that it is very remarkable to discover his complete loss of that fear in crowds. This paradox is really important. The human being sheds the fear of being touched only when he stands closely together with others, when he is surrounded on all sides by other human beings, so that he actually no longer knows who is besetting him. At this moment he no longer fears being touched by others. It is the reversal of the fear of being touched; and I believe that one of the reasons human beings like to form crowds, why they like to surrender themselves to a crowd, is the relief they feel when their fear of being touched is reversed. I think that that is a very real starting point; it assumes a concrete experience that everyone knows from crowd situations. And in subsequent chapters I examine other aspects of real crowds. I discuss open and closed crowds. I emphasize the fact that crowds always want to grow, that this necessity of growth is essential to them. I deal with the feeling of equality within crowds and with many other things that I will refrain from naming here. Then in the fourteenth chapter I come to the concept of the invisible crowd, and on that subject I may perhaps be allowed quite briefly to say something: anyone who has occupied himself with religions, and particularly with primitive religions, will have been especially struck by the degree to which these religions are populated by crowds that people cannot in fact see. We need only think of the spirits that play such an important role in primitive religions. There are countless examples of people actually believing that the air is full of spirits, spirits appearing in the form of crowds. This is still true of our world religions. In Christianity, we know the importance of the idea of the devil and of angels. The Middle Ages provide an astonishing quantity of evidence of this. Devils are assumed to surround us in infinite numbers. One medieval Cistercian abbot, Richalm, said that he felt devils around him as populous as particles of dust, whenever he closed his eyes. Now these invisible crowds play an important role in religions and in the minds of believers. But in spite of that I would not label them unreal, since these people believe in these crowds: for them they are something utterly real. And in order to understand that fully, we need only remind ourselves that we too are familiar with invisible crowds in modern life. They are no longer devils, but they are perhaps just as dangerous, just as aggressive, and inspire just as much fear. After all, we all believe bacteria exist. Only very few people have actually seen them under a microscope, but everyone assumes that he is threatened by millions of bacteria, ever present and potentially ubiquitous; and our imaginary picture of them plays an important role.

Those then would be the invisible crowds that I would deem to be in a certain sense real, and I believe that you will admit, Dr. Adorno, that one can in a way still speak of the reality of invisible crowds.

ADORNO: Yes, if I might say something immediately in opposition to that, I would ask you to forgive an epistemologist's pedantry. First, while primitive consciousness makes no such strict distinction between reality and idea, the educated Western consciousness is really founded on this separation. The fact that archaic, primitive thinking does not yet distinguish between the idea of such jinns (or whatever spirits they may be) and their real existence does not yet mean that they have become objectively real. We cannot stand our worldview on its head, which tells us in God's name that the world is not populated by spirits. Given what you've said, it seems to me that you give a certain priority to the imaginary, to what has already shifted into the world of the imagination, over raw, immediate reality, because I do not believe—and this is perhaps not unimportant, should you go briefly into a clarification of your intentions—I do not believe that you represent the view, as Klages and Oskar Goldberg, each at opposite extremes, have represented it, that these pictures, these imagoes have their own immediate reality as collective entities, comparable in a way with the reality of crowds in modern mass-society.[3]

CANETTI: No, I would certainly not say that. Nevertheless I did manage to establish a concept that seems important to me: the concept of the crowd symbol. And I would like to expound on that. I understand crowd symbols to be collective entities that, while they do not consist of human beings, are perceived in the same way as crowds. These include our ideas of such things as fire, the ocean, the forest, fields of grain, treasure, stockpiles of many kinds—for example, stockpiles of harvested grain. Those are of course entities that exist in the real world, but they serve in the individual's mind to symbolize crowds. One has to examine these symbols in detail and describe why they have this function and what meaning accrues to them. Perhaps, as a practical example, I would say that these crowd symbols play a decisive part in the formation of national consciousness. *(ADORNO: There is no doubt about that!)* When people who consider themselves as part of a nation in an acute moment of their national existence—let us say, in the moment of national excitement such as the outbreak of war—label themselves as English, French, or German, they are thinking of a crowd or a crowd symbol, something that they can take as a point of reference. And that is extraordinarily potent in their mind and of the greatest importance to their actions. I think you would agree that the potency of such crowd symbols for individuals is incontestable.

ADORNO: I would agree fully. I think that you have come across something essential with the discovery of the forest as an imago, a crowd symbol. I take such things to be eminently productive. I believe that one can get much further with such categories than with the rather sparse archaic symbols that one finds in Freud, and with, on the other hand, the somewhat arbitrarily established archetypes of Jung. However, I would still say that even after this explanation—and it is no accident that you have attached central importance to the concept of the symbol—your interest still remains fixed essentially on those categories that have already been internalized and that are already undergoing transformation into imagoes. Now what I would like to ask you is very plain and simple, something that in a certain way should likewise also be asked of psychologically oriented social theory. That is whether you believe that these symbols actually hold the key to the problems of contemporary society, problems that primarily drive both your and my work; or whether real crowds, actual crowds in our world, that is to say simply the enormous pressure exerted by these huge numbers of people (although the organization of society potentially facilitates and hinders their survival), whether this pressure of real crowds on the formation of political will is not more important for present-day society than are the imaginary (in a wider sense social-psychological) things that you have pointed out? I might here simply remind you that it has been shown that there was always—latent even in movements that were apparently extreme dictatorships and that eliminated all democratic regard for the people's will, movements like Fascism and National Socialism—something that the sociologist Arkadij Gurland termed the character of compromise.[4] That is, even in these tyrannical forms of rule, a respect for the real interests of crowds and for their real existence has asserted itself in however concealed a way. And what interests me now, and what you could perhaps say something about, concerns the significance you attach in your understanding of society and of crowds to this weight, the real import of crowds, as opposed to the entire domain of the symbolic.

CANETTI: Yes, of course I would say that the value, the significance of real crowds is far higher. I would not hesitate for a moment. I would even go so far as to say that the dictatorships that we have experienced consist entirely of crowds, that the power of dictatorships would be quite unimaginable without the growth of crowds, which is especially important, and without the deliberate and artificial stimulation of ever larger crowds. That fact underlies my whole examination of this subject. Probably anyone, any contemporary of ours during the last half-century, since the outbreak of the First World War, who has lived through the reality of wars, then revolutions, periods of inflation, and then the Fascist dictatorship, has probably, under the weight of these things, felt the necessity of coming to grips with the question of crowds. I would really be very unhappy if the fact that I have—in the course of many years of study—achieved an understanding of other aspects of the crowd led anyone to think that the significance of real crowds were not the decisive and the most important question of all.

ADORNO: That seems to me to be of fundamental importance for correctly understanding your intention. If I may here express a theoretical thought myself, then it would be a kind of mediation, not in the sense of a compromise, however, but rather in the sense of the concept as it is used in Hegel, to acknowledge that it is given that the real pressure of what you have correctly recognized as the deeply intertwined categories of crowds and power has grown, that for the individual it is infinitely harder to resist this pressure, to assert himself. Because of that the symbolic significance of these categories has also grown. It is only because of that pressure that people in their inner life are at the same time withdrawing, in a state of introversion, into archaic phases, in which such a substantial significance has attached itself to these categories, even as internalized categories. People are identifying themselves completely in relation to them. It is probably only due to this that it is at all possible for them to come to terms with their own disempowerment, resulting from the growth of these two correlative categories; namely by putting it in terms that are to some extent meaningful, numinous, and—whenever possible—irrational. To that extent, I believe there exists a connection between the growing symbolic significance of these things and their reality. Only I would attach a certain value to a subtle distinction: that is, that what then returns to us, namely just the symbolic and irrational, is something that returns under pressure and is not exactly what it once was. Rather it is now, yes, I am tempted even to say, a kind of resultant from the real situation in which people find themselves or from the world of images to which they refer or even regress. I would think that the fatal, mortally threatening tone that accrues so easily today to concepts like *Führer* or crowds, above all when they connect up in a kind of short-circuit, that tone has to do with the fact that the situation in which they originally functioned no longer exists. Rather, the archaic things that are invoked in fact no longer hold any truth and as a consequence of their untruth in the present transform themselves into a kind of poison.

CANETTI: I believe there is much more to be said about that and related questions. With your permission, I might have to correct you somewhat about my meaning. However, I accept what you say. Perhaps I should say, though, that one of the essential points—a point one cannot avoid when thinking about crowds today—concerns the archaic elements that one finds in them. I do not know whether you would agree that these archaic elements warrant special attention. It is not possible to study the crowd in its contemporary manifestations alone, although there is ample and varied material for study. It is also important to trace the connection back to its numerous historical manifestations and formations.

ADORNO: Of course I would agree with you on that, and it is to precisely this archaism, which manifests itself in the formation of crowds, that attention has repeatedly been drawn: firstly by Gustave Le Bon who, in his book *The Crowd,* was the first to frame an analytic description of these archaic, irrational patterns of behavior and then to trace these back to the somewhat problematic and vague category of suggestion; and then by Freud who attempted, in his (at least in my opinion) very important essay "Group Psychology and the Analysis of the Ego," to support Le Bon's descriptions of crowds (with which he concurred) with recourse to a theory of genetic-psychological derivation.[5] Since at this point you confront what is by any standards a considerable tradition of social thought (and the American sociologist McDougall should also be included here), I believe it would be splendid if you cared to outline, even from a typological standpoint, the intellectual context of your thinking and perhaps even to indicate the specific points at which your own theory differs from those of the authors I have named.[6]

CANETTI: For that I would have to take a breath and begin by returning to the question of the form in which the crowd exists in primitive societies, for it is quite clear that primitive societies, which consist of a small number of people, cannot support the crowd formations that we know today.

ADORNO: Exactly this question has been on the tip of my tongue from the beginning: Can one speak at all of crowds in primitive societies, where there were still so very few people? It is splendid that you have broached this topic.

CANETTI: And here, I believe, one must refer to the formation of a new concept. I have spoken of the pack, and I define the pack as a small group of people in a particular state of excitement directly related to the state of excitement of our modern crowds but with the difference that this state, while it can grow unabated in our crowds, is subject to limits. Packs are found in societies consisting of small groups, sometimes of only 10, 20, or 30 people, living as nomads in search of food. The famous examples of such small groups in the literature of ethnology are the hordes of Australian natives. Now, it is striking that under certain conditions such hordes, as they are known today to anthropologists, form into small groups that have a clear objective and that pursue that objective with great energy and in a state of extreme excitement. One of these hordes is the Hunting Pack, for example. The stimulus is either a very large animal that an individual cannot overcome—so that several people have to come together to take this animal—or else a large group of animals that has appeared. One wants to take as many of them as possible at once, not to let them escape; they could disappear again or else a period of drought could set in and there would no longer be many animals. To that end people join forces and go after an animal or group of animals. The concept of the Hunting Pack is, I believe, so obvious that one does not need to say much about it. The second kind of pack—and this is equally clear—is one that directs itself against another, which brings us to the War Pack. When two packs threaten one another, something arises that we know very well today on a very much enlarged, indeed enormous, scale from our experience of war. This situation—fighting between crowds—is, however, already extant in early societies. The third kind, which is less obvious, is what I—perhaps originally—designate the Lamenting Pack. When one person is torn away by death, lost from a group, the group usually closes together in order to mark this death in some way. At first the group will try to hold the dying person back for a while, to hold him in the group; but once he has died, the group will resort to whatever rites are necessary to distance the deceased from itself, to reconcile him with his fate, and to ensure that he does not become an enemy of the group. Countless significant ceremonies exist for this, and scarcely a people on earth does not know them. I identify all the phenomena relating to this under the heading of the Lamenting Pack. Now we come to the fourth kind of pack, which is for us perhaps the most interesting of all: those people who existed in very small numbers always wanted to be more numerous. If they were more numerous, they could also hunt more. If they were more numerous, they could make a better stand in a war against another group of people who attacked them. Countless rites and ceremonies serve the increase of a people's numbers. This increase is not confined only to human beings: it includes also the increase of the animals and plants on which they live. And everything of that order I call the Increase Pack.

These four kinds of pack seem to me to be solidly established. I believe that their existence can be proven in many ways. Also, it seems to me that they have a continuing effect on our age, with the proviso that the first three kinds have a sort of archaic continuation. In modern life the Hunting Pack has become the Baiting Crowd. We know cases of lynch-murders, where people suddenly go after one man.... *(ADORNO: Pogrom packs!)* Obviously that goes back to this early case of the Hunting Pack. War we know only too well. Lamentation we know, perhaps better from the religions than from the very moderate social form in which it functions today. It plays an enormous role in Christianity and in other religions. The Increase Pack has, however, undergone a transformation. This transformation was of course completely independent of the change in the conditions of production. And when one speaks of the significance of the conditions of production, one is thinking, I believe, above all of phenomena relating to the Increase Pack. So it is not only an archaic form but one that has undergone qualitative changes, to the degree that it would no longer be recognized in our society where it manifests itself as production. I believe it is important—and I do not know to what extent you would agree here—to draw a clear distinction between those types of pack that are purely archaic in character and those that have achieved currency in modern life.

ADORNO: Permit me to cream off the best of what you have just said. You hit on something essential: namely, that for you the concept of the crowd, as it appears today in numerous contexts, is not purely quantitative. Rather, by reference to the model of the pack, you determine the concept of the crowd by means of a series of qualitative distinctions, such as they are, which you have mentioned. Thus Hunting; and War, the latter of which is then a kind of more rational, heightened, more highly developed form of hunting; Lamentation; and what you call Increase. I think one should emphasize this distinction, because it exposes the superficiality of today's catchphrases about the epoch of crowds and all these things that really follow the assumption that it is purely a question of numbers. We know something about this from Stefan George: "Your number even / is wickedness," while the wickedness lies not in the number but in the qualitative factors that you have highlighted.[7] Now, of these categories of pack, the first three are obvious, although even you will surely concur that they cannot be so straightforwardly and so inflexibly distinguished from one another but that an interdependence exists between them. So the distinction between Hunting Pack and War Pack may well dissolve, although then again the War Pack, as an organized pack in contrast to the spontaneous Hunting Pack (if one can put it that way), complicates the comparison.

CANETTI: If I may briefly interject something here: I am even convinced that the War Pack really evolves from the Hunting Pack. *(ADORNO: Evolves, precisely!)* Revenge had to be taken on someone, for instance, who had committed a murder, and so people combined forces and set out to avenge this murder. When the group to which the murderer belonged took up arms, a second pack was formed, and there we have the model of the War Pack.

ADORNO: Exactly! I think too that that is probably also the prevalent view of ethnology today on this matter. *(CANETTI: Indeed.)* Frankly, I have a certain difficulty now with the concept of the Increase Pack, because the matter of the will to increase seems to me to be a little problematic. This will is at least ambivalent. It is noteworthy that the commandments to be fruitful and multiply, as they are found in the great religions, particularly Judaism and Catholicism, that these commandments are found in those religions that distinguish themselves from mythical or magical natural religions. One would have to assume that in more primitive stages—whereby I am thinking of the construction of a hetaera phase in the development of humanity—this question of procreation was taken so little to heart that they attached no importance to it at all. And I would be inclined to say that this commandment to multiply has historical origins and is connected to the category of property, of solid, heritable property. Only when such a thing as property is to be preserved, fetishized, understood as such, and passed on to heirs—only at that moment does it become a commandment that one must create heirs who will take possession of this property. The consequent impulse to increase, to grow, is then not primary, but secondary.

It would perhaps be interesting if you could address that topic next. I would then like to say something about the interpretation that seems to me very productive regarding this category of the Increase Pack.

CANETTI: Out of a large number of examples, I would like perhaps to present two: The *Shih Ching,* the classical *Book of Songs* of the Chinese, contains a poem that makes reference to locusts. It equates the number of locusts with the number of one's descendants, positing that as something desirable. I would like to read the short poem to you: "The locusts' wings say 'throng, throng'; Well may your sons and grandsons be a host innumerable. The locusts' wings say 'bind, bind'; Well may your sons and grandsons continue in an endless line. The locusts' wings say 'join, join'; Well may your sons and grandsons be forever at one."[8]

So here one finds three wishes for one's descendents: numerical abundance, continuity in the line of descent, and unity. And it is especially remarkable that locusts are used here to symbolize progeny, because locusts are of course the object of fear. *(ADORNO: They have negative connotations.)* Nevertheless the enormity of their numbers is exactly what one desires for one's progeny.

ADORNO: But isn't that after all a very late stage of an already institutionalized, organized society, of a political system, and of an organized religion, as opposed to a natural state?

CANETTI: One could perhaps say that. The *Shih Ching* is very old, but. . . . *(ADORNO: But nevertheless it presumes a highly advanced, indeed an advanced hier-*

archic society.) That may be right. But for exactly that reason I would like to present another example to you. It is of particular interest because it is concerned with totemic myths that were published only about 15 years ago. They were recorded by Strehlow Jr. among the Aranda.[9] I would like to recount one of them about the origin of the totem of the opossums, which are also known as bandicoots in Australia. It tells the following story. The ancestor of the opossum totem, Karora, is pictured lying at the bottom of a pool in eternal sleep since time immemorial. One day large numbers of opossums emerge from his navel and his armpits and completely surround him. But he remains asleep. The sun rises. He rises, feels hungry, notices that he is surrounded by an immense number of opossums. He gropes all around and grabs one of these opossums, cooks it in the burning sun, and eats it—actually eats one of these creatures that came out of him. He lies down to sleep and, the very same night, from beneath his armpit falls a bull-roarer that metamorphoses into a human being. It is his first son, who then grows up and is acknowledged the following morning as his son. The following night more sons, each dropping out of his armpit. Every night the same thing. Finally 50 sons emerge at once from his armpits, and now he sends these same sons to find opossums, which they catch and cook, and on which they live.

So here we have a kind of double increase: first he is the ancestor of the opossums of which suddenly gigantic crowds appear, then later there come into being a great number of sons out of him, their father. One might actually call him a crowd mother. One could say he consists of sons, of opossums. The relationship between the opossums and his sons is fascinating. The one group feeds on the other. So he has produced the food and also his own sons. He is the ancestral father of the totem, the opossum totem, and this totem means simply that opossums and human beings belonging to this totem are related in the closest possible way. The human beings, his human sons, are so to speak the younger brothers of these opossums. There are many other myths of this kind. I feel it's possible to speak of a very strong compulsion toward increase.

ADORNO: What you have just said could take us very far, and I don't think we could get to the bottom of that now nor that we are concerned with something ambivalent here. There is certainly an archaic element that drives us into diversity, amorphousness, multifariousness of forms. But there is also the counterelement, and it seems to me that it is probably scarcely possible any more to distinguish the primary from the secondary. Generally such questions of what is primary and what derivative do not take us very far at all. Today, at any rate, it appears for the most part that the thought of numerical increase—and that of course has clear and recognized civilizing-economic bases—is both desired and feared, as much by individual people and individual families as by races and by humanity as a whole. In its increasing numbers humanity senses the danger to the continued viability of its present organizational forms and beyond that it torments itself with the surely imaginary doubt about whether the old earth will still be capable of supporting a humanity whose numbers have increased beyond measure.

CANETTI: If I might interject something here: This idea of the earth's over-population is very old and mythical. *(ADORNO: Very old indeed!)* It is found among the ancient Persians, and was also present among races that tended strongly toward increase and that always emphasized the wish to increase.

ADORNO: Surely within this ambivalence exists the very deep awareness that, on the one hand, everything that has any possibility of being has the right to exist, but that, on the other hand, in view of the forms, the institutions under which humanity has lived and still lives up to the present, every newly approaching human being on the farthest horizon represents simultaneously something of a threat to the continued existence of all others. I would say this ambivalence has not only a psychological basis, but also a basis in reality, even if far removed. Let me come to what seems to me a very productive detail in your theory of increase—regardless of how this controversy might be resolved: You discuss at one place in your book how modern production—the increase of goods—has become a kind of end in itself, or, as I would say, how production has become fetishized. Now, from an economic theory of society one can cite very rational—pseudorational—reasons why it has come to be so. That is to say, that under the present circumstances the apparatus of production and, with that, the whole means of production can only sustain themselves by creating an ever broader circle of consumers for their products. And here we are precisely at that remarkable point of reversal between the primary and the secondary, at which the very human beings for whom all this supposedly exists are, in reality, just being dragged along by the machine of which they themselves are the component parts.

I believe your theory performs an important function at this point. That is, one would probably not be able to understand how this cult of production for production's sake thrives everywhere, regardless of differing political systems, if there were not also something in the subjectivity of human beings, in their unconscious, in their whole archaic heritage, that responded to it in a tremendously powerful way. Otherwise the simple objection would have to be raised: why should more and more be produced when in reality what is produced has long since been sufficient to free us from our needs? That this question isn't asked appears to me to prove that the apparatus of production is mobilizing huge libidinal resources, which its own constant and, yes, in the end, very problematic expansion can then draw upon in the masses. For that reason I maintain that this point of view is exceedingly productive, even if one is not inclined, as I am not, to make primary this drive or will to increase, as you do.

I would like to return once again to the still unaddressed question that I directed to you earlier: that of the difference between, on the one hand, your approach and your theories about crowds and, on the other, those of Le Bon and Freud that are after all very well known. In general, a theory's productiveness lies essentially in the smallest differences separating it from adjacent theories.

CANETTI: Perhaps you will allow me instead to emphasize the differences between Freudian theory and my own, since I find. . . .

ADORNO: Le Bon's work is not actually a theory but rather a description of a relatively narrow phenomenon. I believe the crowds that he describes are actually just those that form in very specific situations, such as when buildings or theaters burn, or on other such occasions, and that are of course not at all representative for the concept of the crowd in general. I think too that it is much better if you consider Freud rather than Le Bon.

CANETTI: With regard to Freud, some things need to be said: Freud speaks of two concrete crowds, which he cites as examples. One is the church, the other the army. And the fact that he chooses two hierarchically structured groups (for want of a better term) to explain his theory of crowds seems to me very characteristic of him. I do not consider a crowd to have a hierarchic structure. The army is not a crowd at all. The army is a collection of people held together by a definite command structure that serves precisely to *prevent* its becoming a crowd. For an army it is especially important that a subgroup can be split off by means of a command; 300 men can be deployed somewhere else. The army is always divisible. It can on occasion, at certain moments, in moments of flight or a vehement attack, become a crowd, but in principle the army cannot be considered a crowd in my sense. So it is quite significant that Freud illustrates his theory by reference to the army. Another thing that I would like to raise as an important difference is that Freud really only speaks of crowds that have a leader. He always sees an individual as the reference point of the crowd.

ADORNO: That naturally has a connection with the theory of the original father, the tribal father.

CANETTI: But there are, and here I think that you will perhaps agree with me, also crowds of a quite different kind: a Flight Crowd for example. People in one place are suddenly threatened by. . . .

ADORNO: He understands that, quite logically from his point of view, as the decomposition of the crowd.

CANETTI: No, there, I believe, one must distinguish between a Flight Crowd and a panic crowd. *(ADORNO: Yes, a panic crowd.)* The Flight Crowd is still in a crowd state, like a fleeing herd when all members flee simultaneously. Panic is ... *(ADORNO: A disintegration)* ... a breaking apart of the crowd, where every individual simply wants to save his own life. The Flight Crowd, which is not yet in panic, has no leader. It does have a direction. The direction: away from danger! Nevertheless it does display quite pronounced crowd characteristics that one can explain in detail and that are very important. I do not believe that a Baiting Crowd necessarily has a leader. You will quite correctly point out that Baiting Crowds are very often whipped into a frenzy by certain demagogues....

ADORNO: It has always been historically the case that precisely the Baiting Crowds were not spontaneous but manipulated. That was already the case during the pogroms of the crusades.

CANETTI: That is certainly right. Nevertheless, I believe, there is a Baiting Crowd before and beyond this directed crowd that takes its leader as its point of reference. Then there are other cases. You will recall that I also describe the Feast Crowd. *(ADORNO: Indeed.)* That is something that has nothing at all to do with a leader. It deals with a collection of people and the large quantity of what they have produced that they wish to consume together in a state of joy and excitement. The crowd does not move in any direction, and there is really no question of a leader. I believe that Freud's concept of the crowd depends too much on Le Bon's.

ADORNO: It was his frame of reference. His work is actually a commentary or an interpretation, a genetic interpretation of Le Bon's phenomenology of crowds.

CANETTI: And here I would also say that, even if one thinks of this bounded crowd, as Freud, following Le Bon, seeks to explain it, still more objections arise. For me it is primarily a question of the concept of identification. I consider this concept not fully thought through, not precise enough, not really clear. At many points in his works, when he speaks of identification, Freud says that it is a question of an ideal image that the child identifies with the father, for instance, in its wish to become like the father. The father is that model image. Now that is certainly correct. But what really happens to the model image in this relationship has never been precisely described. You will certainly be astonished that such a large section of my book is devoted to the problems of metamorphosis. The second volume should contain much more on the subject of metamorphosis.[10] There I have really made it my task to examine anew all aspects of metamorphosis, so that I can finally determine what a model image actually is, what really takes place between the model image and the person who takes the image as a model. And only perhaps then will one have clearer ideas about identification. In the absence of that, I would prefer to avoid the whole concept of identification. I am trying to dispense with it as a category. I have now mentioned only some of the points. There are others besides.

ADORNO: To me this criticism seems extraordinarily accurate and helpful. Because of his fundamental tendency to substitute for his theory of society an individual psychology extended to the collective, Freud at this point always returns to the unvarying, the invariable basic quanta of the unconscious. This prevents him from taking essential historical modifications into account; and consequently his social psychology remains somewhat abstract. So I would agree fully that the term "crowd" can in no way be applied unproblematically to the army and the church. Rather they are reactions to it, forms of reaction in which this crowd situation Freud had in mind occurs but is confined and negated essentially by the hierarchic features and also by a certain kind of rationality. And, if one takes that further, one will realize that it is not so easy to see the so-called crowd phenomena with which we are concerned today as primary manifestations of archaic crowds, as Freud did during the First World War. Instead, one glimpses forms of reaction, even regressions to early stages of society, which are actually no longer compatible with the contemporary world.

With regard to festivals, it is certainly quite correct that one cannot speak of leadership in that context. Perhaps I may draw your attention to the very important work on festivals that appeared some years ago by Roger Caillois, the French cultural anthropologist.[11] He traces the festival as a form of reaction, as a reversal of hierarchic, strict rites within barbaric, rigid societies that to some extent are only able to sustain their continued existence by means of a reversal of their rules and, in certain exceptional situations, by allowing, even indeed making mandatory, the very things that are at other times forbidden. In this sense, what you call the Feast Crowd would itself also be a historically contingent phenomenon, rather than a primary one.

If I may say one more thing. What made the greatest impression on me in your book was a point that has less to do with the theory of crowds than with the inseparable, correlative theory of power. It is your theory of the command that to me seems so eminently enlightening and essential because you give voice to something that—and allow me here to recall again our *Dialectic of Enlightenment*—for the most part is hidden behind society's facade. Behind all the social, (in the larger sense) socially sanctioned, socially required modes of behavior, there exists, however obscure it may be, something like direct physical force, the threat of annihilation. And I think that, only if one is clear about the fact that society, and thus the self-preservation of humanity itself, has as its substance the threat of death, only then can one grasp the terrible power of survival (as you call it) and death, as you have formulated those things.

I think it would therefore be very good if you concluded simply with a few more words about your theory of the command, Dr. Canetti.

CANETTI: I would very much like to do so, although it requires more than a few words: I trace the origin of the command—biologically—back to the command to flee. I believe that the threat of an animal that feeds on other animals leads to the flight of those animals. A lion, which ranges out and signals its presence by roaring, causes other animals to flee at its approach. And that seems to me to be the seed from which the command later developed and became an important institution in our world. It drives the endangered away from the danger. And that is very important. Society uses this model. It has actually been built into our society. Orders are issued, perhaps without their recipients' being aware that they contain a threat of death. In whatever way orders are given, however, they conceal that threat. When death sentences—still customary in most societies—are carried out, the command's terrible power is restored. One is warned: if you do not do what is required of you, then what you see played out here before you will happen to you. *(ADORNO: Every execution addresses the others, those not being executed.)*

And then quite briefly, to mention one more point, a consideration of the command led me to understand that the command can be dissected into its impulse, the motive energy that leads to its execution, and a third part that I call the sting of command. This sting has exactly the form and content of the command, and it remains behind in the person who has carried out an order. Thus a person who has executed an order can in no way be happy about it. Perhaps he is unaware of it; perhaps he does not reflect on it. But the sting of command remains in him and this sting is absolutely unchangeable. That is especially important. Human beings can store in themselves stings of command that they received 20 or 30 years ago. It is all present within them, and by means of a reversal, it reappears on the surface. People want to free themselves from these stings. They feel oppressed by these stings and often search for situations that present an exact reversal of the original command situation so that they can relieve themselves of their stings. The consequences are clear. It is simply true that every person who lives in a society is crammed full of all kinds of stings of command. They can become so numerous that this person is driven to quite monstrous deeds, poisoned by his own stings of command.

ADORNO: I think that is noteworthy, particularly because you have expressed in a very original and unconventional manner the idea that, because the threat of direct force lives on in all these transactions, every attempt to move beyond this sphere remains in the spell of this vicious circle, namely of doing to others what has already been done to oneself. And the magnificent sentence of Nietzsche's, that it is essential that man be freed from the bonds of revenge, plays precisely on the issue that you address here.[12] And by addressing it here, by identifying this spell, by naming the magical incantation, by naming the word by which humanity is bewitched, your book seeks, if I understand you correctly, to serve the aim of helping us finally to succeed in breaking that spell.

Notes

1. [The reference here is most probably to the international crisis and the military standoff between NATO and Warsaw Pact forces in Central Europe following the construction of the Berlin Wall in August 1961. *Ed.*]
2. [The use of masculine pronominal forms here and elsewhere in this translation is intended to reflect the scholarly conventions of the early 1960s. *Trans.*]
3. [Ludwig Klages (1872–1956), philosopher and psychologist; Oskar Goldberg (1885–1952), Old Testament scholar. *Ed.*]
4. [Arkadij Gurland (1904–1979), political scientist. *Ed.*]
5. [Le Bon's *Psychologie des Foules* was published in 1895 (*The Crowd: A Study of the Popular Mind* [Harmondsworth: Penguin, 1977]); Freud's *Massenpsychologie und Ich-Analyse* dates from 1921 ("Group Psychology and the Analysis of the Ego," in *The Standard Edition of the Complete Psychological Works of Sigmund Freud*, trans. J. Strachey, vol. 18 [London: Hogarth, 1955], 69–143). *Ed.*]
6. [The reference is to William McDougall, *The Group Mind: A Sketch of the Principles of Collective Psychology with Some Attempt to Apply them to the Interpretation of National Life and Character* (New York: G. P. Putnam's, 1920). *Ed.*]
7. [The words "Schon eure zahl ist frevel" are from Stefan George's poem "Die tote Stadt" ("The Dead City"), in *Der siebente Ring*, vol. 6/7 of *Stefan George: Gesamtausgabe der Werke* (Berlin: Bondi, n.d.), 30–31. The cited translation and one alternative rendering are found in *Stefan George in fremden Sprachen: Übersetzungen seiner Gedichte in die europäischen Sprachen ausser den slawischen*, comp. Georg Peter Landmann (Düsseldorf: Helmut Köpper, 1973), 357, 720–21. *Trans.*]
8. [Cited from *The Book of Songs*, trans. Arthur Waley (New York: Grove, 1960), 173. *Trans.*]
9. [The reference here is to T. G. H. Strehlow's study *Aranda Traditions* (Melbourne: Melbourne University Press, 1947). *Ed.*]
10. [Canetti subsequently abandoned the idea of publishing a second volume of *Crowds and Power. Ed.*]
11. [Roger Caillois's *L'homme et le sacré* appeared first in 1939 and subsequently in expanded form in 1950 (*Man and the Sacred*, trans. Meyer Barash [Glencoe, Ill.: Free Press, 1959]). *Ed.*]
12. [The phrase *"dass der Mensch erlöst werde von der Rache"* is found in *Also sprach Zarathustra: Ein Buch für Alle und Keinen*, vol. 6, no. 1 of Nietzsche, *Werke: Kritische Gesamtausgabe*, ed. Giorgio Colli and Mazzino Montinari (Berlin: de Gruyter, 1968), 124; the English rendition of Adorno's words mostly follows the wording of *Thus Spake Zarathustra: A Book for Everyone and No One*, trans. R. J. Hollingdale (Harmondsworth: Penguin, 1961), 123. *Trans.*]

Mass, Might and Myth

Iris Murdoch

I am not the polymath who would be the ideal reviewer of this remarkable book. To deal adequately with *Crowds and Power* one would have to be, like its author, a mixture of historian, sociologist, psychologist, philosopher and poet. One is certainly confronted here with something large and important: an extremely imaginative, original and massively documented theory of the psychology of crowds.

Using heterogeneous and very numerous sources, Dr. Canetti has built a structure which has the clarity, simplicity and explanatory flexibility of a metaphysical system. His view will not prove easy to "place" in any familiar pattern or genealogy of ideas; nor has he himself given any help to would-be "placers." He quotes the most diverse and esoteric writers, but the names of Freud and Marx occur nowhere in his text (Freud is mentioned once in a note). This particular reticence, which reminds one of Wittgenstein, is the mark of the artist and of the confident, truly imaginative thinker; only whereas Wittgenstein had in fact not troubled to read some of his best-known predecessors, one may be pretty sure that Dr. Canetti has read everything.

The book falls roughly into two halves. The first half analyses, with an amazing wealth of illustration, the dynamics of different types of crowds and of "packs," a term used to denote a smaller, more rigidly structured and purposive crowd. The second part, which discusses how and why crowds obey rulers, deals with the psychology of the despot. The key to the crowd, and to the crowd's master, Canetti finds in his central theory of "command" and "survival."

A simplified account of this theory runs as follows. A fundamental human passion and a key to the nature of all power is the passion to *survive*. There is always satisfaction in the thought that it is someone else who is dead: and this satisfaction may become an addiction. This is something much more positive than a mere instinct of self-preservation. "The lowest form of survival is killing." In one guise or another—the meditation in the cemetery, the general "throwing in another division"—there is deep satisfaction in the notion: "They lie dead, I stand here alive." This is one aspect of power.

Reprinted with kind permission of *The Spectator* (from *The Spectator,* 6 September 1962, 337–38).

A related aspect is "the command." Canetti connects command with the primitive notion of a flight from death. (The herd flees when the lion roars.) "Beneath all command glints the harshness of the death sentence." We are all subject to commands and each command which we obey leaves behind in us its "sting." This alien sting "remains in us unchanged." We do not forget or forgive any command. This in turn provides us with a major source of energy: the desire for a "reversal," the desire to "get rid of our stings" by making other people obey corresponding orders. This has many and varied consequences, some obvious and some not so obvious. Many promotion systems rely quite explicitly upon this primitive aspect of human nature. A man under orders will do anything because "he does not accuse himself but the sting." Our stings are our destiny.

In the last part of the book, Canetti introduces another concept, that of "transformation." This specifically human talent has many uses but is most primitively a kind of protection. It is a danger to any would-be despot, whose corresponding passion is "to unmask." The book ends with a discussion of the case of Schreber, a paranoiac who wrote a detailed memoir of his delusional life. In this account Canetti finds all the characteristics of power and its relation to crowds which he has been analysing. "It is only a step from the primitive medicine man to the paranoiac and from both of them to the despot of history."

How does one judge a large-scale theory of this sort? Clearly there is no point in just saying impatiently, well is it true or not? The question is, how much will it explain, how much light will it throw, what will it connect with what? I think Canetti's theory throws a great deal of light and precisely illuminates places which have hitherto been very dark. Marx has told us much about the dynamics of society. Freud has told us much about the human heart. But neither of them provides us with a satisfactory theoretical explanation of Hitler or an explanation, say, of the political power of a church over its adherents. Let us take two instances from Canetti. Roman Catholicism "sees the open crowd as its enemy." "Communication between worshippers is hindered." Even the communion service gives each man "a precious treasure for himself." "The communion links the recipient with the vast invisible church but it detaches him from those actually present." The only "permitted crowd" is the crowd of the blessed, who are "not imagined as active."

And then (fragment of another discussion) about Germany. The German national symbol is the forest, which means also the army. The prohibition on universal military service robbed the Germans of their most essential closed crowd. This was "the birth of National Socialism." "The party came to the rescue," with its hierarchical order-uttering structure. Canetti concludes the discussion with speculations concerning the persecution of the Jews, which he connects with the German experience of inflation. The Germans felt that they had been "depreciated," and they needed to pass this humiliation on to something else which could be, like the mark, reduced to worthlessness and thrown away by the million.

This sort of quotation and reference cannot do justice to the imaginative subtlety and variety of the analyses which Dr. Canetti produces on page after page; and even if we do not always agree, we have certainly been given something to reflect *with*. One's hesitations, I think, are not at all concerned either with the importance or the scale of what is here presented, but (a characteristically philosophical question) with its relation to other types of theory. Canetti gives us no direct help with this problem, but indirectly presents us with an excellent object of study, since the case of Schreber has also been discussed by Freud. A feature of Schreber's delusion was that he imagined that he was being changed into a woman; this, which at first distressed him, he later decided was part of a plan whereby he was to redeem humanity by entering into sexual relations with God. Freud emphasises the *subsequent* nature of the religious fantasy, and finds the origin of Schreber's condition in repressed homosexuality.

Canetti disagrees: "Processes of power always play a crucial part" in paranoia. He adds a note that "Freud wrote in 1911, before the great wars and revolutions of our century. Had he read Schreber forty years later he would have been the first to see the limitations of his approach." Canetti sees the case of Schreber against a background of power conceived in quasi-political terms. Schreber's sex-change is to be thought of as a device used by Schreber in a power-battle with the Almighty. Here "religion and politics are inextricably intermingled: the Saviour of the world and the Ruler of the world are one.... At the core of all this is the lust for power."

One has here the profoundest hesitations. I suspect that many of us (such is the power of Freud) would tend to regard it as axiomatic that in a delusion about sex-change the purely sexual aspect must be radical. It is eminently salutary to be made to challenge such axioms. For myself, I do not want to be forced to say that Canetti's account necessarily invalidates Freud's, or vice versa. The human mind is an ambiguous thing. One hesitates here between an appeal to "science" and an appeal to a natural metaphysic which lies at the basis of morality and which is not under orders from either science or philosophy. The paradox of our situation is that we must have theories about human nature, no theory explains everything, yet it is just the desire to explain everything which is the spur of theory. The peculiarity of contemporary philosophy is that it is so stunned by "everything" that it has given up explaining.

Ideally a "theory" should be both centripetal and centrifugal, and this I think Dr. Canetti's theory triumphantly is. His book is full of starting points, embryo theories, sudden independent illuminations. When he says of Christianity, for instance, that it is a "religion of lament" in which the "hunting pack" expiates its guilt by turning into a "lamenting pack," or when he speaks of the "frenzy of increase" which in modern capitalism undermines the religion of lament, he is giving us new means of thinking which, as it were, contain their own ambiguities. Dr. Canetti might be the first to agree that concepts as well as men should enjoy the privileges of transformation. Rich concepts have histories. And precisely because Dr. Canetti's concepts are so rich I do not think we should be in too much of a hurry to see them as rigidly systematic.

This problem of the necessary incompleteness of systems occurs to one particularly in relation to the "moral" of *Crowds and Power.* Canetti speaks of power as fundamental to human nature and he analyses power with predominantly "political" imagery: "Canetti's man" appears as a conscious, irritable person ruled by "stings." And it is incidentally a matter of "accident" whether extreme cases turn out to be Hitlers or harmless Schrebers. Our most pressing need, as Canetti very movingly and convincingly argues at the end, is to control the "survivor mania" of our rulers, and the key to this is "the humanisation of command." But how is command to be humanised? Canetti has not given us a psychology with which to picture the humanisation of command. Here rival science and indomitable morality stand ready to enter the argument. How strictly is one to understand the imagery of the "stings"? Command has a sexual aspect which deserves analysis. (This Hegel appreciated. Dr. Canetti is resolutely non-Hegelian.) Also, cannot the pain of stings be removed by love and compassion without any "reversal"? How are we here to conceive the "free" man? No theory of human nature can place itself beyond the attack of purely moral concepts.

Whether or not we agree, we have here that rare sense of being "let out" into an entirely new region of thought. Canetti has done what philosophers ought to do, and what they used to do: he has provided us with new concepts. He has also shown, in ways which seem to me entirely fresh, the interaction of "the mythical" with the ordinary stuff of human life. The mythical is not something "extra"; we live in myth and symbol all the time.

Crowds and Power, one may add, is a marvellously rewarding book even if one were to read it without any theoretical interests at all. It is written in a simple, authoritative prose, splendidly translated by Carol Stewart, and it is radiant with imagination and humour. There are hundreds of memorable things. A matchbox derives its charm from being reminiscent of a forest: a forest fire in a matchbox. "A menagerie of transformed clothes" is mentioned in passing. There is a beautiful discussion of the human hand, and a remarkable section on the psychology of eating. The book is full of entertainments and provocations to thought. It is also a great original work on a vitally important subject, and provides us with an eminence from which we can take a new look at Marx and Freud. A large work of scholarship which is also a completely new work of theory is rare enough: and we should remind ourselves that in the obscure and disputed field of "the study of human nature" we cannot rely only upon the piecemeal efforts of teams of merely competent scientists. We need and we shall always need the visions of great imaginers and solitary men of genius.

Canetti as Anthropologist

RITCHIE ROBERTSON

Crowds and Power is Canetti's central book. The themes of his novel, his dramas, and his aphorisms converge in it. It is presented, however, not primarily as a work of literature, but as a contribution to the social sciences. Yet social scientists and historians have paid it scarcely any attention, and their rare reactions have been lukewarm at best. When the French translation was published, the reviewer in the historical journal *Annales* was typically cool in describing it as "one of those labyrinths from which thought does not escape without bruises."[1] More usually it has been ignored. Recently J. S. McClelland, a political scientist, has devoted to it the final chapter of a book surveying ideas about the crowd since Plato.[2] Even here, however, Canetti is treated primarily in historical terms, and related to the tradition of right-wing thinking on the dangerous character of crowds that dates particularly from Hippolyte Taine's *Origins of Contemporary France*. Does this mean that *Crowds and Power* is already nothing more than a historical document? Do Canetti's ideas on these and kindred subjects possess only historical interest? Certainly, since he began work on the project in the late 1920s, one would expect it to be dated in some respects. But since the book was published in 1960, it is surely too soon to relegate it to the archives. We still need to distinguish what is living and what is dead in Canetti's thought.

In discussing *Crowds and Power* I want to look both backwards and forwards. That is, I want to relate the book to some of the intellectual controversies from which it originated, but also to argue that much of the book anticipates trends in the human sciences that have developed only since its publication, and largely independently of Canetti's work. And, since *Crowds and Power* offers nothing less than a history and theory of human society, I want to narrow my subject down to a few aspects of the book, and a few aspects of Canetti's relations with anthropology.

Most of the material of *Crowds and Power* comes from anthropological and ethnographic works. An impressive list of such works forms the bibliography. In a footnote he promises another work dealing with the crowd in his-

Reprinted from *Elias Canetti: Londoner Symposium,* ed. Adrian Stevens and Fred Wagner (Stuttgart: Hans Dieter Heinz Akademischer Verlag, 1991), 131–45. Reprinted here by kind permission of the publishers.

tory; this second volume has not yet appeared, and we must hope that we do not have to wait for Canetti's death before it becomes available. As it stands, however, *Crowds and Power* may fairly be called a work of anthropology, and I want to make some suggestions about its place in the history of anthropology. By anthropology I mean above all social and cultural anthropology ("Völkerkunde" in German); I do not mean the German tradition of "Anthropologie," which is concerned, not with the study of particular societies and cultures, but rather with elementary modes of human behaviour and categories of human existence which are supposed to transcend particular cultures.[3] It has been suggested that Canetti is indebted to this tradition; but while there may be a very general similarity of approach, none of the eminent practitioners of "Anthropologie" (Scheler, Gehlen, Plessner) are cited in his bibliography. Instead, Canetti displays a markedly Anglo-Saxon preference for the close scrutiny of empirical sources.[4]

Canetti wrote the book in Britain, during a period when British social anthropology was highly productive and successful, but in almost complete isolation from actual anthropologists. He was a close friend of Franz Baermann Steiner, an anthropologist from Prague who had a lectureship at Oxford and died prematurely in 1952. The statement in Dagmar Barnouw's Metzler volume that he also owed some ideas to personal contact with Mary Douglas, the distinguished anthropologist who taught at the University of London from 1951 to 1978, must however be corrected: Professor Douglas tells me that she only got to know Canetti after the publication of *Crowds and Power.* She adds: "for British anthropology it missed its period, since at the time it came out we were in the grip of a narrowly professional frame of mind, arguing amongst ourselves in an esoteric way about lineage segmentation, and allowing ourselves little scope for speculation on the human condition."[5] This may be a rather tongue-in-cheek description of British social anthropology *circa* 1960, but it does allow us to begin setting Canetti in context by relating him to an earlier tradition of anthropological thought.

Early in this century anthropology underwent a paradigm change with the shift from evolutionary explanations to functional explanations. The word "evolutionary" is not intended to recall Darwin but to describe a historical approach to social institutions: one which attempts to understand them by tracing their origins and showing how they had evolved to their present state. This approach goes back to the "philosophical history" of the Scottish Enlightenment. In the late nineteenth century, as the European empires extended across the globe, this method of investigation was applied also to the primitive societies, information about which was coming in from explorers and missionaries. Suppose, for example, you wanted to know why among certain peoples in South-East Africa a nephew is treated with extreme indulgence by his maternal uncle, and is allowed to take any of his maternal uncle's possessions that he fancies. The evolutionary explanation was that this unaccountable custom was a survival from an earlier stage of society, and that these peoples must at some earlier time have been matrilineal. The trouble with this explanation was that there were no facts to base it on. The peoples in question had no historical records, and the previous state of their society could only be guessed at. Here, therefore, an explanation in evolutionary terms was mere speculation.

But the institutions of primitive society could be approached in another way. Bearing in mind another insight of the Enlightenment, that different features of social life are interconnected, one could ask how the relationship between the nephew and the maternal uncle is connected with other features of the societies in question. This step was taken by the British anthropologist Radcliffe-Brown, who found that the nephew spoiled by his mother's brother was at the same time treated very severely by his father's sister: if she chose a bride for her nephew, for example, the nephew was obliged to accept her choice without complaint. Thus Radcliffe-Brown disclosed a structural correspondence between the two relationships and pointed out that this reflected the structure of a patrilineal society in which the father exercises authority and the mother treats children indulgently. Instead of an explanation in terms of origins, he provided one in terms of structure.[6] And this could easily be extended to explain the two corresponding relationships in terms of their function. The new paradigm proved immensely fruitful for British anthropologists, permitting above all the prolonged study of kinship and other social structures. A historian who, in the early 1960s, entered what was then the dark continent of anthropology, noted with some disappointment that its "concern with Africa and with social structure [...] has produced what appears to the outsider as a disproportionate emphasis on law, government and, above all, kinship, with a consequent neglect of psychology."[7]

One should not therefore blame Canetti too harshly for remaining to a large extent within the earlier, evolutionary paradigm. His study of society is very much a search for origins. He shows a particular fondness for two hunting and gathering peoples, the Kalahari Bushmen and the native Australians, who were thought to be the most primitive people surviving and therefore invaluable evidence for the condition of early man. The Bushmen serve to illustrate Canetti's important though obscure concept of "transformation" ("Verwandlung"), while the native Australians provide instances of two types of pack, the group formation in which Canetti claims to find the origin of religion. In order to illustrate Canetti's use and abuse of the evolutionary paradigm, I want to look closely at this concept of the pack.

By the pack Canetti means a relatively small group, seldom consisting of fewer than ten or more than twenty. The pack is not a stable social formation, like the family. It is a group of people who combine for a specific purpose, and are united by a shared focus of attention; the intensity of their concentration helps to hold them together. Unlike the crowd, the pack does not tend to grow in numbers; it resembles the crowd, however, in that its members are equal.

Canetti classifies packs according to their purpose. Since a pack is the same kind of unit whatever its purpose, one kind of pack can easily change into another. Depending on the purpose, the attention of the pack may be focused outwards or inwards. The first two types of "pack," the hunting pack and the war pack, look outwards, concentrating on their prey or their antagonists. Other types, engaged in ritual, focus on an object in their midst. Thus the "lamenting pack" focuses on a dead person who is being mourned. The fourth type is the "increase pack." Its members are united by the desire to increase the numbers, not of the pack itself, but of the community to which they belong. They perform rites or ceremonies intended to bring this about. Canetti suggests that the "increase pack" was necessary from the beginning of humanity's existence in order to increase its numbers. Primitive human beings were presumably few in number; they bred slowly and increased only gradually; to overcome this natural drawback, they needed a cultural means of increasing their own fertility and the size of their food supply. A frequent means was the identification with an animal: Canetti mentions the identification of Australian aborigines with a kangaroo or emu which they suppose to be among their ancestors, and the dance of the Mandan Indians who placed bison skulls over their heads and danced, sometimes for weeks on end, in order to attract herds of bison. Finally, Canetti suggests that the increase ceremony, when successful, led to a feast, in which we can see the origins of the communion feast found in most religions.

This sounds like an ingenious theory. In all essentials, however, this theory about the origin of religion already existed when Canetti was born; various versions of it were advanced by Frazer, Freud, and Durkheim; and it was subjected to damaging questioning as early as 1910. It is better known as the theory of totemism. Totemism, like whisky, the telephone, and radar, was created by Scotsmen. In 1869 an Edinburgh lawyer called John McLennan published an article entitled "The worship of animals and plants." He surveyed evidence that not only the North American Indians but many other peoples associated themselves closely with animals and plants, while also reckoning descent through the female line and practising exogamy. He then argued that traces survived among the myths of the Egyptians, the Indians, the Greeks and the Romans, showing that they likewise had passed through what he called "the Totem stage of development," and proposed that the totemic complex was the primeval religion of mankind.[8] Another Scotsman, Robertson Smith (one of the first people in Britain to absorb the Higher Criticism of the Bible, and one of the last to be tried for heresy), argued that totemism lay at the origin of the sacrifices of the Old Testament, in which worshippers performed a communion with their god by eating the animal supposed to symbolize the god.[9] Robertson Smith was a Fellow of Trinity College, Cambridge, at the same time as another Scotsman, the young James Frazer, and induced Frazer to write the article on "Totemism" for the ninth edition of the *Encyclopaedia Britannica*.[10]

In the late 1890s exciting ethnographic evidence for the totemic complex began coming in from Australia. The biologist Baldwin Spencer, working in collaboration with Frank Gillen, the postmaster of Alice Springs, was compiling extremely detailed and thorough reports on the customs of the native Australians, among whom totemism proved to be widespread. Not only that, but one tribe, the Arunta, near Alice Springs, had an elaborate ritual, called by some of them the *intichiuma,* in which the men of the totem first engaged in ceremonies to bring about the increase of the totem creature, and then, when the ceremonies had been successful, ate the creature in a ceremonial feast.[11] Here surely was evidence that totemism was the primeval religion. Frazer was sceptical, pointing out that the totem was not actually worshipped, but Durkheim, in *The Elementary Forms of the Religious Life,* and Freud, in *Totem and Taboo,* seized on this evidence. After quoting the description by Spencer and Gillen, Durkheim declares that here "we find, in the most elementary form that is actually known, all the essential principles of a great religious institution which was destined to become one of the foundation stones of the positive cult in the superior religions: this is the institution of sacrifice."[12]

Unfortunately, this turned out to be flimsy evidence for totemism as the primeval religion. Spencer and Gillen admitted that the *intichiuma* ceremony (increase rites followed by the eating of the totem) existed only in Central Australia. Increase rites were performed elsewhere, but not in connection with a communal feast. In 1910 an American anthropologist examined the evidence for the totemic complex that had accumulated since McLennan's article forty years previously, and concluded that it was insufficient. Totemism, taboo, and exogamy were found separate from one another more often than together; moreover, the totem was rarely worshipped, so it was impossible that totemism should have been the primeval religion.[13] Anthropologists lost faith, not only in the original totemic religion, but in the very concept of totemism. "It may well be asked," said Radcliffe-Brown in 1929, "if 'totemism' as a technical term has not outlived its usefulness."[14] More recently Lévi-Strauss has maintained that the concept of totemism is a scientific illusion like hysteria, and that the practices it refers to are only part of the system of classification by which primitive people structure their world.[15]

In tracing the origins of religion back ultimately to the increase ceremonies of the Arunta aborigines, therefore, Canetti is fighting a battle that was lost long ago. Not surprisingly, therefore, his argument in this part of the book is peculiarly strained and perfunctory. He lays great emphasis on this typology of packs and on the propensity of one kind of pack to change into another. Yet packs, groups organized for a specific purpose, cannot be as fluid as crowds. The change from a "closed" crowd into an "open" crowd takes place suddenly, as when a demonstration becomes a riot, but one kind of pack does not suddenly change into another. A hunting expedition does not suddenly drop its weapons and begin a ritual of mourning. Rituals require preparation.

The concept of the pack is important to Canetti, not as a means of analysing behaviour, but as part of his evolutionary picture of human society. He wishes us to accept that the "pack" is in some unexplained way derived from group formations among animals, thus grounding human society in animal behaviour. His use of the word "pack" (*Meute*) is tendentious, since the word, like its German equivalent, is normally applied only to animals. It allows him to suggest, without argument, that the close bonding of the pack is in some way derived from the unity of a pack of hounds.

Moreover, Canetti wishes us also to accept an identity between the hunting group and the ritual group. He wants to suggest that the aggressive impulse is intrinsically connected with ritual: that organized aggression and organized religion are in some sense the same thing. Canetti suggests a connection between hunting and lamenting which is independent of the perhaps insignificant fact that both are performed by organized groups. "The hunting or baiting pack," he says, "expiates its guilt by becoming a lamenting pack" (p. 145). Having unleashed their aggression upon the victim, they identify with the victim as a way of freeing themselves from the guilt of killing. Hence the importance of sacrifice and of substitutive death.

Before dismissing these suggestions, we should note that, since the publication of *Crowds and Power,* such speculations have become fashionable in several quarters. Particularly in America, there is the work of the sociobiologists, who profess to derive features of human society, especially violence, competitiveness, and territorial proprietorship, from animal behaviour; while in Europe a group of thinkers, above all the German classical scholar Walter Burkert and the French literary critic turned anthropologist, René Girard, argue that sacrificial rituals originated as a means of controlling and containing the violence ineradicable from human society. Girard maintains that the prototype of sacrificial ritual was the attack by a violent crowd upon a victim, while Burkert suggests that the guilt felt by palaeolithic man at killing an animal was expiated by transforming the act of killing into the sacrificial ceremony.[16]

The work of Burkert and Girard deserves a respectful but searching critique, which would need also to include the related parts of Canetti's work. One would have to acknowledge that all three thinkers are learned, fascinating, and often persuasive. But one might suggest that they are at their least convincing when they talk not of the functions of religious institutions but of their origins. Here, I would argue, they fall victim (as Freud also does) to a fallacy, which might be called the fallacy of origins. The fallacy has two parts. One is to suppose that there was a point in the remote past at which religion (or art, or language) suddenly came into being: that humanity must have crossed a "mental Rubicon," as in the film *2001: A Space Odyssey.* This is like assuming that there must have been a point in one's own life at which one suddenly became an adult, and searching accordingly for the origin of adulthood. The second part of the fallacy consists in supposing that religion (or art, or language, or any other wide-ranging institution) was separate from the rest of human development: as though humanity already had language, art, social organization, and so forth, and then acquired religion as an optional extra. It is more plausible to think that different aspects of culture developed together and conditioned one another; in which case one cannot, even in speculation, separate out any of them and trace it back to its origins.[17]

When Canetti offers to explain the origins of social institutions, I suggest, we should treat his work with the reserve that the first structural anthropologists applied to the evolutionary hypotheses of their predecessors. But what about the accounts Canetti offers of social phenomena which we have all had the opportunity to experience—above all, the behaviour of crowds?

Canetti deals here with the same subject-matter as many present-day anthropologists. Unlike the British social anthropologists discussed earlier, they are no longer primarily concerned with kinship and social structure, but with meaning. They examine above all the cultural symbolism that permeates the entire life of a society. This form of anthropology has a tradition going back to Durkheim. His work, and that of the anthropologists he gathered round the journal *L'Année Sociologique,* was absorbed and mediated to the English-speaking world by Sir Edward Evans-Pritchard in his studies of witchcraft and religion among tribal peoples of the southern Sudan. Durkheim's breakthrough (anticipated by Robertson Smith) consisted in treating religion not as a set of beliefs but as a set of practices accompanied by symbolism. The essential element in religion, according to Durkheim, was not dogma but rather the cult, the ritual, and the myths and symbols surrounding it should be understood not as theories concocted by individuals but as collective representations through which society explains itself to itself. Meanwhile the Belgian anthropologist Arnold van Gennep showed how all the major events of life—birth, initiation, marriage, death—are accompanied in every society by ceremonies which differ in detail but share the underlying pattern of rites of passage. Social life could henceforth be seen as a system of symbolism.

Canetti moves from evolutionary anthropology to symbolic anthropology without paying any attention to structural-functionalist explanations. Some of his sources belong to the structural-functionalist paradigm, but he ignores the explanation and substitutes evolutionary or symbolic interpretations. This procedure may be illustrated from the use he makes of Mary Douglas's essay on the Lele of Kasai. Canetti transcribes and paraphrases large parts of Douglas's account, allowing her material to speak for itself. Thanks to his selectiveness, however, the material now conveys a different message from that of the original essay.[18]

The Lele live in the grassland on the edge of the Congolese forest. They speak of the forest with almost religious enthusiasm. Although they are very fond of meat, they will only eat game which has been caught in the forest; they do not breed goats or pigs. Hunting in the forest is an important practice, and the centre of their religion. It is a communal activity; hunters are surprisingly lacking in individual skills. Evidently hunting is a way of enforcing the Lele sense of community. This is the more necessary because there is no strong authority and no clear organization in village life. Lele shun leadership roles. Moreover, the population of the village fluctuates constantly. Disharmony in the village is thought to result in unsuccessful hunts and infertility in women. Evidently, the hunt is an instance of communal solidarity, which carries the authority of religion. Douglas concludes that, besides its obvious practical purposes, the hunt serves the social function of embodying the social solidarity of the village.

Quoting and paraphrasing Douglas's account, Canetti omits her description of the loose social organisation of a Lele village. He is evidently not interested in the functional relation of the hunt to other aspects of Lele society. The Lele are important to him as offering the best recorded example of a hunting religion, and thus confirming his arguments about the origins of religion. He notes also that the forest, as a mass of trees, is a crowd symbol, which seems to substantiate his theories about the appeal of crowds to the creative imagination. Although he praises Douglas's essay, he ignores the relation it suggests between religion and society, and concentrates on the primitive character and the symbolic meanings of Lele religion.

It is not only the societies conventionally labelled primitive, like the Lele, that interest the student of cultural symbolism. For, if the primitive societies customarily studied by the anthropologist structured their worlds in symbolic terms, the same should in principle be true for complex societies like those conventionally left to the historian. Admittedly, the immense complexity of societies like our own confronts the anthropologist with problems. He needs a manageable unit to focus on. Nevertheless, the past few years have seen the tentative growth of a historical anthropology. Unlike sociology, historical anthropology tends to focus not on general patterns but on specific incidents which lend themselves to close study and interpretation.[19] They are particularly interested in events involving large numbers of people, whether these are organized rituals or the seemingly disorderly behaviour of crowds or a combination of both. To mention just one example, Emanuel Le Roy Ladurie has examined in detail the carnival in the town in Romans in 1580 which ended in a politically-motivated massacre; he has shown how different parts of the carnival celebrations were organized by different social and political groups, who expressed their standpoints by manipulating carnival symbolism. The result is a blend of social history with anthropology.[20]

When Canetti moves from simple to complex societies, he still examines social practices with the eye of an anthropologist. Consider, for example, his descriptions of ritual. *Crowds and Power* includes a detailed description of Catholic ritual, in which Canetti interprets the ritual as a means of domesticating the crowd; or, in other words, as a means of social control. He points out that Catholic ritual is slow and deliberate, describing "the movements of the priests in their stiff, heavy canonicals, their measured steps, the drawing-out of their words" (p. 155). The worshippers are not allowed to communicate with one another. All communication is between the priest and the worshippers. The rituals of confession and communion tend to separate the worshippers from one another and prevent them from forming a true crowd. "The communicant," Canetti points out, "receives a precious treasure for himself. It is for himself that he expects it, and for himself that he must guard it" (p. 155). Processions, like the ceremonial inside the church, are slow and orderly. They present a picture of the ecclesiastical hierarchy; thus they arouse veneration among the onlookers and remind the onlookers of their subordinate position. "The adult spectator," Canetti says acutely, "never sees himself as priest or bishop" (p. 157). This is typical of one of Canetti's favourite procedures. Particularly in the early sections of *Crowds and Power,* he begins with familiar experiences, like attending a football match or a concert, but he defamiliarizes them by revealing their similarities to less familiar experiences. When he describes the highly disciplined attentiveness of a concert audience, Canetti points out that the natural response to music is to move one's body in time to the music, not to sit in motionless concentration. Motionless concentration originates, he suggests, from religious worship; and he compares the Moslem ritual in which pilgrims at Mecca spend half a day standing on the plain of Arafat, in a crowd of six or seven hundred thousand, enduring the blaze of the sun, and listening to a sermon. These comparisons serve to defamiliarize our own culture. They show us that practices that we take for granted are very far from being natural. They are cultural practices, open to sociological and anthropological analysis. The practice of "standing on Arafat" may seem strange to us, but to the eye of the anthropologist it is no more strange than the behaviour of concert-goers.

Canetti's defamiliarizing descriptions of religious practices recall Nietzsche, as does the manner in which they are written. *Crowds and Power* is composed in a style of relentless assertion. Some readers have criticized Canetti for failing to present his interpretations more tentatively, or to back them up by reasoned argument. Tom Nairn complained in 1962: "Dr Canetti never employs his sources to *argue* a case, about crowds, history, psychology, or anything else. He declaims."[21] However, if it is accepted that in these descriptive passages Canetti is practising a kind of historical anthropology, then we can find a similar style in recent anthropological writing, and thus come to understand and appreciate better what Canetti is doing in such passages.

Canetti's mixture of description and interpretation closely resembles the mode of writing known as "thick description." This term was put into circulation by the American anthropologist Clifford Geertz, who took it from an essay by the Oxford philosopher Gilbert Ryle on how to describe behaviour.

Ryle invites us to consider two boys rapidly contracting the eyelids of their right eyes. In one, this is simply an involuntary twitch; in the other, it is a conspiratorial signal to a friend. A description of the physiological event alone would overlook the distinction between a twitch and a wink. A thick description, however, would describe the conspiratorial wink, not just as a physical event, but as a deliberate act of communication conducted according to a socially established code. It would attend not just to the action but to the meaning of the action. The meaning might be very complex. Instead of simply winking to an accomplice, the boy might be imitating someone else's clumsy or exaggerated wink; or he might be practising an imitation of a wink; or he might, for reasons best known to himself, be pretending to practise an imitation of a wink. Challenged to explain what he was up to, the boy might produce a many-layered description such as this: "I am trying to get myself ready to try to amuse my cronies by grimacing like Tommy trying to signal covertly to his accomplice by trying to contract his eyelids."[22] Geertz, having cited this, goes on to argue that in describing the behaviour of people of other cultures, you must not only describe but also interpret. You must produce an account of the meaning of their behaviour. That is thick description: the description of actions in terms of the meaning they have for the actors.[23]

So far, this sounds like sheer common sense; but when Geertz actually does some thick description, he does much more than is allowed for in his programmatic statement. His most famous piece of thick description is his highly influential essay "Deep Play: Notes on the Balinese Cock-fight." The difference between Ryle's wink and Geertz's cockfight is not just that a cockfight is a much more elaborate and complex event. There is the further difference that a boy who winks can normally explain his action fully. The interpretation Geertz gives of the Balinese cockfight, however, is one that no Balinese could possibly deliver. Emphasizing the bloodshed in the cockfight, and the excitement among the spectators who have bet money on the outcome, Geertz asserts that the cockfight is an art form, compares it to the experience of watching Shakespearean tragedy, and describes it as an expression of "death, masculinity, rage, pride, loss, beneficence, chance."[24] Now this particular interpretation may well go too far, as has been suggested; it may be quite wild and fanciful.[25] But it does provide a dramatic illustration of the fact that, in practice, "thick description" normally goes beyond the conscious meanings that actors assign to their actions and explores semi-conscious or unconscious meanings. Where interpretation stops is up to the tact of the interpreter. A more persuasive essay in thick description, which warmly acknowledges the example of Geertz, is the paper on Roman gladiatorial combats by the sociologist Keith Hopkins, which interprets not only the social functions of such combats but also the psychological motives which caused some at least of the audience to find gladiators sexually attractive and to identify with the victory of the aggressor rather than the sufferings of the vanquished.[26] Working with richer material, Le Roy Ladurie, in recounting the carnival at Romans, interprets the carnival symbolism as condensations of political, social and moral meanings: the participants were well able to manipulate and understand these symbols, but could hardly have provided the analysis, indebted to Freud and Lévi-Strauss, which the modern historian puts forward.

Canetti's accounts of Catholic ritual or "standing on Arafat" should be read, I suggest, as thick description. Seen in this light, their assertiveness need cause no offence. In thick description, interpretation and description are interwoven. The persuasiveness of a thick description is not to be established by a separate argument, but depends on the inherent plausibility of the description itself. Such anthropological interpretation is not far removed from the interpretation of literary texts. It is no drawback, therefore, that in most of his thick descriptions Canetti, like Hopkins and Le Roy Ladurie, is interpreting texts dealing with events which he could not himself have witnessed. Since he draws so much on the writings of travellers and anthropologists, the quality of his interpretations will of course depend on the accuracy of the initial description. He is suitably careful in his choice of sources. For example, on the numerous occasions when he mentions the native Australians, he uses particularly the works on aboriginal tribes by Spencer and Baldwin, which were mentioned earlier: books filled with scrupulously careful description, keeping speculation to a minimum, and even illustrated with photographs. It is therefore unfair to accuse Canetti, as has sometimes been done, of an entirely uncritical attitude to his sources.[27]

There are many more anthropological contexts which could be explored, and which I hope to examine in future. For example, where does Canetti stand in relation to controversies about the primitive mentality? How much is his concept of transformation indebted to Lévy-Bruhl's notion of "mystical participation"? What does he owe to specifically German traditions of anthropological inquiry, in particular the work of Frobenius? And what sort of use does he make of the accounts of African kingship which provide so much material for his theory of power?

I hope I have said enough, however, to indicate that despite its highly personal character *Crowds and Power* does contribute something to the social sciences. Admittedly, it is an odd betwixt-and-between book. It carries on some anthropological arguments that were passé long before it was published. But its more successful passages, notably the description of crowd behaviour, anticipate the interpretive turn in social anthropology, and the literary technique of thick description recently adopted by the new breed of historical anthropologists. Although *Crowds and Power* missed its moment when it was published, we may hope that its moment is soon to come.

Notes

1. J. Leenhardt, "Masse et puissance," *Annales E.S.C.,* 22 (1967), 649–50 (p. 649). Canetti's text is quoted from the excellent English version, *Crowds and Power,* tr. C. Stewart (London, 1962).

2. J. S. McClelland, *The Crowd and the Mob: from Plato to Canetti* (London, 1989).

3. See H. Schnädelbach, *Philosophy in Germany.* 1831–1933. tr. E. Matthews (Cambridge, 1984), ch. 8; W. E. Mühlmann, *Geschichte der Anthropologie.* 2nd edn. (Wiesbaden, 1984).

4. J. P. Stern, "Canetti's later work," *London Review of Books.* 8, 3 July 1986, 13–15. [Stern's essay is reproduced elsewhere in the present volume. *Ed.*]

5. Letter to the present writer, 20 Feb. 1989. Cf. D. Barnouw, *Elias Canetti* (Stuttgart, 1979), p. 47.

6. A. R. Radcliffe-Brown, *Structure and Function in Primitive Society* (London, 1952), pp. 15–31.

7. K. Thomas, "History and anthropology," *Past and Present,* 24 (1963), 3–24 (p. 17). See A. Kuper, *Anthropology and Anthropologists: the modern British school,* 2nd edn. (London, 1983).

8. J. F. McLennan, "The worship of animals and plants. Part I: totems and totemism," *Fortnightly Review,* n.s. 6 (1869), 407–27 (p. 408); continued in n.s. 7 (1870), 194–216. On the history of theories of totemism, see A. Kuper, *The Invention of Primitive Society* (London, 1988), chs. 4–6.

9. W. R. Smith, *Lectures on the Religion of the Semites* (Edinburgh, 1889).

10. See R. Ackerman, *J. G. Frazer: his life and work* (Cambridge, 1987).

11. See B. Spencer and F. J. Gillen, *The Northern Tribes of Central Australia* (London, 1904), ch. 9, and the more detailed account given by the same authors in *The Arunta: a study of a Stone Age people* (London, 1927). Canetti draws heavily on both books.

12. E. Durkheim, *The Elementary Forms of the Religious Life,* tr. J. W. Swain (London, 1976), p. 336. Cf. *Totem and Taboo,* in *The Standard Edition of the Complete Psychological Works of Sigmund Freud,* ed. J. Strachey (24 vols., London, 1953–74), xiii. 3–4.

13. A. A. Goldenweiser, "Totemism, an analytical study," *Journal of American Folklore* 23 (1910), 179–293.

14. Radcliffe-Brown, *Structure and Function,* p. 117.

15. C. Lévi-Strauss, *Totemism.* tr. R. Needham (London, 1963); *The Savage Mind* [no translator given] (London, 1966).

16. For an introduction to their work, see W. Burkert, R. Girard, and J. Z. Smith, *Violent Origins: ritual killing and cultural formation,* ed. R. G. Hamerton-Kelly (Stanford, Cal., 1987).

17. See G. Geertz, *The Interpretation of Cultures* (New York, 1973), p. 47.

18. M. Douglas, "The Lele of Kasai," in D. Forde (ed.), *African Worlds* (London, 1954), pp. 1–26.

19. For a definition and illustrations, see P. Burke, *The Historical Anthropology of Early Modern Italy* (Cambridge, 1987), pp. 3–4 and *passim.* For a critical survey of recent approaches, see H. Medick, " 'Missionaries in the row boat?' Ethnological ways of knowing as a challenge to social history," *Comparative Studies in Society and History,* 29 (1987), 76–98. On German counterparts, see T. Nipperdey, "Kulturgeschichte, Sozialgeschichte, historische Anthropologie," *Vierteljahrschrift für Sozial- und Wirtschaftsgeschichte,* 55 (1968), 145–64.

20. E. Le Roy Ladurie, *Carnival,* tr. M. Feeney (London, 1980).

21. T. Nairn, "Crowds and critics," *New Left Review,* 17 (1962), 24–33 (p. 29).

22. G. Ryle, "The thinking of thoughts," in his *Collected Papers* (2 vols., London, 1971), ii. 480–96 (p. 482).

23. Geertz, "Thick description: toward an interpretive theory of culture," in *The Interpretation of Cultures*. pp. 3–30.

24. Geertz, *The Interpretation of Cultures,* p. 443.

25. See V. Crapanzano, "Hermes' dilemma: the masking of subversion in ethnographic description," in J. Clifford and G. E. Marcus (eds.), *Writing Culture: the poetics and politics of ethnography* (Berkeley, Cal., 1986), esp. pp. 68–76.

26. K. Hopkins, "Murderous games," in his *Death and Renewal: sociological studies in Roman history,* 2 (Cambridge, 1983), pp. 1–30.

27. S. Schmid-Bortenschlager, "Der Einzelne und seine Masse: Massentheorie und Literaturkonzeption bei Elias Canetti und Hermann Broch," in K. Bartsch and G. Melzer (eds.), *Elias Canetti: Experte der Macht* (Graz, 1985), pp. 116–32 (p. 118).

Destiny's Herald: Elias Canetti's *Crowds and Power* and Its Continuing Influence

HANSJAKOB WERLEN

We have become more modest in every respect. We no longer trace the origin of man in the "spirit," in the "divinity," we have placed him back among the animals.

Nietzsche

In June of 1995, driving down the splendid Paseo de la Reforma towards Chapultepec Park, I encountered a huge and colorful sign stretching along the wall of the tree-lined avenue: FUEGO, MASA Y PODER. ALREDEDOR DE ELÍAS CANETTI. INSTALACIONES (Fire, the crowd, and power. About Elias Canetti. Installations). With these words the Museo de Arte Moderno of Mexico City announced a series of installations by contemporary Mexican artists in the Galería Gamboa. The exhibition displayed startling and moving reactions to Canetti's magnum opus *Masse und Macht* (*Crowds and Power*). The dozen or so exhibits, personal transformations of the artists' reading experience, gave concrete form to Canetti's analysis of power and, at the same time, provided a forceful critique of Mexico's present political and social conditions.

These days the Museo de Arte Moderno of Mexico City is not the only important cultural institution paying homage to the novelist, poet, essayist, and dramatist Elias Canetti who died in Zurich in August 1994 at the age of 89. From 25 October 1995 to 22 January 1996 the Centre Pompidou was the site of a large exhibition entitled "Elias Canetti, l'ennemi de la mort" (Elias Canetti, the enemy of death). The aim of the exhibit was to present to a larger public a man who, in the words of the Centre's own advertising material, "was a European before it was fashionable, who seized this century from its very center and, within his own life, fully embraced it" (my translation). In the brief announcement of the Centre's show, Canetti is characterized the way he preferred to see himself: as a thinker whose intense intellectual involvement in all the major developments of the twentieth century assumes the quality of a physical embrace of his age. *Crowds and Power* was to be, in

This essay was written specifically for this volume and is published for the first time by permission of the author.

171

Canetti's own estimation, the most important work of his life, one that contained the summary of his deep involvement with the events of our times: to "have succeeded in grabbing this century by the throat" is the boastful and corporeal metaphor used by Canetti to describe his analysis of the crowd and of power, an intimation of an intense physical reaction that goes beyond its merely figurative evocation.[1] For Canetti the corporeality of power is a *Realmetapher,* revealing power's destructive effects in various human postures and, at the same time, inscribing the results of these effects on the actual human body. The announcement of the French exhibit comments on that particular presence of the physical in Canetti's works, while universalizing it by claiming that it speaks for all of us: "For if Canetti is apt to captivate everyone and make people think differently, it is simply because he totally, completely embraces the human condition, explores it in its most minute details, and then fully recreates it."

Canetti is often viewed by critics as the last representative of a tradition that invested the act of writing with the power to reveal a universal human condition. This assessment, too, paraphrases the explicit and implicit claims of the author of *Crowds and Power.* Canetti's status as the last representative of a bygone historical and cultural era finds expression in the anachronistic title of *Dichter* (poet), which he claimed for himself. Reminiscent of Hölderlin's paean to the poet's calling, the meaning of seer and prophet echoes in Canetti's own understanding of his role as a writer. While many are eager to bestow this role upon Canetti, the reception of his oeuvre shows a much more ambivalent relationship between Canetti and the literary public. Even at the time of his "rediscovery" in the late sixties and early seventies, after the novel *Die Blendung* (*Auto-da-Fé*) had been reissued by the prominent Hanser publishing house, Canetti remained a rather obscure figure in German literature. Three years before, in 1960, the publication of his massive work *Crowds and Power* elicited scarcely a reaction, and the silence that greeted the book, whose research and writing had occupied Canetti for more than 30 years, left the author stunned and deeply disappointed. Even though Canetti gained wide official recognition in the form of literary prizes and other honors, a recognition that culminated when Canetti received the Nobel Prize for Literature in 1981, it was not until the publication of the autobiographical trilogy that Canetti found a wider readership, and at the time of his death he was mostly known as an incisive chronicler of European—and specifically Austrian—culture of the period before the Second World War.

A recent flurry of books and articles on Canetti and his works, coupled with museum exhibitions and scholarly conferences, does not necessarily mean that Canetti is now finally receiving wider attention and critical acclaim. A similar surge of interest was evident after his receipt of the Nobel Prize for Literature. It is unclear whether today's renewed preoccupation with this author, who acquired a reputation for being very demanding, is merely a prolonged eulogy or the result of a widening of the influence of his writings.

Canetti's checkered reception history and his reputation for being diffi-cult can be attributed to the nature of his writings as well as to his own self-representation as *Dichter.* While his youthful novel *Auto-da-Fé* can be viewed as an impressive testimony to the ossification of prewar bourgeois Viennese culture and the emergence of modern crowds, its sardonic humor and the chilling antihumanism of its main characters make the book hard to finish for many readers. Canetti's plays, which are mostly based on the dramatization of a single idea, seemed to be better known for the public indecency trial caused by the staging of *Hochzeit* (*The Wedding*) in Braunschweig (1965) than for a broad public reaction to their performances.[2] The reasons for this lack of public recognition are to be found not simply in Canetti's works but also in his persona. As *Der Spiegel,* repeating a commonly heard judgment, opined after Canetti's death: "He never found his niche or pedestal in German litera-ture of this century. He was too individualistic and also always too demand-ing to achieve this stature."[3] What makes the author Canetti so "demanding" are not experimental narratives, complex language, or esoteric erudition but rather an uncompromising understanding of his art, an understanding that demands from the readers, like Rilke's "Apollonian Torso," that they change their lives.

Canetti's texts are interventions into moments of extreme social crisis. Their intent is to reveal the causes of that deep crisis and, by naming these causes, they want also to serve an apotropaic function. As Urs Widmer writes, "as long as he was among us, the hope of stopping wars with words never was extinguished. To say one word, and the murderers would lose their hands. Canetti, too, failed, as so many before him."[4] This statement is much more than the resigned recognition that Canetti's poetic intervention into the sociopolitical realm was unable to change the course of events. In the person of the writer Elias Canetti, the old and often-asked question of the pen versus the sword regained its urgency and importance, even when in the end the sword seemed to triumph.

Canetti, who very early on seemed to have realized literature's ineffec-tiveness as a political tool, forbade himself to write any purely literary works from 1939 on, focusing instead on the comprehensive study *Crowds and Power.* The silence that met the publication of the study led to a disillusioned resig-nation, as evident in Canetti's later aphorisms and, according to his confi-dants, in the comments he made on recent historical developments, especially in the Balkans. Yet from its inception in the 1920s and throughout all the years of writing, Canetti saw *Crowds and Power* as an attack on, and a chal-lenge to, power in all its guises. In this centerpiece of his life Canetti intended to combat even the obviousness and resigned acceptance of death itself.

When *Crowds and Power,* a work that can be viewed as an early example of the now popular genre of cultural anthropology, was published in 1960, Canetti's anatomy of the twin phenomena of crowds and power appeared to be already as anachronistic as its author. Written over a time span of more than 20 years in London, the work found little resonance in sociological and anthropological circles. Of the few responses from those fields most were harshly dismissive, and this almost complete disregard of the book by the disciplines it most closely seeks to emulate has continued. Yet despite the indifference of the social sciences, *Crowds and Power* has become a frequently quoted text for a great variety of contemporary authors. Many of its startling insights are evoked to illustrate a myriad of phenomena, from the psychology of the conductor (in Norman Lebrecht's *The Maestro Myth: Great Conductors in Pursuit of Power* [1991]) to the nature of gender fluidity (in Klaus Theweleit's influential *Männerphantasien* [1977–1978; *Male Fantasies*]). The artists in Mexico City found in it the most revealing diagnoses of their political system, as did the poet Durs Grünbein during the time when he was a citizen of the German Democratic Republic.

What makes *Crowds and Power* such an important book for many contemporary writers and artists and yet, at the same time, an almost completely disregarded contribution to the anthropology of the crowd and the sociology of power? In his study Canetti tried out various narrative strategies and employed many different discourses. A closer look at the unique mixture of these discursive strategies can yield a better understanding both of the book's strengths and of its weaknesses. Ethnographic study and poetic speculation, chemical experiment and symbolic representation, *Crowds and Power* conflates the varying subdiscourses to form a compelling phenomenology of power and the crowd. In this massive essay, Canetti intended to reveal the underlying mechanisms of the sociohistorical developments manifesting themselves in the twentieth century, and most especially in Fascism.

In his collection of notes and aphorisms entitled *Die Provinz des Menschen* (*The Human Province*) Canetti reveals that his obsessive fascination with the phenomenon of the crowd went all the way back to his teenage years. At age 17 he witnessed the large workers' demonstration in Frankfurt after the murder of Walther Rathenau. The intense and uncontrollable experiences of that day filled him with a strong desire to examine the processes behind his altered state during the hours of the demonstration. In 1925 Canetti made formal plans to write a book about the crowd and began collecting material for his study. Six years later, in 1931, he realized that any systematic analysis of crowds had to include a study of power.

Canetti's chronology of the origins of his book points towards a crucial change in his thinking about crowds. While there are only six years between his plan to write a study on the phenomenon of the crowd and the insight that such a project would also require a study of power, the immense changes that affected the sociopolitical landscape of Central Europe attest to the urgency of that decision. Within those few years, the proletarian crowds that Canetti had witnessed in Frankfurt had been replaced by marching brown shirts and huge fascist mass rallies.

As a result of the realization that crowds are inextricably bound to the projection of power, *Crowds and Power* displays a deep ideological caesura. This division in the middle of the work goes far beyond its formal split into part 1 (crowds) and part 2 (power). The positive validation of crowd formation that dominates Canetti's early statements on the subject of the crowd gives way to a heightened awareness that crowds can easily become the tool of rulers who use them to increase their power.

There is no such neutrality in the early chapters of the study, when Canetti depicts the merging of a single person into the deindividuated totality of the crowd and the acompanying loss of the fear of touch as an *Erlösung*. Here, the word's double meaning of dissolution and redemption conveys an idea that was most popular in early modernist Austrian anti-individualism. Canetti moves away from this positive valuation of the crowd when examining the mechanisms of power in the second part of his study. This examination reveals the threat of an inherent complicity between ruler and crowds. Still, this later insight cannot overcome Canetti's early enthusiastic view of the crowd-state as a redemptive alternative to the fate of petrified individuality, and the opening chapters of *Crowds and Power* convey this enthusiasm in the sympathetic descriptions of the individual's disappearance in the crowd. What results is an ideological tension that remains unresolved throughout the entire work. This contradictory tension becomes an aporia at the end of the study when the author's call to resist power is countered by the book's proclamation of the inexorability of the crowd-state.

The long and isolating task of thinking and writing *Crowds and Power* brought with it many self-doubts and a deep suspicion of having wasted time on an impossible project. Numerous entries in Canetti's notes and aphorisms give testimony to this recurrent insecurity. In these (usually) short paragraphs, Canetti oscillates between, at one extreme, the regretful and plaintive self-reproaches of working on an unfinishable and anachronistic book and, at the other, hyperbolic self-reassurance that the finished essay would be the most important publication of its time. While a good part of the self-doubt and self-questioning vis-à-vis his monumental effort to reveal the innermost, perennial laws of the crowd is mainly a rhetorical setup for a final affirmative and triumphant answer, entries written after *Crowds and Power* appeared convey a deep feeling of failure, especially given the minimal response elicited by its publication in 1960.

One of the major reasons why the research for the book took such a long time is Canetti's obsessive desire to observe, learn, and think through everything anew and by himself. This led to a sharp rejection of any predecessor who worked on the nature of the crowd, a rejection that is expressed in Canetti's complaint to Hermann Broch that there existed no even rudimentary inquiries into the phenomena of crowds. This complaint, as is well known, was of course not quite correct. Gustave Le Bon had published his

Psychologie des foules (*The Crowd: A Study of the Popular Mind*) already in 1895, and Freud had published his investigations of *Massenpsychologie und Ich-Analyse* ("Group Psychology and the Analysis of the Ego") in 1921. Neither work appears in Canetti's bibliography at the end of *Crowds and Power.*

In *Crowds and Power* the reader encounters a variety of rhetorical devices, from documentary style and the mode of scientific discourse to the simple stating of apodictic axioms. These axioms are engendered by the individual's physical experiences and observations vis-à-vis encounters with the crowds within and around him- or herself. Personal observations and experiences form the grid of Canetti's theory of crowds and stand as bold assertions at the beginning of the various chapters. In their immediate concreteness, they do not seem to be abstract contentions but appear rather to stem from empirical descriptions of human feelings and actions. It is the immediate physical dimension of these astute observations, oscillating between social behaviorism and the conceptualization of natural instincts, that gives *Crowds and Power* its most convincing quality. Despite Canetti's self-imposed prohibition against "purely literary" writing, *Crowds and Power* is a "poetic" text that differs greatly from the conventions of scientific prose. The expressive quality of the various chapters rests as much on their use of metaphoric language as on the ethnographic examples or observations.

Crowds and Power is often viewed as a more elaborate theoretical continuation of ideas announced in Canetti's novel *Auto-da-Fé.* This is certainly correct for the explicit descriptions of the crowd and of crowd behavior in the novel, but there is a fundamental rupture between the two works with regard to their proposed alternatives to the perceived cultural impasse: while the last part of the novel seems to project a redemptive alternative to the pervasive cultural malaise of petrified subjectivity, the essay, claiming to reveal immutable anthropological facts, no longer shares the optimistic belief in the crowd-state. This shift, which mirrors broader sociohistorical and aesthetic developments, manifests itself most clearly in the different narrative strategies and especially in the modes of address the two works employ toward their readers. The novel's formal features are linked with the theme of cultural rejuvenation in a different social state, but the proposed alternatives are not represented simply as a utopian paragon.[5] They are delineated by a multitude of voices whose ironic and often grotesque discourse renders ambivalent the very solution they purport to project.

Crowds and Power explicitly and implicitly claims to formulate that part of human beings that can be identified as their enduring, unalterable state. Canetti believes that the crowd-state is an innate part of us, an urge comparable to hunger and the libido. His positing of a *Massentrieb* (mass drive) and its demarcation from the libido already explains the major difference between Canetti's analysis of crowds, which is independent of a leader figure, and Freud's theory of the crowd's libidinal attraction to its leader, a reinterpretation of Le Bon's notion of the hypnotic influence exerted by the leader's prestige. Yet even though Canetti's basic understanding of the crowd differs in crucial ways from that of Le Bon and Freud, it seems that the magnitude of his personal investment in the writing of *Crowds and Power* did not allow for even a partial acknowledgment of these important precursors.

When judged from the viewpoint of Canetti's methodology, the bibliographic exclusion of other theorists in *Crowds and Power* is, however, of no particular importance. A cursory glance through the bibliography at the end of the long work reveals a startling way of using sources—startling, that is, if one expects a traditional scientific treatise. The selection of secondary texts in *Crowds and Power* is not dependent on the actual importance of the listed sources for a study about crowds and power. Rather, the selection of these sources is based on their subjective reception by the author. They are quoted by Canetti because they support his axioms, contribute to his train of thought, and, finally, can serve as useful reference works for readers who would like to read more about the distant cultures Canetti deems important for the understanding of his topics. As an indicator of the state of theoretical knowledge about the crowd, Canetti's bibliography is irrelevant. In that regard, the names listed at the end of *Crowds and Power* could easily be replaced by a list of other names. They were, however, very relevant for Canetti's own reading experiences and insights. The axiomatic rules of *Crowds and Power* come first, all other accounts borrowed from ethnographers and anthropologist are mere demonstration material. Despite its abstract-sounding title, *Crowds and Power* is most importantly a book about the personal experiences and obsessions of its author. That is why Canetti can eschew all pretense to traditional scientific rigor and practices. A criticism directed at the relatively small number of listed works in *Crowds and Power,* although valid as a yardstick of academic conventions, misses the point because it neglects to understand the main function of the consulted works. The synopsis of the chosen texts is given in paratactic clarity to furnish a step-by-step illumination of the study's premises. In this way, the powerful contentions of *Crowds and Power* are grounded in ethnological and mythological accounts and become part of that ontologizing strategy of a work that intends to present its revelations as immutable aspects of human nature.

The first part of *Crowds and Power* explains the shift from jealously guarded distances, which circumscribe every person's individuality, to the desires and energies unleashed by an individual's immersion in the crowd. All individual traits are abandoned in favor of a new communal entity when the fear of being touched changes into the desire to become a part of the crowd. Canetti establishes the key characteristics of a crowd by using the discourse of his doctoral field of study, chemistry. The crowd's desire for growth, density, and equality, its sense of direction, its destructiveness, rhythm, eruption, and discharge are described as processes that display the nature of chemical reactions. By imitating the discourse of the biological sciences, Canetti arrives at descriptive terms very similar to those one finds in Le Bon's chapter on "General Characteristics of Crowds." Canetti distinguishes between baiting crowds, flight crowds, prohibition crowds, reversal crowds, and feast crowds. There is a distinction between invisible crowds and double crowds. All crowds have their prefiguration in crowd symbols, such as fire, the sea, rain, and the forest, with which they identify, and which, according to Canetti, continue to exert great influence on the national psyche of many countries.

Canetti makes it clear that the anatomy of the crowd can only be understood if its primordial genealogy in all its divergent forms is traced. All subsequent manifestations of crowds throughout the course of time are already represented in the oldest known unit: the pack. Canetti shows the various transmutations of the pack by citing a plethora of ethnological accounts and historical documents drawn from global history and prehistory. The resulting anatomy of crowds and power includes a wide range of social organizations, from primitive societies (in their German designation tellingly named *Naturvölker*) to the traditional world religions, all exemplifying the underlying mechanisms of power and the crowd. These exempla confirm, in spite of their great geographical and historical differences, that the same basic laws regulate all human behavior.

Most of the collected material, which Canetti lists as evidence of his theory, deals, as mentioned before, with premodern societies. Great importance is attributed to certain "primitive" societies, like the Australian aborigines and the African bushmen, which seemed "untainted" by Western civilization at the time when the first ethnological and archaeological studies and reports were made. There is no critical examination of the possibilities of distortion or the inadequacies of interpreting texts. The huge geographical and historical differences between the various societies used to exemplify the theoretical axioms only make the results more certain because they can independently confirm the assumptions and remove the criticism of local particularity. The unquestioned use of widely divergent materials serves an important purpose in the text: it enforces its central message that the described properties of crowds are not subject to historical or social change, but rather traits of an immutable ontology of the crowd. The small packs of prehistoric times, seemingly far removed from the masses of the twentieth century, nevertheless display the same basic behavior patterns. *Crowds and Power* thus proceeds to unfold a dehistoricized account of its two titular phenomena: as unchangeable entities they retain their global synchronic character through the course of history.

The pack, as described earlier, is the small primordial unit from which all crowds developed. Its appearance goes beyond human time to the animal origins of social formations. The four basic forms in which the pack appears—the hunting pack, the war pack, the lamenting pack, and the increase pack—constitute the generic core of all subsequent historical and social forces of the crowd. In *Crowds and Power* the ineluctable workings of primordial behavioral mechanisms are beyond ethical judgment, just as their authoritative narrative presentation seems to be beyond doubting scrutiny. The mechanisms that characterize the pack function within collective rituals that are much stronger than the powers of the individual and protect the collective from disintegration and incendiarism. The constants of these rituals belie all teleological theories of enlightened historical progress and legitimize the ahistoricity of Canetti's approach.

Connecting the initial outline of the project with sensual perception locates the analysis of crowds in the realm of nature. The characteristics described are natural reactions valid for everybody. This behavioristic approach facilitates the exclusion of history. Crowds are not a product of, for example, capitalist modernization (although Canetti attributes a quantitative change in the nature of crowds to the advent of the industrial age) but a constant entity since the beginning of human history, and the figure of the ruler exerts his deadly power over the crowd in the same fashion from the beginning of time.

The descriptive corporeality of the discourse in *Crowds and Power*, its statements that are striking in their originality and astute power of observation, engender a narrative momentum that carries the reader through the entire text. The cogent and convincing analysis of concrete psychological and physiological human traits and the salient interpretation of myths and ethnological accounts are combined with more speculative and symbolic chapters. The sudden leap from the empirical to the imagined, along with the subsequent fusion of these categories into phenomena of equally important stature for the ongoing investigation, is one of the most original features of *Crowds and Power*. It is also the most criticized. Canetti's equation of the real with the imagined is the topic of a major critical exchange between himself and Adorno.[6]

The observations that stand at the beginning of *Crowds and Power*, and that form the first and immensely interesting chapters of this work, have their corollary in events that influenced Canetti so profoundly that, as we know from his own admission, at the young age of 21 he vowed to dedicate his life to the examination of the phenomenon of the crowd. In all three volumes of Canetti's autobiographical works, the observation and description of crowd phenomena play an important role. Even childhood memories are conveyed in the terminology later used to define the crowd.

The sense of the concrete effected by Canetti at the beginning of his treatise completely captivates the reader through the absolute intelligibility and seeming validity of the introductory accounts. Readers seem to be confronted with their own personal experiences. Everybody can relate to the physical reactions described at the beginning of the voluminous work. The short chapters commencing *Crowds and Power* do not require the reader to mull over abstract conceptualizations but rather, by vocalizing common emotions, provide a sense of instant déjà vu. The familiarity of the initial contentions and their accompanying descriptive elaborations effect the consent of the reader. While traditional scientific discourse addresses the rational faculties of the reader, the narrative of *Crowds and Power* addresses the reader's empathetic acquiescence.

Canetti's clear and paratactic prose is devoid of the prolixity that so often beleaguers scientific treatises. A closer look at the language of *Crowds and Power* shows that the narrative pursues an artful mode of corroborating the unfolding inquiry: original claims reappear as similes, initial arguments are confirmed on a metaphorical level, and contentions made are not critically examined but reappear as accomplished facts.

In the first part of *Crowds and Power* Canetti establishes a genealogy of the crowd by tracing the manifold transformations of the primordial pack in history and religion. Having established the nature of the crowd by observing concrete crowd events, he can confirm his observations through the various ethnographic and historical documents cited. This method of inquiry, which jettisons the traditional scientific mode of conceptual correlations and refuses to weld the wealth of observations and thoughts into a fixed system, provides the reader with a multifaceted spectrum of insights and illuminates surprising connections between crowds and power. The various aspects of the crowd are displayed under different headings that circumscribe a particular area of investigation, but there is no slavish dependence of one chapter on another. This style of inquiry continues in the second part of the work, concerned with the elusive phenomenon of power. Canetti orchestrates a polyphony of observations and accounts, each independently elucidating the contours of power.

"The moment of *survival* is the moment of power."[7] This statement at the beginning of a long chapter entitled "The Survivor" expresses in unsurpassable brevity Canetti's definition of power. In the preceding pages we encounter the physical activities (seizing, ingesting) that keep man alive, and the struggle between predator and prey becomes the metaphor for all aspects of power that always gravitate between the poles of survival and death. This struggle takes place between the giver and the recipient of commands, between sons and fathers, between the ruler and the crowd. It manifests itself in so many aspects of daily life that we have become oblivious to it. The phenomenon of power is all-pervasive. It is inherent in so many different realms that it cannot be hierarchically systematized. Canetti reveals the desire to survive and dominate in the most diverse constellations: in human postures and the psychology of eating, in the person of the orchestra conductor and that of the paranoiac.

Canetti expresses the nature of power in metaphors stemming from the physiological state of human beings. There is no progression to a more abstract level of discourse, because designations like "Entrails of Power" are *Realmetaphern,* simultaneously metaphorical and literal. For Canetti, power ultimately *is* connected to the processes of the entrails. The linkage of the abstraction "power" to concrete functions of the body serves two purposes: it connects power to a physiological realm, and at the same time, as I will show later, the connection of power with the corporeal conveys the sense of the vulnerability and frailty of the victims of power.

As with his descriptions of the crowd, Canetti grounds his theory of power in descriptions of concrete observations. Canetti's own comments about his work on the crowd link the unequivocal rhetoric employed in *Crowds and Power* to external circumstances. The urgency of its content always has as its tacit point of reference the rising Fascist movement and the horrors of the ensuing World War.

In *Crowds and Power* Canetti explicitly claims to reveal the anatomy of authentic human nature, but the inseparable connection of the crowd with the exertion of power invalidates the initially expressed belief in the crowd as the redemptive state for the isolated individual. The primordial forces of the crowd are always subjugated and manipulated by the ruler, the paranoid survivor who needs to kill in order to secure his power. The history of twentieth-century crowds disqualifies the crowd-state as a liberating alternative to the lonely isolation of petrified individuality. The threat of global nuclear annihilation added new urgency to Canetti's project of revealing the mechanisms of power and the psychology of the ruler, whose destructive obsessions with survival now threatened all of humanity. This urgency is reflected in the narrative strategies of *Crowds and Power.* The experimental polyphony of *Auto-da-Fé* is replaced by an unequivocal rhetoric of apodictic didacticism.

Unlike the anthropologist or historian, Canetti is not primarily concerned with providing a systematic overview of his subject matter. With great singularity of voice he creates his own system at the beginning of *Crowds and Power.* The book has no introduction explaining its scope or trajectory, nor is there a foreword that gives readers an insight into the author's intentions. Instead, *Crowds and Power* begins in medias res, with descriptions of physical experiences that every reader can share. Canetti does not represent scientific facts that the audience can refute or accept, rather, he relies on the inherent coherence of a subjective description that evokes in the readers a sympathetic recognition. Canetti does not refute any earlier theories of crowds and of power, rather, he presents the "true" nature of power and the masses in a series of apodictic axioms illustrated with a wealth of anthropological material. Canetti's presentation of the nature of the crowd and of power takes no notice of readers' expectations; on the contrary, he apologizes for destroying many dearly held human illusions with his pitiless analysis of power. The reader is not expected to have any previous knowledge either of the anatomy of the crowd or the secret workings of power. The book in the reader's hands will reveal them once and for all, no other views need intrude. While all personal authorial involvement is elided, readers of *Crowds and Power* will recognize many of its descriptions as recurrent tropes in Canetti's oeuvre.

Despite the wealth of material cited in his essay, Canetti's approach is oddly formalistic. Once the axioms of power or the crowd have been established (and this is done very quickly in the opening chapters), the wide-ranging wealth of secondary materials is interpreted according to the few essential categorical elements announced in the axioms. The elementary structures of the crowd and of power underlie the myriads of myths and ethnographic stories like iron grids holding up innumerable buildings that look different on the outside but that are held erect by identical internal elements.

The crossing of boundaries in *Crowds and Power* is not restricted to the appropriation of various discourses. Canetti's essay crosses all chronological and geographic limits, the demarcation between the real and the imagined, and, most importantly, the schism between Western and non-Western consciousness, between rationalist thought and mythic imagination. It is this appropriation of anything and everything to document the core axioms of *Crowds and Power* that makes the reception of Canetti's essay so difficult. The use of the most heterogeneous sources turns *Crowds and Power* into one of those "sociologically monstrous corpora," to echo Pierre Bourdieu's term. Canetti presses all the variegated sources used in *Crowds and Power* into the service of his theory of the crowd and power.

Canetti's use of ethnographic writing is most selective: it seems that the broad variety of anthropological texts used, rather than widening the field of inquiry, serves only a *quod erat demonstrandum* function: the texts are used, in other words, as supporting materials that justify the axiomatic claims of *Crowds and Power*. With regard to this practice, one could call Canetti's purposeful reinterpretation of more or less well known ethnographic sources "deconstructionist." In his interpretation of these texts Canetti goes far beyond their conventional meaning and purpose. His readings always excavate a particular meaning from the ethnographer's accounts, a meaning that substantiates the theoretical claims of the essay provided to the reader at the beginning of the book. These substantiations are conveyed in a narrative that completely lacks any self-critical questioning either of the status of the source material (e.g., with regard to the conventions of articulation within the discursive field of anthropology that these texts must follow) or of their interpretation by Canetti.

The ethnographic passages that Canetti uses to illustrate his observations in *Crowds and Power* are considered to be factual accounts of other cultures. Canetti does not reflect on the dominant textual conventions underlying late nineteenth-century and early twentieth-century anthropology. For him, the ethnographic descriptions that serve as illustrations of his own axioms are completely transparent. They alone can provide objective facts about distant cultures and undistorted insights into civilizations now long gone. When analyzed in Canetti's text, the descriptions of non-Western cultures by Western ethnographers constitute "white writing" in a double sense: they are written by Europeans in the anthropological conventions of the time, and they also represent "white writing" in Roland Barthes's sense, that is, they are taken as neutrally mimetic of the foreign cultures they present. Steadfast in this belief, Canetti expresses an ideology that, in James Clifford's words, claims "transparency of representation and immediacy of experience."[8] This seeming immediacy separates the writing from the writer. It conveys an aura of impersonal and timeless facts that are expressed in a language whose ability to convey meaning is never questioned.

In its unquestioning use of the writer's privileged position to create meaning out of distant events and cultures, *Crowds and Power* is part of the tradition of European Orientalism as described by Edward Said. For Canetti, who is searching for the paradigmatic exempla of barbarity, the Orient (and other non-European cultures) is the mise-en-scène where the paradigmatic aspects of power can be observed and verified in their clearest representation (e.g., in the trope of the Oriental despot). For Canetti, Hitler is equal to a Mongolian prince, and the most terrifying aspects of power are revealed and unmasked in the senseless cruelty of African kings. In *Crowds and Power* geographically and chronologically distant groups of human beings are invested with the dubious privilege of representing the primordial aspects of human nature in the starkest and most uninhibited manner. Their rituals give an undistorted insight into the workings of the crowd and of power. While centuries of European civilization have softened ritualistic expressions of power, the true face of power still appears unmasked in the customs of the Oriental rulers.

Canetti's use of ethnography can be characterized as an instrumentalization of other cultures through their translation into Canettian theorems. When using these sources, Canetti accepts the authority of the Western ethnographers' representation (Frazer, Mary Douglas), even when he subverts their intended meaning with a reading that is propelled by his own axiomatic insights into the nature of power and crowds. Although Canetti has the benefit neither of experience in the field nor of any firsthand encounters with non-Western cultures (aside from his 1954 trip to Morocco), this lack of immediate contact is of no consequence for the study. The citation of the many exempla from non-Western cultures is first and foremost a device to legitimize deeply felt personal experiences. These experiences provided Canetti not only with the desire to study the mechanisms of power and the crowd but also with a unified interpretive strategy that it is the ethnographic accounts' function to confirm.

As stated earlier, the theories presented in *Crowds and Power* are not expressed in the abstract language of scientific prose. Instead, they take as their demonstration object the human body itself. Canetti's analysis of crowds and power is derived from the observation of physical and psychological processes centered upon the body. In this fixation on the corporeal nature as the core of his inquiry, Canetti's writing resembles that of Nietzsche and Kafka. In Canetti's work power is based on sheer physical coercion. In *Crowds and Power* there is no mention of competing structural forms of power, which, after the social philosopher Émile Durkheim's insight into the phenomenon of "normative integration," could be viewed as instrumental for today's socialization processes. Ironically, Canetti could have found such a differentiated understanding of power in the writings of anthropologists. The nature of the coercive effect of moral socialization leads the anthropologists Ruth Benedict and Margaret Mead to a cultural distinction that sees in the contrastive systems of "guilt cultures" and "shame cultures" an important indicator of whether mechanisms of control are internalized or externally applied.[9] Canetti's monocausal explanation of power misses much of its modern complexity and shows his strong indebtedness to the mechanistic anthropology of Hobbes.[10]

While Canetti erases the traces of progressive socialization processes, he reinscribes the unchangeable marks of power in the continuously vulnerable human body. This inscription—as the mark of the claw or as pain—calls out for an end to the torturous cruelty inflicted on humans by other humans. The locus of Canetti's physiology of power is corporeal, and power manifests itself as violations of the defenseless body. In *Crowds and Power* Canetti can only show and decry the ineluctable destruction of the victims of power: he is unable to offer any hope of resistance. The absence of any alternative to the forces of crowd formation and the abuses of power stands in unreconcilable contrast to Canetti's often expressed claim to speak for the rights and autonomy of every individual.

What type of resistance to power is possible given the ontologically justified archaic desire for deindividuation? Are there any alternatives to counter the biologist-determinist narrative of *Crowds and Power?* In the closed system of power the *Machthaber*—the ruler, the possessor of power—survives continuously as the parasite who eats and is in command. In the hierarchy of power, Michel Serres concludes, "he who is well-placed has the right to eat the others."[11] The victim of power fears intrusion, penetration, and violation of the body, which is helpless in the weakness of the flesh. Yet in *Crowds and Power* an alternative voice can be heard. It is a voice that struggles to be heard through the silencing carapace of power. In the face of the immutable forces of crowds and power, which engulf the individual and erase his consciousness, a subjective voice appears and, speaking as (and for) the mutilated anonymous victim in the crowd, unmasks the deadly domination patterns of power, tacitly legitimized by heroizing historiography.[12]

For Canetti, the writing of history is the apotheosis of the powerful rulers, a written monument to ruthless power. The immense sacrifices of the masses, the towering heaps of bodies that form the fundament of all victories, are not recorded. What survives is the glowing image of the *Machthaber*: The artists who participated in the exhibition in Mexico City understood this central truth of *Crowds and Power* and tried in various installations to wrest the nameless victims of power back into the consciousness of the observer. Unmasking the deadly games of power, they fulfill the tasks that Canetti has set for the artist, a task he had set for himself in the writing of *Crowds and Power.*

Notes

1.   Elias Canetti, *The Human Province,* trans. Joachim Neugroschel (New York: Seabury, 1978), 185.

2.   [The final part of Peter Laemmle's essay, which appears in the present volume, gives an account of the controversy that followed the Braunschweig production. *Ed.*]

3.   *Der Spiegel,* 22 August 1994, 159 (my translation).

4.   Urs Widmer, *Sonntags Zeitung,* 18 August 1994, 18 (my translation).

5.   For a critique of Canetti's novel in the context of modernist writing, see Russell A. Berman, *The Rise of the Modern German Novel: Crisis and Charisma* (Cambridge, Mass: Harvard University Press, 1986), 195–204.

6.   Elias Canetti, "Gespräch mit Theodor W. Adorno," *Die gespaltene Zukunft: Aufsätze und Gespräche,* Reihe Hanser 111 (Munich: Hanser, 1972), 66–92. [This conversation appears in the present book in English translation. *Ed.*]

7.   Elias Canetti, *Crowds and Power,* trans. Carol Stewart (New York: Farrar, Straus and Giroux, 1984), 227.

8.   James Clifford, "Introduction: Partial Truths," in *Writing Culture: The Poetics and Politics of Ethnography,* ed. James Clifford and George Marcus (Berkeley: University of California Press, 1986), 2.

9.   For an explanation of the terms, see for instance Ruth Benedict, *The Chrysanthemum and the Sword: Patterns of Japanese Culture* (Rutland, Vt.: Tuttle, 1954), 222–24.

10.   See Axel Honneth, "Die unendliche Perpetuierung des Naturzustandes: Zum theoretischen Erkenntnisgehalt von Canettis *Masse und Macht,*" in *Einladung zur Verwandlung: Essays zu Elias Canettis "Masse und Macht,"* ed. Michael Krüger (Munich: Hanser, 1995), 123.

11.   Michel Serres, *The Parasite,* trans. Lawrence R. Schehr (Baltimore: Johns Hopkins University Press, 1982), 26.

12.   For a more detailed analysis of this alternative voice in *Crowds and Power,* see my article "Ohnmächtige Hoffnung: Die Stimme des Individuums in *Masse und Macht,*" in *Einladung zur Verwandlung: Essays zu Elias Canettis "Masse und Macht,"* ed. Michael Krüger (Munich: Hanser, 1995), 151–62.

THE VOICES OF MARRAKESH

◆

At the Edge of Silence:
"Mystery" in the Work of Elias Canetti

GERHARD MELZER

The psychiatrist Georg Kien in Elias Canetti's novel *Die Blendung* (*Auto-da-Fé*) is so taken with the "greatness of the distracted" that he does not want to cure any of his patients.[1] Clients who insist on recovery disappoint him, and he secretly hopes that they will soon return to their former condition again. Whenever he meets them on the street, he is really only waiting for their relapse, for small, redeeming remarks like: "*Then* it was nicer!" "How empty and stupid my life is now!" "I wish I were ill again!" or "Sane rhymes with bane!" (*AdF,* 404). What disturbs Georg Kien about the cured is their *lack of mystery*: "Their riddles," he observes resignedly, "had flickered out; earlier they lived for riddles; now for things long ago solved" (*AdF,* 404).

In the context of the novel this strange doctor, who seems to act so completely at cross-purposes to his profession, is a kind of counterfigure to the paranoid scholar Peter Kien. At first that sounds paradoxical, for Peter Kien, the psychiatrist's older brother, is also mad. Georg Kien is therefore no doubt relieved finally to meet with one of the "incurables" who fascinate him beyond all measure. Canetti's novel, however, eludes the simple dichotomy that everyday language sets up between "sick" and "healthy," "normal" and "mad." Basically Canetti opposes two systems of delusion to each other, thereby dissolving the established meanings of normality and insanity and transposing them into a new key. In the course of this revaluation *mystery* takes on a decisive meaning: it becomes the determining criterion for differentiating the two systems of delusion.

To the "distracted," as Georg Kien admires them, there adheres a mystery that remains *inexhaustible.* The picture they convey of themselves never assumes firm, steadfast outlines. It flows, it drifts constantly, and that means that it escapes any grasp that wants to apprehend it. It is just this inconceivable, dark remnant, however, that concerns us here; manifested therein is a

Translated by Paul M. Malone for this volume from Gerhard Melzer, "Am Rande des Schweigens: Zum 'Geheimnis' im Werk von Elias Canetti," in *Elias Canetti: Londoner Symposium,* ed. Adrian Stevens and Fred Wagner (Stuttgart: Hans Dieter Heinz Akademischer Verlag, 1991), 87–103. Reprinted here by kind permission of the publishers.

permanent form of "be[ing] different" (*AdF,* 402), as exemplified by the character of the "gorilla." For Georg Kien this hybrid of animal and human presents a challenge that allows him to test the openness and mobility of his own identity. Thereby occurs an uncomfortable reversal of relationships. For Kien—and no doubt for Canetti as well—the "gorilla" seems to appear as the essence of true humanity: he is only mad in so far as he diverges from what is commonly considered "normal" (cf. *AdF,* 405–6).

This "normality," however, appears embodied and maniacally sharpened in Peter Kien. He is the exact opposite of a drifting, open identity; he does not change, he remains always the same. Determining his identity by fixing *one* sole image of himself, he is, in a frightening way, the *unmysterious* person par excellence. Carefully he seeks to fend off anything that might endanger his rigid identity. He does not read novels because they might drive "wedges ... into the closed personality of the reader" (*AdF,* 42); he dissects dreams immediately into their constituent elements, so that they lose their threatening power over him (*AdF,* 41); and when he briefly loses consciousness once, he is for a long time unable to get over this "weakness" of his controlling and regulating mind (*AdF,* 107). No wonder his brother the psychiatrist declares that he has an "all-devouring lack of imagination," a "brain of lead, moulded out of letters, cold, rigid, heavy" (*AdF,* 449).

Thus Peter Kien and his brother Georg stand, as it were, for two exemplary attitudes toward the sphere of mystery. One of them excludes this sphere from his life with inexorable stubbornness, while the other willingly makes space for it, thus keeping his philosophy and his identity in constant movement. To use a word from one of Canetti's central complexes of ideas, one could say: while the one stubbornly defends the boundaries of his "character"-fortress, the other exercises his capacity for *transformation.*

The fact that the process of transformation occupies a key position in Canetti's poetic anthropology is well known. By contrast, it has hardly been noticed that at the beginning of such processes of transformation there often stands a mystery, that it is therefore in reality the *mystery* that sets the process of transformation in motion. Consistent with the meaning of the word, its content must remain indefinite; it represents rather a kind of productive force, which only becomes tangible by means of its *effects.* In *Auto-da-Fé* the confidence in this productive energy of mystery already forms a kind of utopian counterpotential to the somber and grotesque hopelessness that Canetti displays over long stretches of the novel. What begins as a plot element of the novel develops in time into a literary-aesthetic category of primary importance and ultimately becomes a determinant even of the author's personality.

Canetti likes to surround himself with an aura of mystery. In doing so he goes far beyond the mere protection of his privacy. This becomes most evident whenever he appears to give up his defensive posture. On these occasions, in the notes and aphorisms and particularly in the three volumes of his autobiography, he willingly lays out his feelings, thoughts, and experiences before the reader; and still it cannot go unnoticed that he simultaneously demarcates *zones of concealment* in which further mysteries nest. Canetti is an author who hides, as Claudio Magris attempts to define this double strategy; above all the autobiography, which seems to tell *all,* conceals an absence, a kind of black hole, that threatens to devour the actual truth of the author's life.[2]

Canetti himself, meanwhile, makes no secret of the fact that on principle he does not want to expose this "black hole" to scrutiny. He understands it not only as a private place of seclusion but as a prerequisite allowing the world to remain open to ever more new approaches. It is a matter of extracting the unknown, the dark, the ineffable from the clutches of "irreverent" systematized thinking. "With every thought," Canetti notes in 1943, "the important thing is what it leaves unsaid, how much it loves the unsaid, and how close it comes to it without touching it."[3] This reflection is found further developed in a note from 1947: "A man lives in the belief that everything going through his mind is poisoned and must be avoided forever as of this moment. Reducing all existing things to the unknown is his only salvation. To protect the unknown against himself, he invents a method of *thinking nothing.* He succeeds in realizing it: the world around him flourishes again" (*HP,* 106).

What Canetti anticipates here as a successful experiment certainly hides within itself a momentous contradiction, whose import is obscured by the concentrated form of the aphorism. To be sure, it is again emphasized that only the productive force of mystery can cause the river of transformations to flow or, as it is put here, can bring the world to flower. At the same time, however, it becomes clear that the innermost claim that characterizes this connection of mystery and transformation ultimately excludes any linguistic *designation* and *formation.*[4] Canetti is very conscious of this contradiction, and by reflecting upon it he develops an important dimension of his poetics.

Because he knows that he is incapable of silence, the "fundamental asceticism" of the author (*HP,* 88), he must deal with a double dilemma: He *names* what really should remain *nameless,* and he *captures* what should incessantly change and *transform.* The attempt to get around this dilemma produces a poetological self-image predicated on the tension between silence and speech, concealing and revealing. In a note from the year 1942 this self-image finds perhaps its most succinct expression. "Every language," it is written there, "has its own silence" (*HP,* 18).

What at first sounds merely paradoxical means a specific type of connection between hidden meaning and actual linguistic form, a connection whose particularity appears most vivid and most obvious in a text that deals superficially with something wholly other. To all appearances this text seeks to define the beauty of Greek vases; in fact it specifies how Canetti imagines the silence of language. "The beauty of the figures on Greek vases also comes from their spanning and holding together an empty and mysterious space.

The darkness inside makes their circle brighter outside. They are like hours for time, but rich and various and articulated. While contemplating them, one can never forget the hollowness that they frame. [The events they represent are deeper by the amount of this hollowness.] Each vase is a temple with an undisturbed and uniform holy of holies which is never spoken about, although contained in the very name and form. The figures are loveliest when representing a dance" (*HP*, 82–83).[5]

What Canetti reads from the form of the Greek vases, he also claims for the form that he himself produces. His writing often conceals that which is its innermost determinant.[6] Nevertheless what is concealed is embedded in the shape of the text and constitutes, so to speak, the secret reference point of the form, its "secret heart," as one could say in modification of one of Canetti's own coinages (*SHC*).

Lately, the examination of Canetti's autobiographical texts above all has indicated that this secret heart also beats in texts that allegedly turn their innermost outward. As it becomes apparent that in these works "the equation of life-text and authorial life" is untenable,[7] so the "literary" qualities of Canetti's autobiography become evident, "structures of fashioning" that therefore provide the outermost form of the superficial character of experience of what is fashioned.[8] Friederike Eigler speaks in this connection of the "symbolic organization" of the autobiographical texts, meaning that "pictures, scenes or stories" do not reveal their bare nominal value but rather indicate "a more inclusive structure of meaning" over and above "the event depicted" (Eigler, 27).

While the autobiography thus moves closer to fiction, conversely the voices multiply, saying that ultimately every work of Canetti's is autobiographically anchored, regardless of its classification by genre. All the texts, Dagmar Barnouw finds already in 1979, are "in a simultaneously distanced and intimate way autobiographical," and in 1985 Barbara Meili shows that Canetti's novel *Auto-da-Fé* is in some respects more autobiographical than the autobiography itself (cf. Eigler, 23).[9] Indeed, Canetti's complete oeuvre resembles a scene of fusions. Autobiographical, fictional, and reflective-essayistic elements merge into each other, even if Canetti himself apparently makes strict generic distinctions. By so doing he steers the first examination, which then also promptly confirms an irritating diversity of the work and the absence of a clear authorial identity.[10]

The actual focal point of this diversity, however, is not readily discernible. It is the place where the fusion of the different elements produces the "symbolic organization" of the *textual form*. This textual form disregards not only generic borders but also closed structures of meaning. To be sure, it has the definite, hardened consistency of a form, but it otherwise resembles a revolving door that never really closes and so continually admits new meanings. What is formal about it does not cut itself off from the formless but rather keeps it in mind, and it may be this mute presence of the unformed that ultimately also keeps writing and what is written open to what, in Canetti's conception of himself, is called "transformation."

In Canetti's complete oeuvre there is one text that is exceptionally indebted to the concept of hidden symbolization. The work in question is *Die Stimmen von Marrakesch* (*The Voices of Marrakesh*), a prose volume portraying impressions of a journey to Morocco. At first glance these travel sketches have a graceful, easy, even casual effect (cf. Günther, 117); they appear, unlike Canetti's Greek vases, to encompass no "empty and mysterious space" at all, but rather to display their objects "simply and clearly."[11] Canetti scholarship has largely neglected this text; it counts as a secondary work, and even its author seems to grant it no "proper weight": it was created too "easily and quickly."[12]

On the other hand, and this is the thread that will be pursued here, Canetti insists on the "particular meaning" of his travel experiences.[13] If the particular nature of this meaning could be perceived *directly* in the text, it would not have to be specially pointed out. Canetti therefore evidently refers to a latent meaning, which must first be made accessible. The text itself offers sufficient clues to this end: beyond its episodic character, it develops a dense system of connections and cross-references that overlaps and binds together the loose sequence of chapters in the travelogue (cf. Eigler, 141). To this are added hints from Canetti that illuminate and evaluate the text from the perspective of a superordinate complete oeuvre.

These hints refer first of all to the act of traveling itself, to which Canetti ascribes great meaning. As a child he is already fascinated by the promises of far-off places. Canetti prefers reading "the diaries of great travelers and discoverers,"[14] and a word like the Sephardic "corredor," which his grandfather scorns, thus already represents for him a temptation, because it marks persons who live "in perpetual motion" (*SHC*, 31). This mobility, understood as an openness to everything new, foreign, unknown, later enters into Canetti's idea of transformation as its most essential identifying feature. Not by accident do those who are incapable of transformation, such as Peter Kien or Therese Krumbholz, derive no pleasure from traveling. "If she didn't have to go shopping," Therese would "prefer to stay in all day" (*AdF*, 35), and Kien, of course, goes on journeys but merely through his landscape of books, where he has the feeling "his journey through the unknown was like no journey" (*AdF*, 67). Canetti recognizes in this stubborn holding to one track a kind of "homeland paranoia" (*HP*, 60) and to escape it he recommends a constant change of location. In a note from 1957 he writes: "One advantage of traveling in new areas is *breaking through the ominous*. New places do not fit into old meanings. For a while, one truly opens oneself. All past histories, one's own overflowing life, that is choking on its own meaning, suddenly remains behind as though one had put it into safekeeping somewhere, and, while it stays there quietly, purely uninterpreted things happen: the new" (*HP*, 173).

Put in such a perspective, traveling first of all keeps the world from ever becoming far too cozy and comfortable; it makes space for the uncomprehended, the mystery, the miraculous event: *The Voices of Marrakesh* can be read not least as an attempt to raise the topic of the novelty of this experience.[15] Simultaneously, however, the book makes topical the dilemma that such an attempt necessarily causes; it can be summed up in the question that concerns Canetti generally and fundamentally: How can one *talk about* the mystery without *giving it away?*

Canetti's answer: a symbolic textual form that speaks and is silent at the same time, thereby remaining permeable for new meaning, is tested in the Moroccan travelogue for its usefulness. Because of this, Canetti does not merely utilize the process of symbolization, but he also reflects on it (cf. Eigler, 139–48). In this connection the process of the journey gains a second stratum of meaning, a *poetological* stratum, if you like. In Canetti's self-conception the first, real journey is in fact followed by a second, a kind of *journey of memory and learning,* in which the original experience is transformed and only thereby comes to fruition as a literary work.

It is crucial that this process of elaboration is accompanied by silence; it necessitates a *delay* of the form, yet it does not end in silence and formlessness but rather in a textual form that does justice to the unbelievable novelty of what he experiences on his journey. Canetti sees the model of such asceticism in the Persian mystics: "One feels they have wandered and often been silent and have suddenly spoken with passion after a long silence" (*HP,* 269–70). The reference to the "suddenness" with which a "form" breaks forth from the formlessness of the silence comes up repeatedly (cf. *HP,* 97, 128, 130, 185, 192); it emphasizes that this "form" does not arise from an arbitrary act but rather emerges organically and from internal necessity out of a rather long process of finishing.

It is also ultimately this process that Canetti has in view when he gives *The Voices of Marrakesh* the unusual subtitle "Notes *after* a journey."[16] Thus he indicates not only the *temporal* difference between the experience of his journey and the linguistic record of it but also indirectly the *ontological* difference between experience and textual event. What appears in textual form is *not* identical with the experience but purified and *transformed* through memory. It is memory, as Canetti stresses in the "Dialogue with the Cruel Partner," that "distribute[s] to the days what is theirs" (*CW,* 49). That is to say: memory is understood for its part as a kind of movement that takes up the first, decisive impetus of the experienced journey, develops it further, and drives it to the "blossoming of [its] form" (*HP,* 130).

It is obvious that such a dynamic process of memory and formation must not simply come to a halt with the form *achieved;* like truth, so too is form for Canetti no "rock" but rather "a sea of grass tossed by the wind" (*HP,* 45). The "infinite" quality to which Canetti lays claim in the process of writing (*SHC,* 3) should continue into what is written, and that necessitates a textual form whose meaning goes beyond the meaning of the words and sentences from which it is composed. Such an excess of meaning is what Canetti refers to when he speaks of the "special meaning" of his Moroccan record.[17] Whoever wishes to approach this "special meaning" must accordingly take two things into account: first, that it is essentially a *process of transformation* that produces the excess meaning, and second, that this excess meaning *for its part* is characterized by a call for transformation.

The reader is meant to leave the rut of codified meaning and to turn his attention instead to that subjective system of connections and cross-references in which the "special meaning" takes shape.

The connection of mystery, transformation, and symbolic texture not only finds it way into *The Voices of Marrakesh* as a poetological principle but also forms, as it were, the travelogue's thematic backbone. While the narrative movement appears to follow the more or less random impulses of a roaming tourist, the symbolic subtext develops a dense, suggestive structure of meaning that basically represents a narrative realization of the vase allegory. It constantly deals with hiding and revealing and with the different possibilities of accentuating their relationship to one another. Thereby Canetti succeeds in taking up almost every one of his "lifelong themes" and binding it into the sign system of the symbolic texture.

In short exemplary stories, which however are all intertwined, the talk is of crowds, power, enmity toward death, transformation, and unmasking— and particularly of the dilemma of language. This last is certainly already counteracted by the particular composition of this "talk." It recalls the gorilla's language "of his own" (*AdF,* 401) in the novel *Auto-da-Fé,* where "Each syllable which he uttered corresponded to a special gesture. The words for objects seemed to change. He meant the picture a hundred times and called it each time something different; the names seemed to depend on the gesture with which he demonstrated them. Expressed and accompanied by his whole body no sound appeared indifferent" (*AdF,* 401). This indicates a flexibility in the relationship between thing and word that ultimately also determines the system of cross-references and connections in the Moroccan notes. In the network of meaning created by this system, the signs and ciphers do not have *set* but rather *inflected* meanings, according to the context in which they stand. In this way they appear, so to speak, saturated with a *diversity* of meaning that can never be completely redeemed by the signs themselves.

Thus there is, for example, a symbolic *topography* in *The Voices of Marrakesh* that extends far beyond the atmospheric illustration of the scene. *Squares* of different size and different character form the center of this topography: large and small, empty and animated, cramped and wide. The determining factors are not these comparatively external characteristics, however, but rather the situations that bring the squares to life.

At the beginning of the travelogue, for instance, are three encounters with camels. Each of these encounters confronts the traveler with the death of the animals: they are to be butchered, and the cruelty with which the butchers demonstrate their power over the camels displays in exemplary fashion that connection between killing and the exercise of power whose representation is given particularly close attention in *Masse und Macht* (*Crowds and Power*).[18] The place where the successive encounters with the camels and their butchers occur is a gigantic square, of which Canetti writes that it "would have been difficult to fill."[19] Actually Canetti presents this square as a place of exposure; its size does not give the impression of freedom but rather of threat, and for the camels its immense expanse means that they appear isolated and alone. Because on the other hand one of the butchers emphasizes that "a camel does not like to be alone" (*VM*, 16), the whole constellation acquires symbolic expressive power: in this square the virtue of transformation, which upholds the value of all life, even animal life, is denied. In its place exclusion and ultimately death are decreed. Not by chance, it is a similarly large square that forms the topographical frame of reference for the *final* episode of the travelogue. Here, admittedly, Canetti develops a completely different meaning, although he still first emphasizes the similarity of the constellation. The place of the camels is taken by a being that displays only barely human traits, essentially already standing on the threshold of the animal world. The outlines of this being remain indistinct; its figure and its face disappear behind a dirty garment, and even its size cannot be ascertained because it always cowers on the floor. Perhaps it is blind, perhaps has it no arms, possibly it does not even have a tongue. Nevertheless, without pause it gives forth an unvarying sound that is the only sign of its humanity. During the day this insignificant bundle is all but lost in the hustle and bustle of the great square, but in the evening it is finally *alone,* and the sound that it incessantly emits becomes a manifestation of an unbroken will to live.

The fact that this life can sustain itself, admittedly, has also to do with a certain constellation of power. While the butcher must first *force* the standing camel "to its knees" (*VM*, 15), the bundle has voluntarily escaped the clutches of power: through diminution and reduction. It has shrunk itself "so low, that one would have stumbled over it unsuspectingly, had the sound ever stopped" (*VM*, 102), and it adopts a posture matching, in Canetti's typology of human postures, a complete "disarming" (*CP*, 390).

Thereby the meaning of the last episode deviates in a second crucial point from the initial episode. Not only are life and death opposed to each other but also two opposing forms of survival: in the first chapter the butcher survives as a representative of *power,* in the last the bundle survives as an allegory of *powerlessness.* The expanse of the square offers both forms of survival a kind of surface to be projected on; but while the square in one case strengthens the *deadly threat* of power, in the other it forms an echo chamber for the cry of *life.*

Further shadings of the sign "square" emerge from the circumstance that Canetti, in the tectonic center of the travelogue, yet again takes up and varies the opposition between the beginning and end chapters. This tectonic center is in a way also the thematic center, for it leads the traveler into the Jewish quarter of Marrakesh; that is to say, it plays—however cryptically—on Canetti's *Jewish identity*. In this autobiographically intensified context the contrast between the opening and closing episodes also appears heightened. Again there is a square marked by power and death, but now it is the undiluted *power of death* that becomes evident. It drives the wanderer to the Jewish cemetery. He finds himself "in a very bare, open space where not a blade of grass [grows]" and perceives it as a "lunar landscape of death" (*VM*, 49).

By contrast there is in the Jewish quarter a square that Canetti provides with all the attributes of a utopian place. It is—completely in contrast to the rigor mortis of the cemetery—a place of transformations and fusions. Canetti demonstrates that the breadth and openness of a place have nothing to do with its dimensions; on the contrary, the square described here is "small" (*VM*, 43). What makes it a *special* place is not its size, but its *quality*. It absorbs the diversity of life into itself; that is to say, it becomes the symbolic analogy of Canetti's view of the world.

"In the best times of my life," states a note from 1942, "I always think I am making room, even more room in me" (*HP*, 2). In 1949 he emphasizes, in the context of a detailed examination of the system of paranoiac mania of the judge Daniel Paul Schreber: "In everything I have ever tried, I have always taken precautions against being locked in like that (i.e., like the paranoiac); apertures, space—that was my uppermost thought, so long as there's a lot of space, nothing is lost" (*HP*, 120). In 1975 he finally admits, more emphatically than ever: "So much, so much, and everything wants to exist. Mysterious, the place things find for themselves: so many *penetrations*, and everything preserves its consistency" (*SHC*, 23).

Continuously, therefore, Canetti uses the image of the open, permeable space to define himself and his place in the world. This is the final sense in which this image appears in *The Voices of Marrakesh*. The traveler understands the small, rectangular square to be the "heart" of the Jewish quarter (*VM*, 43) and is so fascinated by the colorful, dynamic vitality that marks it that he fuses into a kind of *unio mystica* with it. "I did not want to leave; I had been here hundreds of years ago, but I had forgotten and now it was all coming back to me. I found exhibited the same density and warmth of life as I feel in myself. I *was* the square as I stood in it. I believe I am it always" (*VM*, 51).

The "square" spoken of here is now only tangentially connected to the actual square that the traveler happens upon. *Together* with the other "squares" that play a role in *The Voices of Marrakesh*, it forms a hierarchical *complex of signs* that admits a correspondingly complex meaning. In the context of this fabric of meaning, central categories of Canetti's life and writings are actualized as stories, and it once more becomes clear that Canetti does not communicate his experiences in unadulterated form but rather processes them, filters them, and finally subjugates them to the telos of his philosophy.[20] What characterizes the autobiography is similarly also suited to the autobiographical travelogue: "personal history and the history of the work" (Eigler, 26) interpenetrate each other and become *fused* or *infused* into a symbolic textual form.[21] In *The Voices of Marrakesh* the sign "square" is only *one* of numerous building blocks that together constitute the symbolic order of the text. Alleys, courtyards, houses, and apartments also mutate into carriers of hidden meaning, and even doors and furniture no longer allow themselves to be taken for granted as props. It makes a difference, then, whether alleys lead further on or not, whether doors hang open or remain closed, whether houses are large and stately or small and unimposing. Even in so doing, however, Canetti guards himself from offering easily comprehensible symbols. "Open" and "closed," for instance, are not categories whose status can be determined in the symbolic frame of reference once and for all. This can be seen itself especially clearly in the case of the women whom the traveler encounters. "In a society . . . that keeps the figures and faces of its women . . . jealously hidden from foreigners" (*VM*, 20), such encounters appear burdened by prejudices from the beginning. Canetti occasionally brings his narrative perspective into line with this tourist's view from outside and notes then with corresponding disappointment that the women do not show themselves on the flat roofs of the city (cf. *VM*, 33) or that they look like "shapeless sacks" (*VM*, 35). His true aim, however, is to correct the self-consciousness of this view.

It transpires that the women whom the traveler meets belong to different cultural spheres. In simple terms one could say: while some of them appear to be defined by the traditional *Oriental* culture of the country, the others demonstrate that they have taken in influences from *European* or *Western* culture. The situations in which the encounters occur underline this difference. There is on one hand the woman who only maintains contact with the outside world through a barred window; and on the other hand Ginette, a girl who, though of Italian-English descent, has never left Morocco and who is forced by her homosexual Moroccan husband into prostitution. Further there are the bread-sellers who withdraw themselves from any forbidden gaze and in contrast to them the local prostitutes who are exposed to this gaze at all times and in a humiliating fashion. And finally there are also in the Jewish quarter two women who embody a similar contrast: the one, a young bride, wears a flowered dress that could originate "from a French department store" (*VM*, 56); the other reminds the traveler of "the kind of oriental women Delacroix painted" (*VM*, 67).

Common to all these oppositions is the fact that they already contain in embryo what is then illustrated by the episodes themselves: European, Western "openness" and Oriental "reserve" invert themselves almost into their opposites. What to the outside looks like cosmopolitanism is in truth accompanied by a withering and reification of all relationships. Conversely it can be seen that the restriction of the *external* latitude of movement does not necessarily have to diminish the *internal* ability to form relationships; on the contrary, the pressure that enforces reserve produces a kind of *secret language* of looks, gestures, and sounds. The traveler does not understand what the woman at the barred window says to him, but he feels that they are tender words. The bread-sellers make the act of selling into a subtle erotic game (cf. Göpfert, 141 ff.), and while the young bride merely stares at the traveler without really communicating with him (*VM,* 56 f.), the Delacroixian beauty answers his look "in response to a natural pull" (*VM,* 68).

The crucial aspect of this sign language is that it knows no fixed code; the code is born from the situation and changes with it. But that means that whoever wants to "understand" must first of all forget all previously known codes. Just as Georg Kien only understands the "gorilla" because he proceeds from no already-existing language, so here too communication only begins once a new quality of language can take hold. Central to this quality is the *mystery* that enters twofold into Canetti's travelogue: both as theme, as for instance in the episodes with the women, and as productive force impressing the entire textual form of the Moroccan notes with its stamp.

Settled at the edge of the silence, it is only the mystery that makes language shine out; it prevents its petrifaction, keeps it alive and dynamic; and it may be that mystery that ultimately gives a text that deals with motion and emotion its innermost justification.

Notes

1. Elias Canetti, *Auto-da-Fé,* trans. C. V. Wedgwood (New York: Farrar, Straus and Giroux, 1984), 403; hereafter cited in text as *AdF.*

2. Claudio Magris, "Der Schriftsteller, der sich versteckt: Canetti als unerreichbarer Autor und als konzilianter Interpret der *Blendung,*" in *Elias Canettis Anthropologie und Poetik,* ed. Stefan H. Kaszyński (Munich: Hanser, 1984), 32. [An earlier version of Magris's essay appears in English translation elsewhere in the present volume. *Ed.*]

3. Elias Canetti, *The Human Province,* trans. Joachim Neugroschel (New York: Seabury, 1978), 29; hereafter cited in text as *HP.*

4. Cf. Harry Timmermann, "Tierisches in der Anthropologie und Poetik Elias Canettis," *Sprache im technischen Zeitalter* 94 (1985): 110: "A valid 'human being' is only someone who has not yet forfeited his absolute capability of transformation, who remains conscious of all his 'animal' and cultural possibilities and is open to new transformations. Poetics, the impulse toward representation, however, demands delimited 'characters,' that is, figures that do not change further."

5. [The phrase in brackets occurs in Canetti's original German but is omitted from Neugroschel's translation. *Trans.*]

6. Cf. Elias Canetti, *The Secret Heart of the Clock: Notes, Aphorisms, Fragments, 1973–1985,* trans. Joel Agee (New York: Farrar, Straus and Giroux, 1989), 41; hereafter cited in text as *SHC:* "It is important in literature that many things remain unsaid. One must be able to sense how much more the writer knows than he says, and that his silence is not a sign of dullness but of wisdom."

7. Friederike Eigler, *Das autobiographische Werk von Elias Canetti: Verwandlung—Identität—Machtausübung,* Stauffenburg Colloquium 7 (Tübingen: Stauffenburg, 1988), 25; hereafter cited in text.

8. Umberto Eco, *The Open Work,* trans. Anna Cancogni (Cambridge, Mass.: Harvard University Press, 1985), 226; cited in Eigler, 30.

9. Dagmar Barnouw, *Elias Canetti,* Sammlung Metzler 180 (Stuttgart: Metzler, 1979), 1; Barbara Meili, *Erinnerung und Vision: Der lebensgeschichtliche Hintergrund von Elias Canettis Roman "Die Blendung,"* Studien zur Germanistik, Anglistik und Komparatistik 115 (Bonn: Bouvier, 1985).

10. Joachim Günther, "Die Stimmen von Marrakesch," in *Elias Canetti,* ed. Manfred Durzak, LGW-Interpretationen 63 (Stuttgart: Klett, 1983), 117; hereafter cited in text.

11. Eberhard Horst, "Elias Canetti: *Die Stimmen von Marrakesch,*" *Neue Rundschau* 4 (1968): 724–27.

12. Herbert G. Göpfert, "Zu den *Stimmen von Marrakesch,*" in *Elias Canettis Anthropologie und Poetik,* ed. Stefan H. Kaszyński (Munich: Hanser, 1984), 135; hereafter cited in text.

13. Elias Canetti, *Die Stimmen von Marrakesch: Aufzeichnungen nach einer Reise,* Reihe Hanser 1 (Munich: Hanser, 1968), 1. [This introductory page does not appear in Underwood's English translation. *Trans.*]

14. Elias Canetti, *The Conscience of Words,* trans. Joachim Neugroschel (London: Deutsch, 1986), 49; hereafter cited in text as *CW.*

15. Cf. *HP,* 160: "To spend the rest of one's life only in completely new places. To give up books. To burn everything one has begun. To go to countries whose language one can never master. To guard against every explained word. To keep silent, silent and breathing, to breathe the incomprehensible. I do not hate what I have learned; I hate living in it."

16. [In the original German; the subtitle of Underwood's English translation is *A Record of a Visit. Trans.*]

17. Cf. *SHC,* 45: "He always says more than he wants to say."

18. Cf. Elias Canetti, *Crowds and Power,* trans. Carol Stewart (New York: Farrar, Straus and Giroux, 1984) 227; hereafter cited in text as *CP:* "The moment of *survival* is the moment of power.... In survival, each man is the enemy of every other, and all grief is insignificant measured against this elemental triumph.... The lowest form of survival is killing. As a man kills an animal for food, and cuts bits from it as it lies defenceless on the ground ... , so also, and in the same manner, he seeks to kill anyone who stands in his way."

19. Elias Canetti, *The Voices of Marrakesh: A Record of a Visit,* trans. J. A. Underwood (New York: Continuum, 1978), 14; hereafter cited in text as *VM.*

20. Cf. Bernd Witte, "Der Erzähler als Tod-Feind: Zu Elias Canettis Autobiographie," *Text und Kritik* 28, rev. ed. (1982): 66.

21. Moreover, this textual form demonstrates striking similarities to Canetti's idea of the "figure" (*CP,* 373–77). To make clear what he means by this, he proceeds from the double figures of old religions, which always represent human and animal simultaneously. Such figures refer to the transformative ability of creatures but themselves mark a provisional "product of transformation" (*CP,* 373); that is, they contain *in nuce* the dilemma of any formation that wants to exorcise what is essentially fluid and flexible. Nevertheless, the possibility of expressing "the process of transformation *and* its result" (*CP,* 374) opens an escape route from this dilemma, and Canetti chooses it by writing the mystery of a "particular sense" into the unmysterious order of his sentences.

The Dignity of Difference:
Self and Other in Elias Canetti's
Voices of Marrakesh

ANNE FUCHS

For a long time Elias Canetti's *Die Stimmen von Marrakesch* (*The Voices of Marrakesh*) was considered marginal in relation to Canetti's major publications, such as *Die Blendung* (*Auto-da-Fé*) or his autobiography. The critical attention the book has received came largely from admirers of Canetti's works who praised it for its poetic quality without, however, placing the narrative in the context of current theories of travel writing.[1] This paper addresses the fallacious innocence of much of the literature on Canetti's *The Voices of Marrakesh* by reading the book with reference to several arguments central to the postcolonial debate. Canetti's journey is an exploration of the dignity of difference that neither appropriates nor colonizes the other in Orientalist terms. Scripting cultural difference, the narrative metaphorizes the repressed underside of all cultural constructs: namely, death and abjection.

Elias Canetti's *The Voices of Marrakesh* is a belated book: although Canetti accompanied an English film team on a trip to Morocco in 1954, his slim record of his Moroccan experience only appeared some 13 years later in 1967. But, as the subtitle suggests, "Aufzeichnungen nach einer Reise" (literally: notes after a journey), this belatedness is intentional: it shows that *The Voices of Marrakesh* is not conceived as a spontaneous notebook registering the traveler's immediate impressions but rather as a carefully orchestrated sequence of poetic vignettes that, according to the critic Manfred Durzak, work like Joycean epiphanies, revealing moments of metaphysical or aesthetic truth through seemingly marginal observations (Göpfert, 142).

The time lapse between the actual journey and the publication—together with the subtitle—thus highlights once more what characterizes the poeticity of Canetti's book as a whole: the voices of the title are mediated not only through the consciousness of the traveler but also through the passage of time. This built-in distance between the traveler and the narrator also creates an attitude of distance toward the world of Marrakesh on the reader's part,

This essay was written specifically for this volume and is published for the first time by permission of the author.

thus undermining the impression of presence and immediacy that is evoked by the sensual allure of the title. According to Cecile Zorach, "this unresolvable tension between the traveler's desire for immediacy ... and his acceptance of distance results in a travel book which tells the reader relatively little about Marrakesh and very much about how Canetti sees man's position in the world at large" (Zorach, 47). In a sense this is true of all travel writing, in that travelogues—ranging from the scientific and ethnographic travel books of the eighteenth and early nineteenth centuries, the *Bildungsreise* (educational tour) à la Goethe or Karl Philipp Moritz, Laurence Sterne's *Sentimental Journey,* Johann Gottfried Seume's alternative *Spaziergang nach Syrakus* (Walk to Syracuse) to Heinrich Heine's extremely subjective *Reisebilder* (*Travel-pictures*), to name just a few important examples of the genre—always articulate an encounter between self and other that is premised upon the traveler's own beliefs and expectations.[2]

In Canetti's case, however, the relative absence of political, economic, and social themes—at a time when the Moroccan National Movement, the Istiklal Party, was fighting for independence (which was finally achieved in 1956)—raises the question of whether *The Voices of Marrakesh* is not just another example in Europe's long tradition of inventing the Orient as "a theatrical stage affixed to Europe."[3] In his seminal study *Orientalism: Western Conceptions of the Orient,* Edward Said argued that Orientalism was not just a field of study but rather "a *distribution* of geopolitical awareness into aesthetic, scholarly, economic, sociological, historical, and philological texts; it is an elaboration not only of a basic geographical distinction ... but also of a whole series of 'interests' " (Said, 12). In Said's view Orientalism always promotes an essentialist difference between self and other, Europe and the Orient, and it engages in inventing an unchanging Orient that is closed off from historical change and absolutely different from the West (Said, 96). The Orientalist attitude therefore shares "with magic and with mythology the self-containing, self-reinforcing character of a closed system, in which objects are what they are *because* they are what they are, for once, for all time, for ontological reasons that no empirical material can either dislodge or alter" (Said, 70).

While Said's analysis has had a pervasive influence on the theory and history of travel writing and on the deconstruction of the white man's gaze,[4] Said's own essentialist set of premises have since been subject to considerable criticism, most notably by Robert Young and the great critic of the postcolonial condition, Homi Bhabha, with the latter arguing that Said paid inadequate attention to representation as a concept that articulates "the historical and fantasy (as the scene of desire)."[5] In the present context Bhabha is of particular interest since he highlights an ambivalence that is fundamental to colonial discourse and that is of relevance for our reading of Canetti's *The Voices of Marrakesh*: applying Freud's notion of the fetish to his analysis of colonial discourse, Bhabha defines the colonial stereotype as "a form of knowledge and identification that vacillates between what is always 'in place' and something that must be anxiously repeated."[6] On the functional level both fetish and stereotype share "the archaic affirmation of wholeness and sameness and the anxiety associated with lack and difference" (Bhabha 1994, 74).

And this brings us back to Canetti's *The Voices of Marrakesh* and the question of whether his narrative is an example of such anxious repetition of that which is already known. Or, to put it differently, does Canetti's vocabulary of "openness and concealment, of knowledge and mystery, of secrecy and curiosity" (Zorach, 56) produce the colonized as a reality "which is at once an other and yet entirely knowable and visible" (Bhabha 1994, 70)? Do we have to agree with the critic who placed Canetti in the Orientalist camp, arguing that *The Voices of Marrakesh* consists of a series of queer, bizarre, and horrific images of an abnormal Orient that is "distinct and removed from the sane and rational West"? And is it true that Canetti's Morocco aims at evoking nothing but "shock, disgust, laughter or pity" in the reader?[7]

If one studies Canetti's *The Voices of Marrakesh* only in terms of its themes and imagery, it appears to be hard to disagree with this scathing critique, since the narrative is indeed heavily peopled with decrepit animals, beggars, and veiled women; in addition, there are many metaphors of secrecy and concealment that, out of context, may suggest an Orientalist outlook on Canetti's part. However, in what follows I want to demonstrate that the book articulates a hermeneutics of otherness based on empathy and reciprocity. This hermeneutics is largely informed by a key concept in Canetti's thinking, namely that of *Verwandlung* (metamorphosis, transformation), which he developed in his anthropological study *Masse und Macht* (*Crowds and Power*) and applied to the poet in his essay "Der Beruf des Dichters" ("The Writer's Profession").

Using anthropological studies as well as literary examples such as *The Odyssey* or Ovid's *Metamorphoses,* myths, and legends, Canetti attempts to show in *Crowds and Power* that the ability to participate with either nature or an other in an intuitive and empathic manner is a uniquely human quality.[8] In the process of civilization, however, this potential is limited and curbed by the opposite tendency toward *Erstarrung* (petrifaction), which is closely affiliated with power (*CP*, 377–79). Canetti analyzes history as a battle between *Verwandlung* and *Erstarrung*: he argues that in totalitarian societies the representatives of power attempt to curb and limit the human potential for *Verwandlung* because *Verwandlung* always contains the promise of change. Since history has the tendency to repress this ability, the poet, in Canetti's view, has to be a "keeper of metamorphosis," a guardian of man's most imaginative ability.[9] By virtue of creative empathy the poet breaks through those tendencies of the technocratic age that applaud petrifaction in the form of professional specialization and impose limits on the individual's horizon of expectation, rendering him or her closed to the diversity and dignity of life. Opposing the rational linearity of the technocratic age, the poet has the task of keeping alive the ability "to become *anybody and everybody,* even the smallest, the most naive, the most powerless person" (*CW,* 162). He is a guardian of *Verwandlung* who imaginatively transforms himself into "every individual thing or person that lives and exists" (*CW,* 165). This is the methodological horizon of Canetti's *The Voices of Marrakesh.*

Obviously, this theory has to be placed in the romantic tradition, which Roland Barthes has attacked for its tendency to convert culture into nature. Canetti's *Verwandlung* is indeed a naturalized concept; likewise he conceives the role of the poet in highly romantic terms as an autonomous and creative subject engaged in the salvation of mankind. However, while one should be aware of the ideological implications of Canetti's romanticism, it seems to me that his theory of *Verwandlung* translates itself in *The Voices of Marrakesh* into a hermeneutics of otherness based on reciprocity. In contrast to the binary straitjacket of Said's *Orientalism* and its closed interpretation of the terrain between Orient and Occident, Canetti's concept of *Verwandlung* represents an approach to the other characterized by openness. For *Verwandlung* can never reach its telos completely; if it becomes an end in itself it reduces itself back to the petrifaction that it seeks to transcend.

The title *The Voices of Marrakesh* reflects the primacy that Canetti attaches to the nonsemantic dimension of experience. It emphasizes those prelinguistic sensual impressions that appeal to an intuitive understanding but ultimately preserve a sense of strangeness. Favoring auditory over visual impressions, Canetti thus detaches himself from the politics of ethnography and travel writing that has systematically privileged the eye as the primary agent in the discovery and colonization of the other.[10] In contrast to such visual colonization, Canetti's use of the term "voices" conjures up an image of sounds. This appeals to the aural sense, however without permitting appropriation by the language and symbolic order of the traveler. Note for instance the chapter "Storytellers and Scribes" in which Canetti captures the paralinguistic expressiveness of the narrator's public performance in the following words: "He arranged them in a rhythm that always struck me as highly personal. If he paused, what followed came out all the more forceful and exalted. I sensed the solemnity of certain words and the devious intent of others. Flattering compliments affected me as if they had been directed at myself; in perilous situations I was afraid. Everything was under control; the most powerful words flew precisely as far as the storyteller wished them to."[11] By being receptive to rhythm, tone, pitch, and gesture, the traveler feels his way into the story, without, however, understanding it. A fine balance between intuition and distance is maintained throughout.

A similar receptiveness is manifest in the traveler's approach to the tortured cries of the camels, the decrepit donkey, the repetitive calls of the beggars, the alluring babble of the madwoman, as well as the call of "the unseen" in the final chapter. Here the voice is reduced to a singular sound emitted by a little brown bundle that cannot be discerned behind a shield of cloth. Both traveler and narrator are deeply affected by this singular voice: "Only for this voice, reduced to a single sound, did I feel something akin to fear. It was at the very edge of the living; the life that engendered it consisted of nothing but that sound" (VM, 101). At the same time as interpreting this bundle as a symbol of life, Canetti voices his respect for its otherness and dignity, both of which are closely affiliated: "I was proud of the bundle because it was alive. What it thought to itself as it breathed down there, far below other people, I shall never know. The meaning of its call remained as obscure to me as its whole existence: but it was alive, and every day at the same time, there it was" (VM, 103). Here and in the other episodes, the traveler and narrator register the voices of Marrakesh with empathy, relating them to the dignity of all life. These voices always remain firmly in the possession of the enunciating subject and are not colonized by the outsider.

The Voices of Marrakesh thus articulates Canetti's awareness that the culture of Marrakesh is only partially accessible to him and that his encounter retains the status of sense perception even at the point of writing. Throughout the book Canetti evokes the enigmatic quality of these voices that yield an intuitive understanding, while at the same time preserving a sense of strangeness, qualities that transcend the boundaries of language: "A marvelously luminous, viscid substance is left behind in me, defying words. Is it the language I did not understand there, and that must now gradually find its translation in me? There were incidents, images, sounds, the meaning of which is only now emerging; that words neither recorded nor edited; that are beyond words, deeper and more equivocal than words" (VM, 23). Canetti's insistence that one must attune one's sense perceptions to a higher pitch, in order to transcend the constraints of a discursive language that is affected by power, is curiously reminiscent of Julia Kristeva's concept of the *semiotic*, the anarchic circulation of sexual energy and impulses, in short "jouissance," which antedates the distinction between subject and object and which is associated with the pre-oedipal drives and the symbiotic space shared by the mother's and child's indistinguishable bodies, all of which is eventually repressed in favor of the symbolic order, the domain of language, hierarchies, exchange, and so on. Suffice it to add that for Kristeva modern art problematizes the symbolic by liberating the unarticulated *jouissance* of the semiotic: "Art—this semiotization of the symbolic— ... represents the flow of jouissance into language."[12] From this angle, Canetti's desire to unlearn all languages reflects his urge to escape the petrifactions of the symbolic order in favor of the archaic resonances of the semiotic state with its fluidity and pulsations. For this reason, in The Voices of Marrakesh, silence can speak as loudly as sounds. The silences that are written into the text are a powerful symbol of the ineffable quality of the semiotic that Canetti tries to evoke in this text. It is given a most succinct expression during the encounter with Élie Dahan's father, who, after having been introduced to Canetti, repeats the latter's full name in such a way that it appears "more substantial, more beautiful" (VM, 74), affecting Canetti deeply: "Awed, I remained perfectly silent. Perhaps I was also afraid of breaking the wonderful spell of the name-chanting. As a result we spent several long moments facing each other. If he only understands why I cannot speak, I thought; if my eyes could only laugh the way his do" (*VM*, 75). This aesthetically charged silence communicates a bond of intense empathy that taps into the semiotic; for this reason it can be only evoked but not interpreted through language.

On the other hand, the silence that hovers throughout the text can also point to a sense of alienation. A good example of this is to be found in the chapter "The Silent House and the Empty Rooftops," where the traveler experiences a sense of frustration at the silence and inaccessibility of the other culture. This theme is reinforced by the image of the wall prohibiting access to the private sphere, which has a mysterious allure for the traveler. For this reason he tries to catch a glimpse behind the walls and climbs onto the roof terrace where he hopes to see women in fairy tales (*VM*, 32). Feigning admiration for the mountains in the distance, he sneaks a furtive glance into the courtyard next door but is caught in the act and severely reprimanded by his friend. This scene and the ensuing dialogue between the traveler and his friend about the function of boundaries serve to parody the traveler's desire to peer behind the walls of this alien society. Canetti's irony here and elsewhere is a reminder of the limitations of the traveler who, by registering his own sense of alienation, maintains a careful equipoise between proximity and distance, empathy and frustration.

In direct contrast to the carefully guarded privacy of the houses and their inwardness is the "greater [literally: intensified] openness" (*VM*, 20) of the bazaar in the chapter "The Souks." Canetti conveys a wonderful image of the rich sensual impressions here, coupled with a semiotic reading of the trading and bartering. The bazaar is a display of abundance, craftsmanship, and dignity, human qualities that reflect the nonalienated relationship between the goods and their vendors; without labels and a fixed price, they are metonymies of the men who produce and sell them. Canetti carefully notes the proximity of the merchant to his goods, interpreting this seductive intimacy as a celebration of pride that affects the goods themselves: "There is a great deal of pride in this exhibition. They are showing what they can produce, but they are also showing how much of it there is. The effect is as if the bags themselves knew that they were wealth and were flaunting themselves in their excellence before the eyes of the passers-by. It would come as no surprise if the bags were suddenly to begin moving rhythmically, all of them together, displaying in a gaily-coloured, orgiastic dance all the seductiveness of which they were capable" (*VM*, 18–19). The image of the dancing bags evokes a carnivalesque atmosphere that highlights the communicative and symbolic function of the bazaar. Instead of describing the goods in terms of their monetary value, Canetti sees them in terms of an emotional value that is derived from the relationship between seller and buyer. Unlike shopping in capitalist societies where "any fool can go out and find what he needs" (*VM*,

21), shopping in the bazaar is a complex game. The price of each item fluctuates according to a number of variables:

> In the souks, however, the price that is named first is an unfathomable riddle. No one knows in advance what it will be, not even the merchant, because in any case there are many prices. Each one relates to a different situation, a different customer, a different day of the week. There are prices for single objects and prices for two or more together. There are prices for foreigners visiting the city for a day and prices for foreigners who have been here for three weeks. There are prices for the poor and prices for the rich, those for the poor of course being the highest. (*VM*, 21)

This passage reads like an illustration of Jean Baudrillard's observation "that an accurate theory of social objects must be based on signification rather than needs or use-value."[13] It is in line with this idea that Canetti describes the act of trading as an artful game between two parties, a communicative praxis that is as important as the outcome, that is, the agreement of a price. The price appears as a reflection of the rhetoric and arguments of the two parties:

> It is desirable that the toing and froing of negotiations should last a miniature, incident-packed eternity. The merchant is delighted at the time you take over your purchase. Arguments aimed at making the other give ground should be far-fetched, involved, emphatic, and stimulating. You can be dignified or eloquent, but you will do best to be both. Dignity is employed by both parties to show that they do not attach too much importance to either sale or purchase. Eloquence serves to soften the opponent's resolution. Some arguments merely arouse scorn; others cut to the quick. You must try everything before you surrender. (*VM*, 22)

Canetti, the tourist, is an "agent of semiotics" who interprets the bazaar in terms of a cultural praxis and a sign system (Culler, 155). Such semiotic mediation does not, however, necessarily colonize the other by appropriating it within the culture of the outsider, but in Canetti's case it is rather an exploration of the dignity of difference. An indication of this is his careful orchestration of proximity and distance throughout.

Whereas the ethnographic chapter "The Souks" offers a close-up of bazaar life and explores it in terms of a meaningful sign-system, the same semiotic approach appears to be jeopardized a little later in the chapter "The Marabout's Saliva" where the cultural distance between self and other is thematized. In a manner of speaking, this episode is a test case for Canetti's respect for the other because the chapter deals with an experience that breaks a taboo of Western culture to such an extent that it provokes disgust. Canetti describes how he watches a beggar chew something with an astounding intensity. He waits until the beggar stops chewing to see what has caused an "enjoyment, which struck me as being more conspicuous than anything I had ever seen in association with a human mouth" (*VM*, 27). When Canetti offers the beggar 20 francs, he notices to his great surprise that the beggar puts the coin in his mouth and chews it with the same delight and intensity as before. Now Canetti's sense of amazement turns into open disgust: "I tried to dissolve my disgust at this proceeding in its outlandishness. What could be filthier than money?" (*VM*, 28).

Julia Kristeva's theory of abjection in *Powers of Horror: An Essay on Abjection* provides an extremely productive horizon of interpretation for this episode, the main tenets of which I propose to outline briefly. When, for instance, a subject experiences disgust for the improper and unclean, this can often be read as a physical reaction against a "threat that seems to emanate from an exorbitant outside or inside, ejected beyond the scope of the possible, the tolerable and thinkable."[14] Since the mapping out of a "clean and proper body" is a basic condition of the subject's constitution as a speaking subject, the improper and unclean—that is, the "abject"—is banished both from the territory of individual subjectivity and the sphere of sociality. Such expulsion has nothing to do with hygiene but much to do with our sense of identity and belonging to the symbolic order. Kristeva illustrates our disgust for all transgressions that threaten our "clean and proper" body with reference to refuse and corpses: "Without makeup or masks, refuse and corpses *show me* what I permanently thrust aside in order to live. These body fluids, this defilement, this shit are what life withstands, hardly and with difficulty, on the part of death. There, I am at the border of my condition as a living being. My body extricates itself, as being alive from that border" (Kristeva 1982, 3). It seems to me that the beggar's chewing of the coin is for Canetti just such a basic violation of the body's clean and proper boundaries. His involuntary revulsion is thus less motivated by an Orientalist ideology but more by the subject's need to protect his own sense of identity and order. Looked at from this angle, Canetti's experience of repugnance is both an expression of a threat to the subject and an expression of the subject's struggle against the intolerable invasion of the abject. What is at stake in this episode for Canetti is the validity of the symbolic order and sociality as such.

At the height of his revulsion Canetti attempts to suspend his reaction in a conscious effort: "But this old man was not I; what caused me disgust gave him enjoyment, and had I not sometimes seen people kissing coins?" (*VM*, 28). Struggling for a position that recognizes the difference between self and other, he tries to reframe the episode as a ritual, the meaning of which he wants to discover. The longer he watches, however, the more clueless he feels: "The longer I looked on, the less I understood why he did it" (*VM*, 29). At this point the narrator reverses the narrative perspective and zooms in on his traveling alter ego that appears to be quite a sight for the natives: "I did not notice that people were also looking at me, and I must have presented a ridiculous spectacle. Possibly, who knows, I was even gaping open-mouthed" (*VM*, 29). Canetti's surprise at the strange beggar is matched by the native's surprise at the tourist's strange behavior. What this ironic reversal of view-points illustrates is the relativity of both cultures.

Eventually an orange dealer assumes the role of cultural translator and explains that the beggar is a marabout, a holy man. However, Canetti's desire for an explanation of the marabout's behavior remains unfulfilled, since the orange dealer simply adds: " 'He always does that' ... as if it had been the most natural thing in the world" (VM, 29). The juxtaposition of the two viewpoints—namely that of the tourist who interprets the other culture in terms of an alien sign system and that of the native who sees it as his normal everyday environment—highlights once more the relativity of cultural inter-pretation. For the natives it is actually the tourist who is the object of curios-ity: "Only now did I notice that behind every stall there were two or three pairs of eyes trained on me. The astonishing creature was myself, who stood so long uncomprehending" (VM, 29).

Canetti leaves, feeling strangely affected by the whole scene. A week later, when he sees the marabout again, the ritual is repeated with Canetti offering a coin, the marabout chewing, and a native who assumes the role of cultural interpreter addressing the marabout in Arabic: " 'That's a marabout. He is blind. He puts the coin in his mouth to feel how much you've given him.' Then he said something to the marabout in Arabic and pointed to me. The old man, his chewing finished, had spat the coin out again. He turned to me, his face shining. He said a blessing for me, which he repeated six times. The friendliness and warmth that passed across to me as he spoke were such as I had never had a person bestow on me before" (VM, 30). Again it is not the meaning of the words but the nonverbal bond of empathy that makes the marabout's blessing so special for Canetti; it is a moment of *Verwandlung* that transforms the abject into the sublime. Such sublimation of abjection is the business of art.

And this leads me to the final point of my analysis. In a manner of speaking, Canetti's *The Voices of Marrakesh* is as much a book about death as about life. For death as the threatening underside of all cultural constructs is evoked throughout. But it is in the central chapter, "A Visit to the Mellah," that death becomes the central theme. The visit to the Mellah, the Jewish quarter in Marrakesh, represents the high point of Canetti's journey; this chapter and the following one on his acquaintance with the Jewish family Dahan are located at the center of the book and make up more than one-third of the narrative. The quest for a Jewish identity is therefore a latent but integral part of Canetti's narrative.

At the opening of the chapter the narrator describes the bazaar life in the Mellah, focusing this time on the diversity of the human faces that is implic-itly set against the pervasive racial stereotype of a Jewish physiognomy (VM, 40). Yet at the same time the traveler identifies a specific quality that charac-terizes the group: he notices that all the Jews have a way of swiftly looking up and assessing any newcomer. Describing these looks as swift, intelligent, and guarded, Canetti then interprets them as an expression of a collective history of persecution: "They were the looks of people who are always on their guard but who, expecting hostility, do not wish to evoke it" (*VM*, 41). Canetti's walk "deeper into the Mellah" assumes an increasingly uncanny quality, culminating in his encounter with an ancient withered crone who, with her eyes fixed into the distance, walks along slowly enough to throw a curse on every living creature (*VM*, 42). When Canetti dares look at her, she feels his gaze and, turning round, "turned her gaze full on me. I hurried on; and so instinctive had been my reaction to her look that it was not for some time that I noticed how much faster I was now walking" (*VM*, 42). This uncanny encounter with this doppelgänger of death is counterbalanced by the description of a lively square, the "heart" of the Mellah. Here the traveler achieves a moment of complete identification, in Canetti's terms, of *Verwandlung:* "I did not want to leave; I had been here hundreds of years ago but I had forgotten and now it was all coming back to me. I found exhibited the same density and warmth of life as I feel in myself. I *was* the square as I stood in it. I believe I am it always" (*VM*, 45). This moment, however, cannot be sustained for long. After a visit to a Jewish school, Canetti comes across the Jewish cemetery. Here Canetti maps out a topography of death that is also one of fear, in Kristeva's terms "that terrifying abject referent" depriving us "of the assurance of being ourselves, that is, untouchable, unchangeable, immortal" (Kristeva 1982, 38). Unlike other cemeteries, this Jewish cemetery has the appearance to the visitor of a barren, threatening wasteland signifying nothing but the annihilation of all meaning: "But in that desolate cemetery of the Jews there is nothing. It is truth itself, a lunar landscape of death. Looking at it, you could not care less who lies where. You do not stoop down, you make no attempt to puzzle it out. There they all lie like rubble and you feel like scurrying over them, quick as a jackal. It is a wilderness of dead in which nothing grows any more, the last wilderness, the very last wilderness of all" (*VM*, 49). This imagery of rubble, a lunar landscape and a desert of the dead, where all meaningful individuality is annihilated, evokes the Shoah without naming it.[15] Here Canetti strips death, the latent subtext of this chapter, of its metaphysical makeup: beyond the borders of our condition as living beings within the symbolic order, the subject is waste. The language of fear is further intensified in the description of the beggars who inhabit this wasteland. Living not only on the margins of society, but, moreover, in this borderland of death, they are the true representatives of the abject, that terrifying nonobject that is opposed to the subject, drawing it to a place where all meaning collapses (Kristeva 1982, 2). Although barely existing on the borders of life, they express a vitality and desire for life that the visitor experiences as threatening. In this context, it is hardly surprising that the visitor tries to escape when a one-legged beggar chases him on his crutches: "Like some threatening animal he came hurtling at me. In his face as it drew rapidly closer there was nothing to arouse sympathy. Like the whole figure it expressed a single, violent demand: "I'm alive! Give!" (*VM, 50*). Amid this landscape of decay such stubborn vitality maintains the ambiguity of the abject. Rather than affirming the meaningfulness of our social constructs, the beggar's desire for life points to its opposite, the meaninglessness of death that infects life. This phobic episode points to the repressed underside of all cultural constructs; it points, moreover, to the fact that language is, in Kristeva's terms, our "ultimate and inseparable fetish," the fetish of life (Kristeva 1982, 37).

After the visit to the small synagogue in the center of the cemetery, Canetti describes another moment of *Verwandlung:* a frenzied crowd of beggars that surrounds and physically touches him, moves him so deeply that he loses himself in the emotion, forgetting his earlier fear (*VM, 52*). This moment of *Verwandlung* can also be read as the transformation of the abject into the sublime. Kristeva's observation about the writer provides a succinct and final comment here: "The writer is a phobic who succeeds in metaphorizing in order to keep from being frightened to death; instead he comes to life again in signs" (Kristeva 1982, 38).

Notes

1.   Of the literature on *The Voices of Marrakesh,* I found the following titles useful. On the poeticity of the narrative: Herbert G. Göpfert, "Zu den *Stimmen von Marrkesch,*" in *Elias Canettis Anthropologie und Poetik,* ed. Stefan H. Kaszyński (Munich: Hanser, 1984), 135–50; hereafter cited in text. For a first exploration in terms of travel writing: Cecile Zorach, "The Outsider Abroad: Canetti in Marrakesh," *Modern Austrian Literature* 16, no. 3–4 (1983): 47–65; hereafter cited in text. For a more recent analysis with reference to "Der fremde Blick auf das Eigene im Spannungsfeld von Sinnstiftung und Sinnentwertung": Axel G. Streussloff, *Autorschaft und Werk Elias Canettis: Subjekt, Sprache und Identität* (Würzburg: Königshausen und Neumann, 1994), 177–208. For a reading with reference to current theories of tourism: Anne Fuchs, "Der touristische Blick, Elias Canetti in Marrakesch: Ansätze zu einer Theorie des Tourismus" in *Reisen im Diskurs: Modelle der literarischen Fremderfahrung von den Pilgerbertichten bis zur Postmoderne—Tagungsakten des internationalen Syposiums am University College Dublin vom 10–12. März 1994,* ed. Anne Fuchs and Theo Harden (Heidelberg: Carl Winter, 1995), 71–87.

2.   For a critical reading of the construction of self and other in paradigms of travel writing from the eighteenth century, see Anne Fuchs, "Sterne's *Sentimental Journey* and Goethe's *Italian Journey:* Two Models of the Non-Perception of Otherness," *New Comparison* 16 (1993): 25–42; Anne Fuchs, "Der Reisende und sein Geldbeutel: Zur Symbolik des Geldes in J. G. Seume's *Spaziergang nach Syrakus,*" *Euphorion* 89 (1995): 392–400; and Anne Fuchs, " 'In Madrid müßten zwei Ochsen an einer Traube ziehen': Fremdverstehen in Karl Philipp Moritz' *Reisen eines Deutschen in Italien,*" *Weimarer Beiträge* 44 (1998): 42–53.

3.   Edward Said, *Orientalism: Western Conceptions of the Orient* (London: Penguin, 1991), 63; hereafter cited in text.

4.   Cf. Mary Louise Pratt, *Imperial Eyes: Travel Writing and Transculturation* (London: Routledge, 1992); and Peter Hulme, *Colonial Encounters: Europe and the Native Caribbean, 1492–1797* (London: Routledge, 1992).

5.   Robert Young, *White Mythologies: Writing History and the West* (London: Routledge, 1990), 126–40; Homi K. Bhabha, "Difference, Discrimination, Discourse of Colonialism," in

The Politics of Theory: Proceedings of the Essex Conference on the Sociology of Literature, July 1982, ed. Francis Barker, Peter Hulme, et al. (Colchester: University of Essex Press, 1983), 200.

6.   Homi K. Bhabha, "The Other Question: Stereotype, Discrimination, and the Discourse of Colonialism," in *The Location of Culture* (London: Routledge 1994), 66; hereafter cited in text as Bhabha 1994.

7.   Rana Kabbani, *Europe's Myth of Orient: Devise and Rule* (Houndsmills: Macmillan, 1986), 126, 128.

8.   Elias Canetti, *Crowds and Power,* trans. Carol Stewart (New York: Farrar, Straus and Giroux, 1984), 337–58; hereafter cited in text as *CP.* For a critical reading of the validity of Canetti's study in anthropological terms, see Ritchie Robertson, "Canetti as Anthropologist," in *Elias Canetti: Londoner Symposium,* ed. Adrian Stevens and Fred Wagner (Stuttgart: Hans Dieter Heinz, 1991), 131–45. [Robertson's essay is reproduced elsewhere in the present volume. *Ed.*] The poetic implications of *Verwandlung* are analyzed by Alfred Doppler, " 'Der Hüter der Verwandlungen': Canettis Bestimmung des Dichters," in *Elias Canetti: Blendung als Lebensform,* ed. Friedrich Aspetsberger and Gerald Stieg (Königstein, Taunus, Germany: Athenäum, 1985), 45–56.

9.   Elias Canetti, "The Writer's Profession," in *The Conscience of Words* (London: Deutsch, 1986) 160; hereafter cited in text as *CW.*

10.   This has been studied by Johannes Fabian in his excellent book *Time and the Other: How Anthropology Makes Its Subject* (New York: Columbia University Press, 1983).

11.   Elias Canetti, *The Voices of Marrakesh: A Record of a Visit,* trans. J. A. Underwood (New York: Farrar, Straus and Giroux, 1984), 77; hereafter cited in text as *VM.*

12.   Julia Kristeva, *The Revolution in Poetic Language,* trans. Margaret Waller (New York: Columbia University Press, 1984), 80.

13.   Quoted in Jonathan Culler, "The Semiotics of Tourism," in *Framing the Sign: Criticism and its Institutions* (Oxford: Basil Blackwell, 1988), 155; hereafter cited in text.

14.   Julia Kristeva, *Powers of Horror: An Essay on Abjection,* trans. Leon S. Roudiez (New York: Columbia University Press, 1982), 1; hereafter cited in text as Kristeva 1982.

15.   This idea is also suggested by Zorach (57).

AUTOBIOGRAPHY,
NOTES AND APHORISMS,
ESSAYS
◆

The Only Sentence and Its Sole Possessor:
The Symbolic Power of Elias Canetti

GERHARD MELZER

One of Elias Canetti's most crucial formative experiences is the torment of physical inadequacy. The fact that his size prevents him from fulfilling a desire is the earliest and most frightening form of this experience, which Canetti undergoes at the age of five: "You're too little! You're too little! You can't read yet!" his older cousin and playmate Laurica mocks him, as he longingly attempts to grab her notebook.[1] The child Canetti cannot know it—and the grown author says very little of how conscious he may be of the incident's meaning—but it cannot be ignored: in the confrontation with Laurica, Canetti learns for the first time what *superiority* is. The girl is *bigger;* she is *older;* and she seems to *know* more.

From the start Canetti begins to doubt Laurica's knowledge. Of course she forbids him to touch the notebook; but once he is, at least, allowed to point at the letters with his fingers and ask what they mean. When Laurica's answers are uncertain, he becomes convinced that her knowledge does not go far: "You don't even know! You're a bad pupil!" (*TSF,* 29). It is more or less irrelevant whether this judgment, which Canetti still believes years later, is correct or not.[2] In the concrete situation it performs the psychohygienic task of *diminishing* his school-age cousin's level of knowledge. Likewise, it also allows Canetti to equalize the age difference of four years. Among the many misogynist statements found in his work, some of the most informative concern his childhood playmate. It is the contemptibility of her *sex* that supposedly justifies the boy in his opinion of Laurica. Her advantage over him in years is, in Canetti's mind, nearly offset by his own membership in the male sex: "I never let her feel," he relates with barely concealed arrogance in the first volume of his autobiography, "that she was only a girl and a youngest child. Since my brother's birth, when I had started wearing pants, I had been keenly aware of my dignity as the eldest son" (*TSF,* 28).

Translated by Paul M. Malone for this volume from Gerhard Melzer, "Der einzige Satz und sein Eigentümer: Versuch über den symbolischen Machthaber Elias Canetti," in *Elias Canetti: Experte der Macht,* ed. Kurt Bartsch and Gerhard Melzer (Graz: Droschl, 1985), 58–72. Reproduced here by kind permission of the Literaturverlag Droschl.

The physical deficit that is the most visible sign of his inferiority, however, is not so easy for Canetti to eradicate. In his tireless pursuit of his cousin's notebooks, it is finally his *smallness* that keeps him from the objects of his desire. Canetti pins Laurica against a wall, where she can no longer escape him; but she uses the advantage of her height and sets the notebooks on the ledge of the wall. "I couldn't get at them," Canetti describes his plight, "I was too little, I jumped and jumped and yelped, it was no use, she stood next to the wall, laughing scornfully" (*TSF*, 29). From the powerlessness imposed upon him by the confines of his body, Canetti knows only one way out; and, choosing it, he seeks to invert the size relationship (and therefore also the power relationship) in the most radical way thinkable. If he succeeds in this, he *himself* will be able to revel in the feeling of superiority that a corresponding height imparts. Canetti abruptly leaves Laurica to get an ax, with which he wants to kill her.

Decades later, in the comprehensive study *Masse und Macht* (*Crowds and Power*), to which he devoted so much of his life, one of his projects is to decipher "the different 'postures of the person,' that is, standing, sitting, crouching, lying, as a code or as a body language of power and powerlessness."[3] The posture that the "little" Canetti wishes to assume relative to Laurica is meant to end—literally at one "blow"—the humiliating state of powerlessness. When he has killed the girl, she will *lie* before him. Despite his lesser height he will *rise* above Laurica, and that once and for all. He will have felled her, and she will *remain* lying while he, standing upright, will enjoy his victory and his superiority. In *Crowds and Power* Canetti defines this situation, where one lays low the other, as the quintessential "moment of power": "Horror at the sight of death turns into satisfaction that it is someone else who is dead. The dead man lies on the ground while the survivor stands."[4]

The show of force so determinedly attempted by the five-year-old Canetti ultimately does not occur, however, thanks to their grandfather's intervention. He wrests the ax from the boy and scolds him angrily. From that moment, Canetti's life and writing are determined by the "original taboo against killing."[5] The most enduring obsessions of his thinking, the struggle against the outrage of death and the scorn for power and those who possess it, can be derived from this taboo. Even though the binding force of this taboo is unquestioned, the destructive energy that seeks to manipulate and limit the taboo has nonetheless gone on working subconsciously, thereby developing a thrust that decisively shapes the attitude and the form of Canetti's work. In *his* way, Canetti has never stopped attacking Laurica; and just as he wanted to strike at her, he strikes at all those who play in a similar way on his powerlessness. He needs no ax for this: for his furtive attacks, Canetti uses a weapon that nobody can strike from his hand. It does its work, and its destructive effect is not to be doubted. It can be summed up thus: Canetti kills by writing. Or better: there are sentences in his texts that carry out symbolically what was forbidden to the boy Canetti. Without blood actually flowing, these sentences execute death sentences; their goal is the annihilation, or at least the submission, of their objects. When Canetti criticizes the satirist Swift for being a "frustrated ruler," so too can this label be applied, almost without modification, to Canetti himself.[6] Like a divine judge he disposes immediate salvation or damnation, and the place where his sentences take effect is his *work*.

In this sense Canetti's power of interdict also extends to his cousin Laurica. He grants her a second appearance in his autobiographical scenario, subtly writing into the representation his judgment on his former adversary. At the age of 20, while staying in Sofia, Canetti meets his "childhood playmate" (*TME*, 96) again. "Something was wrong with her size," he begins his account, "I remembered her as *tall*, high above me; now, she was smaller than I, delicate, coquettish, intent on marriage and a husband. What had become of her dangerous character, her envied copybooks? She knew nothing about them now; she had forgotten how to read, she couldn't recollect the ax I had threatened her with, or her own shrieks" (*TME*, 96).

The encounter with the mature woman thus appears far more harmless than the earlier confrontation with the half-grown girl; and yet Laurica emerges *more lifeless* from the later encounter than from the open conflict of childhood. Why is this?

First of all, it is striking that Canetti—despite the passage of almost 15 years—measures the woman by the same yardstick as he had formerly measured the child. The judgment is correspondingly harsher. If lack of practice, at least, could be put forward in defense of the schoolgirl who revealed the *uncertainty* of her reading before the curious Canetti's probing questions, now there is nothing more at all that excuses the *inability* of the 24-year-old to read. Similarly, Canetti also fosters an increased severity of judgment when he plays up Laurica's fixation on the traditional woman's role; as if her membership in the feminine sex, which had already provoked chauvinistic resentment in the five-year-old, allowed no other expectations of her personality development *from the beginning*. After all, and it is still the first and most urgent thing that Canetti cares to report about the later encounter with Laurica, he emphasizes that she is now smaller than he. To be sure, there is a glimmer of satisfaction there: nevertheless, it is not really important to Canetti that he exceed his cousin in height. On the contrary: if the grown Canetti differs from the "little" Canetti in any point, it is in the disdain of everything corporeal. This includes not only the repeatedly observed scorn of eroticism and sexuality but also—and in this connection this may be more informative—the unconcealed identification with people whose diminished physicality is accompanied by mental superiority (cf. particularly *TME*, 38, 48; *TSF*, 181).

In *Die Fackel im Ohr* (*The Torch in My Ear*) one stumbles immediately upon two examples of such identification. There Canetti returns for the time being to a constellation whose similarity to the Laurica episode is unmistakable. In the course of his chemistry studies he makes the acquaintance of a dwarfish fellow student who compensates for his bodily defect through rhetorical and intellectual ability. Again and again this dwarf speaks of his brother, supposedly a captain in the army, who bears an almost identical resemblance to him but for his disproportionately great height: he is six feet four. Nobody quite wants to believe his stories until one day the brother, who looks exactly as the dwarf has described him, actually appears at the laboratory. He makes an extremely awkward, pitiful impression, and it turns out that he is inferior to the shorter brother in almost every regard. "Fleeing the dwarf's domineering ways and eternal sarcasm," Canetti reports, "the brother had sought refuge in the army. There, orders were at least expected, and he didn't have to fear the little one's unpredictable flashes" (*TME*, 199–200). The dwarf also refers disdainfully to this fear, after the captain has hastily taken his leave. "Well, he was scared long enough," he crows in front of his fellow students, "but he did finally come, after all. And now you've seen the guy! Six feet four—you almost have to be ashamed of a brother so tall. What a scaredy-cat! He's scared of me! When we were children, he was so scared of me, he cried. Now, he doesn't show it so much. But he's still scared of me. Did any of you notice? He's *afraid* of me! What a scaredy-cat! The captain is afraid. What a laugh! I'm not afraid. He could learn something from me" (*TME*, 200.).

The story, as Canetti tells it here, may be authentic. Still, it cannot be denied that he makes a point of playing up its symbolic character: power, he suggests, is a question neither of height nor of hierarchical position. At issue here is another form of power, as Canetti demonstrates in his study of the connection between crowds and power. As manifested in the context of this episode, it is a power over others whose claim to validity rests exclusively on *intellectual* superiority.

Canetti gives a similar shading to his description of the paralyzed philosophy student Thomas Marek. What fascinates him about this physically deformed young man is the strength of his will and his unruly ambition in *intellectual* things. "There were many things that attracted me to Thomas Marek," admits Canetti, "most of all his daily strain to overcome his powerlessness. . . . I admired him because with his intellect he had gained a superiority that transformed him from an object of pity into a person to whom people made pilgrimages" (*TME*, 364).

In his admiration for the paralytic, Canetti goes so far as repeatedly to give him the satisfaction of putting his *own* bodily awkwardness on show. Anyone who knows Canetti's animosity in matters of artistic or intellectual *hierarchy* can easily appreciate that, by fabricating bodily afflictions, he forgoes a superiority that ultimately means nothing to him.[7] It is the exception rather than the rule, when he occasionally also suppresses his *intellectual* superiority over Marek. In these moments Canetti slips to some extent into the role of mentor and teacher, secretly well aware of his knowledge; and he does this all the more willingly when he sees in Marek his own "twin brother," maturing intellectually (Witte, 69). He recognizes in him, as Bernd Witte rightly observes, "the absolute allegorical embodiment" of his own "design for living" (Witte, 69). That is to say: he agrees with Marek in the passionate appreciation of everything intellectual, against which physical states, material realities of any kind, play virtually no part.

In the crippled figure of Marek we see in distorted form the inmost kernel of Canetti's revolt against death. If Canetti wishes a long life for himself, it is because he desires to protect not the matter of the body but rather the mind that dwells therein. He has no illusions about the weakness of the body. What he believes in is the immortality of the *mind.* Because the body is mortal, it is essentially already of no importance during one's lifetime. What counts are the accomplishments of the mind, for they guarantee the only form of survival that Canetti considers valid. In Marek this will to survive confronts him in the flesh: he values, as he says, Marek's "notion of fame and immortality" (*TME,* 354), and that is not surprising, for it is also his own notion. "My greatest wish," he admits in conversation with Horst Bienek, "is that people still read me in a hundred years. That may sound ridiculous today, but I mean it completely seriously."8

What is crucial is that this wish has consequences for the practice of living. Summed up in a sentence, one could say: Whoever wants—like Canetti—to survive in his *works,* must transform his life into his work, his reality into literature. Only in this way can the mortal body become an immortal *textual body.* Of course Canetti avows that he wants to make space for "all who were alive with him here" in this textual body, that he plans to take them with him into an "immortality" in which "all these, the least as well as the greatest, are most truly alive" (*CP,* 278). Such laudable intentions, however, are contradicted by the fact that Canetti differentiates very well between those objects that he literally *saves* by bringing into the work *and* those that he merely lets *occur* therein: not, indeed, as saved but as *conquered, settled, removed* objects. He establishes himself thereby as a sovereign who decrees who or what, in what form and to what extent, is allowed entrance into his symbolic representation of the world.

Seen in this light, Laurica too is ultimately a character by Canetti's grace. We know of her only what Canetti tells us in his autobiographical writings; and since he communicates nothing other than the history of the power struggle that he conducts with her on different planes, in the end we know only of the *defeat* that he inflicts on her. It is not a defeat on the level of biological or physical conflict. The criterion of this defeat is not the physical size to which Canetti alludes in recounting his second meeting with Laurica. While *orders of magnitude* retain their central importance, however, it is a question of intellectual rather than physical magnitude. Even as Canetti describes his former playmate, he pursues her *reduction* and depreciation as an *intellectual* person. It is not enough that she is "merely" a woman and still ignorant of reading: above all—and this must appear to Canetti in this context especially criminal—she meets with no misfortunes that she must "survive" in his sense. While such a will to survive requires *memory*, even if only to be able to *select* from its fund, Laurica appears to occupy herself with *forgetting*: she does not even recall the aggressive attack of the "little" Canetti, as the "big" Canetti notices with obvious bewilderment.

This apparent superficiality or repression has something to do with the *viewpoint* of the perceiver. The experience with Laurica appears exclusively in Canetti's light: it is Canetti who attributes to this experience a certain meaning in the shape of the work that is his life. Laurica herself evidently emphasizes completely different aspects, but these are not mentioned at all in Canetti's version. The "greatest and purest measure of life" (*CP,* 278) that Canetti avers a "work" must contain so that its author can survive with it and in it, turns out in the light of such preparations to be a very "particular" measure of life. For the Laurica episode is no isolated case. The disguised articulation of claims to power attributed to the struggle with Laurica characterizes a whole series of similar strategies of representation in Canetti's work. Obviously he is not only concerned, as Sigrid Schmid-Bortenschlager states, with the *external* control of his masses of text but also with their internal organization.[9] Here as there it is evident that the symbolic exercise of power establishes patterns of manifest power in practice and develops them to efficacy in its own way.

To this point it is relevant, for instance, that Canetti evidently sees the process of forgetting as a mitigated form of *annihilation.* In Laurica's case, however, he stylizes this annihilation into a kind of self-obliteration. Canetti suggests that it is not *he* who through his portrayal devalues his cousin as an intellectual person but Laurica herself. In his examination of Georg Büchner's dramatic technique of portraying people, he calls this process "self-denunciation." "The characters," he writes, and here Canetti refers particularly to the doctor and the drum major in Büchner's *Woyzeck,* "present themselves. They have not been whipped into place. As though it were the most natural thing in the world, they denounce themselves, and in their self-denunciation there is more vainglory than condemnation. They are, in every case, present before a moral statement has been made about them" (*PE,* 16).

What fascinates Canetti about this concept of self-denunciation is the *innocence* implied in the acquittal of the author, just when the impression could arise that he was pursuing the symbolic destruction of a character. Just as the character appears in the work, so he is judged; but there is, at least in Canetti's understanding, no judge who could be made responsible for it: "They accuse themselves," Canetti says, generalizing about such characters, "by representing themselves as they are, and this is self-indictment, it does not come from someone else" (*PE,* 17). Here at the very latest it becomes clear: the concept of self-denunciation that Canetti reads into Büchner's dramas is basically nothing more than Canetti's *very own* strategy of immunization. It is meant to obscure the fact that he by no means saves all his figures and objects equally *intact,* as he claims to do in his transfiguring vision of literary immortality (cf. *CP,* 278). In this light, the *obliviousness* of which Canetti accuses his cousin is ultimately merely the condemnatory *forgetting* that the mature autobiographer imposes on her to punish at last the insult of childhood.

To be sure, Canetti does not always manage so skillfully to harness his occasional destructive energies to the harmless mills of self-denunciation. As unreservedly as he can *admire,* just so ruthlessly comes the rejection when he believes the time for it has come. Susan Sontag indicates in one of her essays that Canetti has a real need for "being challenged by worthy enemies ... [and] being strengthened by an unattainable, humbling standard."[10] Again and again, however, the admiration turns into scorn; and ultimately, even Canetti's great model Karl Kraus is not spared from this scorn.

Canetti reports Kraus's *physical* death in a manner that also destroys Kraus as an *intellectual* authority. Crucially, this time it is not the person in question who aims the weapon of forgetting at himself: Canetti himself decrees the spell, and in this way, to some extent, he makes Kraus "die" once more. Here again, admittedly, he also strives to place the responsibility on Kraus, as for example when he maintains regarding the latter's last years: "It was as if he had gathered his followers together and attacked himself in one of his most eloquent and annihilating speeches" (*PE,* 287). At the same time, however, Canetti's more active, more aggressive participation in this "annihilation" is unmistakable. Joined with the cutting coldness with which he claims to have received the news of his former mentor's death, there is an "obliviousness" that is clearly identifiable as the author Canetti's hostile strategy of representation. He writes, "I heard the news of his actual death—he died in June 1936—without any emotion. I didn't even take note of the date, and I had to look it up just now" (*PE,* 287).

Canetti's rhetoric of devaluation, however, consists not only of a forgetting that erases what once *was* but also of *silence,* or more precisely *leaving unsaid,* and of *ignoring,* all of which give rise to a tendency to obscure undesirable areas of reality from the beginning. We can reconstruct what such processes of reduction must mean to an author like Canetti, for whom reality first assumes its true form in the "work." In the final reckoning he understands himself to be the creator of a "world" that will survive him as a person, and his power consists of his unlimited ability to control admission into this "world."

In the character of the sinologist Kien in the novel *Die Blendung (Auto-da-Fé),* Canetti offers a caricature of such a "creator" authority. Kien lives under the delusion of his absolute *sovereignty* in the empire of books that surround him. This "power" is in fact only the other side of his real powerlessness; it is founded on an almost complete abstraction of the practice of his life, and thereby the attitudes of silence, leaving unsaid, and ignoring provide useful services. That which is not spoken of or perceived, as it were, does not *exist* at all. It reduces the share of the threat from an unmanageable reality and, if successful, it imparts a sense of power and superiority. His purposeful silence and his strategic blindness are defensive reaction and arrogance in one. In this sense, Claudio Magris considers Kien's silence a "defense of his own identity," a "withdrawal from power," and yet at the same time also "a heavy block, a means of exercising power in order to put the status quo in chains and to immortalize it."[11] And Kien himself claims that the overlooking he unceasingly practices is almost in a scholar's blood: "Learning is the art of ignoring."[12] Kien expands this "art" into a "theory of ignoring" meant to help him successfully avert the onward surge of reality, as embodied in the robust housekeeper Therese (Piel, 28).

In the novel this "ignoring" seems grotesquely exaggerated, but it is also by no means completely foreign to Canetti himself; as in general the character of Kien is not only the *terrifying vision* of his author but also his—precisely exaggerated—*likeness*. "It is impossible," as Susan Sontag, for example, pointedly suggests in this regard, "not to regard Kien's derangement as variations on his author's most cherished exaggerations," and she counts among the parallels that she claims to have found maniacal and cunning "schemes of orderliness" (Sontag, 186–87). The fact that such ideas of orderliness, albeit in diluted, disguised form, again and again determine Canetti's relationship to the people he portrays, is made clear particularly in his nonfictional writings, where reorderings, stylizations, and reductions of factual occurrences are of more consequence than they are in fictional texts.

In this sense, Wolfgang Hädecke is irritated by the strategy of leaving unsaid that he occasionally sees at work in *Crowds and Power*. Thus, observes Hädecke, the name of Camus goes unmentioned, although there are unmistakable intellectual parallels to his philosophy; and also the names of the theoretician of crowd psychology, Le Bon, or of the founder of psychoanalysis, Sigmund Freud, are oddly suppressed and correspondingly do not appear in the bibliography, which is otherwise very exact.[13] This process corresponds to a personal attitude of Canetti's of which he informs us in the third volume of his autobiography. This attitude shows him to be at least as skilled in the "art" of ignoring as his fictional caricature Kien in the novel *Auto-da-Fé*.

Canetti had lived in the Viennese suburb of Grinzing since September 1935, and whenever he took a walk he had to go by the house of Ernst Benedikt, the publisher of the *Neue Freie Presse*. Canetti's views, despite his rejection of Kraus, were still clearly preformed by his great model. Because of Benedikt's connection with the *Neue Freie Presse,* he was for Canetti a nonperson. Canetti wanted nothing to do with him, despite never having met him. For Canetti, the judgment that Karl Kraus passed on Benedikt's father in the *Fackel* was sufficient, and he based his behavior toward the son on this judgment:

> I adjusted to the situation in my usual [!] way. I cast an interdict on the Benedikt house and from then on I *didn't see it.* I couldn't have seen it anyway

from the window of the room where I wrote and where I kept my books, which looked out on the front yard and on Himmelstrasse. The Benedikt house was farther down and its number was 55. It couldn't be seen from *any* room in our apartment, not even from the unoccupied ones. To see the interdicted house you had to go out to the garden terrace.... And when I went down to the village, usually to take the streetcar, I automatically turned my face to the left until number 55 was behind me. (*PE,* 217–18)

Such episodes as this disclose to what extent Canetti tends to engage in the composition of reality, to reinterpret it, to reorganize it, to stylize it at his discretion, to the point of arbitrarily obscuring it. In so far as this attitude finds its way into his writing, it forms the dark side of Canetti's poetics. The light side, morally inspired, is well known for asserting with untiring emphasis that it wants to "save" everything that lives and is mortal in the immortal textual form of the work. From the dark side it can be seen that the authority that decrees this "saving" can also occasionally decree its *opposite.* In general, it is the "lacunae" of forgetting, leaving unsaid, and ignoring that throw into relief what is preserved in his work. In this way an "orderliness" of the text arises, constituting in symbolic form the ultimate goal of every ruler: manageable structures, hierarchies, meaning, and context, therefore an *order* of life and reality that keeps *chaos* and *diversity* at a distance.

His first lengthy stay in Berlin in 1928 awakens in Canetti a sensitivity to chaos; he experiences the big city as an impenetrable jungle of situations and connections; at the same time, the stay in Berlin seems to impart to him a sharpened consciousness of the chaos and of the abysses within himself. It is then certainly characteristic of Canetti that he does not expose himself to this confusion but determinedly sets out "to find my bearings, take things apart, set their direction and thus gain understanding of them" (*TME,* 317). He begins to write, for the time being working on the "Human Comedy of Madmen," then on *Auto-da-Fé,* and, as he outlines this work in *The Torch in My Ear,* he comprehends it as a single great process of seizing power over reality, of stylizing and arranging unconnected realities that appear threatening to him, above all because of their "centrifugal pull" (*TME,* 318).

If there are at first still "eight remote, exotic territories" that he seeks, as their "lone arranger and surveyor" (*TME,* 366), to redeem and delimit from this "jungle" of reality, so his organizing attention is ultimately concentrated on a single character who will later be named Kien. "I had never encountered it," Canetti recounts, "It disconcerted me to a terrifying degree, pounced on me, squatted on my shoulders, crossed its legs around my chest, steered me as fast as it pleased to wherever it pleased.... I was frightened and yet aware that the only thing that could save me from the chaos I had brought along was now happening. What saved me was that this was a figure that had an outline, that kept going, that gathered the senselessly scattered things and gave them a body" (*TME,* 320–21).

The concentration on a single figure is recognizable as an attempt to bring "perspicuity into the mass of experiences" (*TME,* 323). Thereby Canetti projects as exemplary a view of reality that he also expresses elsewhere and in connection with other things. He notes about 1943 in his journal that he is "scornful of reality"; it reminds him of "a jungle, growing before [his] eyes, and while it grows, everything belonging to the life of a jungle takes place within it." Canetti's conclusion: "Thus I must guard myself against too much reality, otherwise my forests will burst in me" (*HP,* 45). Similarly, in an entry from 1945: "The chaos of voices and faces in which I used to be at home has become hateful to me. I like to experience people individually. When there are several of them, I want to have them sitting next to one another, in an order, as in a train, and I wish to decide what I look at first. Chaos has lost its attraction. I want to order and form and not lose myself in anything anymore" (*HP,* 57–58).[14]

In such a need for dissociation and orderliness there is a logical consistency that moves Canetti dangerously near to—and makes him dangerously similar to—the victor and survivor, the ruler in the narrower sense. In Canetti's characterization of the primal situation of survival it is important that, "whether the survivor is confronted by one dead man or by many, the essence of the situation is that he feels *unique.* He sees himself standing there alone and exults in it; and when we speak of the power which this moment gives him, we should never forget that it derives from his sense of *uniqueness* and from nothing else" (*CP,* 227).

The taboo against killing forbids Canetti to lay claim to his *own* uniqueness in this way. Nonetheless, that is secretly his goal. He achieves this not only *abstractly,* by working toward the survival of his work, but also *concretely,* by continually writing into this work allegories of his uniqueness. An instance of this is the *one* sentence of old Kokosch ("And then he pulled me to th' altar 'n' kissed me 'n' he was so sweet"), for whose sake Canetti claims to have written his first drama *Hochzeit* (*The Wedding*); another is the continual crying out of the faceless and shapeless bundle in *Die Stimmen von Marrakesch* (*The Voices of Marrakesh*), which for him becomes the "only sound" that will "[outlive] all others."[15] Such moments always appear more effectively saved in the "work" than anything else of which the work otherwise consists. "A sentence by itself is clean," Canetti proclaims in his journal: "The very next one takes something from it" (*HP,* 52).

Seen in this light, Canetti does not gather the sentences of his work into a disordered mass of text but rather sends them into battle against one another so that a hierarchy emerges among situations and stories, above which the symbolic representatives of his uniqueness can ultimately rise as truly "saved." How very similar these symbolic survivors are to the ruler who enjoys the triumph of victory before a mountain of corpses is made clear by an episode Canetti relates in the third volume of his autobiography. He is staying in Strasbourg, and because the garbage collectors have been on strike for weeks an intolerable stench rules the streets. One day he has a vision that plague has broken out. In all the houses people are dying; only Canetti survives by identifying himself with the Cathedral, the symbol of permanence and immortality:

> The processions of supplicants ended at the Cathedral, and against the Plague they were useless. For in reality the Cathedral existed for its own sake; you could stand in front of it, you had been inside it, that was the help it provided: it was still there, it hadn't collapsed in any of the plagues. The movement of the old processions communicated itself to me; we had assembled in every street and made our way together to the Cathedral. And there we all stood, I stood alone[!], perhaps not to entreat but to give thanks, thanks that we could still stand here, for nothing had fallen on us, and the glory of glories, the spire, was still pointing heavenward. Last but not least, I had the privilege of climbing it, and of looking down[!] on everything that was still intact, and when looking down, I breathed deeply, it seemed to me that the Plague, which was once again trying to spread, had been thrust back into its old century. (PE, 66)[16]

It is the *towering* quality of the work of art from which the artist derives his uniqueness. It is many times taller than he is and it preserves his substance. In order for us to know of his uniqueness, however, not only must he himself survive but also all those whom he has survived in life must live on in his writing. To apply this to Canetti: so that he can finally climb to the "spire" of his work, he must first have stacked countless sentences one upon the other; in the final analysis only that *one* should survive that includes in itself all the others. And *that one,* if we take Canetti's word, should be the only *truly* "saving" sentence.

Notes

1. Elias Canetti, *The Tongue Set Free: Remembrance of a European Childhood,* trans. Joachim Neugroschel (New York: Seabury, 1979), 29; hereafter cited in text as *TSF.*
2. Cf. Elias Canetti, *The Torch in My Ear,* trans. Joachim Neugroschel (New York: Farrar, Straus and Giroux, 1982), 96; hereafter cited in text as *TME.*
3. Edgar Piel, *Elias Canetti,* Autorenbücher 38 (Munich: Beck, 1984), 72; hereafter cited in text.
4. Elias Canetti, *Crowds and Power,* trans. Carol Stewart (New York: Farrar, Straus and Giroux, 1984), 227; hereafter cited in text as *CP.*
5. Bernd Witte, "Der Erzähler als Tod-Feind: Zu Elias Canettis Autobiographie," *Text und Kritik* 28, rev. ed. (1982): 71; hereafter cited in text.
6. Elias Canetti, *The Human Province,* trans. Joachim Neugroschel (New York: Seabury, 1978), 15; hereafter cited in text as *HP.*
7. Cf. for example Canetti's sensitive reaction to the slightly schoolmasterish mannerisms of the conductor Wladimir Vogel, for whom Canetti was supposed to write a opera libretto. The project fell through because Canetti could not bear being "humiliated" by Vogel:

"It was one of those puzzling situations that have occurred time and again in my life; I was offended in my pride, though the 'offender' couldn't possibly have guessed what had happened. Perhaps he had given me an almost imperceptible impression that he felt superior to me. But if I was to subordinate myself to anyone, it had to be of my own free will. And it was for me to decide to whom. I chose my own gods and steered clear of anyone who set himself up as a god, even if he really was one; I regarded such a person as a threat" (Elias Canetti, *The Play of the Eyes*, trans. Ralph Manheim [New York: Farrar, Straus and Giroux, 1986], 173–74; hereafter cited in text as *PE*).

8. Elias Canetti, *Die gespaltene Zukunft: Aufsätze und Gespräche*, Reihe Hanser 111 (Munich: Hanser, 1972), 95–96.

9. Cf. Sigrid Schmid-Bortenschlager, "Der Einzelne und seine Masse: Massentheorie und Literaturkonzeption bei Elias Canetti und Hermann Broch," in *Elias Canetti: Experte der Macht*, ed. Kurt Bartsch and Gerhard Melzer (Graz: Droschl, 1985), 127.

10. Susan Sontag, "Mind as Passion," in *Under the Sign of Saturn* (New York: Farrar, Straus and Giroux, 1980), 182; hereafter cited in text.

11. Claudio Magris, "Die rasenden Elektronen," in *Canetti lesen: Erfahrungen mit seinen Büchern*, ed. Herbert G. Göpfert (Munich: Hanser, 1975), 47.

12. Elias Canetti, *Auto-da-Fé*, trans. C. V. Wedgwood (New York: Farrar, Straus and Giroux, 1984), 387.

13. Cf. Wolfgang Hädecke, "Die moralische Quadratur des Zirkels: Das Todesproblem im Werk Elias Canettis," *Text und Kritik* 28, rev. ed. (1982): 31.

14. [Melzer's original German mistakenly attributes this observation to 1954 rather than 1945. *Trans.*]

15. Elias Canetti, *The Voices of Marrakesh: A Record of a Visit*, trans. J. A. Underwood (New York: Farrar, Straus and Giroux, 1984), 103. [The line from *The Wedding* has been translated anew to suit the context of the article: Gitta Honegger's translation divides the line into two sentences. Cf. Elias Canetti, *The Wedding*, trans. Gitta Honegger (New York: PAJ Publications, 1986), 83. *Trans.*]

16. [The phrase "I stood alone" is in Canetti's original German but omitted from Manheim's English translation; it has been silently reinstated here because Melzer's point is partly dependent on its presence. *Trans.*]

The Individual and His Literature:
On Elias Canetti's Conception of the Writer

BERND WITTE

1

Elias Canetti: his name, like his writing, is that of a prophet. And it is with a prophet's fury and devotion that he speaks of literature, the most ephemeral thing of this world. He once described the writer as a "dog of his time," a dog that picks up and follows the scent of everything that moves.[1] Canetti was still young then, but he had already hunted down the grotesque characters needed for his "Human Comedy of Madmen" (*CW,* 126) and, in ripping apart the perverse relationship between an unworldly sinologist and his sly house-keeper, he had already exposed the nature of the fascist personality. That was in 1936. Forty years later Canetti describes the writer—the *Dichter*—differ-ently: he has become the "keeper of metamorphoses" (*CW,* 161), a name that suggests reverence, respect, responsibility for the greater whole, a mystical quality.[2] The hungry young novice from Vienna has become an international author, the future Nobel laureate. What is implied by this?

The "keeper of metamorphoses": the attentive reader of Kafka's works—and Canetti was just such a reader from early on—will be reminded here of the "doorkeeper" in the parable "Vor dem Gesetz" ("Before the Law"). The doorkeeper interrogates the man from the country who has come to seek admission to the law, and he "frequently has little interviews with him."[3] And just as the supplicant explains that he has, over the years, studied the door-keeper down to the smallest detail, to the point where he "has come to know even the fleas in his fur collar" (Kafka, 4), so too the reverse can be assumed to be true. During their long time together the doorkeeper has also applied himself to the most detailed study of the man from the country. And at the end of the story, when he goes to close the door, he explains why he has been standing there. He has not stood before the entrance in order to protect the

Translated by Nancy Bray and David Darby for this volume from Bernd Witte, "Der Einzelne und seine Literatur: Elias Canettis Auffassung vom Dichter," in *Elias Canetti: Experte der Macht,* ed. Kurt Bartsch and Gerhard Melzer (Graz: Droschl, 1985), 14–27. Reproduced here by kind permission of the Literaturverlag Droschl.

law; rather, like the entrance itself, he too had been "made only for you," for the simple man from the country (Kafka, 4).

Read in this unusual manner, the parable "Before the Law" evokes a moral very different from the one usually inferred. The doorkeeper stands with his back to the law, facing away from what he knows to be inaccessible. Instead he faces the man who has appeared before his door. He is thus not the keeper of the door but rather the keeper of the metamorphoses of the man assigned to him, whom he patiently observes growing older and more child-like. In 1969, in his notes and aphorisms, Canetti offers the following reading of this moral: "Goodness, he says. But what does he mean? ... He means openness and spontaneity, a never-tiring curiosity for people, which takes them in and understands them. He means gratitude for those people who haven't done anything for one, but who come towards one, they see one and they have words. He means memory that omits nothing and releases noth-ing.... He especially means everything that is more stupid than oneself. He means powerlessness and never power.... He means concern for people *here,* no petitioning for their souls."[4] The origin of power and the exercise of power within society—the threat of death directed toward other individuals to ensure one's own survival, archetypically represented in the biblical story of Cain and Abel—are neutralized here and turned on their head. "Am I my brother's keeper?" Yes, asserts Canetti in this allegorical interpretation, in which Kafka's doorkeeper assumes the role of the writer, I am the keeper of my brother's metamorphoses.

2

When Canetti speaks about the writer, he is speaking about himself. He is driven by the same curiosity—"not bound by anything, it jumps from every-where, on everything"—that he admires in Lichtenberg (*HP,* 240). The "urge for universality," which he detects in Broch's novels, becomes a self-imposed law governing Canetti's own works (*CW,* 5). His *Masse und Macht* (*Crowds and Power*) teems with distant myths and forgotten characters. In his 20 years of work on this gigantic work, he fed this "hunger for myths" from the most obscure of sources (*HP,* 35). But why did Canetti go to this excessive and—judging by the hollow chord the book struck with readers—absurd effort? This enormous essay is nothing more than an adaptation, a retelling of earlier texts. This active remembering of forgotten experience, which has lain buried in arcane scientific research, is in itself influenced by the oldest mythical ideas. The dead swarm around the writer like shadows and plead with him to be brought back to life through his living blood. But he too lives only from their words, which we need "in a different way, but no less than, our daily bread" (*CW,* 160). To feed on the dead: what does this mean in the context of our century's cult of fetishizing the dead? To feed on the dead means to over-come the threshold of mortality that separates each generation from the next. It denotes a process whereby one can keep alive what theology has always accounted for under the heading of "tradition." Through this medium of tra-dition, which remodels and renews the past, the individual can find his own voice, can invent his own language, and can thereby invent himself and his world. Without this language he remains mute, imprisoned in a public lan-guage, a language that belongs to those in power and that threatens death to so many, if not—as our daily reality suggests—to all.

Poetry as the authentic language, as the "original language" of human-ity, the poet as its first speaker: these are reformulations of an old utopia pro-moted by Herder and the romantics. Its realization is as unlikely now as it was at that time. Serving as a warning against an all-too-hasty optimism is the figure upon whom Georges Kien places his hopes in *Die Blendung* (*Auto-da-Fé*), the brother of a Parisian bank director who has regressed into a gorilla-like existence. Here individualism is pushed to an extreme. This fig-ure's language is so much his own that he has become incomprehensible to those around him. His world, intended as an alternative to the one governed by public language, emerges instead as a regression into the archaic. The "mythical tale of passion" between the gorilla and his secretary, of which Georges hears "a few powerful words, hurled into the room like living tree trunks," is subject to the ambivalence of the mythical to the same degree that it accommodates the reimposition of the power structures of the everyday world within itself.[5]

The longing remains, however, for a language other than the one steeped in power and death that we utter every day.

3

Myths are stories of metamorphosis. In his autobiography Canetti shows how the Mesopotamian epic of Enkidu and Gilgamesh, with the "enormous con-frontation" between its heroes, on the one hand, and death, on the other, has "decisively determined" his life (*CW,* 161). Likewise Odysseus, "the first char-acter in world literature to enter its most central existence" (*CW,* 160). Through the example of these characters the reader learns that it is only by means of continual and cunning metamorphoses that one can escape the threat of death. Myth, therefore, is not simply a meaningless return to some-thing unchanging but rather the memory of what saves us. Odysseus, an Enlightenment hero before the fact, transforms himself into the lowliest of all things, dirty and old, a beggar held in contempt by everyone, and as such he teams up with his last servant, the swineherd, to destroy Penelope's suitors. In this way he escapes death, punishes the insolent usurpers of power, and returns to his home and ancestral bed.

Writers—*Dichter*—have, according to Canetti, the same function. He describes their "gift of metamorphosis": "That gift, once universal, but now doomed to atrophy, has to be preserved by any means possible; and the *Dichter,* thanks to that gift, ought to keep the accesses *between* people open. He should be able to become *anybody* and *everybody,* even the smallest, the most naive, the most powerless person. His desire for experiencing others from the inside should never be determined by the goals of which our normal, virtually official life consists; that desire has to be totally free of any aim of success or prestige, it has to be passion in itself, the passion of metamorphosis" (*CW,* 162). In *Die Fackel im Ohr* (*The Torch in My Ear*) Canetti has traced his own path to this destination. His guides were Karl Kraus, from whom he learned to pay attention to the individuality of speech, a phenomenon he later calls the "acoustic mask," and Isaac Babel, whom he met in Berlin 1928 and whose curiosity for "all kinds of people" inspired the great project that would come to dominate Canetti's life: that of " 'learn[ing]' human beings."[6]

Canetti puts this plan into action in his autobiographical writings. These texts consist of a series of sharply demarcated portraits of people whom the author has encountered in his life. His memory is admirable, retaining characteristic details of even the most insignificant figures—schoolfriends, teachers, fellow boarders, or chance acquaintances—who have crossed his path. With a storyteller's equanimity he sees that justice is done to them all. In this process the individuality of each single character is emphasized to the point of caricature. At the same time, however, they seem so tailor-made to fit the life of the individual who has written the text that one could mistake them for freakish products of the author's imagination. This paradox exposes both the dialectic nature of memory and what autobiographical writing that relies on such memory can achieve: the author shapes himself and finds his identity by transforming—in his own image—the people, animals, and things that he encounters.

As an Apollonian satirist, Canetti sketches stark outlines of the figures that populate his life. The collection of these characters into an epic universe constructed by the author excludes nobody, not even the most lowly and insignificant. So what Canetti says about Stendhal in *Crowds and Power,* under the subheading "Immortality," applies also to how he himself—by means of a process of active recollection—saves the people who have passed through his own life: "But whoever opens Stendhal will find him and also everything which surrounded him; and he finds it *here,* in this life. Thus the dead offer themselves as food for the living; their immortality profits them. It is a reversal of sacrifice to the dead, which profits both dead and living. There is no more rancour between them and the sting has been taken from survival."[7] In this passage, which transposes the mystical content of the *communio* onto the secular process of the author's memory work, we witness the fulfillment of Canetti's often-cited assertion that literature is capable of saving humanity from death.

4

Canetti's books do not talk of love, for the reason that love has been completely absorbed into their design. As at the mysterious, theological center of *Crowds and Power,* the writer is the antiruler, the messiah who brings redemption to a godless world. The "law" guiding his conduct is formulated thus: "One shall repulse nobody into nothingness who would like to be there. One shall seek nothingness only to find a way out of it and one shall mark the road for everyone. Whether in grief or in despair, one shall endure in order to learn how to save others from it, but not out of scorn for the happiness that the creatures deserve, even though they deface one another and tear one another to pieces" (*CW,* 166). These are the words of a voice calling in the wilderness, preparing the way for the coming of the messiah.

But is it not blasphemous to apply these words to writers? Can we really equate literature and theology so simply? In the passages where Canetti undertakes a concrete analysis of the writer's position, as opposed to making a moral appeal and evoking mystical qualities, the picture looks very different. Take for instance the picture of Kafka in the essay *Der andere Prozeß* (*Kafka's other Trial*). According to Canetti, Kafka frees himself from his suffocating ties to his family by frantically writing love letters to Felice Bauer, whom he had met only once before at Max Brod's. This liberation enables him to compose his first stories of real value. This love, however, which was itself a fiction and was initiated by Kafka, soon comes to make its demands in the form of the wedding plans devised by Felice. Kafka, in attempting to escape these plans and thereby defend his creative freedom from this new threat, resorts to excuses, lies, and malicious behavior. Historical fact here refutes the idealized description of the writer's role provided in *Crowds and Power.* The writer, who in his own work assumes the role of the positive adversary of the ruler cannot, in real life, be differentiated from his opponent. Worse still, he desecrates his writing to achieve power over the woman who loves him.

Canetti offers no resolution to this paradox. He does not possess the dialectic ability to synthesize points of view. His unconditional and abstract negation of death leads him to overlook the fact that it is only by accepting death's position as the ultimate possibility of human existence that we can free ourselves from domination and from death itself. Canetti's fixation on life denies him the radical insight that Kafka formulates in a letter to Max Brod at the end of his life: "I have not bought myself off by my writing. I died my whole life long and now I will really die."[8] Writing, Kafka suggests, can oppose the exercise of power only if it detaches itself from all natural connections. One can "break ranks with the murderers," as Kafka describes writing, only in death. Only in death are all illusions, all abuses of power erased. Kafka writes to Felice: "What I need for my writing is seclusion, not 'like a hermit,' that would not be enough, but like the dead."[9]

5

All metamorphoses end in death. Kafka's story "Die Verwandlung" ("The Metamorphosis") proves this. In this story a man metamorphoses into the lowliest of all beings, a gigantic insect, and is in the end swept away like a piece of garbage by his family. Canetti does not acknowledge this final possibility, but he hints at it when he speaks of the "prestige that writers [*Dichter*] draw from their martyrs: from Hölderlin, Kleist, Walser" (*HP,* 229). He writes: "They wound up extinguished and suffocated, and they have the choice between burdening others as beggars or living in a madhouse. The writer who asserts himself, who knows that they were purer than he, can't endure having them around for long, but he is quite prepared to venerate them in the asylum. They are his split-off wounds and keep on vegetating as such. It is exalting to contemplate and know the wounds so long as one does not feel them in oneself anymore" (*HP,* 229). Is this Canetti's indictment of those who have attained success—of Goethe, who dismisses Kleist and Hölderlin—and thus also his indictment of himself? Or even the expression of a cynical, riven consciousness? The latter seems hardly imaginable in an author of such uncompromising moral rigor as Canetti. It is more likely an admission that the two overwhelming imperatives—on the one hand, one's own entitlement to life and happiness, and, on the other, the entitlement of others to life and happiness—cannot be completely reconciled even in literature.

Something like that is the case when literature aims to save the individual, who is more voiceless today than ever. Literature may be able to contribute by helping the individual find his or her own language, thus helping to repair the destruction wreaked by the exercise of power in society and by the media industry, and thereby creating a fully intact individual, a person with his or her own language. There are points on which such a writing process may orient itself: on the one hand, past literature, which serves as both the object of meditation and the means of finding one's own language, and, on the other, the historical position of the individual who wishes to be actualized and understood in the text. This individual's creativity must be stimulated by the forms of literature and supported by its institutions. To achieve this modest goal, literature would have to give up its last semblance of aura, its wish to immortalize humanity and the world in text. In the face of the possibility of global annihilation this wish is wrongheaded. Instead, literature must find a way to point each individual toward his or her own salvation through the work of writing.

6

What is called for first and foremost is the abandonment of the closed literary work whose traditional narrative configuration posits an all-powerful and all-knowing author and an anonymous and passively receptive reader. Even Canetti's most recent narrative works, the three volumes of his life story that have appeared to date, belong formally to this tradition of narrative. They are texts that, with their sweeping anecdotic gestures, offer readers very little opportunity to exercise their own creative faculties. They are overwhelming in their completeness, and their suggestive power allows the reader little breathing space.

This traditional mode of narration is quietly concealed beneath Canetti's musings in these texts on the profession of writing. In particular, the third part of the autobiography, *Das Augenspiel* (*The Play of the Eyes*), contains a profound revision of Canetti's conception of the role and function of the writer. Here the figure of Hermann Broch, who appeared in the 1936 speech as a revered role model, is viewed much more critically from the perspective of the older Canetti.[10] It is true that in the autobiography he is still surrounded by the mythic aura of one who writes "breath-picture[s]" and who can instinctively capture the essence of all living beings (*CW,* 12). And he is the only listener who understands when Canetti reads his still-unpublished drama *Hochzeit* (*The Wedding*), his eyes simply inhaling what he hears. Nevertheless, Broch's appropriations seem to go too far for Canetti. He characterizes Broch as a man who cannot refuse any request, who thus surrenders himself to the influences of his world. Canetti interprets his quick gait and his perpetual lateness as means of escaping these incessant impositions.

In retrospect Canetti faults Broch's work on its tendency to psychologize, and he faults Broch on his unconditional belief in the validity of Freud's theories and on his dependence on his analyst. Canetti goes so far as to criticize Broch, whom he had revered as a master in his youth, calling him a writer without substance whose texts consist of nothing but appropriations: "When Broch could not resist someone else's impulses or intentions in any other way, he simply took them over."[11] It is suggested that the determination with which the younger writer devoted himself to the study of crowds moved Broch to work on his own psychology of crowds. The malicious superiority with which the survivor has his teacher speak of "the impossibility of developing a psychology of the masses," and thus has him condemn his own later works in advance, is a strategic ploy in a literary power struggle, a ploy of which one would have liked to believe Canetti incapable (*PE,* 40–41).

The antipodes of Broch in the autobiography is Robert Musil. The young author, who at the beginning of the 1930s had still not published any of his work but who, nevertheless, emphatically laid claim to the status of a writer, sees a kindred spirit in Musil. Canetti admires Musil's commitment to the one great work for the sake of which he is willing to forgo both his contemporaries' recognition and any financial security. Consequently, *Der Mann ohne Eigenschaften* (*The Man without Qualities*) is an exemplary literary work for Canetti, a work whose fundamental inconcludibility is justified for Canetti by Musil's attempt to immortalize the whole of Austria and every last one of its citizens. Once again Canetti sees in the novel—consistent with his own theory of the writer in *Crowds and Power*—a place where humanity can overcome death, not only the writer's death but that of all whom he takes up in his text. The literary work remains the only path toward salvation, a statement that becomes all the more paradoxical when applied to a text whose methodical skepticism evades all such demands.

7

The Play of the Eyes is quietly dominated by a third character, whom Canetti calls Dr. Sonne and about whose life the reader is never informed. These details are withheld with good reason since this man, whom Canetti meets through Broch and whom he and Broch believe to be the archetype of a "good human being," becomes for him a character of emblematic significance. It is his silent presence in a café and his resemblance to Karl Kraus that initially, over a period of a year, attracts Canetti's attention. Canetti later has long conversations with him about current political issues, about philosophy and religion, and about literature. In these conversations Canetti discovers with amazement that Dr. Sonne understands everything, finds connections between everything, and finds a place for all voices in his own speech. The young writer falls completely under the spell of this universality of the spoken word: "When he had made a complete statement, one felt enlightened and satisfied. . . . Dr. Sonne *spoke* as Musil *wrote*" (*PE,* 136).

If one looks back from this central figure to the first two parts of the autobiography, one can see that other such universal interlocutors had already stood at the center of those works. In *Die gerettete Zunge* (*The Tongue Set Free*) it is Canetti's mother who, in a very close symbiotic relationship with her son, passes on her German language and her love of literature: "It was an intimate togetherness of wonderful warmth and density. All intellectual matters were preponderant, books and conversations about books were the heart of our existence."[12] This is the prototypical relationship upon which all others are patterned. After his mother's life is destroyed by the exclusivity of her relationship with her son, men supersede her in Canetti's life, men who have rejected the world of power and influence, men such as the paralyzed student Thomas Marek, the author's partner in philosophical discussions in *The Torch in My Ear.* These talks with a real person spoil imaginary conversations for him, conversations that he wants the insane characters in his "Human Comedy" to have: "Even my picture of this conversation had dimmed since I was having conversations full of surprises" (*TME,* 369). The exchange of looks and gestures, of speeches and rebuttals, saves the young author from losing himself completely in the world of fiction.

In *The Play of the Eyes* Sonne assumes the original function of Canetti's mother. By spending time each day with Sonne, Canetti realizes his personal utopia: the perfect metamorphosis of life into word. Unlike the symphilosophizing of the romantics, these "endless conversations" that the writer has with his mother and her surrogates do not address the personal relationship between the two interlocutors. As a person, the figure of Dr. Sonne is not developed. Canetti, however, creates in this figure an allegory of dialogue and incorporates in it the essence and function of unending speech.

Sonne's discussions address everything: nothing is suppressed or excluded. He speaks in the service of pure knowledge: "what mattered was *insight* and nothing else" (*PE,* 134). His speech is thus contrasted with that of Karl Kraus in which the word is always used as a means of judgment. When Dr. Sonne spoke, his word was "not an opinion concerning realities; it was their law" (*PE,* 135). In this way Canetti frees himself from the role of satirical world judge, a role he inherited from Kraus, and slides into the role of the prophet, as played by Dr. Sonne. "I tremble for the cities" (*PE,* 298): Canetti interprets this sentence, which Sonne utters in response to the bombing of Guernica, as prophetic, the clairvoyant vision of an individual who can already see future disasters while the rest of the world is cradled in security.

Living in words means abstaining from action. The reader learns nothing about Dr. Sonne's professional or social activities. He appears only in the role of reader or speaker. This abstinence makes it possible for him to withdraw from "the blood feud of history" (*PE,* 299): "He detested every instrumentality directed by men against men; never has anyone been farther from barbarism" (*PE,* 137). Sonne's dedication to the exchange of the living word is thus revealed as a rejection of power relations within society: dialogue as the antithesis of the world of power.

Dr. Sonne takes this asceticism so far that he renounces his own writing and the fame that attaches to it. Whereas Canetti's mother attempts to realize her own ambitions through her son and his literary creations and, similarly, Marek is obsessed with the idea of writing "thick" books, Sonne has given up any literary ambitions. Canetti recounts that, as a young man, Sonne published a few hymnlike poems in Hebrew under the name Abraham ben Yitzhak, poems that in their perfection stood comparison with those of Hölderlin. After this effort, however, Sonne remained silent as a poet.

Nevertheless Sonne's discussions often encompass all earlier works of world literature. Canetti is amazed at his, the Jew's, "mastery of the Hebrew Bible. He could quote any passage from any book verbatim, and translate it without hesitation into a supremely beautiful German that struck me as the language of a poet" (*PE,* 142). Later discussions on the Spanish Civil War reveal Sonne's sure knowledge of Spanish and Moorish poetry. In these examples one sees how the infinite breadth of world literature has become an integral component of Sonne's discourse.

A discourse free of power necessarily also implies that speech is gratuitous. Sonne's conversations serve no social purpose, not even a pedagogical
one. They serve solely to form and confirm the identity of the speaker. As
Canetti notes, it was through Dr. Sonne that he first learned what "a man's
integrity" means, namely "that he will not be swayed by questions, even by
problems, that he will go his own way without revealing his motives or past
history" (PE, 145).

One might think that Canetti had simply invented this all-knowing, all-
understanding godlike figure. In fact he has, while revealing nothing of the
real person behind it, condensed under this one name everything that one
could call "poetic discourse": completely free, liberated language, which
knows no exclusions or restrictions, which accepts all things and people with
an equal openness and liberates the potential of their true being. This language can never be fixed in any work because that would necessarily mean
selection, restriction, ossification, and deathly petrifaction.

Canetti both did and did not create this balanced, idealized figure. Like
all the characters in Canetti's "life stories," he is based upon an encounter
with a real person.[13] Sonne's name is mentioned several times in Martin
Buber's letters: "Abraham Sonne (1883–1950), known also as the Hebrew
poet Abraham ben Yizchak, teacher at the Jüdisches Pädagogium in Vienna,
Secretary General of the Zionist Executive in London (1919–1920), lived
from 1938 on in Jerusalem."[14] This is undoubtedly the same person. In this
figure of the wise poet without poetry, Canetti is once again "exaggerating
precisely." He distorts this character until it becomes recognizable and, in
doing so, he makes its law understandable.

In this process Canetti proves to be Sonne's best student. He surrepti-
tiously hints at the connections when he quotes the dedication that he wrote
in Dr. Sonne's copy of Die Blendung: "To Dr. Sonne [Sun], to me still more.
E.C." (PE, 205). Canetti takes Sonne's name literally, suggesting that his conversations with Dr. Sonne were more essential to him than sunlight itself.
More explicitly, he suggests the importance of his quasi-paternal acquaintance by only once mentioning the secret name that he has given Sonne:
"Archangel Gabriel."[15] In the Bible it falls to Gabriel, "the strong one of
God," to deliver the joyous message. At the beginning of Luke he proclaims
the coming of the Messiah. Who, we might ask, is the bringer of salvation
whose coming Dr. Sonne announces in Vienna in 1936? Is it the writer—is it
Canetti himself?

Canetti is unfaithful to his teacher on only one point: he has continued
to write texts that, by virtue of their formal closure, fetter the productivity of
others, of his readers. Canetti did indeed remain silent for many years of his
life, but following that he has published one new work after another, most
recently his series of "life stories," a substitute for and reworking of the
"Human Comedy" that he planned in his youth but never completed. Moreover, in The Play of the Eyes he has formulated his poetic ideal in a way that

exposes the deep internal contradictions in his conception of the literary text. Even though he calls it a "quite impossible" undertaking, the reader can nevertheless sense the attraction that "writ[ing] Sonne's *Man without Qualities*" has for him: "Such a book would have to be as clear-headed and transparent as Musil; it would command one's full attention from the first to the last word; far removed from sleep or twilight, it would be equally engrossing regardless of where you opened it" (*PE*, 142–43).

This tension between free poetic speech and the overwhelming desire to produce literary work, the latter predicated (albeit against the author's will) on a position of power within society, could not be formulated more clearly than it is in Canetti's utopian hybrid. Only if it were possible to write a text that surrendered its closed form and thus reestablished the primogenital right of the reader to creative freedom could the tension be overcome. Only then would the writer, the "keeper of metamorphoses," no longer be the doorkeeper, the protector, the warden, the superego of the reader but rather the provocateur, the liberator, the instigator of a wild poetic dance. Writing would fulfill itself by helping one produce one's own ego and by encouraging as many others as possible to do likewise. And even if writing were no remedy against our natural deaths, it would still save us from the other, far more insidious deaths that we die each and every day.

Notes

1. Elias Canetti, *The Conscience of Words,* trans. Joachim Neugroschel (London: Deutsch, 1986), 3; hereafter cited in text as *CW.*
2. [The richly loaded word "Dichter" implies in particular a writer of poetic texts. *Trans.*]
3. Franz Kafka, "Before the Law," trans. Willa and Edwin Muir, in *The Complete Stories,* ed. Nahum N. Glazer (New York: Schocken, 1971), 3; hereafter cited in text.
4. Elias Canetti, *The Human Province,* trans. Joachim Neugroschel (New York: Seabury, 1978), 255; hereafter cited in text as *HP.*
5. Elias Canetti, *Auto-da-Fé,* trans. C. V. Wedgwood (New York: Farrar, Straus and Giroux, 1984), 402.
6. Elias Canetti, *The Torch in My Ear,* trans. Joachim Neugroschel (New York: Farrar, Straus and Giroux, 1982), 291, 313; hereafter cited in text as *TME.*
7. Elias Canetti, *Crowds and Power,* trans. Carol Stewart (New York: Farrar, Straus and Giroux, 1984), 278.
8. Franz Kafka, *Letters to Friends, Family, and Editors,* trans. Richard and Clara Winston (New York: Schocken, 1977), 334.
9. Franz Kafka, *Letters to Felice,* trans. James Stern and Elisabeth Duckworth (New York: Schocken, 1973), 279.
10. [The speech in question is published in English under the title "Hermann Broch" (*CW,* 1–13). Ed.]
11. Elias Canetti, *The Play of the Eyes,* trans. Ralph Manheim (New York: Farrar, Straus and Giroux, 1986), 22–23; hereafter cited in text as *PE.*
12. Elias Canetti, *The Tongue Set Free: Remembrance of a European Childhood,* trans. Joachim Neugroschel (New York: Seabury, 1979), 140.

13.   [The term "Lebensgeschichten" (life stories) is drawn from the subtitles of the second and third volumes of Canetti's autobiography. These subtitles are omitted in the English translations. The term "Geschichte" (story, history) is also found in the subtitle of the first volume of the autobiography. *Trans.*]

14.   Martin Buber, *Briefwechsel aus sieben Jahrzehnten,* ed. Grete Schraeder, vol. 1 (Heidelberg: Lambert Schneider, 1972), 506 n. 1.

15.   [Ralph Manheim's translation renders the name simply as "the angel Gabriel" (*PE,* 189). *Trans.*]

Canetti's Later Work

J. P. Stern

In *The Conscience of Words* Elias Canetti has collected 15 mainly literary essays and addresses written between 1964 and 1975 (the German edition, first published in 1975, contained a slightly different selection). *The Human Province* (first published in 1973) consists of aphorisms and reflections from Canetti's notebooks, most of them written while he was working on *Crowds and Power* (1960), which he regards as his most important contribution to 20th-century thought. Both books contain material published in previous volumes. They have thus something of the quality of paralipomena, things omitted from, but appertaining to, earlier and perhaps weightier writings.

A remarkable air of self-confidence informs the work of this author. Long before the old men of Stockholm bestowed their accolade on him (in 1981), Canetti wrote with the authority of one determined to make his readers take him at his own valuation: he saw himself as a major German author of his time, which is the half-century since 1936, when *Die Blendung* (*Auto-da-Fé*), his only novel, appeared. Whether or not it is justified, such overt self-confidence is unusual among his contemporaries. The best of them, in Central Europe at all events, were beset by profound doubts about themselves, their calling and its relevance in an age which saw the rise of the Third Reich, the defeat of European humanism, the Second World War and its aftermath. Even Bertolt Brecht, little given to public self-doubt or literary self-deprecation, questions (in the most famous of the *Svendborg Poems* of 1939) any man's right to equanimity in an age when

> A conversation about trees is almost a crime
> Because it implies silence about
> So many misdeeds.

Canetti understands and occasionally shares such doubts. He has an essay, "The Poet's Profession," on the question of what justifies a man (women don't seem to come into it) in devoting his life to literature. It cannot be sheer love of writing—"formulation as an end in itself"—which he rejects as "mere literary vanity." It must be something more weighty, "for, in reality, no man

First appeared in *The London Review of Books*, vol. 8, no. 12, 3 July 1986, 13–15.

can today be a writer, a *Dichter,* if he does not seriously doubt his right to be one"; and Canetti goes on to quote an anonymous diarist (it may have been the Berlin poet Oskar Loerke) who wrote ten days before the outbreak of the Second World War: "But everything is over. If I were really a poet, I would have to be able to prevent the war." Paying homage to the sense of responsibility that makes a poet commit himself to such a noble illusion, Canetti offers an interpretation of those moving words: "It is precisely this irrational claim to responsibility that gives me pause to think and captivates me. One would also have to add that words, deliberate and used over and over again, misused words led to this situation, in which the war became inevitable." The original lament—*Es ist aber alles vorüber*—contained no such explanation. Setting up a causal connection between "misused words" and "war," Canetti is following in the footsteps of Karl Kraus, to whom he devotes two of the essays in *The Conscience of Words.* The claim that words are the causes of deeds—and the only causes the satirist is interested in—provides the theoretical foundation for the satirical element in Kraus's work, and satire, unlike the anonymous *cri-de-coeur,* is involved in fiction. But if the causality set up between words and deeds is at least partly fictitious (a truth plus a vast exaggeration of what happens in the world), the conception of "responsibility," too, becomes a fiction, a metaphor rather than a literal truth, leaving the writer's—Kraus's *or* Canetti's—self-confidence unimpaired.

The point of these remarks is not to question the seriousness of Canetti's ambitious literary undertaking, but to introduce the thought that it is cast in arguments, and that the majority of these arguments—in the books under review and even more so in his magnum opus—live just such uneasy lives in the uncharted territory between extended metaphor and literal truth, between fact and fiction. The complex and fascinating edifice of *Crowds and Power* reminds one of the complex and fascinating edifices of M. C. Escher. The first impression one receives from either oeuvre is of a detailed, painstaking realism, but this impression soon gives way to the recognition that nothing here works quite the way it does in ordinary life: perspectives deceive, clouds turn into birds, leaves into frogs, embryos into corpses, spheres into hollows. But whereas in Escher all this happens through the deliberations of irony, sophisticated parody and wit, Canetti's constructs defy realism not by design but by inadvertency.

Crowds and Power is a huge and, after its own fashion, systematic enquiry into human conduct, its biological, zoological and anthropological origins and/or parallels, its psychopathological oubliettes, the social and moral values it exhibits and the catastrophic consequences it entails—and all this astonishing collection of true insights and oddities is both sustained and vitiated by its mixed status on the borderline between the fictional-metaphorical and the literal-empirical. Conversely, Canetti's novel *Auto-de-Fé* contains scenes in which the fictional guise is torn asunder by an authorial loathing that reveals moments of horrifying, matter-of-fact cruelty. The book may well be—as

John Bayley has called it, in the *London Review of Books* of 17 December 1981—an "attempt at an intellectual imagination of the true nature of the 20th century," though it is very far from being "the most remarkable" of such attempts. To speak of it as "an apotheosis of the immensely weighty and serious Faust tradition of German letters" is to mistake Goethe's *Faust* for one of those latterday "Faustian" abstractions—among them, Spengler's *Decline of the West*—which may have influenced Canetti. Almost thirty years after *Auto-de-Fé*, in the essay "Power and Survival" of 1962, Canetti wrote: "Among the most sinister phenomena in intellectual history is the avoidance of the concrete." *Auto-da-Fé* is a book about life "lived in the head"—it was Canetti's friend, Hermann Broch, who saved him from the vulgarity of calling its hero "Kant"—and abstraction is certainly not its dominant mode. But the book does pose the question by what margin it succumbs to the dangers it describes.

In the morning paper of 15 July 1927 Elias Canetti, then a 22-year-old student of chemistry in Vienna, read of the acquittal, by a Viennese jury, of a number of right-wing thugs who had attacked working-class demonstrators, killing a disabled war veteran and a child. In protest against this outrage, the workers of Vienna downed tools and converged on the Ministry of Justice in the Ringstrasse. Despite attempts by a few social-democratic leaders to pacify the crowd, extremists entered the building and set fire to it, while other demonstrators prevented the firemen from getting at the flames. Police opened fire and in the ensuing massacre, which lasted until the evening, they killed 88 people, including children and passers-by; and, forcing their way into the hospitals, they manhandled some of the doctors who were tending the wounded. Canetti followed the crowd on his bicycle. The burning of the Justizpalast is the seminal experience of his life, and he has presented it as such more than once. In its two aspects—the fire and the crowd—it is the biographical occasion and literary source of *Auto-da-Fé* and *Crowds and Power* respectively. The event is the provider of Canetti's central imagery—the connection between crowd and fire is one of his recurrent themes:

> Of all means of destruction, *fire* is the most impressive. It can be seen from afar and it attracts ever more people. It destroys irrevocably; nothing after a fire is as it was before. A crowd setting fire to something feels irresistible. So long as the fire spreads, everyone will join it. Everything hostile will be destroyed. The fire is the strongest symbol we have of the crowd. After the destruction, crowd and fire die away.[1]

The principal interest and strength of *Crowds and Power* derive from the book's precise analyses of the physical phenomenon—the very feel—of human crowds. (The German word, *die Massen,* is more expressive and carries the connotation of evil more surely than does the English.) What we are given here is a series of functional descriptions—a sort of phenomenology—

of the human condition under the aspect of crowds; their density or looseness, whether they are moving or at rest, aimless or directed by a leader, led by a pack or driven on by it, surrounded or surrounding, organised or thronging in chaos, festive or lamenting, intent on increase or on destruction, calm and patiently waiting or spreading panic like wildfire: the variations seem almost endless. Of "the method" Canetti uses in elaborating his central insight it can be said that it enables him to present *die Massen* without deciding on their actual status, as an archetypal phenomenon from which an astonishing variety of human activities is to be inferred or extrapolated: indeed, the tacit implication is at hand that the totality of human conduct is to be accounted for in this way.

Even though the writings of Gustave Le Bon and especially of Ortega y Gasset on the function of crowds in modern Europe were very much part of the mid-European intellectual atmosphere (they are not mentioned in Canetti's book), the decision to choose what may be called the phenomenological method and to apply it to his central image or concept is largely original. The method itself, however, places the book squarely in the context of that philosophical anthropology which, in the wake of Herder, of Kant's *Anthropology with a Pragmatic Intent* and of Husserl, formed one of the major schools on the German philosophical scene between the wars. Again, no acknowledgement of this is made. Mercifully undramatic, not given to startling vatic pronouncements and free from political influences or consequences, "philosophical anthropology" is a movement which has not, as far as I know, had much of a following outside Germany.[2] It aims to answer the question "What is man?" by considering the actual ways in which our organism as well as our intentions and drives relate to the human environment; or, attempting to bridge the Cartesian gulf, philosophical anthropology relates our states of mind to our vital powers and through them to our being in the world; or again, it investigates the ways in which man in his status of "defective creature" compensates for his vulnerability and "openness to the world." All such enquiries proceed by reflecting on data which derive from our concrete and sensuous experience of the "life-world" that surrounds us and of which we are a part. Kurt Stavenhagen's seminar in Göttingen in 1947 on "the phenomenon of physical revulsion," known as *das Ekelseminar*, is a case in point: the aim was to show how our feelings of revulsion to mud, to serried crowds of people or herds of animals, and to some invertebrates, arise at the point where we expect to touch or see hard and firmly delimited single things, but instead come into contact with a soft, inchoate, indistinct mass or mess of things.

Canetti's section on man's postures, repeated in a slightly shortened form in the essay "Power and Survival" in *The Conscience of Words*, provides a vivid example of the fascination the method yields, as well as the limitations of his use of it. Each of our postures—standing, sitting, lying, squatting and kneeling—is seen in terms of its vulnerability: that is, in its relationship to the threat of death. "Man's pride in standing consists in being free and needing no support," we read, and: "A man lying is a man disarmed ... [so much so] that it is impossible to understand how human kind has managed *to survive* sleep" (Canetti's italics); "Squatting expresses an absence of needs, a turning in on oneself"; and "kneeling is a gesture of supplication for mercy ... [It] is always a rehearsing of a last moment, even if in reality something quite different is involved." The claim that man is the most vulnerable of creatures, germane to many parts of Canetti's book, is central to the writings of the "philosophical anthropologists."

The trouble with these picturesque arguments is that the reduction of such postures to an "essential" or "fundamental" meaning which is then generalised simply doesn't work (e.g. there is no "fundamental" sense in which the accused who is made to stand facing the court is "free," or superior to the sitting judge). Their meanings, like the meanings of most other phenomena assembled in *Crowds and Power,* are bound to be determined by the contexts—social, moral or whatever—in which they occur—that is, by something other than the postures themselves: but Canetti's argument leaves no room for such contexts. Thus when he repeatedly expresses his conviction that any man's "real" or "true" or "essential" reaction in the presence of another's death is a feeling of satisfaction and relief (a view which in any less serious writer one would take to be a piece of smart-aleck cynicism), this is, in this scheme of things, not a disconnected or gratuitous opinion. On the contrary, it is an illustration of Canetti's view that the act of standing is a sign of strength entailing satisfaction; and that, in the presence of a body lying prone *and therefore* defenceless on the ground, satisfaction is joined by a feeling of relief—relief at not being the body on the ground. Why, to one side of such "anthropological" inferences, should satisfaction and relief in the presence of the dead be a truer or more fundamental attitude than sorrow? Why should sorrow always be an expression of fear of not being "the survivor"? And how is one to decide what meaning to give to the claim that one view rather than the other is *right*?

To conclude that Canetti's use of the method of philosophical anthropology is uncritical—that is, unphilosophical—is to advert to the fact that at no point in the book does he (or indeed, more surprisingly, Iris Murdoch in her enthusiastic review of 1962) show any interest in providing a validation for his insights and claims.[3] Relying (presumably) on the evidence of a certain kind of robust and aggressive common sense, the book contains no truth-criteria by which to assess its arguments. It was Kant—not Kien, the central character of *Auto-da-Fé*—who observed that there is nothing wrong with the appeal to common sense so long as that appeal is not challenged.

Our common-sense perception that in a crowd men are apt to behave differently from the way they behave when on their own—Canetti's experience at the burning of the Justizpalast—is radicalised to the point where *die Masse* is seen as the normal condition of existence. The reaction against

Freudian psychology, seen as the analysis of individuals, is obvious. More interestingly, it is the European experience of crowd-manipulation, in Mussolini's Italy and especially in the Third Reich, that provides the undertone of the entire book, and becomes explicit in two essays, "Hitler, According to Speer" and "The Arch of Triumph" (1971), in *The Conscience of Words*. The essays offer powerful illumination and insight into aspects of Hitler's personality and rule which many historians and sociologists have ignored. However, the Hitlerian experience as Canetti describes it does not provide a political paradigm. The formation and politically effective function of crowds presupposes the proclamation and acceptance of certain values and goals. These values were accepted largely because they belonged to, and were parasitic on, a traditionally legitimated German and European ethos. Of those values and of that ethos we hear nothing in Canetti's account, so that we get the impression that crowds form spontaneously, without a common belief, without any purpose other than conquest and its complement, destruction. This was not true even of Hitler's Germany, where other motives were at work; in almost any other political situation Canetti's account offers scant illumination. Political parties are always seen as warring "double crowds." "The Essence of the Parliamentary System" is defined as the immunity of the House of Commons from the violent death which such crowds aim to inflict on each other: a remote historical origin is identified with "the essence" or "true nature" of a complex modern practice. But origins and essences of such remoteness "explain" everything in general and nothing in particular. "A simile that has been absorbed into the forms of our language," writes Wittgenstein, "produces a false appearance, and this disquiets us. 'But *this* isn't how it is!'— we say."

Why is "the crowd" as Canetti presents it always evil, potentially destructive, threatening death or suffering it? What precisely is the relationship between all those many, often very lengthy episodes and myths he quotes from the papers and journals of anthropologists and explorers, on the one hand, and our modern Western experience, on the other? Are these episodes to serve as parallels to and illustrations of our conduct, or as accounts of its origins, or again as rudimentary prefigurations of it? Why is power seen always in its relationship to the crowd? Why is all power whatever seen as evil, concerned only with dealing death to others in order to ensure survival of the self? Why is survival always an outliving that entails the death of others? And what is the ontological status of Canetti's *Masse*—when does it cease to be an actual crowd and become a metaphor?

These are Hobbesian themes and questions. Indeed, Thomas Hobbes is almost the only philosopher mentioned by name and the only one spoken of, in *The Human Province,* with modified approval—it is mainly his longevity that Canetti admires. Yet Hobbes's criticism of writers who "use metaphors, tropes and other rhetorical figures, instead of words proper" has left no trace in Canetti's writings. It is among the many paradoxes of this idiosyncratic author that although he spent his formative years in the Vienna of the Twenties, he shows no interest whatever in the critical linguistic philosophy that was going on there throughout that time. When Miss Murdoch writes, "Canetti has done what philosophers ought to do, and what they used to do: he has provided us with new concepts," she seems to take it for granted that something significant corresponds to the "concepts" Canetti has formulated. She never asks whether phrases like "the fundamental nature of power," or "a man's *true* reaction," or "the essential feeling"—phrases which tend to be used when disclosures are introduced of a disagreeable or humanly discreditable kind—amount to more than strong personal opinions energetically expressed; she never asks whether Canetti's self-assured conviction that every one of his "concepts," however contingent its coinage or arbitrary its metaphorical extension, has something in the world to correspond to it. Given his great skill in making up a terminology that will serve his obsession, and the facility of German for the expression of such a skill, the absence of truth-criteria gives free play to the erstwhile novelist's imagination.

Among the unnumbered sections of *Crowds and Power* there is one entitled "The Forms of Survival," which I take to be typical of Canetti's procedure. The scientific statement with which the section opens is immediately framed with an evaluative hypothesis and followed by one of his insistent claims to originality: "The earliest event in every man's life, occurring long before birth and surely of greater importance, is his conception; and this process has never yet been considered under the important aspect of survival. We already know a great deal—indeed pretty well everything—about what happens once the spermatozoon has penetrated into the egg cell. Scarcely any thought, however, has been given to the fact that there are an overwhelming number of spermatozoa *which do not reach their goal,* even though they play an active part in the process of generation as a whole." I have italicised the anthropomorphic part of the argument, which, taken literally, leads on to the analogy upon which this entire excursus into genetics is based. The passage continues:

> It is not a single spermatozoon which sets out for the egg cell. It is about 200 million. All of them are expelled together in a single ejaculation and then in a single mass [*dicht gedrängt*] they move together toward one goal. Thus their number is immense. Since they come into existence through partition, they are all equal; their density could hardly be greater, and they all have one and the same goal. It will be remembered that these four traits [partition, equality, great density and singleness of goal] have been described as the essential attributes of the crowd.

And then, with some unease, the methodology is invoked: "It is unnecessary to point out that a crowd consisting of spermatozoa cannot be the same as a crowd of people. But an analogy between the two phenomena, *and perhaps more* than a mere analogy, is *undoubtedly* given." It is hard to know how seriously to take an argument which relies for conviction on the ambiguities I have emphasised. In the next paragraph, the elimination of other cells is described in emotive terms (*sie gehen zugrunde* is italicised by the author) while the one surviving cell is designated as their leader:

> All these spermatozoa perish, either on the way to the goal or in its immediate vicinity. One single seed alone penetrates the egg cell, and this cell may very well be described as a survivor. It is, so to speak, their leader, who has succeeded in achieving what every leader, either secretly or openly, hopes for: which is to survive all those he leads. To such a survivor; one out of 200,000, every human being owes its "existence."

By now the free-floating analogy has moved into the centre of the argument and starts pretending it has become a proof.

Such passages make it difficult to avoid an obvious association with the "genetic" metaphors in Hitler's *Mein Kampf,* with that leader's penchant for phoney analogies and relish of loaded images of doom. Whatever their overt purpose, all naturalistic arguments derived from *Sozialdarwinismus* end up offering "scientific" grounds for "inevitable" destruction and thereby reducing the area of human responsibility in favour of the operations of some biological mechanism. This is a matter not only of retrospective criticism but of contemporary concern. Can we really rest content with designating Freud or Lévi-Strauss—or Nietzsche, for that matter—as mythopoeicists? The uncritical use of "anthropological" fictions, our heritage from the troubled Twenties and Thirties, has acquired a new academic respectability: then and now we are surrounded by enquiries in which metaphors replace theory and analogies explanation. Anyone intent on doing away with distinctions between fiction and philosophy should read *Crowds and Power* to see what discord follows.

In a notebook entry for 1948, included in *The Human Province,* Canetti writes:

> How many credible utterances of hope and goodness we would have to find, to balance those of bitterness and doubt we have thrown around so generously! Who can dare think of death knowing he has only increased the sum of bitterness, albeit from the best motives? Had one always kept silent, one could at least die. But one wanted to be heard and one shouted out loud. Now it's time to say the other thing and yet be heard, for it cannot be shouted.

And again, in an entry for 1952: "he thinks in amazement of that period in his life when he dashed off his characters with hatred and bitterness." This is one of many reflections which suggest a change in Canetti's attitude. Throughout his career he has been deeply concerned with death. *Auto-da-Fé* and *Crowds and Power* (and two minor satirical plays à la Karl Kraus) are dominated by a spirit of obsession: in the later writings a spirit of reconciliation prevails.

Reconciliation to what? At no point does Canetti reconcile himself to death. Throughout he upholds a spirit of protest: unlike Freud, for instance, he regards death, not as "natural, inevitable, the necessary conclusion of all life," but in the manner of the Psalmist and the Gospels, as an abomination.

Enough of the argument of *Crowds and Power* has been shown here to suggest that it is its author's fascination with infliction of death, rather than with protection against it, which constitutes the book's dominant theme. And in *Auto-da-Fé*, too, he shows no compunction in depicting violent death with a relish which I find deeply offensive. (John Bayley doesn't seem to be bothered by scenes which include the slicing-up of a hunchback's hump with a kitchen knife.) The pornography of violence was rife in the literature and art of the "Neue Sachlichkeit" of the Twenties, when Hermann Unger's *Die Verstümmelten* (*The Mutilated Ones*, 1923) was published—a novel which contains almost the same horror scenes.

The reconciliation I have in mind, which is present in Canetti's writings from the end of the war onwards, concerns not death but the humanity that must suffer it. Death is unavoidable, but at least protesting against the idea of its unavoidability makes us ashamed of our death-dealing sentiments, and brings to the fore some that are less shameful. His formulation of what, in these mortal circumstances of ours, will stand the test of experience and remain valuable is careful, and is worth careful attention, because he goes out of his way to take into consideration much that might be said *against* all affirmations of value:

> With the growing awareness that we are perched on a heap of corpses, human and animal, that our self-confidence actually feeds on the sum of those we have survived—with this rapidly spreading awareness we find it harder and harder to reach any solution we would not be ashamed of. It is impossible to turn away from life, whose value and expectation we always feel. But it is equally impossible not to live on the death of other creatures, whose value and expectation are no less than ours ...
>
> The good fortune of relating to a remoteness, on which all traditional religions feed, can no longer be ours ...
>
> The Beyond is within us: a grave piece of knowledge, this, but it is trapped inside us. This is the great and unbridgable chasm in modern man; for the mass grave of creatures is within us too.

Unlike the fee-fo-fi-fum of the Existentialists, such reflections take no pride in our predicament. Canetti fully understands the pitfalls of the "death-where-is-thy-sting-aling-aling" mentality, of the Rilkean transformation of lament into praise. Yet there are, in *The Human Province*, surprising affinities with Rilke's thinking.

The only positive value mentioned in *Crowds and Power* is the human capacity for "transformation" or "metamorphosis." Here again one may point to the philosophical anthropologists, who, in Gladys Bryson's words, insist that for man alone "it is natural to make an order of life different from that in which the race was nurtured earlier." Under this heading of "transformation" Canetti includes, not only the poetic and artistic creation of shapes and meanings different from those that surround us in our daily lives, but also man's ability to change himself into another, to empathise with another, to think in metaphors; and in the context of our crowd-existence, he describes it as the mechanism men adopt to enable them to flee from the pursuing pack. Less is made of the positive aspect of our capacity for transformation in *Crowds and Power* than of its abuses and evil consequences: creativity, in our world of "increase crowds," turns into pointless, senseless productivity, the human capacity for change into dissimulation and deceit, masks of protection and play into masks of terror. And the book ends in a long analysis of a famous case of paranoia (the Schreber case, discussed by Freud in 1911), where the pathology of a heightened capacity for transformation is related to the crowd theme: here again we aren't told at what point, if any, this portrait of madness ceases to serve as a valid image or analogy for less extreme mental dispositions.

But Canetti's later work *is* different. Even though the positive concept of "transformation" is not worked out nearly as fully as the negative concepts of crowd and power, and even though it is in the nature of the aphorisms and reflections in *The Human Province* that a systematic elaboration of it is not attempted (his unstinting praise of G. C. Lichtenberg provides good reasons why such an attempt is not made), enough of an outline is given to indicate how close to Rilke's images of *Wandel* and *Verwandlung* this notion of transformation really is. None of Rilke's extravagant claims are made for it. But it leaves us less at the mercy of the evil and violence that are in us than did Canetti's earlier, more self-confident writings.

Notes

1. Here and elsewhere I have amended the English translation of *Crowds and Power* by Carol Stewart (1962) wherever it alters or omits parts of the original text.

2. A very clear account of it is given in the last chapter of Herbert Schnädelbach's *Philosophy in Germany, 1831–1933,* translated by Eric Matthews (1984). The relevant authors discussed are Max Scheler, Arnold Gehlen and Helmut Plessner, to which I would add the name of Kurt Stavenhagen.

3. [Murdoch's review is reproduced elsewhere in the present volume. *Ed.*]

A Passion for People:
Elias Canetti's Autobiography
and Its Implications for Exile Studies

Harriet Murphy

In his short piece from 1979 on "Methodological Problems in German Exile Literature Studies," Joseph Peter Strelka suggested that the main and "entirely proper" way out of the dilemmas confronting scholars of literature known as exile literature was to treat *exile* literature as exile *literature*.[1] This route, Strelka maintains, leads us away from sociological and political divergences, from methodological chaos, pedestrian journalism and population statistics, to a country of the mind, an "inner country," worthy of investigation because of its timeless beauty, grandeur and significance. This concept of timeless artistic significance may appear old-fashioned, but it does draw attention to the one-sidedness of positivistic approaches to exile studies.

Elias Canetti's three-volume autobiography, which covers the years from 1905 to 1937, ends at a critical moment, just before Canetti's decision to flee Vienna at the time of Hitler's annexation of Austria, a flight which subsequently led to the choice of London and Zurich as his new, long-term homes. Interestingly, considering the popularity of autobiography among those living in exile, Canetti's three volumes were not written in close temporal proximity to the events which they actually chronicle. *Die gerettete Zunge* (*The Tongue Set Free*) appeared in 1977, although it chronicles life between 1905 and 1921. *Die Fackel im Ohr* (*The Torch in My Ear*) appeared in 1980; it chronicles life between 1921 and 1931. Finally, *Das Augenspiel* (*The Play of the Eyes*) appeared in 1985, although it chronicles life between 1931 and 1937. Richard Critchfield notes that Ernst Toller, Stefan Zweig, Klaus Mann, Heinrich Mann, Alfred Döblin, Gustav Regler and Ludwig Marcuse all, by contrast, produced their autobiographies or memoirs almost immediately after the initial decision to live in exile.[2] While this issue of the timing of publication may partly explain Canetti's absence from so many of the major collections of essays or studies of exile literature,[3] it may also explain why Canetti's autobiography

Reprinted by permission of the Edinburgh University Press from *Austrian Exodus: The Creative Achievements of Refugees from National Socialism,* ed. Edward Timms and Ritchie Robertson, Austrian Studies 6 (Edinburgh: Edinburgh University Press, 1995), 134–46.

has not been taken seriously as a historical text. My contention in this chapter will be that Canetti's near-exclusion from exile studies is suggestive of two interconnected points, which may help to qualify Strelka's contention that critics should elevate artistry above thematics.[4]

While the near-exclusion of Canetti's work from exile studies is the responsibility of scholars and critics, it also suggests that Canetti's writing may be resistant to the critic's desire that narratives should also be impersonal metanarratives, offering conceptual paradigms of human experience. For Canetti's narrative has little to say about the virtue of giving priority to the collective, whether in terms of racial, linguistic, religious or cultural groupings. It is thus implicitly critical of the very methodological criteria which critics use to justify their choice of subject matter on the basis of national or ethnic premises. Authors are taken seriously because they can provide documentary or testimonial evidence of what it might mean to survive as a Jew or as a German-speaking intellectual in exile from some kind of original homeland as a consequence of the ideology of National Socialism. Exile studies further identifies home in impersonal and spatial terms, and as synonymous with language, race, religion or culture.

If one isolates points relating to language in Canetti's autobiography, however, it is clear that language is always presented as if it were an aspect of Canetti's personal biography. Although the autobiography is written exclusively in German, it is hardly a sustained attempt to promote the German language as such. Its references to the fact that German was specifically chosen as Canetti's literary language, and one chosen from a number of possible languages, do not indicate that Canetti felt particularly moved by the ideological debate about how "proper" it would be to use a language so apparently devalued by the National Socialists. The polyglot members of Canetti's family in Rustschuk are not primarily presented as if they were linguists (the fact that Canetti's grandfather spoke seventeen languages becomes a relatively incidental detail). Rather they are shrouded in charisma, remembered as they are through the eyes of an impressionable child who is entranced by the aura that surrounds the adult world. A fair amount of narrative space is dedicated to the gruelling experience of acquiring German in Lausanne, yet only in terms of Canetti's extraordinary awareness of the extent of his mother's passion for high standards. That Canetti has chosen to write exclusively in a language, German, which was not his first language, *can* be read as an almighty tribute to his mother and to the punishing experience of learning from her. By the same token, the fact that German was a private language between his parents is recorded in terms of Canetti's appreciation of its role in the development of their love. There is a plain and simple appreciation of the theatrical aspects of language, particularly of "Wienerisch." Above all, there is an appreciation of the way in which words can be used economically and with power, a point which will become clear in my discussion of Canetti's relationship with Fritz Wotruba.

Canetti's narrative shows by example that the desire to appropriate narratives for metanarratives is reductive. His fascination with highly personal details suggests that such an attitude is destructive of the inalienable uniqueness of each human experience, and each human subject. Indeed, his attention to the inalienable truth of detail undermines the abstract, totalising drive of metanarrative. There is thus little in Canetti's autobiography on what it "means" to have to leave, or to choose to leave, a linguistic, cultural, religious or national home, not least because Canetti rejects definitions of home which equate home with geographical *space*.[5] His concept of *resistance* is not directed towards sociopolitical issues, as in the case of authors like Ernst Toller and Klaus Mann, for whom existence is primarily a matter of taking on sociopolitical causes.[6] Canetti's aesthetics and politics of resistance are of a different kind, and have little in common with the idea of resistance normally encountered in exile studies, where it is usually equated with resistance to political or racial persecution.

Canetti's narrative works with a very challenging assumption, namely that the individual should make a priority of those personal details of his life which are *emotionally* meaningful to him, as a way of *preserving* the full integrity of the self and protecting it from violation by sociopolitical ideology of any kind. This is a substantially different point of departure from the view that the priority should be with *defending* the self against impersonal forces in the world beyond the individual's imagination. By being brutally clear about the wealth and depth of each individual human experience, Canetti also becomes capable of defying and celebrating as life-giving, in terms of dynamic human relationships, something that other exiled authors tend to assume only exists in the sociopolitical realm, namely power. Canetti chooses to meet and negotiate the challenge of power as it is embodied in individual personalities. Finally, in denying that identity should be constituted by impersonal factors and repudiating membership of those communities founded on very general notions of purity or exclusivity, whether of language, culture, religion or nation, he reveals how we can open up possibilities for ourselves related to an ideal freedom, which celebrates personal identity. Such possibilities preserve the uniqueness of each human subject. As such, they cannot seriously promote discrimination.

The silent subtext of the autobiography is thus very aware of the fact that all thinking which makes an issue of the determinants of human behaviour and experience in terms of race, sex, class, colour or creed is vulnerable to exploitation by the very evils which it wishes to combat. The subtext is shot through with the knowledge that the repeated use of common denominators stifles the scope for uniqueness and originality: repeatedly to make an issue of the impersonal may imply a failure of the imagination as an instrument of creativity, above all of happiness.

Despite the attempts made by critics, like Sander Gilman, to isolate aspects of the Jewish "issue" in Canetti's autobiography, and to appropriate his insights for metanarratives, the bulk of narrative space in Canetti's autobiography is actually dedicated to human relationships and what sustains them.[7] The narrator is fascinated by those highly personal communities of self-selecting, elect sister souls, so boldly promoted by his hero, Stendhal.[8] Canetti, like Stendhal, does not believe, emotionally, in the state or experience of exile. He firmly believes in the possibility of freedom and happiness at all times, in spite of the endless constraints that may be imposed on individuals in the course of their lives. Canetti, throughout his narrative, promotes "the happy few," those individuals who love one another because they share a delight, both personal and social, in self-creation. Such people choose one another because they enjoy cooperating with those who make a priority of the humanist goal of subordinating social culture to the goal of personal culture, especially with those who believe that identity is best constituted by the uniquely personal experience. The only justification for this strategy for living lies in the way in which it yields practical fruits in terms of personal happiness and pleasure: personal culture tends to nourish, complement and perpetuate natural bonds, such as those of love. Finally, a survey of Canetti's favourite people indicates, rather unusually in terms of the history of love in Western literature, that his "passion for people" is really love, which may also be construed as a synonym for friendship.[9]

While it is obvious that very little in the autobiography lends itself to documentary interpretation, partly because of Canetti's easy cosmopolitanism, one could nevertheless reply that this can be accounted for by the kind of socioeconomic privileges which Canetti inherited at birth. He may simply have reacted positively to his new surrounding after 1938, when he first settled in "exile" in London, because of these privileges. This ability to create a sense of home is corroborated, amusingly, by John Willett, who writes that Canetti, when he lived in London, was able to transform an ordinary English café in Hampstead into a Viennese-style literary coffeehouse.[10] And the same idea must have been in Steven Beller's mind when he coined the witty phrase: "If you like: is not London NW6 one of the last bastions of the Habsburg Monarchy?"[11] While this would be an easy way of dismissing the achievement of the autobiography, the passages which I have chosen should reveal that the rhetorical drive of the narrative questions such a response.

Canetti's refusal of the categories which are common in exile studies and susceptible to exploitation is expressed by implying that the details of his life are unique to him as a named individual in the first instance, and then unique as such in the second instance. This curious ability to see *both* the general in the particular *and* the particular in the general is reflected in the very way in which the narrative assumes that the reader is a creator himself, and a believer in the power of creativity. The details of Canetti's life are narrated in ways which appeal to the imagination of his readers in terms of inventiveness and resilience and in terms of the reader's ability to appreciate the art of self-preservation as a necessary life-skill.[12]

If the autobiography asks, primarily, to be read in terms of the relationships which it depicts between two individuals, it does so in ways which turn all aspects of relations between individuals into powerful rituals, fuelled by the power which lies at the heart of the personalities which Canetti celebrates in his life-story. In the classic account of the death of his father, the representation of his mother's reaction enacts the violence of shock and, in doing so, asserts the importance of passion as a way of life:

> He went down to breakfast as usual. Before long, we heard loud yells. The governess dashed down the stairs, I at her heels. By the open door to the dining room, I saw my father lying on the floor. He was stretched out full length, between the table and the fireplace, very close to the fireplace, his face was white, he had foam on his mouth, Mother knelt at his side, crying: "Jacques, speak to me, speak to me, Jacques, Jacques, speak to me!"[13]

The breathtaking, ruthless authority and determination of Canetti's mother as a teacher are likewise remembered in ways which both ritualise the experience itself and make her power as a creator and passion as a human being self-evident:

> I don't know how many sentences she expected to drill me in the first time; let us conservatively say a few; I fear it was many. She let me go, saying: "Repeat it all to yourself. You must not forget a single sentence. Not a single one. Tomorrow, we shall continue." She kept the book, and I was left to myself, perplexed. (pp. 67–68)

That this encounter between mother and son, so punishing in itself, resulted in the exclamation "My son's an idiot!" is not an invitation to self-pity or pathos (p. 68). It is simply proof of the extent to which Canetti abhors any of the emotions which are debilitating in terms of self-preservation. Hence the frequency of laconic understatement in the course of the narrative. At the conclusion of the above episode, for instance, the sentence "She regarded the terror I lived in as pedagogical" states the obvious—only a wantonly fantastic reading of the scene could conclude otherwise (p. 69). At the same time it refuses, utterly, to indulge in the business of recrimination, thus expressing a vote of confidence for dignity in the face of power. Here, Canetti's mother's power is really a synonym for an ability to do things with passion, *as if you thought they were worth while;* and the power of her son is enshrined in his dignified acceptance of his mother's power and passion, and in his refusal to minimise the extent of either. There is no explicit commentary and no analysis of the implications of her behaviour in terms of theory. It is simply given, as power is given.

There are also countless examples of the way in which Canetti's intersubjective encounters are productive of a sense of life. Whereas Sander Gilman dredges the text for themes pertinent to the cause of promoting the categories dear to exile studies—in the case of his survey in *Jewish Self-Hatred,* the apparent hostility of the Western Jew to the Eastern Jew—the autobiography actually excels at the artistry involved in creating and sustaining human relationships.[14] It does so, not primarily in the sense that it is admiring of the relationships which formed the substance of Canetti's actual life, but in terms of the way in which the text relates to its readers. The text presupposes the kind of reader who relishes intersubjective encounters of all kinds.

Dominating the story of his life is Canetti's relationship with his mother, a relationship which has inevitably attracted attention on account of its strength and intensity, and on account of the way in which it inverts the normative conventions usually thought to inform mother-son relationships.[15] Waltraud Wiethölter sees in the relationship evidence of Elias Canetti's omnipotence fantasy, of a rivalry between mother and son and of an Oedipus complex.[16] Friederike Eigler sees in the autobiography, more generally, evidence of Canetti's psychological need to define himself in opposition to other selves, as a way of protecting his own ego and his unquestioning sense of his own superiority. While it goes without saying that theory has a wonderful ability to deny individuality in favour of blank anonymous ideas about the workings of the human mind, it would be appropriate to remember the number of times that Canetti pays tribute to his mother's power as a creative influence, in terms of small, local details. His mother's amazing fear of mice makes her particularly human, when it is set alongside her terrifying strength of character. Her withering hatred of anything resembling secular success or material ambition, and her overriding passion for all pursuits of the mind and intellect, for anything which could be seen, heard and discussed, for all human beings who have any kind of character, above all her idealism—these qualities are all felt very powerfully. Indeed, Canetti's autobiography is so capable of distilling her spirit that one feels personally implicated in her almighty challenge to her son, as she lies on her death-bed, punishing him with her eyes for having hurt her by having married the woman he loved, Veza, and kept it a secret:

> That was her face again with the insatiable nostrils. Her enlarged eyes rested on me. She didn't say: "I don't want to see you. What are you doing here! I didn't send for you!" She recognized the scent, and I had crept into it. She asked no questions, she surrendered wholly to the smell. Her forehead seemed to widen, I fully expected her unmistakable words, hard words that I dreaded. I heard her words of bitter reproach, as though she had repeated them: You've married. You didn't tell me. You deceived me.[17]

That elusive quality which Henry James called the sense of "felt life" characterises the autobiography, in the sense that the enactment of experience flatters the reader's own ability to live life intensely. Yet the autobiography does not make a virtue out of Canetti's own uniqueness by implying that he is exceptional or superior, as so many autobiographies do: it assumes that we are all equal in our capacity to live life to the full. The extent of the intensity of experience in the autobiography is such that one soon forgets that Canetti is *re*membering or *re*collecting the past. On balance, far more creative and imaginative energy is committed to the dramatic enactment of scenes already experienced, *as if* they were still real, not just to the Canetti who is remembering as he writes and writing as he remembers, but to the reader as (s)he reads. In this sense they have been salvaged, altogether, from the possibility of loss and destruction.

We can turn now to the relationship with another loved one, Veza. First and foremost, given that Canetti married Veza and that *The Torch in My Ear* is dedicated to her, the story of the relationship is fiercely protective of itself, a feature of the narrative which has caused Bernd Witte to comment that the portrait of Veza is "strikingly abstract and impersonal."[18] Veza is known to us as a lover of books, and as an independent spirit, not as Elias Canetti's lover. Again, a feature of this close relationship is the sense in which it is possible to cooperate with another person's powerfully individual, unique and idiosyncratic differences. One can argue that Canetti tends to equate love with intellectual intimacy and friendship above all, not sentiment as such: while he admired Gogol and Stendhal, Veza liked Flaubert and Tolstoy and the two positively relished intellectual combat: "There were battles, but there was never a victor."[19] Veza's delight at Elias's ignorance of Büchner's *Woyzeck* underlines the sense in which a relationship is positively enriched by differences of opinion and differences in experience. It also leads on to another important point about the way in which experience is treated in the autobiography.

My example here is taken from the passage in *The Play of the Eyes* where Canetti relates how he ran to visit Veza and wake her up one night, after he had read *Woyzeck* for the first time. Veza appears to be full of contempt, and Canetti expects her to indicate that she does not think much of Büchner's work. He is proved wrong:

> "And you don't think much of it?" There was anger, menace, in my voice. Suddenly she caught on.
> "What?! Who doesn't think much of it? Why, I think it's the greatest play ever written in German."
> I couldn't believe my ears. I stammered the first thing that came into my head: "But it's only a fragment."
> "A fragment? You call it a fragment? What's missing from it is better than what's present in any other play. We could do with more such fragments."
> "You never mentioned it to me. Have you known Büchner long?"
> "Longer than I've known you. I read him long ago. I came across Büchner at the same time as Hebbel's *Journals* and Lichtenberg."

"But you never said a word about him. You often showed me passages from Hebbel and Lichtenberg. But not a word about *Wozzeck*. Why?"[20]

Canetti makes frequent use of what Henry James described as the "scenic method"—the exploitation of dialogue in prose to make experience seem as vital as it is in non-literary life. It is the use of dialogue which makes it possible for the reader to experience what Canetti describes with absolutely no loss of intensity. Not only has the very spirit of life been successfully distilled from the historical moment to which the details of his life are linked: it has been preserved intact. It is in this way that Canetti's autobiography is in a class of its own: it destroys the division of time into mutually exclusive units—the past, the present, the future—a division absolutely crucial to those writers who believe in Exile and its corollary Loss. And it does so to demonstrate that linear time can be transcended in favour of something like the perpetual present of the imagination, a perpetual present which has very little to do with memory as a place where memories are stored, and everything to do with the way in which the imagination is endlessly capable of creating/recreating the past *as if it were still present*.[21] The timelessness of Canetti's autobiography, to which Strelka obliquely refers in his insistence on the importance of the kind of literature which has the status of art, has, therefore, nothing to do with linear time at all. The timelessness is Canetti's attitude to life, and that attitude to life implies an unusual degree of pride, as indeed love. The two combine in favour of the idea that preservation is crucial to survival on qualitative terms: you can preserve what you love and keep its sense of life and meaning intact by an act of the imagination, and without having to sell out to the devils lurking in the shadows. Canetti's imagination is alive enough not to be vulnerable to apocalyptic thinking, and it never degenerates into melancholia.

In *The Play of the Eyes*, Canetti discusses at length his relationship with the sculptor Fritz Wotruba. I have implied that the narrative of Canetti's relationships with his mother and with Veza are tributes to them as people, and the narrative space dedicated to Fritz Wotruba, his "twin brother," is no exception.[22] Here, one can marvel at Canetti's ability to approve of another person's being. Wotruba's creation of the sculpture "Der schwarze Stehende" itself becomes the centrepiece of their relationship. Canetti marvels at the discriminating *man* in him, the creator who does not reserve his creativity for sculpture, who knows that there is an art to life:

His words were charged with the strength that enabled him to hold them back. He was not a silent man and he expressed opinions on many matters. But knew what he was saying, I have never heard idle chatter from his lips. Even when he was not talking about his main interest, his words always had *direction*. ... Perhaps Wotruba's language had only one thing in common with Nestroy's: its hardness, the exact opposite of the sweetness for which Vienna is famed and ill-famed throughout the world.[23]

This analysis of the most important relationships in Canetti's life has indicated that his life-story is all about personal culture, about the rituals of life with one's loved ones. It has become clear that the *way* in which Canetti narrates his life-story is symbolic of his conviction that his readers are capable of living life intensely: he stages his scenes in ways which appeal to our artistic skills as creators, capable of negotiating power when it is at work in personalities around us and of using such dynamic intersubjective encounters to create and perpetuate bonds of love. This achievement may also be read ideologically, as a vote of confidence in our ability to sustain a sense of the uniqueness of ourselves and our experiences, if we want to survive and resist discrimination.

In so many of the accounts of exile literature, as in so many of the primary texts on which they focus, the silent view taken, if rarely expressed, is an opposed one, namely that the possibility of sustaining the self under pressure does not exist. The focus on loss, on rootlessness, on non-assimilation, on the failure of sociopolitical commitment and the problem of "being" a German in a post-1945 world, conspires to suggest, especially in autobiographical narratives, that those writers who were more directly affected by 1939–45 than Canetti effectively lost their faith in the purpose of life and in humanity as a whole. While this is obviously understandable, it seems that exile studies may be doing violence to the dignity of those testimonial accounts of loss, in its rigorous determination to exploit such accounts for other purposes. The first generation of writers to chronicle the experience of loss has now given way to a generation of critics, whose preoccupation with the spoils of the destructive past is suspect. Exile critics tend to privilege the works of writers who identify themselves racially or nationally as exiles. Because of the prominence given to race and nationality as "methodological" criteria for selection, this has the effect of perpetuating the very ideology which such writers found abhorrent when it took the form of National Socialism. Yet the implications of this ideology remain hidden because such critics tend to celebrate their subjects as victims, making them into martyrs to the cause of truth. The recent dramatic increase in the number of publications which have been produced under the rubric of exile studies may indeed reflect a belated awareness of German guilt about the Second World War.

Adorno and Horkheimer attempted in their *Dialektik der Aufklärung* to attribute the rise of National Socialism to the spirit of the Enlightenment, identified as the evil which fostered the dogmatic mind-set which produced the ideology of fascism, and hence also its human victims. Yet the very paradigm which they develop in the course of their survey is one which instates the model of innocent victim and guilty aggressor: reason is identified as guilty of the evils associated with National Socialism, just as reason gave birth to innocent human victims. This binary thinking has been used repeatedly since 1945 by intellectuals on the political left, especially in Germany. Heinrich Böll and Günter Grass created the framework for "critiques" of German society based on a relentlessly naive and imaginatively paralysing model of innocent victim and guilty aggressor. Exile studies form part of this large and diffuse phenomenon, which tends to *encourage* people to think in binary terms that render combative action or thinking redundant. Some of the most prestigious German newspapers implicitly endorse this binary model. *Die Zeit* thought it pertinent to republish Adorno's essay "Erziehung nach Auschwitz" in the wake of the racist attacks in Rostock. In doing so, it further endorsed the links which intellectuals on the left like to see between Auschwitz and the present, yet in terms which do not allow for *negotiating* ways out of chaos and disorder. And in an article published in 1994 in the same newspaper, Ulrich Greiner, commenting on the popularity of Spielberg's *Schindler's List,* bemoaned the way in which "Germans" still have to learn "about" "Auschwitz" from Hollywood. In so doing, he endorsed the polarised model on which the film was based, according to which all Jews are victims deserving of our sympathy and almost all Germans are perverse and worthy of our condemnation. The recent reminder by Rafael Seligmann in *Der Spiegel* that the continued identification of the Jews with Auschwitz would constitute the formal triumph of Hitler's thinking, and his emphasis on the tendency among those who reflect on Auschwitz to be intellectually numbed by the details of the Holocaust, only goes part of the way towards disentangling these deep confusions.[24]

Canetti's continued vote of confidence in creativity, his celebration of artistry and his insistence on the inviolable uniqueness of personal detail, can be read as a reminder, therefore, of the vulnerability to abuse of so many of the largely thematic criteria invoked by exile studies. There is a danger not simply of sustaining a perverse romance of Exile and Loss, but also of sustaining a perverse romance of covert racism and covert nationalism based on the model of aggressor and victim. Canetti admires power when it becomes a synonym for passion, and in his willingness to negotiate power in the spirit of passion he not only celebrates those who treat life seriously as a challenge, but also reminds us that power and passion produce the kind of systematic commitment which is creative of life. He reminds us that power and passion are destructive of the debilitating drive of that melancholy which induces the paralysis which has led to the continued, widespread acceptance of the binary model as a way of "negotiating" the world. Ernst Toller ends his autobiography with a series of rhetorical questions which reinstate German nationalism, and the possibility of a messianic comeback by Germany. Klaus Mann ends his autobiography with a series of rhetorical reflections on the "meaning" of German national identity. In Canetti's autobiography, we have a sustained use of rhetorical *devices,* all of which bespeak the conviction that to identify oneself as a unique individual, without recourse to race, religion, creed, nationhood or colour, is to secure both the possibility of non-discrimination and the advantages of compelling personal encounters with other human beings.

Notes

1.   Joseph Strelka, "Material Collectors, Political Rhetoricians, and Amateurs: Current Methodological Problems in German Exile Literature Studies," in *Protest—Form—Tradition: Essays on German Exile Literature,* ed. Joseph P. Strelka, Robert F. Bell and Eugene Dobson (Alabama, 1979), pp. 1–14 (p. 11).

2.   Richard Critchfield, "Autobiographie als Geschichtsdeutung," in *Deutschsprachige Exilliteratur: Studien zu ihrer Bestimmung im Kontext der Epoche 1930 bis 1960,* ed. Wulf Koepke and Michael Winkler (Bonn, 1984), pp. 228–41 (p. 228).

3.   See Reinhold Grimm and Jost Hermand (eds), *Exil und Innere Emigration: Third Wisconsin Workshop* (Frankfurt, 1972); Peter Uwe Hohendahl and Egon Schwarz (eds), *Exil und Innere Emigration II: Internationale Tagung in St Louis* (Frankfurt, 1973); Ingeborg Drewitz, *Die zerstörte Kontinuität: Exilliteratur und Literatur des Widerstandes* (Vienna, 1981); John M. Spalek and Robert F. Bell (eds), *Exile: The Writer's Experience* (Chapel Hill, 1982); Joseph Strelka (ed.), *Exilliteratur: Grundprobleme der Theorie: Aspekte der Geschichte und Kritik* (Bern, 1983); and Andreas Dybowski, *Endstation, Wartesaal oder Schatzkammer für die Zukunft: Die deutsche Exilliteratur und ihre Wirkung und Bewertung in der westdeutschen Nachkriegsrepublik* (Frankfurt, 1989) for examples of the way in which Canetti has been formally excluded from consideration. In a volume edited by Manfred Durzak, *Die deutsche Exilliteratur 1933–1945* (Stuttgart, 1973), a short article by Viktor Suchy entitled "Exil in Permanenz: Elias Canetti und der unbedingte Primat des Lebens," pp. 282–90, only celebrates the autobiography in terms of something as vague as its sense of life.

4.   For a recent attempt to look at the autobiography in terms of its artistry and internal tensions, see David Darby, "A Literary Life: The Textuality of Elias Canetti's Autobiography," *Modern Austrian Literature,* 25 (1992), 37–49.

5.   For a reading of Canetti's own relationship to the German language, see Yaier Cohen, "Elias Canetti: Exile and the German Language," *German Life and Letters,* 42 (1988), 32–45. See also Hans Fabian, "Die Sprache bei Elias Canetti: Exil als Asyl," in *Das Exilerlebnis: Verhandlungen des Vierten Symposium über deutsche und österreichische Exilliteratur,* ed. Donald Daviau and Ludwig Fischer (Columbia, 1982), pp. 497–504.

6.   For a review of the various branches within exile studies, consult Wulf Koepke and Michael Winkler (eds), *Exilliteratur 1933–1945* (Darmstadt, 1989), in particular Werner Mittenzwei, "Ästhetik des Widerstands" (pp. 141–65), who argues for the creation of the aesthetic category of resistance writing to honour those who used writing as a means of fighting against fascism.

7.   See Sander Gilman, *Jewish Self-Hatred: Anti-Semitism and the Hidden Language of the Jews* (Baltimore, 1986) for evidence of Canetti's distancing himself from the "Ostjude" in *Die Fackel im Ohr.* By classifying Canetti as a polyglot, Westernising, assimilated Jew and referring exclusively to the chapter involving Eva Reichmann and Backenroth (the Ostjude), Gilman tends to perpetuate binary thinking, ignoring the possibility that Canetti's non-response to Backenroth might just be an unusual case of his passivity.

8.   See Ingeborg Brandt, " 'Stendhal war meine Bibel': Gespräch mit Elias Canetti, dem Autor der *Blendung,*" *Welt am Sonntag,* 8 November 1963. Also see Christine Meyer, "La vie de Henry Brulard comme modèle pour l'autobiographie de Canetti," *Austriaca,* 33 (1991), 89–107.

9.   Elias Canetti, *The Play of the Eyes,* trans. Ralph Manheim (New York, 1986), p. 138. [This essay has been edited for this volume to include quotations in English only; in the present version all references to Canetti's works are to the published English-language translations. *Ed.*]

10.   See John Willett, "Die Künste der Emigration," in *Exil in Großbritannien: Zur Emigration aus dem nationalsozialistischen Deutschland,* ed. Gerhard Hirschfeld (Stuttgart, 1983), pp. 183–204 (p. 186).

11.   Steven Beller, "The Jewish Intellectual and Vienna in the 1930s," in *Austria in the Thirties: Culture and Politics,* ed. Kenneth Segar and John Warren (Riverside, 1991), pp. 309–27 (p. 323).

12.   See Harriet Murphy's study of Canetti's *Die Blendung* (forthcoming with the State University of New York Press). [*Canetti and Nietzsche: Theories of Humor in "Die Blendung"* (Albany, 1997). *Ed.*]

13.   Elias Canetti, *The Tongue Set Free,* trans. Joachim Neugroschel (New York, 1979), p. 56.

14.   See note 7 above.

15.   The most important full-length or detailed studies of the autobiography look at Canetti ahistorically and psychologically. See Barbara Saunders, *Contemporary Autobiography: Literary Approaches to the Problem of Identity* (London, 1985); Madeleine Salzmann, *Die Kommunikationsstruktur der Autobiographie mit kommunikationsorientierten Analysen der Autobiographien von Max Frisch, Helga M. Novak und Elias Canetti* (Bern, 1988); and Friederike Eigler, *Das autobiographische Werk von Elias Canetti: Verwandlung—Identität—Machtausübung* (Tübingen, 1988).

16.   Waltraud Wiethölter, "Sprechen—Lesen—Schreiben: Zur Funktion von Sprache und Schrift in Canettis Autobiographie," *DVjs,* 64 (1990), 149–71.

17.   Elias Canetti, *The Play of the Eyes,* p. 320.

18.   Bernd Witte, "Der Erzähler als Tod-Feind: Zu Canettis Autobiographie," *Text und Kritik,* 28 (1982), 65–72 (p. 72).

19.   Elias Canetti, *The Torch in My Ear,* trans. Joachim Neugroschel (New York, 1982), p. 219.

20.   Elias Canetti, *The Play of the Eyes,* p. 11.

21.   Wolfgang Paulsen, *Das Ich im Spiegel der Sprache: Autobiographisches Schreiben in der deutschen Literatur des 20. Jahrhunderts* (Tübingen, 1991), misses the point when he merely marvels at the capacity of Canetti's memory, in his cursory glance at the autobiography (pp. 162–5). Alfred Doppler also marvels at the epic breadth of the autobiography in terms of its ability to realise a whole period and to remember so many details: Alfred Doppler, "Gestalten und Figuren als Elemente der Zeit- und Lebensgeschichte: Canettis autobiographische Bücher," in idem, *Geschichte im Spiegel der Literatur: Aufsätze zur österreichischen Literatur des 19. und 20. Jahrhunderts* (Innsbruck, 1990), pp. 197–204 (p. 204).

22.   See Harriet Murphy, "Fritz Wotruba: The neglected master of stone," *The European,* 12 October 1990.

23.   Elias Canetti, *The Play of the Eyes,* pp. 110–11.

24.   Rafael Seligman, "Republik der Betroffenen," *Der Spiegel,* 14/1994, pp. 92–3 (p. 93).

"Fissures in the Monument": Reassessing Elias Canetti's Autobiographical Works

FRIEDERIKE EIGLER

1

In his 1976 lecture "Der Beruf des Dichters" ("The Writer's Profession"), Elias Canetti is critical of authors who write the same book over and over again.[1] Canetti himself penned, over the course of 60 years, a relatively small number of very different works: the early novel *Die Blendung* (1935; *Auto-da-Fé*), several dramas, the monumental anthropological study *Masse und Macht* (1960; *Crowds and Power*), a travelogue of his trip to Marrakesh (1968), numerous essays, a three-volume autobiography (1977–1985), and several volumes of *Aufzeichnungen,* that is, collections of notes and aphorisms.[2] Despite this heterogeneous production, which spanned a large part of the twentieth century, the reception of his works is dominated by the assumption of a homogeneous oeuvre. This applies to the earlier phase of academic and journalistic attention—following the award of the Nobel Prize to Canetti in 1981—which was predominantly laudatory in tone and affirmative in content. It also applies to the reception since the mid-1980s, when a number of scholars began critically to examine Canetti's works, arguing that its powerful means of (self-)representation are anachronistic in an era of critical examinations of the subject, the author, and language.[3] Both approaches, though resulting in opposing assessments of Canetti's works, tend to homogenize Canetti's works. One of the more recent examples is Ursula Ruppel's intriguing study *Der Tod und Canetti* (1995; Death and Canetti), which compares Canetti's work to a seamlessly built memorial that is hermetically sealed from the outside world.[4]

The assumption that the name of the author guarantees a certain degree of thematic continuity and stylistic consistency not only marks Canetti's critical reception but, more generally, also continues to inform a large part of literary criticism. Whenever connections between distinct works are not readily

This essay was written specifically for this volume and is published for the first time by permission of the author.

detectable, literary critics assume the role of (re)constructing continuities and consistencies. In his oft-quoted essay "What is an Author?" Michel Foucault has traced this hermeneutic activity to the biblical exegesis of Saint Jerome in the fifth century.[5] This notion of the author-function (i.e., as the guarantee of a work's coherence and unity) and the related notion of the role of literary criticism have largely survived theoretical discussions that challenge hermeneutical approaches to literature as well as unitary concepts of the author/subject.

By abandoning the assumption of an underlying continuity and coherence uniting Canetti's works, I seek to avoid what I see as two pitfalls in the critical literature: affirmative praise that confirms the presumed singularity of his oeuvre on one hand and dismissive criticism on the other. In order to explore what I contend is the heterogeneous character of Canetti's works, I look at the relationship between Canetti's three-volume autobiography and the collection of notes and aphorisms *Das Geheimherz der Uhr* (1985; *The Secret Heart of the Clock*), which he wrote during roughly the same period. While my approach challenges those critics who assume coherence throughout Canetti's work, it does not entirely discard the traditional notion of the author. Exploring discrepancies and discontinuities only makes "sense" if one continues to presume that a privileged relationship exists between the various writings of the same author. I thus suggest a revised author-function in which the name of the author remains the point of reference but is no longer seen as a guarantee for the homogeneity of the oeuvre. The approach I propose here allows not only for a careful reassessment of the heterogeneous character of Canetti's works; it also opens up new avenues of research that can look at his writings in the context of contemporary literature and thought. In the last part of this essay, for instance, I briefly examine the relationship of Canetti's works to the writings of the French philosopher Emmanuel Levinas, in particular those addressing his notion of ethics. The relationship between Levinas's ethics and Canetti's poetics cannot be fully explored in the context of this article, but I seek to locate an ethical dimension in Canetti's *Aufzeichnungen* that is inherent to and not separate from its poetic dimension. I thereby challenge those critics who look exclusively at Canetti's imposing rhetoric and style. But before I consider the heterogeneous aspects of his works and their relation to Levinas (parts 2 and 3), I first explore those aspects of Canetti's works that seem to suggest continuity.

Arguably, the particular sequence in which Canetti's works were published tends to support homogenizing efforts despite the heterogeneity of individual works. After the publication of *Crowds and Power* in 1960, Canetti almost exclusively published texts that either explicitly or implicitly comment on some of the main issues explored in this anthropological study. For instance, according to Canetti the main function of his 1000-page autobiography is to reconstruct the biographical circumstances within which the project of *Crowds and Power* emerged.[6] Many sections of his life story indeed comment on the genesis of his major study and on the continued pertinence of his analysis of power, crowds, death, and metamorphosis. This self-referential dimension of Canetti's works has contributed to approaches that treat Canetti's writings as an organic whole.

The four volumes of *Aufzeichnungen* published during Canetti's lifetime represent another dimension of his extensive self-commentary. The majority of notes collected in *Die Provinz des Menschen* (1973; *The Human Province*) were written during the same time as *Crowds and Power* and comment on issues related to that study; the notes in *The Secret Heart of the Clock* have accompanied the writing of his autobiography and constitute another layer of his self-commentary. In the following decade Canetti published two more collections of notes, *Die Fliegenpein* (1992; *The Agony of Flies*) and *Nachträge aus Hampstead* (1994; *Notes from Hampstead*). Neither of these two volumes is, however, a chronological continuation of the previous ones. Instead, *The Agony of Flies* includes a cross-section of notes from previous decades, and *Notes from Hampstead* includes additional texts from the years 1954–1971, the period that was already covered in *The Human Province*.

The particular sequencing of Canetti's publications and their self-referential dimension suggest continuity among his works. Like the different layers of a palimpsest, Canetti has gradually exposed various layers of his writings, always reminding the reader both of the existence of other writings that are not intended for publication and of the selective nature of the notes that he did publish (*CW,* 54, 59). This carefully controlled publication process lasted until his death in 1994 and has in some ways continued even beyond his death. Canetti's daughter Johanna oversaw the posthumous publication of yet another volume of notes that Canetti had selected for publication just prior to his death.[7] It seems almost as if Canetti, who throughout his life refused to accept the finality of death, managed to guarantee his own survival in his writings by presenting them in a carefully delayed and selective manner to his readership.

Based in part on the self-referential dimension of his works, Ursula Ruppel argues that Canetti has created a body of texts sealed from contemporary social, cultural, and political concerns. As an example she mentions *Crowds and Power,* which fails to address in any direct manner the ideologies in whose name the most extreme abuse of power in this century took place, namely Communism and Fascism. Regarding the self-referential character of Canetti's entire work, Ruppel comments: "In a continuous movement, Canetti's work turns within itself and around itself.... This process, in which the work interprets and comments on itself, at the same time seals it hermetically from the outside. With each new text, it hardens and thickens into a monument that confronts death. A tombstone of enormous size, erected during life, in which single pieces fit together seamlessly like the square blocks of a pyramid" (Ruppel, 94, 99 [my translation]). In this categorical pronouncement, Canetti is defeated with his own analytical tools. By comparing

Canetti's writings with the erection of a monumental tombstone, Ruppel evokes the imagery of death that Canetti relies on in his own analysis of the archetypical "dictator" in *Crowds and Power.* She declares Canetti, the self-declared enemy of death (*Tod-Feind*), to be an enemy of life. While I find Ruppel's analysis generally convincing, I question her assumption of continuity among Canetti's works. It is this assumption that allows her readily to relate the early novel to the autobiography, published almost half a century later, and to suggest similarities between the author and his figure of the paranoid scholar and misogynist Peter Kien in the novel *Auto-da-Fé.* Regarding Canetti's works, I maintain that the assumption of continuity obscures other important aspects of his writings. It may well be that Canetti sought to build a "perfectly smooth monument," as Ruppel argues, but my exploration in the next part of this article is of discontinuities and contradictions: the "fissures" and "cracks" that mark this written monument.

2

Similar to *The Human Province, The Secret Heart of the Clock* includes, in terms both of content and style, a broad variety of entries. Compared with the entries in *The Human Province,* those in *The Secret Heart* are generally shorter and more concise, sometimes to the point of being enigmatic, thus requiring the active involvement of the reader in the reading process.[8] There are aphorisms critically reflecting on language and prefabricated phrases, a tradition that harks back to Georg Christoph Lichtenberg, Marie von Ebner-Eschenbach, and Karl Kraus;[9] commentaries about particular books, his own works, and the reception of the first volumes of his autobiography; observations about animals; critical observations about human behavior; and reversals of conventional patterns of thought, a figure frequently employed by Lichtenberg.[10] Many entries reflect on topics familiar to readers of Canetti's other works (e.g., crowds, power, metamorphosis, and language), but comments on death and the finality of life are *the* central topics. Yet contrary to what Ruppel's allegory of a seamless memorial suggests, the entries in *The Secret Heart* do not merely reiterate and affirm already known topics and positions. *The Secret Heart* is informed by new perspectives, probing questions, and deep skepticism concerning some of Canetti's previously well-established arguments and views. Thus *The Secret Heart* discloses some of the contradictions and disparities that Canetti's autobiography carefully obscures.

Canetti penned the entries included in *The Secret Heart* between 1973 and 1985; that is, during the same period in which he wrote and published the three volumes of his autobiography: *Die gerettete Zunge* (1977; *The Tongue Set Free*), *Die Fackel im Ohr* (1980; *The Torch in My Ear*), and *Das Augenspiel* (1985; *The Play of the Eyes*). The autobiographical narrative is set against the political and social turmoil of the early part of the twentieth century. In three volumes Canetti captures roughly 30 years of his life (1905–1937). The last volume concludes with the death of his mother and merely alludes to the political events leading to the annexation of Austria by Nazi Germany in 1938, when Canetti was forced to leave Vienna. While Vienna had been Canetti's major domicile since 1924, he had also lived in Frankfurt and Berlin, following his childhood years in Bulgaria, England, and Switzerland. These frequent moves, some of which were involuntary, do not amount to ruptures in his autobiography. Instead, the teleological organization of Canetti's autobiography renders every single event of the past meaningful.[11] In sharp contrast to most (post)modern autobiographies, Canetti's autobiography addresses the processes of writing and of recalling and interpreting earlier events only in passing.[12] The autobiography can be read as his attempt to transcend temporality and challenge death through the written word. By contrast, Canetti's aphorisms and notes include what the autobiography excludes or seeks to overcome: the irreversibility of time, the inevitability of (his own) death, the threat of global destruction—issues that undercut the seminal arguments of his life and works. To explore these discontinuous and disruptive dimensions of *The Secret Heart* further, I discuss in more detail three different types of notes: (a) sociopolitical entries, such as comments on current events; (b) self-referential entries, such as commentaries on the process of remembrance; and (c) self-critical entries, such as remarks that question central arguments of *Crowds and Power.*

Sociopolitical Entries

Contrary to what Ruppel's assessment of Canetti's works suggests, the five volumes of *Aufzeichnungen* do include references to contemporary social and political issues. In *The Human Province* there are comments about the aftermath of the Second World War; *The Secret Heart* includes numerous comments about torture, starvation, the threat of global destruction and the end of humanity, nuclear weapons, and the related threat of another world war in the Cold War era of the 1980s. While most of these comments refer to the state of humanity and world politics in general, there is one entry that refers to a particular event, the downing of a Korean airliner by the Soviets in 1983, which brought the superpowers to the brink of war (*SHC,* 122). Seen against the backdrop of this specific reference to a particularly dangerous moment of the Cold War, the more general comments about the future of humanity increase in urgency. In the following entry Canetti reconfirms his concern about humanity while pondering the adverse effects of a fatalistic outlook: "More and more often he catches himself thinking that there is no way to save humanity. Is this an attempt to rid himself of responsibility?" (*SHC,* 25).

In *The Secret Heart* Canetti displays not only an increasing concern with worldwide political and social crises, he also expresses increasing skepticism with regard to his own role as a writer. The following note suggests the writer's complicity with contemporary humanitarian crises, while it insists that writing remains his only possible form of resistance: "While others starve, he writes. He writes while others die" (*SHC*, 89). This chiastic figure underscores an unresolvable tension between, on the one hand, the moral responsibility Canetti attributes to the writer and, on the other, those social problems that render this claim for responsibility meaningless or, at the very least, questionable. Explicit remarks about contemporary society in *The Secret Heart* are sparse but display a deep concern with the multiple threats to humankind. This dimension of the *Aufzeichnungen* stands in marked contrast to Canetti's official life story, which lacks references to contemporary societal problems and which therefore seems to have been written in a historical vacuum.

Self-referential Entries

Self-probing comments about the processes of remembering and writing are another dimension that distinguishes *The Secret Heart* from the autobiography, a dimension that is relevant to the questioning of the assumed homogeneity of Canetti's oeuvre. In his autobiography Canetti contends that remembrance and writing—the very activity of writing his life story—have the power to revitalize the past. The grand revitalization project of the autobiography seeks to ignore temporality and disruptive aspects of memory. This seemingly unshattered belief in the resurrecting power of language is probed in many entries in *The Secret Heart.* Numerous notes comment on the process of remembering, as for instance the following two: "I don't want to know what I was; I want to become what I was" (*SHC*, 58); "The paralyzing effect of reading early notebooks. It is better, it is more correct, to remember freely. The old crutches get in the way of memory [i.e., remembrance], get stuck in its spokes" (*SHC*, 54).

A close analysis of these notes sheds light on their disruptive effect vis-à-vis the autobiography. Both notes posit an opposition between the retrieval of factual information ("to know," "early notebooks") and vivid recollection ("to become," the act of remembrance). Biographical documents are seen as incompatible with the act of remembering. The accounts of the past do not assist the process of recollection. They have a "paralyzing" effect, and they interfere with the process of remembering precisely because they are fixed documents, signs of an irretrievable past. This opposition recalls Hegel's distinction between *Gedächtnis* (memory), the faculty of mechanical repetition, and *Erinnerung* (remembrance), the process of internalization (*Verinnerlichung*). According to Hegel the two realms complement one another; but the incompatibility Canetti addresses is closer to Paul de Man's reading of Hegel.

De Man contends that "memory" hinders and ultimately derails any act of "remembrance."[13] In the entries quoted above, Canetti reaffirms the objective of his autobiography—to resurrect the past—but he acknowledges at the same time the impossibility of ever fully living up to this stated objective. Instead of reconfirming an unmediated access to the past that informs the autobiographical project, the notes emphasize the mediated nature of remembrance. Or, to draw once more on Ruppel's allegory: instead of sealing together the blocks of his monumental memorial, the notes draw attention to its cracks and fissures.

Self-critical Entries

Canetti's attempt to overcome or to ignore the mediated character of remembrance (and of writing)—an attempt that shapes the autobiography and that is both reaffirmed and undercut in the notes—corresponds with his lifelong unwillingness to accept death.[14] The written word, he contends, is the only way to preserve "life" beyond death and to circumvent the human inclination to dominate others. This resistance to death informs the central argument of *Crowds and Power,* namely that the finality of life is the origin of all (ab)uses of power; by seeking and abusing power, Canetti maintains, humans attempt in vain to negate or overcome the finality of life. The autobiography reconstructs and thereby reconfirms the genesis of Canetti's fight against death. His life story is from the very beginning informed by the experience of death. The first volume of his autobiography is dominated by the untimely death of Canetti's father—he died in 1912 when Canetti was seven years old—and by Canetti's refusal to accept any rational explanation for this (or any other) death.

Several notes in *The Secret Heart* refer to the life-shaping effect of this early experience of loss, as for instance: "A person who has opened himself too early to the experience of death can never turn away from it again; a wound that becomes like a lung through which one breathes" (*SHC,* 40). Through metonymic substitutions, this note evokes the image of a coexistence of life and death; life depends on the experience of death. Contrary to the autobiography, this and several other notes suggest the "productive" effect of the experience of death: "Death, which he will not tolerate, carries him" (*SHC,* 131). There are entries in *The Secret Heart* that go even further and question what is arguably Canetti's principal conviction and the founding argument of *Crowds and Power,* namely his unwillingness to accept the finality of life. For instance the following entry: "To cling to life like this—is it stinginess? When it's the life of others—is that all the more stingy? He looks for arguments against the fundamental conviction of his existence. What if that very conviction is the worst kind of slavery? Would it be easier to regard life as a gift that can be taken back? So that nothing is *part* of you, just as nothing belongs to you?" (*SHC*, 38). In this entry, the figure of reversal—which Canetti, like Lichtenberg, employs to call into question petrified patterns of language and thought—is directed against the author's own position, his lifelong fight against death. Instead of reiterating his previous arguments, Canetti turns into his own most severe critic when he considers the possibility that his rejection of death is nothing more than the self-centered and powerful attempt to hold onto life as one's property. Self-critical entries like the one quoted above can be found next to other entries that emphatically insist on the validity of his previous positions: "It's coming out. What? Something he always shied away from imagining. Is it all moving toward a declaration of love for death? ... Renounce all the words that were the meaning and pride of his life and profess the only true faith of the church of death? It is possible, everything is possible, there is no miserable self-betrayal that did not at some time become truth; therefore, in place of the history of words, the words must stand for themselves, independent of everything after or before them" (*SHC*, 53). In this dramatic staging of a dispute with himself, Canetti seeks to annul his own (present and anticipated future) doubts. He thus assumes the role of executor of his own literary estate. Canetti, the self-declared enemy of death anticipates in this entry his own death and, in an attempt to determine for posterity how his works are to be read, reaffirms his lifelong resistance to the acceptance of death. In a self-ironic twist, the very assertion that the "words should speak for themselves" serves to undercut his attempt to privilege some of his views over others. As exemplified in Canetti's multiple and contradictory remarks about death and his unwillingness to accept death, *The Secret Heart* stands not only in marked contrast to *Crowds and Power* and to the autobiography (demonstrating the heterogeneity of his works), but the notes themselves are heterogeneous and defy any conclusive answers.

Both the insistence on the validity of his previous arguments and the awareness of their futility have shaped the enigmatic title *The Secret Heart of the Clock*. There are two entries that are related to the title and suggest a particular reading: "He sacrifices the clock and eludes the future" (*SHC*, 98); "Unknown to all, the secret heart of the clock" (*SHC*, 120). The first quotation can be read as imagining that temporality and, by extension, death can be overcome. The second one seems to invoke, in the combination of an organic trope (heart) and a mechanical trope (clock), both the finality of life and, at the same time, the ignorance of humans regarding the exact duration of life. Arguably, the collection of notes and aphorisms as a whole represents Canetti's confrontation with finality, his own death, and the futility of his previous efforts, issues that are carefully excluded from his autobiography. Thus, this volume of notes can be considered the "secret center" or the "heart" of the official life story.

In the notes, as one of the entries states, "he has written himself to pieces" (*SHC,* 51). The notes effectively decenter the narrative unity of the official life story, they expose the unified self presented in the autobiography as a carefully crafted construct, and they call into question language's capacity to bring the past back to life. This disruptive effect of the notes coincides with what Jacques Derrida has described as the double effect of the "supplement": the supplement is rarely a mere addition, instead it challenges or even replaces that which it ostensively complements.[15] *The Secret Heart of the Clock* provides space for alterity and renders questionable the attempt to close off the life story in a teleological narrative.

3

It is precisely the heterogeneous character of the *Aufzeichnungen* and their decentering effect vis-à-vis the autobiography that invite their exploration in relation to the writings of Emmanuel Levinas. Levinas's approach to the question of ethics is of special interest to literary criticism, firstly because he sees the origin of language intertwined with primordial ethical behavior and secondly because Levinas posits a nonnormative notion of ethics, a notion that is in constant conflict with legal and political notions of justice. I intend to explore intersections between the works of Canetti and Levinas regarding the relationship between language and ethics. Most specifically, I argue that Levinas's ethics illuminates the relation of the aesthetic to the ethical in Canetti's notion of *Verwandlung* (metamorphosis), a notion that informs, in turn, the content and structure of Canetti's *Aufzeichnungen.*[16]

Levinas, like Canetti, is critical of the Western philosophical tradition. Levinas maintains that Western thought is marked by a pervasive search for lucidity and total comprehension that assimilates the "Other" to the "same" and ignores the irreducible alterity of human life. Yet while Canetti has entirely turned away from any established system of thought, claiming to rethink humanity from scratch in *Crowds and Power,* Levinas's critique evolves out of his continuous engagement with these philosophical traditions. In contradistinction to the primacy of ontology in Western philosophy, Levinas posits the primacy of ethics—which, in the context of this article, I can only introduce in the most schematic manner.[17]

Levinas distinguishes the "ontological Said" from the "ethical Saying." The "ontological Said" signifies the "thought of comparison, of judgement" and harks back to the "Greek tradition" of antiquity. Levinas concedes that we cannot do without this language of instrumental reason, that we have to rely on "Greek" language even when criticizing it (or when "unsaying the Said," as he terms it). The "ethical Saying," by contrast, is shaped by the

Judaic tradition and specifically by the commandment "Thou shalt not kill."[18] According to Levinas, the irreducible alterity of another human being—for which he frequently employs the figure of the face—calls for our response and by the same token for our responsibility. He argues that this response to the Other's face can be considered the origin of both language and ethics (Levinas 1988, 169).

One of the childhood memories central to Canetti's autobiography literally enacts the prohibition underlying Levinas's ethics. The entire first volume, *The Tongue Set Free,* is shaped by the inscription of the primordial prohibition of killing. When the five-year-old Canetti, furious because his cousin refuses to share the secret of writing with him, intends to kill her with an ax, his outraged grandfather pronounces the absolute interdiction against committing murder.[19] Canetti presents this memory—symbolizing two principles central to Judaism, the importance of scripture and the sanctity of life—as the founding event of his life story.[20] The interdiction pronounced by the patriarchal figure in *The Tongue Set Free* visualizes in a protoreligious fashion what Levinas transforms into a universal secular principle. He posits the Other's face, which calls for a response and for responsibility, as the primordial ethical relation.

Levinas's notion of ethics emerged against the backdrop of violence and murder as the final consequence of disrespect for the other. Continuing a secular version of the Judaic tradition, Levinas, like Canetti, refuses to assign any metaphysical meaning to death. Both consider death to be a violent rupture; ultimately any death carries with it an element of murder.[21] While *Crowds and Power* can be considered Canetti's implicit attempt to grapple with Fascism, Levinas is more explicit than Canetti in his references to recent history, namely anti-Semitism, the Second World War, and the Holocaust.[22] For instance, in *Otherwise than Being,* a study that is dedicated to the victims of National Socialism, Levinas mentions anti-Semitism as a trope for the refusal to respect and respond to the alterity of the other person. In an interview Levinas states that Auschwitz is the implicit point of reference for his attempt to develop a nonnormative ethics. The central question that emerged after the Holocaust, he maintains, is whether we can "speak of morality after the failure of morality?" (Levinas 1988, 179). In his essay "Useless Suffering," Levinas responds: "It is this attention to the Other which, across the cruelties of this century—despite these cruelties, because of these cruelties—can be affirmed as the very bond of human subjectivity, even to the point of being raised to a supreme ethical principle."[23]

In recent debates concerning the relationship of aesthetics and ethics, Klaus Scherpe, among others, has drawn on Levinas's notion of a nonnormative ethics, grounded in the response to the distinctive face of the Other. Questioning what he considers to be a false dichotomy between the aesthetic and ethical realms, Scherpe suggests a conception of art that, instead of perceiving the ethical dimension as distinct from the aesthetic (e.g., fiction with a political "message"), considers the two dimensions inseparable from one another. Literary texts that correspond to this notion of aesthetics—Scherpe mentions texts by Peter Weiss, Alfred Andersch, and Hans Magnus Enzensberger—further the awareness of the irreducible alterity of the Other and thus work against homogenization and marginalization.[24] The etymology of the term "aesthetics" underscores this ethical dimension of art: "aisthesis" means awareness or perception. What is at stake is not a moral evaluation of art but art's potential to increase our awareness of the incommensurability of the Other and the world.[25] Focusing on "aisthesis" as the intersection between the ethical and the aesthetical realms opens up a new perspective in an otherwise deadlocked debate, a perspective I find useful in discussing Canetti's poetics.[26]

The notion of *Verwandlung* is central to Canetti's anthropology and poetics. According to Canetti, the ability of the artist or the storyteller to enact and preserve by means of *Verwandlung* the multiplicity, changeability, and the specificity of human life is the only way to counter the pervasive accumulation and abuse of power.[27] The notion of *Verwandlung* rests on the potentially problematic assumption that the writing subject is able to efface the powerful aspects of authorship by assimilating itself to that which it represents.[28] Yet I argue that, within the open-ended and dialogic structure of the *Aufzeichnungen*, Canetti avoids this risk by adapting multiple and often contradictory subject positions and perspectives, and he does so by enacting multiple *Verwandlungen*. As demonstrated above, Canetti's *Aufzeichnungen* provide space for the representation of the irreducible multiplicity of the outer world as well as for the conflicted and contradictory inner world of the writing subject.

The autobiography and the long essay on Franz Kafka, *Der andere Prozeß* (1969: *Kafka's Other Trial*), represent Canetti's fascination with other humans. *Crowds and Power* and *Die Stimmen von Marrakesch* (1968; *The Voices of Marrakesh*) represent his interest in other cultures. The *Aufzeichnungen* display both—his fascination with other humans and his interest in other cultures— but they also provide space for exploring the "other" in the "self." It is in this twofold representation of alterity, I maintain, that the aesthetical realm of the notes coincides with an ethical realm. In a related sense, the author and literary critic Rudolf Hartung, who has regularly commented on Canetti's works since the 1950s, uses the term "the moral" in a review of the *Aufzeichnungen;* Hartung refers to Canetti's disregard for abstractions and his genuine respect for the concrete and the distinct aspects of "reality."[29] The ethical dimension of Canetti's *Aufzeichnungen* can be located, however, not merely on the level of content, as Hartung seems to suggest, but also on the level of style. Rhetorically the aphorisms and notes are governed by repetition and metonymic substitution, features that underscore their fragmentary and open-ended character. The autobiography, by contrast, relies heavily on metaphors and a symbolic organization of events implying a meaningful telos and closure.

The heterogeneous character of Canetti's *Aufzeichnungen* and their ethical dimension challenge those critics who simply dismiss Canetti's work as inaccessible and hermetic. Yet Ursula Ruppel, one of Canetti's strongest and most convincing critics, bases her argument concerning the hermetic character of his oeuvre in part on the role attributed to the feminine. She argues that the absence of woman and the stereotypical representation of femininity are not marginal phenomena in Canetti's works but essential aspects of his notions of life and death (Ruppel, 72–87). Canetti's desire for immortality, she contends, finds it counterpart in the virtual nonexistence of his own body in the autobiography and the explicit contempt for the mortal body that always has feminine connotation—the most graphic example being the figure of Therese in the novel *Auto-da-Fé* (Ruppel, 74).

How, then, are women and the "feminine" represented in *The Secret Heart*? Women are for the most part strikingly absent. Canetti consistently employs the term *Mann* (man) whenever one would expect the term *Mensch* (human being). For instance: "The fragments of a man, worth so much more than he" (*SHC*, 145); "The land without brothers: no one has more than *one* child" (*SHC*, 19). Inadvertently, these notes expose the androcentric bent dominant in most of Western thought. By *explicitly* excluding women, they draw attention to the long tradition of *implicitly* excluding women, that is, the tradition of speaking of humans (*Menschen*) when in fact only men are being considered.

The few notes that explicitly refer to "woman" generally reiterate pervasive stereotypes, like the self-centered or vain woman or the woman as seductress (*SHC*, 10, 67, 136). These notes confirm the mostly stereotypical ways in which the feminine is represented in Canetti's other works.[30] Thus Canetti's representation of women reveals a blind spot in the respect for alterity that the aphorisms and notes otherwise espouse. This tendency underscores the validity of Ruppel's feminist critique of Canetti, but I do not subscribe to her wholesale dismissal of his works, a dismissal that is grounded in moral indignation. While I share her disapproval of the misogynist aspects of Canetti's writings, I find it ultimately more productive to expand Levinas's notion of ethics to the role of the critic: it would then be the "responsibility" of the critic to recognize the heterogeneity of Canetti's works in general and the heterogeneous character of the *Aufzeichungen* in particular.[31]

Notes

1.   Elias Canetti, *The Conscience of Words* (London: Deutsch, 1986), 156; hereafter cited in text as *CW.*
2.   In view of the unwieldiness of the English translation "notes and aphorisms," I frequently use the German term *Aufzeichnungen* in this essay.
3.   The following collections of essays exemplify the two trends in the reception: the volume *Hüter der Verwandlung: Beiträge zum Werk von Elias Canetti* (Munich: Hanser, 1985),

compiled by Canetti's own publisher, includes predominantly affirmative contributions (*Essays in Honor of Elias Canetti,* trans. Michael Hulse [New York: Farrar, Straus and Giroux, 1987]); and the volume *Elias Canetti: Experte der Macht,* ed. Kurt Bartsch and Gerhard Melzer (Graz: Droschl, 1985), includes several very critical contributions. [Essays by Gerhard Melzer and Bernd Witte that appear in translation in the present volume first appeared in the collection *Elias Canetti: Experte der Macht. Ed.*] There are excellent articles in both volumes, and my over-all critique of homogenizing tendencies, which mark both approaches, is not meant as a whole-sale dismissal of individual articles. My critique extends to my own hermeneutic approach in *Das autobiographische Werk von Elias Canetti: Verwandlung—Identität—Machtausübung,* Stauffen-burg Colloquium 7 (Tübingen: Stauffenburg, 1988), a study that displays aspects of both trends, affirmation and critical distancing; hereafter cited in text.

    4.   Ursula Ruppel, *Der Tod und Canetti: Essay* (Hamburg: Europäische Verlagsanstalt, 1995); hereafter cited in text.

    5.   Michel Foucault, "What is an Author?" trans. Josué V. Harari, in *Textual Strategies: Perspectives in Post-Structuralist Criticism,* ed. J. V. Harari (Ithaca: Cornell University Press, 1979), 141–60.

    6.   Elias Canetti, *The Secret Heart of the Clock: Notes, Aphorisms, Fragments, 1973–1985,* trans. Joel Agee (New York: Farrar, Straus and Giroux, 1989), 40–41; hereafter cited in text as *SHC.*

    7.   Elias Canetti, *Aufzeichnungen, 1992–1993* (Munich: Hanser, 1996).

    8.   See Ingo Seidler, "Bruchstücke einer großen Konfession: Zur Bedeutung von Canettis 'Sudelbüchern,' " *Modern Austrian Literature* 16, no. 3/4 (1983): 1–21; and Stefan H. Kaszyński, "Im Labor der Gedanken: Zur Poetik der Aufzeichungen von Elias Canetti," in *Elias Canettis Anthropologie und Poetik,* ed. Stefan H. Kaszyński (Munich: Hanser, 1984), 151–62.

    9.   Regarding the tradition of aphoristic writings, see Wolfgang Mieder, " 'Die falschesten Redensarten haben den größten Reiz': Zu Elias Canettis Sprachaphorismen," *Der Sprachdienst* 6 (1994): 173–80.

    10.   Two brief examples: "If you had traveled more, you would know less" (*SHC,* 46); "Newspapers, to help you forget the previous day" (*SHC,* 48). The social critique inherent in the critique of language and in the figure of reversal is discussed by Jürgen Söring, "Die Liter-atur als 'Provinz des Menschen': Zu Elias Canettis Aufzeichnungen," *Deutsche Vierteljahrsschrift für Literaturwissenschaft und Geistesgeschichte* 60 (1986): 645–66; and by Thomas Lappe, *Elias Canettis Aufzeichungen, 1942–1985: Modell und Dialog als Konstituenten einer programmatischen Utopie* (Aachen: Alano, 1989), 60.

    11.   In my book on Elias Canetti, I argue that the mechanisms of power Canetti ana-lyzes in his major anthropological study *Crowds and Power* shape his extensive autobiography. Canetti's masterfully crafted life story, I maintain, is directed toward the telos of becoming a writer (specifically, the author of *Crowds and Power*) and posits the author's own written cosmos against the catastrophic events of twentieth-century history and politics. In other words, his autobiography projects both in terms of style and content an anachronistic and powerful image of a writer and his works (Eigler, 30–77). The unshattered sense of identity Canetti posits in his life story seems closer to Goethe's *Dichtung und Wahrheit* (*Poetry and Truth*) than to most twentieth-century autobiographies; cf. Robert Gould, *"Die gerettete Zunge* and *Dichtung und Wahrheit:* Hypertextuality in Autobiography and its Implications," *Seminar* 21 (1985): 79–107.

    12.   See Eigler, 71–77. Cf. Waltraud Wiethölter, "Sprechen—Lesen—Schreiben: Zur Funktion von Sprache und Schrift in Canettis Autobiographie," *Deutsche Vierteljahrsschrift für Literaturwissenschaft und Geistesgeschichte* 64 (1990): 168. While it is accurate, as David Darby maintains, that Canetti comments frequently on the mediated and selective character of remembrance in his autobiography, the processes of remembrance and writing are not seen as problematic; they confirm rather than threaten the identity of the writing subject (Darby, "A Literary Life: The Textuality of Elias Canetti's Autobiography," *Modern Austrian Literature* 25, no. 2 [1992]: 37–49).

13.   Paul de Man, "Sign and Symbol in Hegel's *Aesthetics*," *Critical Inquiry* 8 (1982): 761–75.

14.   *The Secret Heart* includes numerous entries in which books and writing are metonymically related to life and living (for instance, *SHC*, 3, 84, 97). The metonymic relation of writing/remembrance to life can be read in two different ways: as emphasizing the immediacy of the act of writing or, conversely, as underscoring the mediated character of life. The entries thus emphasize at the same time as they undercut Canetti's magic notion of language; that is, his attempt to overcome the difference between signifier and signified by associating language with life. The very fact that his notes insist over and over again on the revitalizing power of language and remembrance signifies the difficulty of holding on to this premodern notion of language in a postmodern age.

15.   Jacques Derrida, *Of Grammatology*, trans. Gayatri C. Spivak (Baltimore: Johns Hopkins University Press, 1976), 141–64.

16.   I use the German term *Verwandlung* because of the central role this particular term occupies in Canetti's writings.

17.   For an introduction and overview, see Emmanuel Levinas, *Ethics and Infinity: Conversations with Philippe Nemo*, trans. Richard A. Cohen (Pittsburgh: Duquesne University Press, 1985).

18.   "The Paradox of Morality: An Interview with Emmanuel Levinas," in *The Provocation of Levinas: Rethinking the Other*, ed. Robert Bernasconi (London: Routledge, 1988), esp. 174–78; hereafter cited in text as Levinas 1988. For a more detailed elaboration of his ethics, see Levinas, *Otherwise than Being or Beyond Essence*, trans. A. Lingis, (The Hague: Nijhoff, 1981).

19.   Elias Canetti: *The Tongue Set Free: Remembrance of a European Childhood*, trans. Joachim Neugroschel (New York: Seabury, 1979), 214–15.

20.   Bernd Witte, "Der Erzähler als Tod-Feind: Zu Elias Canettis Autobiographie," *Text und Kritik* 28, rev. ed. (1982): 71.

21.   Emmanuel Levinas, *Totality and Infinity*, trans. A. Lingis (Pittsburgh: Duquesne University Press, 1969), 236.

22.   In a 1965 interview with Horst Bienek, Canetti contends that every single page of *Crowds and Power* deals with Fascism (Elias Canetti, *Die gespaltene Zukunft: Aufsätze und Gespräche*, Reihe Hanser 111 (Munich: Hanser, 1972), 98.

23.   Emmanuel Levinas, "Useless Suffering," in *The Provocation of Levinas: Rethinking the Other*, ed. Robert Bernasconi (London: Routledge, 1988), 159.

24.   Klaus Scherpe, "Moral im Ästhetischen: Andersch, Weiss, Enzensberger," *Weimarer Beiträge* 42 (1996): esp. 114–15.

25.   Cf. Introduction, *Ethik der Ästhetik*, ed. Christoph Wulf, Dietmar Kamper, and Hans Ulrich Gumbrecht (Berlin: Akademie Verlag, 1994), xi.

26.   The false dichotomy between *"engagierte Literatur"*—that is, politically or socially engaged literature that is presumed to have little aesthetic value—and "pure" art, supposedly detached from any political or social concerns continues to dominate post-1989 literary debates in Germany. The ongoing discussion of the relationship between ethics and aesthetics was provoked by questions about the complicity of East German writers in a repressive socialist state.

27.   Canetti's notion of *Verwandlung* is far more complex and ambiguous than it may appear at first. According to Canetti's anthropology in *Crowds and Power*, *Verwandlung* is the trait that distinguishes humans from animals. On the one hand, the ability to turn into different personae has assisted humans in the subjugation of nature. On the other, Canetti refers to Ovid's *Metamorphoses* as a literal example of how *Verwandlung* has been employed to escape from violent or hostile encounters. It is this latter aspect that Canetti underscores in the poetological notion of *Verwandlung*. The writer as the "keeper of metamorphoses" (*CW*, 161) accomplishes two things: he preserves the very notion of *Verwandlung* as *the* human essence in his writings

and, in doing so, he avoids becoming entangled in a society reigned by (ab)use of power. For a critical assessment of this rather idealistic notion of the writing subject, see Eigler, 90–105.

28.   Canetti's anthropological study *Crowds and Power* exemplifies the risks involved in the assumption that it is possible to transcend one's own set of "prejudices" (in Hans Georg Gadamer's sense, as a given set of presuppositions): this assumption may result in a more biased or otherwise skewed representation than if one were to acknowledge the position from which one speaks.

29.   Rudolf Hartung, "Ansturm gegen die Grenzen: Überlegungen zu Canetti's Aufzeichnungen aus drei Jahrzehnten," in *Elias Canetti: Ein Rezipient und sein Autor,* ed. Bernhard Albers (Aachen: Rimbaud, 1992), 124. This review first appeared in the *Süddeutsche Zeitung* (27–28 October 1973).

30.   See Eigler, 175–90; Ruppel, 50–87; and Kristie A. Foell, *Blind Reflections: Gender in Elias Canetti's "Die Blendung"* (Riverside, Calif.: Ariadne, 1994).

31.   This conflict between moral judgment and Levinas's call for responsibility regarding the alterity of the "Other" points to a dilemma that came to the fore in the controversy surrounding Paul de Man's wartime journalism. Jacques Derrida guarded against condemning the whole person by defending "de Man's right to differ from others and from himself" (See Derrida, *Memoirs for Paul de Man,* trans. Cecile Lindsay, Jonathan Culler, and Eduardo Cadava [New York: Columbia University Press, 1986], 50–56). Yet, as some of de Man's critics pointed out, unconditional respect for the "Other"—which according to Levinas precludes judgment—may become "irresponsible" in a broader sociopolitical sense.

IN LIEU OF A CONCLUSION
◆

The Writer in Hiding

CLAUDIO MAGRIS

The Nobel Prize awarded to Elias Canetti honors two writers: the writer who disappears and the one who reappears; the writer who withdraws from the world and the one who opens himself to public scrutiny. One of these two writers is a mysterious and extraordinary genius who has vanished into his secrets, perhaps ever to remain beyond our reach. This is the writer who, at the age of 30, quickly and quietly published one of the greatest books of the century, *Die Blendung* (*Auto-da-Fé*). Both Thomas Mann and Robert Musil liked the book—perhaps Canetti's true masterpiece—which was intelligently received but then disappeared from the literary scene for 30 years. With its republication in 1963 the book was rediscovered as the work of a new and unknown author, previously unrecorded in the annals of literary history. It was not until the mid-1970s that Canetti attained true recognition, the publication of other essential works such as *Masse und Macht* (*Crowds and Power*), *Der andere Prozeß* (*Kafka's Other Trial*), and other essays having in the meantime likewise failed to propel Canetti immediately to the fame and stature that their greatness warranted.

As the author of *Auto-da-Fé,* one of the masterpieces of the century, which fell into total obscurity for almost 30 years, Canetti undoubtedly suffered as a consequence of this marginalization. He accepted his position, however, with a calm composure that hid, behind a gentle modesty, an absolute and unshakable confidence in his own genius. The shadows to which he had been relegated were, moreover, an indication of Canetti's radical consistency: these shadows were Canetti's truth. In *Auto-da-Fé,* a high-modern parable of an intellectual who senses that he is unequal to the chaos of life and who destroys himself by means of his own mad defensive strategy, Canetti has given expression to the dreadful unendurability of existence, the grotesque and paranoid collapse of an individual who is besieged by the crowds growing around him, who is oppressed on all sides by them, and who fears—but also secretly dreams of—being absorbed into these same crowds.

Translated by Nancy Bray and David Darby for this volume from Claudio Magris, "Der Schriftsteller, der sich versteckt," *Modern Austrian Literature* 16, no. 3/4 (1983): 177–95. Reprinted here by kind permission of *Modern Austrian Literature*.

Auto-da-Fé is an icy and merciless parable of a contemporary terminal illness—delirium—which appears to have shaken the reason of our century to the core. It is the grotesque tragedy of a "Head without a World," of the intellectual who, out of fear of living, obsessively barricades himself against the threats and temptations of life and who, in his maniacal and finally self-destructive defense of his world, offers himself up to death.

The novel is the simultaneously tragic and tragicomic story of an individual who steels himself to the point where he consists of nothing more than his suit of armor. He is destroyed as he puts an end to the vibrant life of the world in the cemetery-like order of the library, and as he stifles the seed of every desire and temptation out of fear that the magic of love could tear off his suit of armor and wrench him from the security of his books and cultural classifications, pulling him into the chaotic and ever-changing flow of reality. Doctor Kien, the protagonist of the novel, teaches himself to be blind so that he does not have to see the multifaceted aggression of things: he is pleased that the heavy spines of his bound books conceal and restrain, with the appearance of permanence, the billions of "furious electrons" of which they consist.[1] It is a frightening and painful portrait of any one of us, a mirror of the phobias and rituals with which life slips away from us as we struggle to keep our fear under control.

Auto-da-Fé portrays, with absolute consistency, a total lack of love, a world that is insanely desiccated and sterilized against every desire. Paranoia prevents the characters from projecting their emotions onto their surrounding reality and from viewing things, bodies, and faces with the passion that imparts magic into those objects. Their reactions to this fear, their fear of death, and their desire for power have robbed them of any strength of emotion. By showing the iciness of the absence of love and by allowing this absence to evolve brilliantly into the distorted and blind perspective—a perspective that refuses to see the material world of things—of the novel, Canetti demonstrates, as very few other writers have done, what a life without love means and, consequently, what love itself means. This radical achievement, upon which the humane and stylistic greatness of the novel is based, confuses many readers.

Auto-da-Fé is a book that provokes only extreme opinions. There are readers who are capable of a total and complete identification with the novel—as though they were looking into a fun house mirror—and who read it daily as a sort of Bible; and there are those who retreat from the book, disconcerted and shocked.

Auto-da-Fé is an angular, unthinkable book that makes no concessions and that cannot readily be assimilated by the institutions of culture. Its rejection by the arbiters of literary taste—with their preference for moderation in their role as benevolent guides to literary history—was predictable. It was a truly heterogeneous and indigestible book, an Other in relation to the business of intellectual production and consumption, an Other, moreover, that, unlike that which had been preprogrammed and precoded by the avant-garde, carries no seal to warn of its Otherness.

The author of *Auto-da-Fé*, who has vanished whole, would never have won the Nobel Prize alone. He would not have won it for this work, which is anything but compliant and which refuses to be forced into any literary canon. Canetti's other great works would have been equally incapable of forcing the literary world to grant them the place and the role that was their due. *Crowds and Power*, for example, which appeared in 1960, fascinates but mostly confuses readers and critics who do not know how to accommodate or classify this book, which, with its daring and unusual method, descends to the very roots of existence. Perhaps not even *Kafka's Other Trial* or Canetti's other essays are capable of making his voice heard. In order for Canetti and *Auto-da-Fé* to be understood and accepted, another writer was necessary: the writer who, 30 years later, stepped into the spotlight acting as though the book were enjoying its success after the author's death. This is the Canetti of some of the essays and, above all, of the autobiography, the interviews, and the speeches; the Canetti who, with great alacrity, illustrates and interprets his own life from his birth in 1905 in Rustschuk, Bulgaria, as the child of a Jewish family through his subsequent experiences in many different countries and languages; the Canetti who offers commentary on his own work, as if we had discovered, after decades, Kafka's *The Trial*, and Kafka, kinder and older, appeared as the guide to lead us through his own labyrinth.

This allowed Canetti to express publicly what *Auto-da-Fé* withheld and repressed: a love of every life and every breath of life; a desire to protect the process of transformation and becoming against any power that seeks to repress and stop it; the utopian fight against death, whose power Canetti refuses ever to accept and from whose grasp he wants to steal every living being. The *ex negative* is articulated in *Auto-da-Fé per negationem*, that is to say, by means of negation, through the novel's great portrayal of the lack of all love and of all life. In *Auto-da-Fé* the narrative consumingly and longingly points toward life not lived and toward irretrievable, suffocated love. In contrast, it is in his later works that Canetti speaks of the positive values of love, goodness, and friendship.

The great negation of *Auto-da-Fé* is one of self-protection, of a life composed only of fear and of protection from life itself. "I know this truth is a lie; help me," pleads Peter Kien during the grotesque questioning in the police precinct duty-room: "I know she [Therese] must vanish" [*AdF*, 305].

At this point, having been thrown out of his library, Peter Kien has only the books in his head. He has married Therese and is being persecuted by her, by life, by the world, by reality. At this moment in the interrogation, the reality that Kien has held at bay for years presents itself (Therese's blue skirt, the blue of life), seeking to fend off its own obliteration. The otherwise arrogant and independent Kien waits for help from the scorned and anonymous faces of humanity that surround him, almost as if he were asking them to support him in his attempts at repression that, once so habitual and natural, have suddenly become problematic and difficult.

In the episode mentioned above Peter Kien battles to extinguish reality, the world that has suddenly broken into his head. His is a defensive battle, an abnormal protection of an ego from everything that threatens its precarious and fictitious existence. Canetti is above all a poet of defensiveness, of the absurd and negative defense of a doomed, bourgeois ego against the overwhelming richness of life. This defense signifies self-destruction, like Karl Kraus's Great Wall of China that, to use Canetti's image, suffocates the very realm that it is trying to protect from the barbarians with its stones, continuing until the kingdom is swallowed by the walls, is buried underneath them, and comes itself to consist of no more than wall.[2] In this sense Canetti's work is a clairvoyant and astute parable of the self-destructive delirium into which Western reason is heading in our century, forced in this direction by the crises that are laying siege to it. This embittered defense leads to death, like Kafka's underground passages, which are designed to help the animal that dug them in its escape from an unknown and deadly pursuer, towards which, however, the constructed tunnels always lead.[3]

The existence of Canetti's characters—from Kien, to the African and Mongol kings in *Crowds and Power,* and finally to Franz Kafka in *Kafka's Other Trial*—is composed of a series of automatic responses, a single reactive impulse. Life becomes a complex reaction, a complicated and logical structure built on a foundation of fear for the purpose of both containing fear and holding it at a distance. "Wherever he sets his foot," Canetti writes about Kafka, "he senses the uncertainty of the ground."[4] This uncertainty, which spans the totality of life from the most private to the most public spheres, arises primarily from the uncertainty of individual personalities and the flowing and changing frailty of the boundaries of the ego.

The ego that sets its foot on uncertain ground exposes itself to the most varied and contradictory of dangers and reaches out for the most varied and contradictory of weapons—weapons that ultimately only intensify the uncertainty to the point where they become a part of it, increasing its strength and volume. On his systematic walks, his excursions into the outside world, Dr. Kien has devised a system of pressing his bag to his ribs and under his arms in such a manner as to maintain constant physical contact with his books. A book, Valéry said, helps men not to think: a stiff book protects one from one's own thoughts, from the living spirit, from reality. For Canetti as for Borges, books stand in contrast to life: they are simultaneously the poison and the remedy.

The ego reacts to the shapeless temptation of the outside, the external world, the streets in their multifarious chaos, by erecting boundaries and barriers and by withdrawing into a tried and trusted shell.

Peter Kien is the antihero of an antilife or, better said, of a desperate, self-destructive counteroffensive, which he feels compelled to mount in order to protect his own threatened life and in whose name he undertakes a massive amputation of his own life. In *Auto-da-Fé* Canetti has written the most complete and distressing tragedy of the decline of the subject. The most violent and impressive motif in *Auto-da-Fé* is the total, icy absence of any emotion, heartbeat, or momentum. Paranoia has eliminated the appeal of any object, and the ego does not have the slightest libido to project. Only Kafka could paint an equally devitalized and parched picture of life.

Peter Kien is the embodiment of the ego, a suit of armor built to protect an integral whole that does not exist as such. In reality the ego is a crowd, a changing agglomeration of elements whose continuity we can trace only by approximation and convention, and which, like the population of a city, we continue to identify by the same name for the sake of convenience, regardless of yesterday's dead and today's newborn children.

In order not to lose himself in this multifariousness, Kien reduces it to a monolithic and thin unity; he eliminates the world so that he can consist just of a head. Peter Kien dips his face in water to find his way back to the silent solitude of his past, to reverse the present that has invaded the deathly freedom of this emptiness. He teaches himself to be blind in order to divert as much of the overflowing stream of life as possible, since he is incapable of resisting its current. Only blindness allows him to withstand the collective assault of countless things, the simultaneous perception of which would numb every organ of perception.

The static page of a book is made up of a dizzying number of restless and "furious electrons." To ward off this attack, there is no alternative but to crush them beneath the motionless weight of hard book covers and heavy spines. Refusing to be defeated, the ego denies plurality, especially that which it senses in itself: the plurality that identifies its center and its very own being and that the ego therefore must not recognize. The whole of Austrian culture, under the influence of the teaching of Ernst Mach and the philosophy of Friedrich Nietzsche, questions the unity of the ego and exposes its centrifugal plurality.

Peter Kien counters the impending atomization of his self by compressing his being, squeezing himself until he is as compact as a crushed sponge in a fisted hand. Kien wrings out nature, the force of plurality par excellence. Because of the heavy skylights in his library, physical appearances are softened and distanced. A dull blue announces to Kien that the sun is shining, but the sunshine does not penetrate his world. The pale gray of rain lets him know that it is raining, but it does not rain on him. He hears only a soft noise that cannot move him, cannot touch his skin. There remains only a vague knowledge of the reality of nature as every concrete experience has faded away: "It was as if he had barricaded himself against the world: against all material relations, against all terrestrial needs, had builded [*sic*] himself an hermitage, a vast hermitage, so vast that it would hold those few things on this earth which are more than this earth itself, more than the dust to which our life at last returns; as if he had closely sealed it and filled it with those things alone" [*AdF,* 67].

Above all, Peter Kien seeks to historicize the Otherness that presents itself as a disturbing threat. He traces new and unknown phenomena back to the reassuring categories of the known, already neutralized by the fossilization of knowledge. Kien identifies the violent caretaker with the prototype of the sixteenth-century peasant soldier; he recognizes the smell of a rose because it was adulated in Persian poetry; he underpins his misogyny with an endless quantity of insane scientific proof. Instead of coming to terms with his own past, he replaces it with the general past of humanity that he has learned from books. He even tries in vain to allocate Therese a place in his tried and trusted cultural gallery.

Canetti brilliantly depicts the psychology of this monomaniacal ego as it seeks to shield itself in the struggle against its own dissolution. Kien's resistance to the world manifests itself in an anarchic contempt that supports and subscribes to social conventions, rather than denying them. This rejection nevertheless contains a strong and direct relationship to reality: it remains its partner; whereas straightforward contempt represents a form of distancing, of turning away. Kien would rather pay his insurance premiums than endure the appearance of the agent who would descend upon him if he did not pay. To demonstrate his low opinion of the worthless book dealers, he acknowledges them with a silent yet deep bow. His proud scorn hides Kien's refusal to make choices within the parameters of reality. In his intricate and grotesque account of his experiences with Fischerle, he feels compelled to describe the four canaries (which have no connection to his experience) only "in the interests of accuracy" [*AdF,* 264].

Kien's anarchism—deeply imbued with a hatred for the law ("Everything brings you into collision with the law," Fischerle shouts [*AdF,* 241])—becomes a flight into regression and into a need for power. The deeply rooted mistrust of any type of order forces him to flee into an all-encompassing and grotesque routine. Kien aspires to the freedom of an inanimate object, to its invulnerability to commands: "A *thing* ... can be pushed or pulled about, but it cannot receive or store up commands," writes Canetti in *Crowds and Power.*[5]

The exaggerated and frenetic division of labor has intensified the enslavement of the individual in a terrifying way. The individual is bombarded with commands from all sides by the totalitarian reality of industrial society, and these leave behind deadly stings in both body and psyche. In the face of these provocations and commands that, like an increasingly intense artillery barrage, are incessantly being imposed by society, the personality of the individual proves defenseless and inadequate. The contemporary ego can no longer claim, as in Tolstoy, to be "compact" and "monumental" [*CW,* 97]. It reacts by objectifying itself in order to escape the guilt-laden, monstrous machinery. To dodge Therese's blows, Kien turns to stone; he becomes as motionless and insensitive as a statue; he is as silent as any inanimate object.

The negativism of schizophrenics becomes, as with all so-called sociopaths depicted by Canetti, a sociohistorical symptom. It is the behavior of an individual who feels attacked by all kinds of commands and who denies himself every command, connection, or contact.

In this sense, Kien's parable follows in the tradition of the other great and tragic negative visions of twentieth-century literature, particularly the literature that is closest to Canetti's, such as that of Franz Kafka and Robert Walser.

In his essay *Kafka's Other Trial* Canetti examined this "freedom of the weak person who seeks salvation in defeat," which Kafka also expresses in a letter to Felice: "I stretched myself ... and experienced the joys of being déclassé."[6] This joy of the déclassé, this desire for disintegration, which Kafka overcomes thanks to his alert and revolutionary self-control, ensures this flight into dissimulation, into the margins, and into obedience beyond the reach of commands. As part of this strategy, Kafka "atrophied in all directions" in order to concentrate on the intangible dimension of writing; and, in doing so, he exaggerates the very vulnerability that he is trying to overcome [*K,* 23]. To avoid the tentacles of power, he dispenses with passion and self-assertion. At the moment of Kien's self-destructive involvement in Fischerle's deceitful machinations, Kien feels "relieved ... and resolute because he was under another person's orders," because he subjects himself to a sole authority that protects him from the uncontrollable waves of besieging powers and that, above all, protects him from the illusory freedom and the martyrdom of responsibility and choice [*AdF,* 254].

Underneath his hard shell Kien is waiting like a mollusk, inert in face of the biological mutation of the subject prophesied by Nietzsche and inert when, as Foucault predicts, the sandy face of the ego washes into the sea. Canetti's protagonist hardens and resists this mutation, this metamorphosis of the individual. For Kien, any movement or any temptation that life offers endangers the integrity of the boundaries of the self. In this light it is understandable that, for Kien, the greatest danger lies in women, in eros: Women are "the Second, the Other, the Evil, the Misfortune" [*AdF,* 444]. In the grand mythological and misogynistic portrayal offered in the penultimate chapter, Kien condemns the vanity of God and Eve, whereas he laments the selflessness of Adam. Adam's guilt, Kien believes, lies in his not loving himself, as God loved himself in his creation, but in loving Eve, the second being, the strange and different opposite: "He forgives her for what she is: an expanded rib. He forgets, and of One, Two are made. What misery for all time!" [*AdF,* 444]. Kien would like to be God, the perfect example of the holder of absolute power revealed in *Crowds and Power.* He regrets that humans, despite their *libido gubernandi,* have chosen eros, the multiformity of things, and life. He abhors "these greedy creatures; could they not be satisfied with the life they had had?" [*AdF,* 40]. He dreams of molding them into a gigantic book that will hold the entire world within its covers.

In this Kien is only a victim. Melancholy overcomes him: the melancholy of one who has become, inescapably at this point, the victim who has no alternative but to lay down his arms and who must, for better or worse, see himself "first as prey, then as food, and finally as carrion or excrement" [*CP,* 347]. Melancholy, writes Canetti in *Crowds and Power,* is experienced as guilt. Depression—which envelops the entire person and permits no escape—manifests itself in a feeling of unworthiness that is hard to define. With this diagnosis, which is also incidentally a sweeping interpretation of Kafka's work, Canetti captures the image of the consummate tragedy of the persecuted individual.

Auto-da-Fé is, however, not only the story of Peter Kien and his petrifaction. It is also that of Georges Kien and his metamorphosis. As a psychiatrist, Georges Kien seeks to dissolve himself in others and "perpetually to lose himself" [*AdF,* 411]. He masters an unusually high number of roles, a talent that is reflected in the extraordinary mobility of his facial muscles, which can adapt instantly to diverse situations. He forces himself through the tiniest cracks in the souls of others, especially those torn souls of his patients.

The important motif of metamorphosis and psychic turmoil, which the pages dedicated to Georges Kien elaborate, is directly tied to Kien's conception of language. It is no coincidence that the mentally deficient gorilla, whom Georges envies, always uses a different sign to signify the same object. He thus defies the power of fixed and invariable definitions and resists the petrifaction that would result from the fixing of his own secret code.

The gorilla's own language is fundamentally different. Every characteristic of the linguistic sign is alien to this language. It does not function by substitution since it does not name objects. The gorilla's acts of linguistic creation interrelate perfectly with a "magnetic field of passions" [*AdF,* 403]. Every convention is alien to the gorilla's language because it needs no code and is continually being reinvented. Moreover, it is devoid of any arbitrariness: it takes shape out of a profound and absolute necessity. In the moment of experience its expression of the "mythical tale of passion," coming "from depths a thousand feet deeper than any he [Georges] had ever dared to plumb, could take no form other than the one it does take" [*AdF,* 402].

The "depths"—into which the gorilla's mythical tale of passion sinks in his language—are the undifferentiated and collective ground of the crowd, the "one single flood, one ocean" that foams with "[supposed] . . . individuals" [*AdF,* 411] and that is destined to overflow at any moment, drowning every distinction between "I," "you," or "he." It is the termite colony—"the blind cells of a fanatic whole"—whose order is threatened only by an orgy and by the deceptive desire for individuation [*AdF,* 432].

The mental patient is close to these depths: he is free from the illusion of culture, free from the "*cordon sanitaire* for the individual against the mass in his own soul" [*AdF,* 411]. Peter Kien, by contrast, suffocates in this *cordon san-*

itaire of that institutionalized language that is the basic foundation of culture. Georges is resolved not to cure the insane patients from whom he has so much to learn. He does not want to simplify them, to humble these hearts that beat outside the world of material objects and that descend upon them like alien conquerors.

This living language is the language of metamorphosis, of life. Peter Kien, by contrast, clings to what is in print, to what is set in stone, to books. But not even books are capable of resisting life. The only possible salvation for the ego threatened by life remains death. In the devastating and grandiose finale Peter Kien breaks into roaring laughter: the triumphant laughter of one who is certain of his prey for all time, the laughter of one who possesses power and who knows how to incorporate into himself the objects and goods of his world for all eternity. Indeed, he takes these objects with him into death.

Auto-da-Fé is the portrait of a delirium that continues to blind mortally and that dreams of saving life while at the same time destroying it. It is the portrait of a delirium that faces the future wearing an insane historical grin, having swallowed up and eradicated every trace of existence. Canetti has written the parable of a man who denies himself the present and in doing so steers himself into catastrophe as either executioner and victim. Walter Benjamin's Angel of History, who faces the future and who piles up rubble behind himself, is not so very dissimilar to Canetti's protagonist who dreams of the totality of the past as an immense, immobile realm, a space that is always full and in which he would be immune to the pain of the senses.

The past is, however, a desolate space and the realm of the dead. In Canetti's novel the desired transformation of life into memory simultaneously constructs a refuge and a prison for the divided ego frantically struggling to preserve its own integrity:

> The future, the future, how was he ever to get into the future? Let the present be past, then it could do no more harm to him. Ah, if only the present could be crossed out! The sorrows of the world are, because we live too little in the future. What would it matter in a hundred years if he were beaten to-day [*sic*]? Let the present be the past and we shall not notice the bruises. The present is alone responsible for all pain. He longed for the future, because then there would be more past in the world. The past is kind, it does no one any harm. For twenty years he had moved in it freely, he was happy. Who is happy in the present? If we had no senses, then we might find the present endurable. We could then live through our memories—that is, in the past. In the beginning was the Word. He bowed for the supremacy of the past.... God is the past. He *believes* in God. A time will come when men will beat their senses into recollections, and all time into the past. A time will come when a single past will embrace all men, when there will be nothing except the past, when everyone will have one faith—the past. [*AdF,* 158–59]

The nonexistence of the present is a dominant theme in European and especially Central European literature. It is a motif that emphasizes the nihilism of modern life. "When is the present?" Rilke asks himself in a letter to Lou Andreas-Salomé. Life never *is*: it already has been or is about to be. It belongs to the past or to the future: in other words, it belongs to the irreal. "When does one live," Oblomov had already asked himself.[7] Concrete, immediate life with all its slings and arrows becomes the obstacle to true, essential life. Life prevents life, and Oblomov complains that life attacks us from all sides: he rolls around sleepless in bed. In his masterpiece *La persuasione é la rettorica* Carlo Michelstaedter exposes this inability to live in the present, in the moment. One only lives in the future, in the hope that the present will soon pass, and in the hope of the advent of a total future in which one will no longer hope for anything. But this flight is also a refuge against "gruesome, real life," as Italo Svevo calls it. By fixating on the future, one escapes the deadly present. One desires to live as the chronicler in Doderer's *Die Dämonen* (*The Demons*) does, whose life has already passed and can no longer cause pain. In longing for the future one seeks an empty space—a dead space as protection against the cruelty of life. Death arrives to save one from being killed. With this grandiose portrayal of the horrifying love of death, Canetti himself becomes the mythical hero championing humanity in a duel with death.

Even this Canetti who helps us to live better, more humanely, and more solidly conceals himself. Beneath the surface clarity of his autobiography and his public conduct, which seems to have nothing in common with the monstrosity of *Auto-da-Fé,* there is an inaccessible Otherness, a shadowy entity. In his autobiography, which supposedly tells all, the author hides and dissimulates. Behind the mask of humanity and objective representation there is an emptiness, a black hole, in the autobiography.

Today's Canetti tries to hide or even to erase the traces of yesterday's Canetti. The Nobel Prize pleased him, but it also caused him displeasure. He feels like an animal who can no longer hide in the undergrowth and whose silhouette is now clear against the sky, exposed to hunters and to the pack.

In a complex, Kafkaesque, Chinese ritual Canetti is now organizing his defense. He is working out how both to disappear completely and yet to reappear at will, to remain available for dialogue with a friend or even a stranger while, at the same time, evading the deadly and alienating machinery of the business of culture. Unlike many world-famous personalities, Canetti does not allow himself to be overwhelmed by the mechanisms of fame, and he is capable of defending himself against its pressures with a simple "no." He knows that these pressures constrict one's breathing, stealing that airy and primary freedom to which, as he knows and we know, he clings tightly. To remain himself, he must hide himself, wear a mask, metamorphose, and disappear. The writer who hides in order to catch his breath wages his great battle not only to defend himself but to defend life per se, which is constantly under threat of expropriation and disempowerment.

In this desire to escape, which has been forced upon him, there is perhaps another sting that is more disquieting. In his writing Canetti has brilliantly exposed the paranoid fear of an individual who feels threatened from all sides to such an extent that he fears any contact, is afraid of being touched, and tries to imagine that he is all alone in the world, like God before Creation or like the mad Judge Schreber, about whom Canetti writes masterfully [*CP*, 434–62]. Perhaps a hint of this fear of being touched also affects the writer himself, who from time to time seems to resemble those men of power in his books and who shares their desire to keep life under control, a desire that he has brilliantly investigated and exposed. Now that fame has taken away his authority over his own image, Canetti seems to be trying to recapture this control, to present an interpretation of himself and to impose it on others, to make sure that this version of himself is strictly adhered to—all actions of a man whose secret wish is that only Canetti be allowed to speak about Canetti.

As in the years before his success, when he remained in obscurity, Canetti is still, despite the fame that has been accorded to him, a magnificent example of individual resistance against the world. Granted, the price for this resistance, of which so few are capable, is very high and has left its mark on him. Kafka—the author of the story "The Burrow" in which an underground animal that is being pursued by a mysterious enemy digs escape tunnels that however, ultimately lead to the mortal enemy—knew only too well that the individual who stands up to the world has to pay a high price. This resistance demands constant attention and vigilance to the point of mania, an eternal calculating and weighing of the dangers and the escape routes, a vigilance that sucks up energy and prevents one from dedicating oneself to life, an intricate calculation of debit and credit. Canetti himself speaks of this danger with regard to Karl Kraus and his Great Wall of China that—built to protect the empire and therefore life—spreads itself out so far that ultimately it covers the entire empire with stone. Alongside his generous availability for others, Canetti, out of necessity, also projects an aura of suspicion. He is particularly suspicious of initiatives such as books, conferences, and debates that address and celebrate his life. In Canetti's conduct we can discover his truth: every great writer is besieged by the very demons that he exposes. He knows them because they are within him. He denounces their power because he himself is in danger of succumbing to them.

The autobiography, to which Canetti owes the greater part of his recent success, stems from his desire to construct and impose his own image and to dictate the interpretation of his own work. In this sense the autobiography is fascinating and ambiguous, rich in flashes of intuition and calculated acts of concealment. The second volume, *Die Fackel im Ohr* (*The Torch in My Ear*), for example, encompasses the years from 1921 to 1931, decisive years for both the author and Europe. These were years that were full of unforgettable experiences such as meeting Veza, who would later become the woman whom he loved above all; the great inflation of the early 1920s; the 1927 burning of the Viennese Palace of Justice, which drew Canetti's attention to the new face of the crowd; his fanatical fascination with Karl Kraus, whose seething, red-hot words both attacked the lies of those years and enslaved his audience's spirit while exposing the power of the word, the universal falseness of the period, and the connection between the unconditional demand for truth and the calling to power; the frenetic milieu of Berlin animated by the avant-garde of Bertolt Brecht and George Grosz; the conception and writing of *Auto-da-Fé*.

Reading this book, written in his typically crystal-clear style, which shrouds an enigmatic secret, one senses how European culture exploded, collapsing an order that had stood for centuries. A love of life and a rejection of death make it possible for Canetti to convey the unfading intensity of his experiences, the singular, unique meaning of every face and every gesture that memory and word hold onto forever and, in doing so, to rescue them from time, history, and death. But this autobiography, which seems to say everything, contains an absence, a type of black hole that appears to have swallowed the actual truth of Canetti's life. Canetti purports to describe his inspiration for writing *Auto-da-Fé*, but in reality he says nothing about this grotesque and magnificent book and tells us just as little about its unexpected author, the 30-year-old who he was at that time and whom we cannot imagine standing before a catastrophic abyss or total void. That individual may well have disappeared, but he may also be smoldering beneath the amiability of the 78-year-old writer of today; an individual whom Canetti withholds from us and indeed who does not appear within these pages.

This autobiography appears to suppress the substance of the life of which it purports to tell, perhaps because this substance is extraordinary and inexpressibly Other. At the center of the book is a void, a vortex, an implosion that sucks up its own innards and that appears to destroy the ordered material of the narrative. At the edge of this vortex of the unsaid the writer piles up eagerly and patiently—and often with brilliant evidence—memories, anecdotes, contemplations and special episodes, places and people. *Auto-da-Fé* also contains this void. Indeed this dizzying absence was identified as the central absence, as the insanity of life hidden beneath a credible and conciliatory gesture of dissimulation that attempts to assure us that everything is all right. Like every book of real substance, Canetti's autobiography must be read with both fascination and suspicion; it must be examined for what it says and also for what it does not say. In a splendid passage from *The Torch in My Ear* Canetti remarks that in the face of reality we all resemble Samson, blinded and shattered, as he looks upon the world for the last time, a world that is fading and sinking. Perhaps Canetti also feels this fear, but he masters it brilliantly in his autobiography.

Below the gentle and smooth surface of the autobiography, which stands in such contrast to the angularity of *Auto-da-Fé* and which deceptively appears to tell all, there is a restraint that conceals an unpredictable, flickering, and camouflaged Otherness, an unimaginable and incomprehensible identity. Behind the loving father of a newly established family and behind the friendly gentleman who devises overly polite public utterances in order to protect his privacy, there is another man, extraordinary and imaginable.[8] Both of them teach us daily how the sickness of power and death needs to be exposed and both remind us that "every one of us is the center of the world," as Canetti writes, "every last one."

Notes

1. [Elias Canetti, *Auto-da-Fé,* trans. C. V. Wedgwood (New York: Farrar, Straus and Giroux, 1984), 71; hereafter cited in text as *AdF. Ed.*]

2. [The reference is to Karl Kraus's story "Die chinesische Mauer." Canetti makes implicit reference to this story in *The Conscience of Words,* trans. Joachim Neugroschel (London: Deutsch, 1986), 35–36; hereafter cited in text as *CW. Ed.*]

3. [The reference is to Franz Kafka, "The Burrow," trans. Willa and Edwin Muir, in *The Complete Stories,* ed. Nahum N. Glazer (New York: Schocken, 1971), 325–59. *Ed.*]

4. [Elias Canetti, *The Human Province,* trans. Joachim Neugroschel (New York: Seabury, 1978), 98. *Ed.*]

5. [Elias Canetti, *Crowds and Power,* trans. Carol Stewart (New York: Farrar, Straus and Giroux, 1984), 383; hereafter cited in text as *CP. Ed.*]

6. [Elias Canetti, *Kafka's Other Trial: The Letters to Felice,* trans. Christopher Middleton (New York: Schocken, 1974), 108, 106; hereafter cited in text as *K. Ed.*]

7. [The reference is to the protagonist of Ivan Gonchorov's 1859 novel *Oblomov. Ed.*]

8. [Canetti had remarried in 1971, the year in which he began work on his autobiography. His wife, Hera Buschor, bore a daughter, Johanna, the following year. *Ed.*]

Index

◆

acoustic mask: in *Auto-da-Fé*, 19–20, 21, 26,
  50, 123; in Canetti's dramas, 19, 27,
  93–96, 125–27; in *Crowds and Power*,
  115; in *Earwitness*, 21; and
  Grundeinfall, 101; theory of, 49–50,
  94–99, 110, 112–16; and transformation, 27. *See also* mask switching
Adorno, Theodor W., 6, 179, 258; on *Crowds
  and Power*, 8, 137–53; on dramas, 116,
  118; Horkheimer and, 138, 151, 257
akustische Maske. *See* acoustic mask
alienation effect, 97–98, 100
anti-Semitism, 270
Aristophanes, 43, 100, 110, 115
Aristotle, 105–6, 111
Auer, Annemarie, 67
Auschwitz, 258, 270

Babel, Isaac (or Isaak), 17, 45, 230
Baermann Steiner, Franz, 27, 159
Barnouw, Dagmar, 192; on *Auto-da-Fé*, 61,
  65; on Canetti as poet and intellectual,
  3, 15–34; on Canetti's dramas, 5,
  121–34; on *Crowds and Power*, 6–7
Barthes, Roland, 204
Baudrillard, Jean, 207
Bayley, John, 240–41, 247
Beckett, Samuel, 54, 68
"Before the Law" (Kafka), 227–28
Benedict, Ruth, 184
Benjamin, Walter, 287
Berlin, 17, 44–46, 223, 290
Bhabha, Homi, 202–3
Bischoff, Alfons-M., 119 n. 20
Bloom, Harold, 74

Böll, Heinrich, 257–58
Book of Songs (*Shih Ching*), 146–47
Brecht, Bertolt, 97–101, 239; in Berlin, 44,
  290; on drama, 111; *Galileo*, 131; on
  Hitler, 21
Broch, Hermann: on Canetti, 47; Canetti
  on, 228, 233; as Canetti's mentor, 4,
  48, 241; *The Death of Virgil*, 104
Bryson, Gladys, 247–48
Büchner, Georg, 117, 124–25, 220, 255–57
Burkert, Walter, 163
"Burrow, The" (Kafka), 282, 289
Busch, Günther, 61

Caillois, Roger, 151
Camus, Albert, 222
Canetti, Elias: as anti-Freudian psychologist,
  111 (*see also* Freud; Freudian psychology); on *Auto-da-Fé* (conversation with
  Durzak), 41–54; central themes of, 3;
  cosmopolitanism of, 252, 271; critical
  reception of oeuvre, 1–3, 172, 261; on
  Crowds and Power (conversation with
  Adorno), 137–53; on drama (conversation with Durzak), 93–108; and German language, 16–18, 53–54, 250;
  humanism of, 74, 88, 117; later works
  of (Stern), 239–48; life and work of
  (Barnouw), 15–34; mother of, 16, 18,
  20, 31, 234–35, 253–54; overall configuration of oeuvre, 2–4, 246–47,
  261–75 (Eigler), 281, 288; on own life
  and work, 1, 7, 11; Peter Kien, compared to 222, 264; as poet-thinker,
  3–4, 6, 8–10, 28; as power-figure, 10,

293

The Volume Editor

◆

David Darby is a professor of German and Comparative Literature at The University of Western Ontario. He is the author of *Structures of Disintegration: Narrative Strategies in Elias Canetti's "Die Blendung"* (1992) and of a number of critical essays on modern German and Austrian literature. In addition, he has served as the inaugural editor of *Arachne: An Interdisciplinary Journal of Language and Literature / Revue interdisciplinaire de langue et de littérature*.

The General Editor

♦

Robert Lecker is professor of English at McGill University in Montreal. He received his Ph.D. from York University. Professor Lecker is the author of numerous critical studies, including *On the Line* (1982), *Robert Kroetch* (1986), *An Other I* (1988), and *Making It Real: The Canonization of English-Canadian Literature* (1995). He is the editor of the critical journal *Essays on Canadian Writing* and of many collections of critical essays, the most recent of which is *Canadian Canons: Essays in Literary Value* (1991). He is the founding and current general editor of Twayne's Masterwork Studies and the editor of the Twayne's World Authors Series on Canadian writers. He is also the general editor of G. K. Hall's Critical Essays on World Literature series.